THE STANISLAVSKY SYSTEM OF ACTING

Konstantin Stanislavsky, the Russian director, actor and co-founder of the Moscow Art Theatre, was the originator of the most influential system of acting in the history of western theatre. Many of Stanislavsky's concepts are widespread in popular thought on acting; this book offers a timely evaluation of the basis of his ideas, discussing whether the system has survived because Stanislavsky made discoveries about acting that are, and always have been, scientifically verifiable, or whether his methods work on a practical basis despite an outdated theory. Drawing on information that has become available in recent years in Russia, the book examines how the development of Stanislavsky's system was influenced by scientific discoveries in his lifetime, and compares Stanislavsky's methods with those of Evgeny Vakhtangov, Michael Chekhov and Vsevolod Meyerhold. A full understanding of these ideas is crucial for anyone interested in acting and actor training today.

ROSE WHYMAN lectures in Drama and Theatre Arts at the University of Birmingham. Prior to her academic career she worked in community and experimental theatre, most recently with Open Theatre Company and with Hocus Pocus Theatre Company. She makes regular trips to Russia and Poland to undertake archival research and to run community arts projects, and reads Russian fluently. She is a member of the Professional Association of Alexander Teachers. This is her first book.

THE STANISLAVSKY SYSTEM OF ACTING

Legacy and Influence in Modern Performance

ROSE WHYMAN

University of Birmingham

CAMBRIDGE
UNIVERSITY PRESS

CAMBRIDGE UNIVERSITY PRESS
Cambridge, New York, Melbourne, Madrid, Cape Town, Singapore, São Paulo, Delhi

Cambridge University Press
The Edinburgh Building, Cambridge CB2 8RU, UK

Published in the United States of America by Cambridge University Press, New York

www.cambridge.org
Information on this title: www.cambridge.org/9780521886963

© Rose Whyman 2008

First published 2008

Printed in the United Kingdom at the University Press, Cambridge

A catalogue record for this publication is available from the British Library

Library of Congress Cataloguing in Publication data

Whyman, Rose.
The Stanislavsky system of acting : legacy and influence in modern
performance / Rose Whyman.
p.   cm.
Includes bibliographical references and index.
ISBN 978-0-521-88696-3 (hardback : alk. paper)
1. Method (Acting)   2. Stanislavsky, Konstantin, 1863–1938.   I. Title.
PN2062.W49   2008
792.02'8–dc22   2007051676

ISBN 978-0-521-88696-3 hardback

For Brian Door
with all my love and thanks

Contents

Illustrations

Photographs 1–8 are reproduced by kind permission of the Moscow Art Theatre Museum.
Photograph 9 is from the University of Bristol Theatre Collection.
Photograph 10 is reproduced by kind permission of the Meyerhold Museum, Moscow.

The photographic material dates from the 1920s to the 1930s and the quality of the images is the best it can be.

Preface

'The history of the theater is a history of ideas'[1]
'Delsarte, Stanislavski, Meyerhold and a host of their disciples each developed 'systems' which used languages of acting based on the assumption of an objective science (of the mind and/or body)'[2]

The main innovators of actor-training, from Konstantin Sergeevich Stanislavsky onward, have claimed that their methods were supported by scientific hypotheses and discoveries current at the time of their work.[3] My purpose is to analyse the extent to which Stanislavsky's *system* was corroborated by scientific information available to him and to examine whether Stanislavsky adapted his training methods in the light of advances in science in his lifetime. Stanislavsky's methods can be compared with those of Evgeny Vakhtangov, Michael Chekhov and Vsevolod Meyerhold. Stanislavsky taught all of them, and all had access to the information he had, but all took different directions in their work, and Chekhov and Meyerhold claimed different theoretical bases from those of Stanislavsky to corroborate their own methods.

The question as to whether the *system* in fact had a verifiable scientific basis has long provoked conflict of opinion. Joseph Roach claims that Stanislavsky adjusted his theories in accordance with the emerging psycho-physiological theory of his time and that 'his System, therefore, cannot be comprehended without his science'.[4] On the other hand, as

---

[1] Joseph Roach, *The Player's Passion: Studies in the Science of Acting* (Newark: University of Michigan Press, 1993), p. 11.
[2] Philip B. Zarrilli (ed.), *Acting (Re)Considered*, 2nd edn (London: Routledge, 2002), p. 10.
[3] The Russian word *nauka* can, like the English word 'science', mean in a wide sense 'knowledge', and in a narrower sense 'knowledge ascertained by observation and experiment, critically tested, systematised and brought under general principles' (*Chambers Dictionary*). Unless specified, the term is used in the narrow sense.
[4] Roach, *The Player's Passion*, p. 206.

Eric Bentley argues, the references to science may be, as he puts it, just a ruse: 'theatre people have been invoking scientific terminology *for the sake of its authoritative sound:* anything with a scientific name must have a scientific basis. Once we see through this fallacy, we realize that 'exercises' given to actors may not actually do the work they are supposed to do. But this is not to say they have no value.'[5] These polarised views result from a lack of understanding of the scientific basis of the *system* in its time, and the significance of that basis now. Many of Stanislavsky's concepts are widespread in popular thought on acting; it is time for an evaluation of the basis of that thinking.

After all, Stanislavsky's is the most influential actor-training system in the western world. He trained Meyerhold and Michael Chekhov, whose methods are also still taught today. For example, the Russian directors Alexei Levinsky and Gennadi Bogdanov use Meyerhold's *biomechanics*,[6] and there are Michael Chekhov centres in Britain, America and Germany. Stanislavsky's *system* was the basis for the Method, which was developed by Lee Strasberg in America and was taught at the Actors Studio from 1950 onwards. Stanislavsky's work has been considered of such high status in Russia that it was used to endorse the work of such Soviet physiologists as P. V. Simonov in the 1960s.

How has his work stood the test of time? Has it survived because he made discoveries about acting that are and always have been scientifically verifiable, or do his methods work on a practical basis despite an outdated theory? Did Stanislavsky's writings ever, in fact, constitute a 'theory' of acting? If the methods work practically, how could they be validated scientifically now? In order to begin a consideration of the scientific basis of the *system* we need to see beyond the notions that have developed around the man and his work.

Stanislavsky became an iconic figure in Russia, and particular views of him have been perpetuated in Soviet hagiographies and traditions. The mythologising of his work in the West has also obscured some fundamental issues. My purpose is to challenge these views and to examine the conflicting perceptions of the *system*, in the hope that this will lead to a new appreciation of Stanislavsky's work and its value today.

---

[5] Eric Bentley, 'Who was Ribot? Or: Did Stanislavsky Know Any Psychology?', *Tulane Drama Review*, 7:2 (1962), p. 129.
[6] Both Alexei Levinsky and Gennadi Bogdanov are based in Moscow, where Levinsky works as a director. Bogdanov teaches *biomechanics* in Russia at Mime Centrum Berlin, and works annually on a production with Talia Theatre, Manchester.

In *The Player's Passion: Studies in the Science of Acting*, Joseph Roach makes use of Thomas Kuhn's concept of a 'paradigm' and Michel Foucault's term 'episteme' (a body of knowledge), to examine how scientific models have influenced acting, stating that both 'reject the view that knowledge steadily progresses by accretion'.[7] Foucault warned that the episteme of each epoch is not necessarily continuous with that of the next. This gives rise to the question of whether teachers of Stanislavsky-based acting, or the methods of the other Russian actor-trainers today, take into account changes in scientific knowledge.

Discussing how scientific thought actually proceeds through different epochs, Kuhn describes the role of paradigms in scientific research in *The Structure of Scientific Revolutions*. He defines these as 'universally recognized scientific achievements that for a time provide model problems and solutions to a community of practitioners'.[8] They provide frameworks for traditions of scientific research until there is a shift to a new paradigm. 'The resulting transition to a new paradigm is scientific revolution.'[9] From Stanislavsky's lifetime, the theory of evolution, the development of psychology and the theory of conditioned reflexes may all be said to be paradigms. It can happen that paradigms may be a limitation; they may form a straightjacket around the science of a period but, nonetheless, that appears to be the way that scientific thought progresses. Ivan Pavlov's theory of conditioned reflexes was definitive in many ways as the science of the Russian revolution, but it has largely been disregarded since then and Stanislavsky's attempts to grapple with reflex theory have been also disregarded or misrepresented.[10] Changes of thinking on science were concomitant with shifts in the cultural policy of the USSR, which affected all artists. This points to the need for a contextualised reading of the *system*

[7] Roach, *The Player's Passion*, p. 13.

[8] Thomas S. Kuhn, *The Structure of Scientific Revolutions*, 2nd edn (University of Chicago Press, 1970), p. viii. In *The Essential Tension: Selected Studies in Scientific Tradition and Change* (University of Chicago Press, 1977), Kuhn discards the term *paradigm*, replacing it with *disciplinary matrix* (p. 296).

[9] Kuhn, *The Structure*, p. 90.

[10] The Russian word 'uslovnyi' is generally translated as 'conditioned' in the phrase 'uslovnye refleksi', that is, conditioned reflexes, or perhaps learned reflexes. However, it can also mean 'conditional' and I think it is useful to consider that may have been what Pavlov meant by the phrase, at least in part. The dog is trained to salivate on the sound of a bell as initially the dog is given food at the same time. The dog's reaction to the bell is in the event conditional on the food appearing. Though the dog may salivate just to the sound of the bell, if no food appears after a number of presentations of the stimulus, the dog will no longer react. Salivation when food appears is unconditional and unconditioned. Cuny notes that towards the end of his investigations Pavlov considered 'conditioned' was the better translation. See Hilaire Cuny, *Ivan Pavlov: The Man and his Theories*, tr. Patrick Evans (London: Souvenir Press, 1964), p. 11.

and its scientific basis and an examination of the cross-fertilisation in the period of cultural, political and scientific ideas.

Paradigmatic ideas of the machine, the emotions and the spirit, in relation to acting, were part of the body of knowledge of Stanislavsky's time (that is, in the late-nineteenth century and early-twentieth century). These ideas shifted and changed over the period of his life. In fact, ideas circulated from one discipline to another and in the case of theories of acting, as well as in other spheres, ideas were appropriated, renamed or disguised in order to conform to dominant political and scientific ideologies. A dominant concept emerged as the end of the nineteenth century heralded the age of the machine, with the rapid growth of industrialisation, the invention of motor cars in 1886, the first motion pictures in 1895, and aeroplanes in 1903. The modernist preoccupation with the machine extended to the way the human body was conceptualised, as a machine with a spiritual dimension. The influence of this on the views and theories of acting propounded by Stanislavsky, Chekhov, Meyerhold and others led to the conceptualisation of the actor, as it were, as an emotional machine, a dualistic entity who could and should be trained to work to full capacity according to scientific laws of mechanics, while being required at the same time to be emotionally, even spiritually expressive – this being a more capricious capacity. This fascinating dichotomy pervades the thinking on acting of the epoch, with various solutions being explored in order to resolve it.

Stanislavsky, Meyerhold and Chekhov had different solutions to the problem spirit/emotion/machine and different emphases in their work as a result of their beliefs about art, science, philosophy and politics, which can be identified as the reason for their disputes and entrenched positions. Although all three were concerned with problems of spiritual and emotional expression and technical expertise, Chekhov's emphasis in his training work was on enabling the actor to access the spiritual directly, whereas Meyerhold's was on the actor as machine – on technical mastery as the primary means enabling expression of the spiritual. Taking Meyerhold and Chekhov as opposite ends of a spectrum in relation to Stanislavsky and the development of the *system*, draws out, in comparison, some further features of Stanislavsky's view of the actor as an emotional and spiritual machine.

Something of the differences in approach of the three men is highlighted by their individual standpoints towards the 1917 Revolution. After the revolution, ideas of the revolutionary actor and the machine circulated and influenced the avant-garde artistic movements of futurism and constructivism. There was a demand for the 'root and branch' renovation of everyday life. In Bolshevik propaganda, parades and spectacles, 'new symbols and rituals were introduced and infused with anti-capitalism, the collective spirit, atheism and machine-worship'.[11] After the revolution, the suppression began of avant-garde art and its replacement by totalitarian art. Richard Stites writes:

As the Bolsheviks saw it, cultural power had been used in the recent past by the emerging bourgeoisie for its own purposes – profit, exploitation and obscurantism. Like religion, it was a drug for the masses. But culture also possessed the power to enlighten and ennoble the masses. This was essentially an ecclesiastical view of culture's place in society. For the state, ideological correctness was paramount, mass appeal was important and artistic excellence was desirable to the extent that it fit the other two.[12]

The question of how the work of Stanislavsky, Meyerhold and Chekhov fitted with Bolshevik and then Stalinist perceptions took some resolving. In terms of ideology, Stanislavsky was criticised in the twenties and early thirties but, despite having come from the bourgeoisie, he was canonised by the late thirties. On the other hand, Chekhov was driven to emigrate in 1928 and Meyerhold, a leading figure in theatre and the revolution in the twenties, fell into disfavour and was executed in 1940.

In 1934 the All-Union Congress of Soviet Writers endorsed socialist realism. This was founded in Tolstoyan didacticism and Lenin's doctrine that literature and the arts should reflect the spirit of the class struggle, the overthrow of capitalism and the dictatorship of the proletariat. Bernard F. Dukore writes:

the subjects of art – the ideals the Communists were trying to create or the previous conditions from which socialism would emerge – should be expressed in terms worker-audiences could understand; writing should be realistic, represent revolutionary processes, and contribute to educating audiences in the nature and spirit of socialism.[13]

Stanislavsky's work was used to support Stalinism and socialist realism, which was part of the episteme of the post-revolutionary epoch in Russia. This involved distortions which Jerzy Grotowski referred to as Stanislavsky's 'assassination after death'.[14] Further complications and obscurities have

[11] Richard Stites, *Russian Popular Culture* (Cambridge University Press, 1992), p. 39.
[12] *Ibid.* pp. 38–9.
[13] Bernard F. Dukore, *Dramatic Theory and Criticism*: Greeks to Grotowski (New York: Holt, Rinehart and Winston, 1974), p. 911.
[14] Jennifer Kumiega, *The Theatre of Grotowski* (London: Methuen, 1987), p. 110.

arisen. The different accounts of Stanislavsky's work, from actors who had worked with him at different periods, have brought about confusion. Lee Strasberg's Method, a reinterpretation of Stanislavsky's *system*, gained fame and has been equated (in popular thinking) with the *system*. There is a growing recognition that in both Russia and the West Stanislavsky's work has been misinterpreted and reinterpreted in various ways and for various reasons, from simple misunderstandings to political expediency. Sharon Carnicke and others have explored some of these distortions.[15]

All this emphasises how important it is to look at Stanislavsky's work as clearly as possible in relation to its context, in order to see beyond the misinterpretations and appropriations. Stanislavsky drew from a wide range of sources and was subject to a number of influences and these have not been sufficiently examined so far.

Chapter 1 of *The Stanislavsky System of Acting* discusses Stanislavsky's development in the scientific and political context and identifies a central problem for Stanislavsky and the other actor trainers, that of internal experience and its external expression. This throws some light on Stanislavsky's views of emotion and action, including the rehearsal technique called the Method of Physical Actions. Chapter 2 develops this discussion, focussing on the internal, or what Stanislavsky called *experiencing*, and his views of acting as an expression of the emotional and the spiritual. Chapter 3 goes on to discuss how Stanislavsky experimented with training the actor's external means of expression; he calls this *incarnation* and this section includes discussion on his ideas on habit or second nature, and the actor as machine. Chapter 4 further elucidates the theories on which Stanislavsky's methods were based, in terms of training the actor to express emotional and spiritual truths. This elucidation is achieved by means of a comparison with the work of Vakhtangov and Michael Chekhov.

Similarly, Chapter 5 compares Stanislavsky's work with that of Meyerhold; Stanislavsky taught and directed all three men, initially. Meyerhold's professional career began with the foundation of the Moscow Art Theatre and later Vakhtangov and Chekhov learned the *system* from Stanislavsky, but they all went on to develop their own training theories and practice, to some extent rejecting Stanislavsky's work. Chapter 6 assesses the scientific basis of Stanislavsky's work, including the claim made by P. V. Simonov and others that Stanislavsky's work

---

[15] Sharon M. Carnicke, *Stanislavsky in Focus* (Amsterdam: Harwood Academic Publishers, 1998) and Anatoly Smeliansky, 'The Last Decade: Stanislavsky and Stalinism', *Theater*, 12:2 (1991), pp. 7–13.

validated Pavlov's, and the significance of this in relation to the theory and practice of the *system* both in its own time and in the present day.

In this discussion I make reference to the main texts by Stanislavsky. *My Life in Art* (*MLIA*) was first published in Russia in 1926, and is a history of the development of his theory and practice of acting from his childhood until the early period of the existence of the Soviet Union. I also refer to the three books which comprise his manual on acting. These are: *The Actor's Work on Him/Herself in the Creative Process of Experiencing* (*AWHE*), *The Actor's Work on Him/Herself in the Creative Process of Incarnation* (*AWHI*) and *The Actor's Work on a Role* (*AWR*). They were based on Stanislavsky's earlier writings, begun in 1902, which he began to edit and prepare for publication in consultation with his advisor, Liubov' Iakovlevna Gurevich, in the late twenties. However, they were not published in Russian until the late thirties, after Stanislavsky's death. Jean Benedetti and Carnicke have detailed the reasons for the inaccuracy and inadequacy of the English versions.[16] Therefore, I use only the Russian texts. The translations from Russian are my own unless otherwise specified.

I refer also to writings from both editions of Stanislavsky's *Collected Works*, the first published between 1954 and 1961, the second between 1988 and 1999 (references are to the second edition unless otherwise stated); notes on Stanislavsky's lectures and rehearsals of *Werther* (1918–1922) at the Bolshoi Opera Studio that were taken by one of the singers, Konkordia Antarova, and translated by David Magarshack as *Stanislavsky On the Art of the Stage*; *Iz Zapisnich Knizhek*, the two volume edition of excerpts from Stanislavsky's notebooks, and Stanislavsky's notebooks and manuscripts from the archives of the Moscow Art Theatre (MAT) which include material that has never been published.

The trilogy forming the acting manual is written in novel form, as were other works, such as the unfinished *A Pedagogical Novel* (the story of an actor's work on a role) begun in 1923 and included in *AWHI*. By adopting the novel form, with a narrator and fictional characters of teachers and students at a drama school, Stanislavsky found a way to bring writing about practice to life. As such, theoretical concepts are embedded in the text and sources, and as a rule they are not named. Tortsov, and Kostia (the diminutive form of Konstantin, Stanislavsky's first name) can each be seen as an alter ego of Stanislavsky, the teacher of the *system* and the enquiring student. Other students include Maloletkova, Sonia and

---

[16] See Carnicke's *Stanislavsky in Focus*, Chapter 4, and Jean Benedetti's 'A History of Stanislavski in Translation', *New Theatre Quarterly* 6: 23 (1990), pp. 266–78.

Govorkov, among others. The names often have meanings: Maloletkova is 'the young one', Govorkov 'the talker' and Kostia's surname, Nazvanov, approximates to 'sworn brother'. He is one of the few students prepared to commit to learning the *system* in depth. Tortsov was initially 'Tvortsov', the 'creator'.

Stanislavsky's personal library, from his home in Leontievsky Pereulok in Moscow, was divided up sometime after the house became the Stanislavsky House Museum in 1948. Some books were left in the House Museum; other books and Stanislavsky's notes and papers were sent to the Moscow Art Theatre Museum, but many volumes, which are now in the possession of his heirs, have not been catalogued. The available texts and notes, which include scientific literature of the time, are an important source of information on the development of the *system* and have not previously been analysed sufficiently, which situation I aim to begin to redress in this book.

Acknowledgements

My thanks go to Professor Edward Braun, Professor Maggie B. Gale, Professor Russell Jackson, Mike Pushkin, Dr George Taylor, Professor Bill Marshall, Associate Professor Andrei Kirillov, Marina Ivanova, Dr Lyuba Gurjeva and staff of the Moscow Art Theatre Museum, especially Olga Alexandrovna Radishcheva. I am grateful also to Liz Tunnicliffe, Diane Willetts, Kevin Edwards, Janyce Hawliczek, Dr Vicki Cooper, Hocus Pocus Theatre Company, and friends and colleagues in the Professional Association of Alexander Teachers. Lastly, I would like to acknowledge the support of my family, John, Lynne, Laurie and Georgia Whyman and in particular my parents, my father Lawrence Whyman, who died in 1977, and my mother Rose Lilian Whyman, both of whom dedicated themselves to ensuring that I had educational opportunities.

A grant from the Arts and Humanities Research Council made it possible for me to make study trips to Moscow to work in the Moscow Art Theatre archives.

Note on transliteration

In references and in transliterating Russian terms and names into English I have used MLA System II as described in J. Thomas Shaw, *The Transliteration of Modern Russian for English-Language Publications* (The University of Wisconsin Press: Madison, Milwaukee and London, 1967), except where spellings of Russian names have become standard for readers of English. For example, I have used the 'y' for the masculine endings of Russian names within the text, as in 'Stanislavsky'.

CHAPTER I

Science, nature and acting: the context for Stanislavsky and the system

INTRODUCTION

Throughout his life Stanislavsky sought to resolve two key questions in acting: how the actor can infuse a role with emotional or spiritual content, and how he or she can repeat a performance without it becoming tired and mechanical. In order to achieve this resolution he developed methodologies for training the actor. Crucial to his exploration was Stanislavsky's view of the 'machine', that is, the external training of the actor's voice and physicality, and the inner training of the mechanisms for generating emotion and communicating spiritual truths to an audience. The question of what Stanislavsky understood as 'internal' and 'external' over the course of his career is therefore important and the latter part of this chapter will examine his exploration of this in *MLIA*. The discussion is illuminated by two crises of confidence in Stanislavsky's acting career, the first of which occurred when he was playing Dr Stockmann in Ibsen's *An Enemy of the People* in 1905/06 and the second when playing Salieri in Pushkin's *Mozart and Salieri* in 1915.

Stanislavsky experimented in his own acting, as well as in his training and directing work at the Moscow Art Theatre. He consulted scientific and artistic works, was influenced, of course, by contemporary ideas, and in the Soviet period he was guided by his editor as to how he should theorise about some aspects of acting. It is necessary, therefore, to delineate the ideological context for Stanislavsky's work and some of its dominant themes. His lifespan, from 1863 to 1938, straddled two phases of Russian history – before and after the 1917 Revolution. The emancipation of the serfs in 1861 was an emblem of human progress at the beginning of Stanislavsky's epoch and the start of Stalin's purges towards its end was an emblem of inhumanity. The early period of Stanislavsky's life was marked by civil unrest, with the influence of Karl Marx increasing (*Das Kapital* was translated into Russian in 1872), and the assassination of Tsar

Alexander II in 1881. The first revolution in 1905 was followed by a period of repression until the revolution of 1917. The age of modernism and its vast new cultural movements began in the late-nineteenth century and high modernism emerged from 1910, midway through Stanislavsky's career. In these times of change, scientific, political, philosophical and artistic ideas crossed domains, influencing the development of Stanislavsky's aesthetic theory and theatre practice and how it has been interpreted.

Sometimes there was a disjunction between the received ideas of the early part of Stanislavsky's lifespan and the ideas burgeoning in the revolutionary period, and at other times a continuity of thought. Stanislavsky inherited ideas from Russian artists of the nineteenth-century golden age of Russian literature, such as Alexander Pushkin and Nikolai Gogol, and also the ideas of such thinkers as Vissarion Belinsky and Nikolai Chernyshevsky, all of whom continued to be acclaimed after the revolution. Leo Tolstoy, one of Stanislavsky's icons, was a leader in aesthetic thought at the beginning of Stanislavsky's life and some of his views were embraced in socialist realism at the end. The silver age of Russia, from the 1890s to the 1917 Revolution, was a period when Russian music, dance, literature, theatre and fine art were celebrated in Europe and America; the symbolist movement emerged, with which Stanislavsky engaged. Other avant-garde movements such as futurism and constructivism came to the fore but were later seen as suspect by the Soviet authorities.

Science

Stanislavsky's life spanned remarkable changes in scientific thought and his *system*, though he wished it to be rooted in nature, developed in a period of shifting views of natural science, human nature and behaviour. Significantly, the end of the nineteenth century saw the beginnings of psychology as a science as it emerged from the work of philosophers with a psychological bent, such as Wilhelm Wundt and Gustav Fechner.

Before Marx, the idealist philosophy of first Johann Gottlieb Fichte (1762–1814), then Georg Hegel (1770–1831), held sway in Germany. This philosophy, which studied ideas and saw consciousness as the foundation of reality, was very influential in Russia, as were other aspects of German culture. Romanticism, a predominantly cultural movement in other countries, also pervaded the fields of philosophy, science and medicine in Germany. The philosopher Friedrich Wilhelm von Schelling (1775–1854) founded a school of romantic philosophy called Nature Philosophy, asserting, 'Nature is visible Spirit, Spirit is invisible Nature.'[1] This meant that nature was to be understood not only in terms of mechanical and physical concepts, but also in terms of its underlying spiritual laws. This resonates with many of Stanislavsky's pronouncements on nature: 'Art is in great harmony with [nature]' (*AWHE*, p. 200); or, 'How do you penetrate the spiritual depths of a role, an actor, an audience? This is achieved with the help of nature itself' (*AWR*, p. 141); and 'A human being is nature . . . Human beings, their spiritual and physical creative apparatus, their genius, creative inspiration and so on and so on are the highest incomprehensible manifestation and expression of the creative force of nature' (*AWR*, p. 220).

Notably, these views of nature, consciousness and spirit were also subject to influences ostensibly from the East, as in, for example, the emergence of theosophy and anthroposophy. The last part of the nineteenth century saw the development of occult movements in Russia along with

the beginnings of analytical psychology, new interest in comparative religion and myth and the East. Growing out of romanticism's interest in mythology and religion (Schelling, Schopenhauer, Friedrich Creuzer and others) this interest exploded in the second half of the nineteenth century in the works of Orientologists Friedrich Max Müller and Paul Deussen, the ethnologist Sir James Frazer and the Cambridge School, and in the work of Wilhelm Wundt, Gustav Fechner, Edouard von Hartmann, and Harald Hoffding on the philosophy and psychology of religion.[2]

Hindu works were translated into many languages including Russian. Michael Chekhov famously became an anthroposophist and, most importantly, Stanislavsky had an interest in yoga, to which he was introduced by Leopold A. Sulerzhitsky, his close friend and assistant at the Moscow Art Theatre.

Into the melting pot of ideas about nature and consciousness came those of Friedrich Nietzsche, one of the German philosophers from whose work psychology emanated. In the modernist period, inspired by Nietzsche and, in particular, by *The Birth of Tragedy* (published in 1871), there was a utopian belief in Russia that the new man, the *Übermensch*, would be created in Russia. As psychology developed, Nietzsche proposed that there were hidden realities within human beings and ideas began to

[1] Henri F. Ellenberger, *The Discovery of the Unconscious: The History and Evolution of Dynamic Psychiatry* (New York: Basic Books, 1970), p. 202.
[2] Maria Carlson, *No Religion Higher than Truth* (Princeton University Press, 1993), p. 34.

circulate about the subconscious and unconscious, which could be touched or unmasked through art. Nietzsche defines various art forms including music and tragedy as 'Dionysiac', dealing with the fundamentals of love and death.[3] Some of Nietzsche's ideas were reflected in the work of Meyerhold, who, along with others, transformed the idea of the new man into that of the new actor.

Significantly, by the time Stanislavsky was forming his views on acting in the first decade of the twentieth century, associationist psychology had become established. One of the main subjects of psychological research was the *unconscious*. Through the influence in Russia of German philosopher Edouard von Hartmann, Stanislavsky inherited and appropriated pre-Freudian concepts of the *unconscious*. Although there is evidence of the Freudian paradigm in Russia, it came later and had a far lesser impact than in European countries. Emotion, and what were seen by some as its subconscious processes, was also being investigated by psychological theories of the time, such as those of Charles Darwin, William James, Herbert Spencer and Alexander Bain, all of which concentrated on the physiological basis of emotion, as did the work of associationist Théodule Ribot, whose importance for Stanislavsky has been widely acknowledged though not sufficiently examined. The influence of William James, more indirect yet still significant, has not to date been acknowledged. The meaning of Stanislavsky's slogan for the *system*, 'the subconscious creativity of nature itself – through the artist's conscious psycho-technique', should be considered in the light of all these ideas.

A paradigm shift in science occurred, emblematic of which was the publication of Darwin's *Origin of Species* in 1859.[4] The assertion of the theory that human beings evolved, as opposed to the widespread western belief in God's creation, radicalised thinking in many domains, particularly natural science. Darwin's impact in Russia was different from in the West.[5]

---

[3] Friedrich Nietzsche, *The Birth of Tragedy*, tr. Shaun Whiteside (London: Penguin, 1993), p. 9.
[4] See Peter J. Bowler, *Charles Darwin: The Man and his Influence* (Oxford: Basil Blackwell, 1990), Chapter 1, for an informed discussion of how Darwin and his work came to represent a shift from ideas of creationism to evolution, and also how the work was misrepresented.
[5] Darwin's work was subject to censorship and was smuggled in, with that of Thomas Huxley, in the 1860s. Dmitri I. Pisarev, the literary critic and radical, promulgated *The Origin of Species* in Russia, publishing an idiosyncratic summary and commentary on it in 1864, the year after Stanislavsky's birth. However, the idea of 'the struggle for existence' was glossed over as Darwin's ideas rippled through Russia in the late-nineteenth century. It was thought that the term was unnecessary and a reflection of capitalist views. Nature was not so cruel. The nihilist Chernyshevskii, and also Tolstoy, were very much against Darwinian evolution, favouring Jean Baptiste Lamarck's theories on heredity instead. See Loren Graham's *Science in Russia and the Soviet Union* (Cambridge University Press, 1993), Chapter 3.

It was believed that scientific law was discoverable – and Stanislavsky's search was characterised by this – and progress in science could cure the ills afflicting humankind. This had, of course, influenced Russian science of the nineteenth century, which was undeveloped in comparison with that of other countries. Darwin's theory of evolution and its arguments about animal behaviour encouraged materialistic analyses of mental events and Stanislavsky grew up in an increasingly secular Russia, where ideas of the material evolution of humankind were gaining influence and paving the way for the dialectical materialism of the Bolsheviks.

Darwin was revered by Ivan Petrovich Pavlov, who achieved world fame for his scientific work, and it was because of Darwin's theory that Pavlov and his contemporaries thought they could extrapolate findings about human beings from the study of animals. In 1872, significantly, in relation to the influence of science on acting theory, *The Expression of the Emotions in Man and Animals* was published. Darwin argued here, in a detailed study of animals and people that included photographs by Guillaume Duchenne,[6] that our expressions of emotion are universal (that is innate, not learned) and the product of our evolution. Darwin discussed facial expressions, holding that gestures are socially learned, although other scientists were to include gestures as part of the supposed universal language. This idea was to be incompatible with later theories of behaviour, which stated that inheritance plays no part in explaining our social behaviour, but it was extremely influential in Russian thought in the early-twentieth century, particularly in acting, while theories of conditioned reflexes were developing.

Politics and science

After the revolution, pre-modernist intellectual culture was regarded as suspect, prevailing ideas centring on the materialism and determinism of Marxist philosophy. In his funeral oration on Marx, Frederick Engels asserted that Marx's materialist conception of history was comparable with Darwin's theory of evolution as a discovery, that is, it was a scientific discovery of a law.[7] The Bolsheviks' embrace of Marx's historicism was such that, after the revolution, Marx's dialectical materialism was the basis for Communist society and its particular utopianism. The new philosophy brought with it an expectation that human nature could be

---

[6] The French neurologist Guillaume Benjamin Duchenne du Boulogne's pioneering study, *The Mechanism of Human Facial Expression*, was published in 1862.

[7] Peter Singer, *Marx* (Oxford University Press, 1980), p. 38.

radically transformed and that there were methods to enable that to happen. New men and new women of the revolution would build a new, happy, equal society on a scientific basis, where the worlds of work and leisure would be changed for the better. As people were the product of their environment, it was thought, social and economic forces could be controlled to produce the new Soviet man. Darwinism was appropriated, along with Pavlov's endorsement, as part of Soviet Marxism, which, it was claimed, was rooted in nature. Amy Sargeant writes that Lenin's view of nature derived via Engels from Hegel:

There is no matter without movement any more than there is movement without matter. The study of movement is therefore the essential object of the science of nature.[8]

The study of reflexes, à la Pavlov, became the focus of the study of movement and in it, it was believed, lay the key to understanding and controlling behaviour. It was, in fact, essential for the political leaders that Pavlov's work was central to the developing ideology, although there was a conflict here between ideas of science and politics:

Yet very early, in the midst of the Civil War, the highest leaders went out of their way to persuade Ivan Pavlov that there was an exceptionally honored place for him in revolutionary Russia, in spite of his strongly expressed disapproval of Bolshevism.[9]

The work on physiology, first by Ivan Mikhailovich Sechenov and later by Pavlov, introduced the materialist notion of the human organism which led to the paradigm shift in thinking of human behaviour in terms of reflexes, particularly as a result of Pavlov's work. Pavlov had received the Nobel Prize in 1904 and his theory of conditioned reflexes placed Russian science on the world stage from the beginning of the twentieth century. This was important for Stanislavsky as for other acting theoreticians. The idea that the individual's behaviour is a constant series of interactions with the environment grew widespread within Stanislavsky's lifetime.

The 1917 Revolution ushered in a period of utopianism and science, but at the same time the new science of the twentieth century placed Bolshevik leaders under pressure:

---

[8] Amy Sargeant, *Vsevolod Pudovkin: Classic Films of the Soviet Avant-garde* (London: I. B. Tauris, 2000), pp. 81–2.

[9] Abbott Gleason, Peter Kenez and Richard Stites (eds), *Bolshevik Culture* (Bloomington: Indiana University Press, 1985), p. 101.

The Bolsheviks claimed that they and their culture were 'scientific', but those who were in the process of making the most important Russian contributions to science could not accept the materialist metaphysics of the nineteenth century, any more than the avant-garde artists who were drawn to the Revolution could easily come to terms with nineteenth-century realism as the basis for their art.[10]

Accepting and enshrining Pavlov's work became the project of the Bolsheviks, leading later to the recognition of Pavlov's 'teaching' as the only correct embodiment of Marxism-Leninism in psychology, and the suppression of other kinds of psychology. Richard Stites writes that Pavlov's dogs salivating to ringing bells were a symbol of the scientific way to understand the mind by reducing it to associative functions of the nervous system.[11] Pavlov's bells rang across domains and continents as his ideas spread and there was much cross-fertilisation of scientific ideas in the Soviet Union, America and Europe after the revolution, including the preoccupation with the machine and the concern with 'the making of men'. Ideas on physical culture proliferated and so did ideas on scientific approaches to work.

In fact, Stanislavsky attempted to incorporate reflex theory into his work, no doubt believing it had been proved, and this affiliation was one of the reasons why Stanislavsky's *system* was recognised as authoritative in the thirties, because it was seen to corroborate current political and scientific thinking. Although Pavlov's ideas had been of great importance for Meyerhold (though in a different way), his work, on the other hand, became increasingly incompatible with Soviet ideology.

The Bolshevik project did not discard the past entirely, which was significant for Stanislavsky:

Lenin was a traditionalist in artistic taste and a political realist. He thought it was essential to 'grasp all the culture which capitalism has left and build socialism from it.' Proletarian culture . . . had to evolve organically out of the past and the present.[12]

Here is evidence for Foucault and Kuhn's view that knowledge does not advance by accretion, but that progress can be made by consciously accepting or rejecting cultural ideas. Rather than proletarian culture evolving organically, however, this was a period of extensive state intervention in culture. Narkompros, the Peoples' Commissariat for Education

[10] *Ibid.* p. ix.
[11] *Ibid.* p. 102.
[12] *Ibid.* p. 17.

and the Arts, was set up after the revolution under Anatoly Vasilievich Lunacharsky, who, with Aleksandr Aleksandrovich Bogdanov, encouraged *Proletkult*, the Proletarian Cultural Enlightening Organisation. State subsidies for the arts disappeared with the New Economic Policy in 1921, which caused problems for all organisations from futurist and proletarian arts groups to theatres such as the MAT. Subsidies were found later for certain kinds of art and in the late 1920s a new proletarian-cultural organisation, the Russian Association of Proletarian Writers (*Rossiskaia Assotsiatsiia Proletarskikh Pisatelei*, RAPP), which had connections in the party leadership, achieved power in the short term and established the pattern for state intervention in art.

Within this ferment of ideas there were contradictions: ideas of organic, beneficent nature and natural law, including the truths of behaviour about to be discovered, were juxtaposed with the view that the state or scientists or even individuals could intervene and shape human nature. There was the assumption that humanity was in the care of nature, and simultaneously it was thought that human beings could be engineered or trained. As time went on there was an insistence, for political reasons, on distinguishing the aspects of natural science that were ideologically correct from those that were not. The socialist realist precept that the function of art is to further the aims of Socialism gained currency during Stalin's rise to power, affecting all artists and, of course, Stanislavsky.

STANISLAVSKY, THE NATURAL SCIENTIST

Stanislavsky claimed human nature was the subject of his study, writing that his books 'have no pretensions to science. Their aim is exclusively practical. They attempt to convey what long experience of being an actor, director and teacher has taught me' (*AWHE*, p. 41). This may well be Stanislavsky's disclaimer after the revolution when ideas had changed and the definition of what was 'scientific' had become more circumscribed. For his approach, within the parameters of the time, is scientific. In fact, as Moore points out, he made a study of human behaviour over a period of forty years.[13] His methodology, like that of the associationist philosophers, was based on introspection and observation. He extrapolated from the results of his examination of his own experiences in acting and from his experiments in directing and training other actors, though

---

[13] Sonia Moore, *The Stanislavski System*, 2nd edn (London: Penguin, 1984), p. 17.

after 1917 he did not create a new role and stopped acting in 1928, at the age of sixty-five. In an article written in 1935 entitled 'October and the Theatre' he refers to the need for a theatre laboratory (*Collected Works* vol. 6, p. 387) from where, perhaps, Grotowski took the term.

Stanislavsky emphasised that his terminology arose from his practical work: 'Do not look for scientific roots in it . . . it is true that we also use scientific words, for example, "subconscious," "intuition" but they are used by us not in the philosophical, but in the most simple everyday meaning' (*AWHE*, p. 42). Despite his disclaimers he read and drew from scientific works, including texts on experimental psychology. He complained that stage creativity had been neglected by science in that it had not been researched (*AWHE*, p. 42), and elsewhere, discussing what he calls the 'logic and consistency of feelings', he again complained that these complex psychological questions were still little researched by science, which had given the actor neither practical instruction, nor foundation. He states he had no option, therefore, but to take a purely practical rather than a scientific path relying on 'our human nature, life experience, instinct, feeling, logic, consistency and the subconscious itself' (*AWHE*, p. 262).

The practical, introspective methodology could be claimed as scientific then but it was difficult for Stanislavsky to continue to claim this later, as the approach was based on pre-revolutionary science. An important reference work for him was Tikhon Faddeev's *Psychology*, published in 1913, from which he made brief but significant excerpts. Faddeev asserts experiment as the most complete scientific method in science and industry, but notes that experimental research cannot be conducted fully on consciousness, though some aspects, such as perception, association and memory, can be researched experimentally to some extent. Self-observation, he says, is the basis of psychological research. As 'everyone constantly studies his own soul . . . everyone is to a certain extent a psychologist'.[14] From separate observations, the psychologist must pick out constant manifestations and formulate them as laws, creating a system. The criteria for trustworthiness of the conclusions are 'logical feeling' or 'healthy sense' and indirect experience, that is, practical conclusions verified by experience, where plans lead to a desired end. As well as self-observation we draw our observations from others. We cannot observe their inner life directly but can make judgements about it from observation of their words

---

[14] Tikhon Faddeev, *Shkhol'naia Pedagokika; Kniga 1, Psikhologia* (Moscow: Tipografia Sutaba Moskovskogo voennogo okruga, 1913), p. 4.

and behaviour. This is clearly the process Stanislavsky attempted to employ in the development of his *system*. The validity of scientific laws, as Faddeev indicates, can be tested by seeing whether the consequences they predict actually occur. There were, therefore, parameters that Stanislavsky could adopt in a scientific study of acting.

Faddeev goes on to state that it is important to study psychic manifestations from a physiological point of view. His first rule is that psychology is the science that studies the laws of the life of the human soul; it does not attempt to define what a soul is in essence. His second rule is that the life of the human spirit appears in the constant changing of states of consciousness: feelings, images, voluntary manifestations and the indefinite states of consciousness and psychic overtones that accompany them.[15] Faddeev also writes that feelings and images, which are linked, and psychic states, such as desire or volitional effort, lead to action. The manifestation of spiritual life is reducible to the alternation of images, feelings and voluntary manifestations in the stream of consciousness, which is James's phrase.[16] Faddeev's psychology was empirical in the way that Ribot's and William James's was, and this was exactly what Stanislavsky took as the theoretical base of his *system*.

Moreover, for Stanislavsky, psychology is a natural science, a study of laws established by nature. Stanislavsky read and marked a pamphlet by Evgeny Bezpiatov, the proprietor of the A. S. Suvorin Drama School in St Petersburg, where Michael Chekhov trained. *Elements of Scientific Psychology in the Theatrical Art in connection with general questions of Theatre*, published in 1912, makes the case for empirical as opposed to rational psychology as the science on which acting should be based:

Psychology, according to James (and Ladd)'s best definition, is a natural science, concerning the description and interpretation of states of consciousness... Empirical psychology as a positive science studies the external manifestations of spiritual activity of a person. At its basis is a law, 'to each psychic manifestation corresponds a nervous-mechanical manifestation, which is inextricably linked with it.' Since the actor on stage produces in fact the external manifestations of spiritual (hidden) work, then in fact empirical psychology is also the science that is necessary for the actor.[17]

---

[15] *Ibid.* p. 12. 'Psychic overtones' is James's phrase. An example is a sensation of a forgotten word where we cannot remember the word itself but have some idea of it, such as the letter it begins with.

[16] *Ibid.* pp. 10–11.

[17] Evgenii Bezpiatov, *Elementi Nauchnoi Psikhologii v Teatral'nom Iskusstve* (St Petersburg: I. V. Leont'ev, 1912), pp. 7–8.

Bezpiatov refers to a correspondence between psychical and physical manifestations, an inextricable link between the inner and spiritual and the outer mechanical expression of the actor, the workings of which can be uncovered by psychology. This was similar to Stanislavsky's view of the inner and outer aspects of acting.

Stanislavsky and the laws of nature

Stanislavsky asserts that although for great artists 'inspiration' is a gift from Apollo, there is something else,

small but important, which to some degree is necessary and compulsory for both a Chaliapin and a chorister, because both have lungs, a respiratory system, nerves and a whole physical organism, in the one perfect, and in the other less so, which exist and work for the production of sound according to laws which are the same for all human beings. And in both the realm of rhythm, plastique, the laws of speech and the realm of the placing of the voice, breathing, there is much that is the same for all and therefore necessary for all. The same applies to the realm of psychic, creative life, as all artists without exception receive spiritual sustenance from laws established by nature, preserve this in the intellectual, affective or muscle memory, work on material in their artistic imaginations, give birth to the artistic image with all its internal life included in it and reincarnate it according to known and natural laws which are compulsory for all. These laws of creativity which are the same for all human beings and accessible to our consciousness are not very numerous, their role is not respected much, and confined to subservient tasks but nonetheless they . . . should be studied by every artist, as only through them can the superconscious creative apparatus be set in motion, the substance of which, it seems, will always be a mystery to us . . . These elementary psycho-physical and psychological laws have not until now been studied as they should (*MLIA*, pp. 494–5).

It is important to note that Stanislavsky asserts the necessity of what he calls psychophysical and psychological laws – the laws of creativity. He does not doubt that what he discovers through his introspective method must be true for all. Others, such as James, were more circum-spect, but Stanislavsky's life's work was a study of the workings of the human organism in acting, incorporating initially, as Natalie Crohn Schmitt states, the 'enthusiastic belief that scientists were rapidly dis-covering the laws of nature's single unified system'.[18] This outlook was reinforced by the psychology of his day and also what he believed to be

---

[18] Natalie Crohn Schmitt, 'Stanislavski, Creativity and the Unconscious', *New Theatre Quarterly*, 2: 8 (1986), p. 346.

transcendent philosophies. Stanislavsky's view of nature's beneficence was also reinforced in what he read of yoga. Discussing magnetism, Ramacharaka writes in *Hatha Yoga*,

So, by all means, apply the nature test to all theories of this kind – our own included – and if they do not square with nature discard them – the rule is a safe one. Nature knows what she is about – she is your friend and not your enemy.[19]

In Stanislavsky's 1909 edition this statement is marked; his faith in nature was corroborated here. Ramacharaka equates nature with the 'Life-Principle',[20] a vitalism shared by some schools of psychology in Stanislavsky's time.

Although Stanislavsky may have subscribed to the view that science would eventually define the laws of nature, at the same time he viewed human nature as having mysterious hidden depths (*AWHE*, p. 61). As these are not accessible directly, he states on many occasions that 'the conscious psycho-technique of the artist . . . is the ground for the growth of the subconscious creative processes of our organic nature (*AWHE*, p. 439). The actor must find a way to control nature, to harness it:

Electricity, wind, water and other involuntary forces of nature demand a knowledgeable and clever engineer to subjugate them on behalf of humankind. Our unconscious creative power also cannot go without its own kind of engineer – without conscious psycho-technique (*AWHE*, p. 61).

He writes elsewhere that only nature can do the work of creativity, 'it alone possesses in perfection the internal and external creative apparatus of experiencing and incarnation . . . but we can help our creative nature' (*AWHI*, p. 14). This has to be achieved through indirect means, through psycho-technique. The actor has to develop *second nature*. This is a key term in the theory of the *system*, the concept owing a debt to James, who thought that we should make many of our everyday actions habitual or *second nature* so that we can free our minds for higher work.[21]

Although nature is mysterious and spiritual, as Schelling asserted, for Stanislavsky there are mechanical aspects of human nature that can be trained and developed as *second nature*. As Milling and Ley write:

Conceived in this way, the study of acting is a natural science like any other. The process of acting already exists as an organic entity, both physical and spiritual, and as such it has both truth and beauty: all that remains is for the natural

[19] Yogi Ramacharaka, *Hatha Yoga, or the Yogi Philosophy of Physical Well-being* (London: L. N. Fowler, 1917), p. 11.
[20] *Ibid.* p. 20.
[21] William James, *Principles of Psychology* (London: Macmillan, 1890, reprinted 1950), vol. I, p. 122.

scientist to discover its originating sources or inspiration, and to chart the stages of its progression and natural development.[22]

There remains the problem that nature does not solve all the performer's problems; it must be harnessed and controlled and the actor's body must be trained. Yet nature is the source of truth, of truthful, lifelike acting.

STANISLAVSKY'S AESTHETIC THEORY AND NATURALISM

For Stanislavsky, art does not represent or imitate nature – art should be nature, it should be life, or natural *truth*:

All together this made you live on the stage naturally, according to the laws of nature . . . now you have correct life, which is not only psychical but also physical. In it is truth. You have believed it not with the mind but with the feeling of your own organic, physical nature (*AWHE*, p. 265).

Stanislavsky's aesthetic theory, his view of the artist and his 'naturalism' are all based in 'nature' and so are his ideas of actor training. Before Stanislavsky there was a call for a more 'natural' Russian acting style. In the mid-nineteenth century Ostrovsky's essays discussed realism and naturalism, and Pushkin and Gogol discussed 'truth'. Stanislavsky referred to their work, Tolstoy's, and critics such as Vissarion Belinsky in the development of his ideas. The Russian actor Mikhail Shchepkin, the German Saxe-Meiningen Court Theatre and Anton Chekhov were also formative influences.

Stanislavsky's view of aesthetics coincides with that of Tolstoy. In *What is Art?*, which was written in 1897, Tolstoy makes a survey of ideas about the purpose of art, from Aristotle, Plato and Socrates to writers on aesthetics from Alexander Baumgarten (1714–62), to Tolstoy's contemporaries.[23] In many theories the definition of the purpose of art is predicated on ideas of beauty and pleasure. Tolstoy rejects these and adduces his own argument, beginning with a practical definition given by French critic Eugene Véron (1825–89) in *L'Esthétique*, which was published in 1878. According to Tolstoy, Véron states:

Art is the manifestation of feelings (*émotion*), conveyed externally by a combination of lines, forms, colours or a sequence of gestures, sounds or words subject to certain rhythms.[24]

---

[22] Jane Milling and Graham Ley, *Modern Theories of Performance* (London: Palgrave, 2001), p. 9.
[23] Baumgarten first applied the word 'aesthetic' to a specific science, and has therefore been termed the founder of aesthetics.
[24] Leo Tolstoy, *What is Art?* tr. Richard Pevear and Larissa Volokhonsky (London: Penguin, 1995), p. 28.

Tolstoy writes that art should be considered one of the conditions of human life and in considering it this way, 'we cannot fail to see that art is a means of communion among people'.[25] It can convey feelings such as merriment, joy, sadness, despair, cheerfulness, dejection or the feeling of self-denial and submission to fate or God in a drama, the raptures of lovers in a novel, the feeling of sensuousness in a painting, the briskness of a triumphal march in music, the peace of an evening landscape. Its aim, he believes, is to convey the 'loftiest and best feelings people have attained to in life', thus uniting people.[26] Much of the rest of Tolstoy's work is devoted to condemning art that perverts this spiritual aim. According to R. F. Christian, Tolstoy's sources as well as Véron were Max Schassler's *Kritische Geschichte der Ästhetik*, published in 1872, and *The Philosophy of the Beautiful*, by William Angus Knight (1836–1916).[27] To the thesis that art is the expression and communication of feeling, Tolstoy added the assertion that others experience the same feeling as the artist; it is, in Tolstoy's term, *infectious*, and the artist can not only transmit feelings that he has experienced, but also ones that he has imagined. Gurevich explained the latter idea with reference to an essay by Tolstoy written in 1861, in an article she wrote in 1911 entitled 'Tolstoy's Artistic Behests'.[28] (Meyerhold and Michael Chekhov both subscribed to this idea.) She writes that Tolstoy also distinguished between feelings, which are transmitted by art, and thoughts, which are transmitted by words. This was important for Stanislavsky.

Although not all the playwrights produced by Stanislavsky would have met with Tolstoy's approval (for example, Ibsen, Hauptmann and Maurice Maeterlinck), Stanislavsky adopted Tolstoy's aesthetic framework and terminology. He considered feeling the subject matter for art:

In transmitting the facts and the plot of the play the artist involuntarily transmits the spiritual content contained within them; he conveys the life of the human spirit itself that flows like an underwater current under the external facts. On stage all that is necessary are facts containing spiritual content, which are the final result of internal feelings, or on the other hand, facts which are the cause, giving birth to these feelings (*AWR*, p. 93).

He also used the terms *experiencing* for what the artist undergoes, *infectiousness* and *transmission* to describe how this is conveyed to the audience,

[25] *Ibid.* p. 37.
[26] *Ibid.* p. 53.
[27] R. F. Christian, *Tolstoy: A Critical Introduction* (Cambridge University Press, 1969), p. 248.
[28] Liubov' Gurevich, 'Khudozhestvennie Zaveti Tolstogo', *Russkaya Misl'*, 4 (1911), p. 127.

the *sense of true measure*, which he describes in *MLIA*, and *communion*.[29] Gurevich, Stanislavsky's editor, adds of Tolstoy, 'he sought the teleological basis of art, defining its existence in correspondence with its purpose in the general course of human life'.[30] This is Stanislavsky's shared teleology: art has a spiritual purpose in enabling *communion* between people.

Stanislavsky's concept of the artist's spiritual vocation coincides with that of the critic Vissarion Belinsky (1811–1848), whom Stanislavsky would have studied at school. He refers to him on a number of occasions in his writings. Benedetti writes that Belinsky's vision was of

the artist as missionary whose task was to declare the poetic nature of the world itself. Contemporary literature written in the age of science had to abandon the realm of myth and legend and the subjective expression of emotion to address itself to the problem of describing the world of external reality . . . To describe the sun as a natural phenomenon, a star travelling through infinite space rather than as Phoebus' chariot driving across the sky was not to abandon poetry . . . but to exchange one kind for . . . the poetry of the real . . . and present the world in all its truth and nakedness.[31]

Science and art both tend to the improvement of society and the artist must conform to the highest moral and ethical standards. Laurence Senelick writes that according to Belinsky, drama uses individuals to exhibit all humanity and is therefore the art form closest to its audience: 'As we the public become more engrossed in the emotions and fate of other human beings on stage, our egoism evaporates and we become better persons and better citizens.'[32]

German romanticism was the source for this conception of the role of the artist in society, the artist as prophet and spiritual leader of his nation, with the purpose of art being to serve the truth.[33] In the 1830s Belinsky found that Schelling's idealism suggested a way of viewing Russia's problems and the possibility of resolving them in an optimistic way. For Schelling, the world is an expression of a single eternal idea, which takes its form in history and everything has a purpose. Belinsky went on to explore Fichte's egocentric idealism, and then Hegel's philosophy. Throughout

[29] *Ibid.* p. 157.
[30] Gurevich, 'Khudozhestvennie Zaveti Tolstogo', *Russkai Mysl'*, 3 (1911), p. 125.
[31] Jean Benedetti, *Stanislavski: His Life and Art*, 2nd edn (London: Methuen, 1999), pp. 35–6.
[32] Laurence Senelick (tr. and ed.), *Russian Dramatic Theory from Pushkin to the Symbolists* (Austin: University of Texas, 1981), p. xxviii.
[33] Joe Andrew, *Writers and Society During the Rise of Russian Realism* (London: Macmillan, 1980), p. 118.

his changes in thinking, however, Belinsky (who, like Pushkin and Gogol, revered Shchepkin) considered the artist to be a superior being with a quasi-religious responsibility in the expression of his art. Again, it was Schelling who inspired the idea that artists were more sensitive to their times than ordinary, rational beings. Belinsky called the artist to sacrifice himself, to relate to the universal idea 'to reproduce... the idea of the general life of nature'.[34] Poetic creation is viewed here as analogous to the creative power of nature, and by the 1840s Belinsky was also advocating the educative value of art.

Throughout his life, Stanislavsky maintained both a view of the artist's task as sacred, and a reverential attitude to Tolstoy. He produced Tolstoy's plays and Sulerzhitsky, Stanislavsky's close assistant, was also influenced by Tolstoy. If a performance did not have the desired effect on an audience, Stanislavsky would blame himself rather than question the theory. In 1917, just after the revolution, a gathering of carriers and draymen at a tearoom on Taganskaia Ploshchad' in Moscow had asked for the 'great actor'. Stanislavsky read to them from Griboedov's *Woe from Wit*, but the men did not know the classic play and it did not move them. Stanislavsky is reported to have said that he needed to work on himself more:

The greatest reward for an actor is when he can captivate any auditorium with his experiencings and for this, unusual veracity and sincerity of communication is needed, and if they didn't understand me in the tea room, then I am guilty for not leaping over the spiritual bridge between them and me.[35]

The main precept that Stanislavsky shares with Tolstoy, therefore, is that feeling is the subject matter of art. Feeling, for Stanislavsky, is 'natural' and his task therefore was to find the way for this natural truth to be expressed on stage.

The inheritance of these concepts of truth and nature for acting and actor-training resulted in various experiments and searches on Stanislavsky's part. Goethe wrote in *Rules for Actors* (which Stanislavsky later studied), 'first of all the actor must understand that he should not only imitate nature but also reproduce it in an ideal way and consequently combine the truth with the beautiful in his performance'.[36] This could be seen as Stanislavsky's basic tenet.

[34] *Ibid.* p. 139.
[35] I. N. Vinogradskaia, *Zhizn i tvorchestvo K. S. Stanislavskovo, Letopis*, 2nd edn (Moscow: Moskovskii Khudozhestvennyi Teatr, 2003), vol. 2, p. 569.
[36] Johann Wolfgang von Goethe, *Rules for Actors*, tr. into Russian, *Maska*, 3 (1912), p. 515.

INTERNAL AND EXTERNAL WORK

Stanislavsky's preoccupations in developing the *system* as a means to natural, truthful expression were the actors' work on themselves (that is, training), and the actor's work on a role (characterisation). The process of characterisation is divided in *AWR* into three periods: the period of *analysis*, of getting to know the role, the period of *experiencing* and the period of *incarnation*. Therefore, in both training and characterisation, considerations of what Stanislavsky calls 'internal' and 'external' work are important. *MLIA* recounts the development of the stages of Stanislavsky's thought on this issue in the first four periods of his career and introduces some key terminology. He is writing retrospectively and perhaps with the benefit of hindsight on occasion, but this account is illuminating in many ways and captures the spirit of discovery, which enlivens his style of writing. He entitles the four periods 'Artistic Childhood', 'Artistic Adolescence', 'Artistic Youth' and 'Artistic Maturity'. The final period of his work was after the publication of *MLIA* in 1928.

Stanislavsky's 'Artistic Childhood', 1863–1877

Stanislavsky was born Konstantin Sergeevich Alekseev, in tsarist Russia in 1863, the year of the death of the famous Russian actor Mikhail Shchepkin and two years after the emancipation of the serfs. He was of the merchant class, as his father owned a factory in Moscow that made gold and silver thread, and the family were immensely wealthy. From an early age, Stanislavsky took part in productions with other household members and eventually Stanislavsky's father, Sergei Vladimirovich, had a theatre built at the family's country home in Liubimovka. The family were enthusiastic patrons of the theatre, ballet and opera flourishing in Moscow at the time. Stanislavsky's education was conducted by tutors, and included gymnastics, music and ballet. Roose-Evans states that he was taught by Ekaterina Sankovskaia, one of the most famous of Russia's ballerinas.[37] At the age of eleven he went to a school that offered a classical education, then the Lazarev Institute for Oriental Languages. In *MLIA*, Stanislavsky describes his appearances as a child in the family entertainments. On the first occasion, as a small child, he was dressed as

---

[37] James Roose-Evans, *Experimental Theatre from Stanislavsky to Peter Brook*, 4th edn (London: Routledge, 1989), p. 10.

winter in a tableau, and did not understand where he should look or what he should do. 'I experienced unconsciously a feeling of awkwardness at this meaningless lack of activity (*bezdeistvie*) on stage even then and since then I am more afraid of it than anything when I am on stage.' He was given a stick and told to mime putting it into the real fire, but he actually put it in, starting a blaze:

This seemed a completely natural and logical action to me . . . Since that evening I retain on the one hand the impressions of how pleasant it was to be successful and to be and act on stage purposefully and on the other the unpleasantness of failure, the awkwardness of inactivity and sitting for no reason in front of a crowd of spectators (p. 55).

Whether Stanislavsky could really remember this incident as clearly as he describes it is a matter for conjecture but the point is that he is anxious to prove that his *system* is based on truths of behaviour that are observable even in childhood, and also that action is crucial to acting.

The year 1877 saw Stanislavsky's acting debut in the family theatre at Liubimovka in two one-act plays, *A Cup of Tea* and *The Old Mathematician or Waiting for a Comet in a District Town*. Stanislavsky's first method of acting, as a young man, was imitative; he copied the voice, gesture and movement of famous actors in order to develop a characterisation. In *A Cup of Tea* he imitated Nikolai Ignat'evich Muzil, a comic actor from the Maly Theatre, who had a hoarse voice and made funny facial expressions. This external route into the character gave him a feeling of confidence, and he experienced what he took to be inspiration (*MLIA*, p. 94). However, he was told that his performance was lacking and his inspiration false, a result of his nervousness and lack of restraint. In the other role, where he had struggled, not knowing what to do, he did better. However, in imitating another Maly actor, M. P. Sadovsky in Ostrovsky's *Artists and Admirers*, the imitated mannerisms became habitual and then he made them his own, that is, they became *second nature*. They were sincere and *experienced*, and therefore he was more successful in his acting. Stanislavsky writes that what was external became infused with something from the inside; there was more to his characterisation now than mere imitation, but he did not yet know what this was. Stanislavsky's experimentation was predicated on this concept of internal and external.

Emotional memory was the first of the keys to internal experiencing (Tolstoy's term). Some emotional experiences from childhood were as alive in Stanislavsky's memory as if they were present experiences, and when he recalled them, he experienced the emotion again (*MLIA*, p. 57). Although Stanislavsky had not at this stage discovered Ribot, he claims that his practical experience bore out what he later sought to validate theoretically. He also writes that impressions of famous Italian singers, such as Patti, Cotogni and Giametta, whom he saw at the Bolshoi theatre, were sealed, not just in his aural or visual memory but, as he saw it, also physically, in his whole body, and hence were not conscious, but organic, spiritual and physical. Again he is writing retrospectively and perhaps with an eye to how such physiologists as Sechenov described impressions being stored in the memory, but for Stanislavsky there was always a spiritual dimension. His famous descriptions of memory as a 'storehouse' (*AWHE*, Chapter 9, 'Emotional Memory') are based on what he claimed to have experienced practically. His purpose in recounting these experiences is to continue to emphasise that his acting methods developed from 'organic, natural laws'.

Stanislavsky's 'Artistic Adolescence', 1877–1888

The Alekseev Circle, an amateur company, was formed by the family, household and friends in 1877. Stanislavsky worked on productions (largely operettas), both as actor and director. He worked intensively on himself to correct what he perceived as vocal and postural problems (he was 'tall, clumsy, graceless and mispronounced many letters', *MLIA*, p. 130) and continued to observe great actors and study acting methods. Sometimes professional actors would perform with the Alekseev Circle and in 1877 he was invited to take part in a semi-professional production of Gogol's *The Gamblers*, directed by Aleksandr Fedotov, an actor from the Maly, where the teachings of Shchepkin lived on. Mikhail Semenovich Shchepkin (1788–1863) was a serf actor, released from serfdom in 1821. He achieved great renown on the Moscow stage, and mixed with such writers as Pushkin, Gogol, Lermontov, Griboedov and Turgenev. Stanislavsky learned much from actors who were of Shchepkin's school, such as Fedotov and Glikeria Fedotova, about professional behaviour, the ethics of acting and communication with the stage partner and later read and annotated several books on Shchepkin. In a letter dated 1848, Shchepkin wrote:

In order to check yourself and your advice always keep nature in mind; crawl, so to speak into the skin of the character, study carefully his particular ideas, if there are such and do not lose sight of the society of his previous life. When everything has been studied, when whatever positions have been taken from life, then you will act truly. You may sometimes act weakly, or sometimes satisfactorily to some degree (this often depends on your spiritual state), but you will play truly (*AWR*, 1st edn, p. 493, n57).

The latter statement Stanislavsky took as axiomatic and also adopted the aphorism, 'There are no small parts, only small actors' and other principles which emerge in the *system* as the notions of 'truth from one's own experience', ensemble and discipline. Shchepkin said that the actor should play simply and naturally. Shchepkin was once rehearsing Molière's *Sganarelle* in the conventional declamatory style, but as he had rehearsed it that way hundreds of times before, he spoke the lines in his own voice for a change, instead of 'declaiming'. He decided that this was more effective, and based his acting career on this discovery.

It may be that what was considered 'natural' in Shchepkin's epoch was not the same in Stanislavsky's. However, Stanislavsky took Shchepkin's recommendations into his theory. Shchepkin said: 'it is so much easier to play mechanically – for that you only need your reason', and 'an actor of feeling must begin by wiping out his self . . . and become the character the author intended him to be'.[38]

Clearly, Stanislavsky developed Shchepkin's ideas. As Vladimir Nemirovich-Danchenko wrote in a letter:

though Stanislavsky established himself in the actor's art on the basis of 'Shchepkinism' this did not stop him bringing concepts into art that would have made Shchepkin's hair stand on end if he had heard of them. Shchepkin would have thought that Stanislavsky with his 'rhythm', his 'prana', and his 'kernel' encroached on Shchepkin's realism and with [Stanislavsky's] actual truth encroached on the nobility of his art.[39]

Stanislavsky was not very successful academically and in 1881 he went to work for his father's business, pursuing as an amateur his interest in performance, studying the art of famous performers and taking lessons from them when possible. His first aim was to be an opera singer and he studied with Fedor Kommisarzhevsky, professor at the Moscow Conservatoire, but abandoned this aim because of vocal problems. He became director of the Moscow branch of the Russian Musical Society and the

---

[38] Jean Benedetti, *Stanislavski: An Introduction* (London: Methuen, 1989) p. 8.
[39] Vinogradskaia, *Letopis*, vol. 3, p. 468.

Moscow Conservatoire in 1885, meeting many famous figures from the musical world of the day. The importance of music to Stanislavsky throughout his career should not be underestimated. He became well known in amateur circles and took the stage name of Stanislavsky in 1884, to protect his family, from whom he concealed his intentions. As Benedetti writes:

It never for one moment occurred to Sergei Vladimirovich that his son harboured ambitions to become a professional actor. Such a notion was unthinkable. The status of the professional actor was even lower in Russia than the rest of Europe. Actors, including the great Shchepkin, had been serfs within living memory, the property of the nobility; humiliated and beaten when they did not come up to standard. To be an actor was to be legally disqualified from any form of public office. The taboo against turning professional was absolute.[40]

In 1885, he auditioned for the Moscow Theatre School and was accepted, but left within three weeks, disappointed with the standard of training. The methodology was based on the students copying the teachers, and Stanislavsky had formed his views on the imitative method already. If the students had been allowed to do it in their own way it might have been at least sincere, natural and truthful (*MLIA*, p. 125).

At this stage of his development Stanislavsky recognised the importance of training the body and voice, in order to correct problems. He noticed that Virginia Zucchi, an Italian professional ballet dancer who was involved with the Alekseev Circle for a time, had 'freedom and a lack of tension in her muscles at emotional high points...whereas I was always tense on stage' (p. 145). He goes on to say he was still copying other actors' interpretations of roles:

I did not give my attention to what was happening on stage at a given moment but to what had happened at some time on other stages, from where I took my models. I did not do what I myself felt, but repeated what someone else had felt...I copied the external results of someone's experiencing. I strutted and tensed myself physically.

In seeking the heightened energy necessary to sustain a performance, he tried to make himself speak louder and act more energetically, but this resulted in performances that in his view were embarrassingly bad. The result of being physically present on stage but giving his attention to theatre performances by others in the past (that is, trying to remember

---

[40] Benedetti, *Stanislavski: His Life and Art*, p. 21.

how someone else had performed the role), resulted in a split, a *dislocation* (*vyvikh*), and in straining to overcome it he created tension; his muscles, it seemed, were in rebellion against him. This term is important to an understanding of Stanislavsky's work.

Stanislavsky's 'Artistic Youth', 1888–1906

In 1888 Stanislavsky met Maria Perevosshchikova (who later took the stage name Lilina) when they worked together on a comedy by the popular playwright Ivan Krylov for a conservatoire charity, and they married the following year.[41] The Moscow Society of Art and Literature was founded in 1888 by Stanislavsky, Kommisarzhevsky, Fedor Sollogub, a well-known artist, and Fedotov, the director, writer and actor who had directed Stanislavsky in plays by Racine and Gogol and had encouraged him to consider raising his sights, despite his family's views, beyond amateur performance. Glikeria Fedotova was also one of his advisors. Stanislavsky subsidised the work of the society from his own private fortune. He visited the Comédie Française and the Paris Conservatoire in 1889 but overall was not impressed with the training methods, which were based, again, on students imitating their teachers.

When Stanislavsky was rehearsing for Pushkin's *Miser Knight*, Fedotov and Sollogub performed, as he calls it, an operation on him, that was 'both an amputation, a disembowelling and a cleansing of all the theatrical rottenness, which remained in its hiding places'. His image of the Knight, was what he called a 'stencil', a stereotype of the operatic, elderly nobleman, whereas Fedotov's image was of an ancient, nervous old man, far more interesting than Stanislavsky's. Over the course of the rehearsals Fedotov and Sollogub taught him many valuable lessons (*MLIA*, pp. 154–61) mostly, in Grotowski's phrase, *via negativa*, the clichés and falseness that must be stripped away to achieve truthful acting. As he continued in his quest, Stanislavsky attempted to find something *internal* for the character of Pushkin's Miser Knight, who lives in a castle, by getting himself locked up in an old castle overnight. He discovered that the actor's memory does not work in this way, that is, by trying to record actual experiences and feelings, which can then be revived in a role. A period of confusion ensued, where he wanted to stop 'acting' and

---

[41] Stanislavsky's relationship with Lilina is discussed in Maria Ignatieva's 'Between Love and Theatre: Young Stanislavski', *Theatre History Studies*, 25 (June 2005), pp. 173–90.

producing stereotyped and melodramatic characterisations. When working on Pisemsky's *Bitter Fate*, he confirmed his earlier important discovery (which he was later to see corroborated by Ribot) that muscular tension is a barrier to feeling and emotion:

when real creative feeling is needed . . . the body tenses from lack of strength of will, there is an abnormal tension everywhere, in all the centres there are knots and spasms, thanks to which the legs stiffen and can hardly move, the hands are wooden, the breathing forced, the throat constricted and the whole body is dead. Or, on the other hand, because of the lack of power of feeling there is anarchy through the body: muscles contract involuntarily, bringing about lots of movements, poses and gestures that have no meaning, and nervous tics and so on. Feeling itself runs and hides away from this chaos (*MLIA*, p. 169).

Secondly, he knew that you cannot 'act' an emotional state, that is, you cannot 'be angry' in general without a reason. And in learning some external restraint, getting rid of superfluous gesturing and movement, he practised the difficult task of standing still on stage. He would 'place all the tension in one centre', pressing his nails into his palms, sometimes drawing blood. Eventually, he says, he was able to release this tension, freeing himself from strain and gaining praise from his director (*MLIA*, p. 170).

He experimented with replacing gesture by working on his intonation, giving attention to what he was looking at, and his facial expression. Then he was rebuked for grimacing. Then, serendipity led to true creative work. He found that emotion could appear if he allowed the atmosphere of a scene to affect him and then it could rise to a crescendo (*MLIA*, p. 171–2). The make-up he wore for the roles of Sotanville in Molière's *Georges Dandin* and Paratov in Ostrovsky's *The Dowerless Bride* also helped to bring the external image to life. A mistake in make-up, where half his moustache was glued on higher than the other, gave him the idea of slyness for a character in *The Rouble* (p. 181). In Pisemsky's *Usurpers of the Law* in 1889, he created the character of a general – an image appeared: he did not know where it came from.

Technical means of acting pushed me towards the truth and the feeling of truth is the best stimulus to feeling, experiencing, imagination and creativity (*MLIA*, p. 177).

Still, Stanislavsky's naturalism in this period was very much influenced by the Saxe-Meiningen Court Theatre. This was a company dedicated to producing classics with meticulous historical accuracy in every detail of costume, set and properties. It was a new departure to have designs specific to a production in the theatre world in Europe and Russia that relied to a large extent on stock sets and costume. There were lighting effects and other naturalistic stage effects and actors were on occasion chosen for their physical resemblance to a character rather than their acting ability or status in the company. They were also renowned for the authenticity of their crowd scenes. Ostrovsky wrote, 'What we saw at their theatre was not art but skill or, in other words, craftsmanship', and complained that the external truth did not guarantee an inner truth in acting.[42] At this stage Stanislavsky found their external methods compelling. In 1890 the second visit of the Saxe-Meiningen Court Theatre to Moscow had a great influence on Stanislavsky's production and directorial methods and in 1891 Stanislavsky undertook his first independent production of a serious play, Leo Tolstoy's *Fruits of Enlightenment.* Stanislavsky drew attention for his performances and productions, which in this period included Karl Gutzkow's *Uriel Acosta*, Gerhardt Hauptmann's *Assumption of Hannele*, and Shakespeare's *Othello.* While Stanislavsky's amateur work and work at the factory continued, from 1894, when Nicholas II became Tsar, a period of famine, strikes and civil unrest ensued.

The first characterisation in which Stanislavsky considered he had achieved success was as Rostanev in his own adaptation of Dostoevsky's story *The Village of Stepanchikovo.* Here he became Rostanev whereas 'in other roles I had to a greater or lesser extent, "teased" (copied, imitated) others or my own images' (*MLIA*, p. 196). He still did not know the technical means of achieving this – it had just been luck. Then for the role of Othello he studied the movement and poses of an Arab he had met in Paris, but though he had made the outward characteristics his own he found he was not really up to the emotional demands of the part and strained his voice:

For a young, inexperienced actor to be playing a tragic role was like being in a lion's cage or having to jump across a chasm; the actor resists what has to be done and strains excessively. The actor has to laugh or cry when he doesn't want to. The only way out is to adopt conventions, which soon become actors' stencils (*MLIA*, pp. 183–4).

An example he gives is that of the Russian folk-hero, the *bogatyr*, with its swaggering walk, poses with the hands on the hips, tossing the head back. Some progress was made, working with the Maly actors; he learned the craft of acting and gained stage experience and practise in projecting his voice.

[42] A.N. Ostrovskii, *Polnoe Sobranie Sochinenii* (Moscow: Iskusstvo, 1973–80), vol. 10, pp. 427–30, quoted in David Magarshack, *Stanislavsky: A Life*, 2nd edn (Westport, Connecticut: Greenwood Press, 1975) p. 40.

The Moscow Art Theatre

Stanislavsky had dreamed of a theatre of his own and in 1897 he met Vladimir Ivanovich Nemirovich-Danchenko, a playwright and drama instructor at the Moscow Philharmonic School (where Meyerhold was studying). They formulated their theatre ethic, rejecting the old methods of acting and forming the Moscow Art Theatre (MAT) in 1898, which was to be a 'people's theatre', dedicated to high standards of acting and production. This was a professional theatre and marked the end of Stanislavsky's work with amateur groups. He had appeared in seventy-five different roles as an amateur and was to create only twenty-eight under the auspices of the MAT.[43] However, he continued to maintain his interests in the family business until 1917. He did not subsidise the MAT in the way he had the Society of Art and Literature, his main financial investment being in studio work.

At the beginning they produced plays by Ibsen, Pushkin and adaptations of Dostoevsky's work, mostly directed by Nemirovich-Danchenko. Stanislavsky describes the stages of development of the theatre as 'lines' (*MLIA*, p. 274). There was the 'Line of Historical-Everyday Life' where great care was taken with the accuracy of the creation of historical images. He and the MAT were heavily influenced by the Meiningen performance style and the methods of their director Ludwig Kronegk. This line included plays by A. K. Tolstoy, Shakespeare, Hauptmann and Sophocles (p. 276). In 1902, Briusov published an article entitled 'Unnecessary Truth', commenting on 'the unnecessary truth of material objects and cluttered stages . . . obscuring the spiritual aspect of life on stage, the performer's creative emotion'.[44] This, and the need to find a way to produce symbolist drama, encouraged Stanislavsky to begin to seek for theatrical truth in a different way. The 'Line of the Fantastic' was begun in 1900 with Alexander Ostrovsky's *Snow Maiden*. Then there was the 'Line of Symbolism/Impressionism', with plays by Ibsen, Maeterlinck and Knut Hamsun, and also the 'Line of Intuition and Feeling' and the plays of Anton Chekhov. In this period there was sometimes inspiration but Stanislavsky complained that

We could not then create for ourselves at will a genuine, normal, natural state of being on stage. We could not create in our souls the right sort of ground for the superconscious (*MLIA*, p. 287).

---

[43] Magarshack, *Stanislavsky: A Life*, p. 139.
[44] V. Briusov, 'Nienuzhnaia Pravda', *Mir Iskusstva*, 4 (Petersburg, 1902).

It was the work on the plays of Anton Chekhov that led Stanislavsky to important discoveries about acting, that is, it was about the creation of life in a role on stage, not *representing* a role, and the creation of 'mood' as a way to get the actors to sense external truth by means of authenticity in set, costume and effects from which internal truth in the acting should emerge. The success of the MAT was inextricably linked with Anton Chekhov. Stanislavsky's first Chekhov productions, beginning with *The Seagull* in 1898, were dominated by naturalistic detail in the attempt to create truth for the audience and the actor. Stanislavsky was battling with the problem of stage fright, and how the actor could avoid muscular spasms when standing in front of an audience:

In an attempt to overcome these contortions, Stanislavsky turned to 'slice-of-life' evocation. Perhaps it was his attentive analysis of Chekhov's stage directions in *The Seagull*, which, at this stage in his artistic development, caused Stanislavsky to perceive naturalistic details as a key to liberating the actor from convention and contortion. With naive fervour, he took such details to excess, with tolling bells, crashing storms, breaking glass and barking dogs.[45]

In fact, Stanislavsky found the play problematic because there was so little action and he wanted things for the actors to respond to and to do. Chekhov complained about the excessive sound effects and other details. But what the two had in common was a desire to express truth. Chekhov's work became defined as 'poetic realism' and Stanislavsky later developed the concept of 'spiritual realism',[46] which could be compared with Belinsky's formulation.

In *The Seagull*, the set, *mise-en-scène*, lighting, music and sound created an external mood:

Often this acted on the souls of the actors. They felt the external truth and intimate memories from their own lives connected with it arose in their souls and lured from them the feelings Chekhov spoke about. Then the artist stopped acting and began to live the life of the play, became a person in the drama (*MLIA*, p. 294–5).

He recognised that he still needed a method of working from the 'external' to the 'internal', as this inspiration did not occur consistently.

Later on, the sound of someone scratching on a chair in rehearsal, which sounded like a mouse scratching, suggested the mood of ennui for

---

[45] Bella Merlin, 'Which Came First: The System or "The Seagull"?' *New Theatre Quarterly*, 15: 3 (1999), p. 223.
[46] Vinogradskaia, *Letopis*, vol. 2, p. 362.

Chekhov's *Three Sisters*, stirring personal recollections from childhood in Stanislavsky (p. 306). In both these situations, emotion appeared when not forced. Stanislavsky began to allow himself to be guided by intuition, while still being convinced that there must be a technical, not just intuitive route to the truth, to feeling, *experiencing*, imagination and creativity. However, he was still working from the 'external' to the 'internal', from *incarnation* to *experiencing*, from form to content. He used images from life to achieve external veracity and also *emotional memory*. He was seeking ways to overcome the problem of *dislocation*, so that internal *experience* was manifested in external truth and vice versa.

The method of imitation could be classed with *craft*, as in the Meiningen approach to acting, as Stanislavsky saw it, or *representational* acting, where the actor skilfully recreates the external form of emotion, but does not *experience* it. Having moved away from this as a young actor, Stanislavsky departed utterly from the model in his encounter with Chekhov. 'You cannot "act" or "represent" in the plays of Chekhov... you must be, or exist, proceeding from the main spiritual artery established deeply inside' (*MLIA*, p. 290–91). What is more, the Stanislavskian actor, as well as having a physical, emotional and spiritual dimension, possesses an *unconscious*, a *subconscious*, and also a *superconscious* from which creative solutions can emerge by means of intuition. Of course, these concepts were derived from ideas current at the time, such as those of von Hartmann. Stanislavsky wrote, 'The superconscious comes out of its hiding place only when the spiritual and physical life of the artist on stage develops genuinely, normally, according to the laws of nature' (*MLIA*, p. 287).

During what Stanislavsky called the Socio-political Line, plays by Gorky and Ibsen were produced. Stanislavsky's acclaimed portrayal of Ibsen's Dr Stockmann was developed in 1900 and was even more successful with audiences after the 1905 Revolution than prior to that. The pattern for long rehearsal periods was established, with some plays taking over a year of rehearsals. Despite the MAT's success, Stanislavsky and Nemirovich-Danchenko began to have disagreements from 1899 onwards, which worsened as time went on. In 1905 Stanislavsky funded a studio on Povarskaia Street and invited Meyerhold to work there, to develop appropriate means of expression for symbolist plays, recognising his own lack of success in this area. This, however, was a short-lived experiment with inexperienced actors that ended, in Stanislavsky's view, in failure.

So he had found that the path of intuition and feeling from the *external* through the *internal* to the *superconscious* could work but was still not the definitive method (p. 230). Stanislavsky then describes what represents the epitome of acting for him, that is, *fusion* or *merging* (*slianie*) with the role, which was also very important for Vakhtangov and could be contrasted with Michael Chekhov's *transformation*. *Fusion* is a Tolstoyan concept; Gurevich writes, 'we are freed from our solitude, and the main attraction and quality of art is in such *fusion* with others'.[47] However, Stanislavsky applies the term to the actor's relationship with the character, rather than the audience.

In *fusion* with the role, the external image proceeds from the internal one. In the role of Stockmann, Stanislavsky found the necessary spiritual material and memories of feelings from life that were 'analogous to the role. The soul and body of Stockmann and Stanislavsky fused organically with each other' (p. 320). Stanislavsky only had to think of Stockmann's cares and worries and the character's stoop and hurried walk appeared instinctively, or subconsciously. Some years later, Stanislavsky relates that he met up again with two men whom he had encountered prior to developing the role of Stockmann. He realised that he had retained several of their mannerisms in his *subconscious* and used these for the role, not remembering, at the time of creation, from where the mannerisms had come. He used memories which had been, as he saw it, recorded in the *subconscious* as well as factual research, in conceptualising the character, and found that on this occasion, if he thought what the character would think, the external form of the characterisation appeared.

Stanislavsky's rehearsal notes to the MAT actor I. M. Moskvin (written much later, in 1916), when working on a dramatisation of Dostoevsky's *Village of Stepanchikovo*, expand on the process of *fusion*:

You will not acquire the souls of the general's wife or Opiskin. Remember this. Your soul will remain yours. But you will take into your soul the conditions of the character, its stimuli, and basis – an organic process . . . The tasks and aims of Foma, for example belong to Foma, and the execution of them to Moskvin. You will not become Foma, be Moskvin-Foma.[48]

Stanislavsky appears to drop the term from his later writings, although obviously at this stage it was an important concept for him.

Stanislavsky's 'Artistic Maturity', 1906–1926, and the system

The 'Finland crisis' occurred in 1906, when Stanislavsky was on holiday in Finland. He realised that his acting of the role of Dr Stockmann had

[47] Gurevich, 'Khudozhestvennie Zaveti Tolstogo', p. 127.
[48] Vinogradskaia, *Letopis*, vol. 2, p. 498.

become mechanical and as an actor he did not know how to prevent that from happening. For example, Stanislavsky copied Stockmann's naivety but, he writes, he was not truly naive. Again there was a *dislocation*, a split between internal and external:

the internal content with which I had invested roles since first creating it and that external form into which the roles had degenerated as time passes were as far away from each other as heaven and earth. Before, everything had come from beautiful, exciting, internal truth. Now all that was left was the empty shell, the dust and rubbish, which had remained, stuck in the soul and body for various accidental reasons, which had nothing to do with genuine art (*MLIA*, p. 371).

Stanislavsky had created Stockmann from memories of actual people but had thrown away the 'living memories, which should have been his unconscious guide'.

The solution to the problem of preventing a role from degenerating was in spiritual preparation, that is, in the development of the *creative feeling of the self*. He then began to work on what became known as the *system*, and continued to do so for the rest of his life. The *system* was designed to enable the actor, through techniques of *belief* and the *magic if*, to develop the ability to pay attention and to be fully alive on stage, *experiencing*, in the present moment. By full concentration on the *task* they have on stage, actors develop and practise the *feeling of truth* and *freeing the muscles*, which enables them not to react to the audience, not to stiffen in fear or to show off. All actions are internally *justified*, not *incarnated* externally. Crucial to this is the *task*. The *task* touches the actor's will: a spiritual *task* will evoke internally the actor's conscious or *superconscious* emotion. This is the path to the unconscious through the conscious. In 1906, Leopold Sulerzhitsky became Stanislavsky's assistant and staunch supporter in the period when the MAT actors were resistant to Stanislavsky's experiments with the *system*. He was responsible for many of the developing ideas and introduced Stanislavsky to yoga practices which he found helpful in 'spiritual preparation'.

However, as the system developed, further problems emerged. In Hamsun's symbolic play, *The Drama of Life*, produced in 1907, Stanislavsky emphasised internal technique and did not allow the actors external means of *incarnation*; gestures and movements were restrained in order to facilitate 'incorporeal passion, straight from the soul of the actor' (MLIA, p. 386). However, the actors became more fearful about what was required of them, too focussed internally and there was no *justification* for the absence of gesture. It appears that in one rehearsal Sulerzhitsky tried to get an actor to find the required emotional expression by sitting astride him and hitting and shouting at him as he lay howling on the floor – a method that was not repeated. Another problem Stanislavsky was investigating was how the actor's sense of himself when standing on stage is unnatural and an obstacle to creativity:

Imagine you are put on show on a high platform on Red Square in front of a crowd of hundreds of thousands beside a woman you have perhaps just met. You've got to declare your love for her publicly, so that you could go out of your mind and kill yourself for love. But you can't think of love . . . you are confused; 100,000 eyes are on you wanting you to make them cry . . . and they've paid money for it. You've got to shout tender things to this woman so they can all hear . . . and see your gestures (*MLIA*, pp. 373–4).

The solution is the *creative sense of the self.* Stanislavsky discovered that if he gave his attention to the sensations of the body he stopped being afraid of the audience. In the creative feeling there was a connection between muscular freedom and greater general concentration. 'Creativity is first and foremost full concentration of the whole of the spiritual and physical nature' (*MLIA*, p. 378). He began systematically to develop his ability to pay attention.

In his speech in October 1908, on the tenth anniversary of MAT, Stanislavsky stated that the Art Theatre was based on Shchepkin's behests and the innovations of Chekhov:

In this way Shchepkin, Chekhov and our theatre have merged into a general aspiration for artistic simplicity and truth on stage . . . After a whole series of . . . researches in the region of the psychology and physiology of creativity we have arrived at a whole series of conclusions, in the study of which we must temporarily return to the simple and real forms of stage productions. In this way, going from realism and following the evolutions of our art, we have completed a full circle and after ten years we have returned again to realism, enriched by work and experience . . . this period will be consecrated to creativity, based on simple and natural principles of the psychology and physiology of human nature.[49]

On other occasions, Stanislavsky equated naturalistic theatre, with truthfulness (AWHE, p. 61). Truth was the truth of the actor's *experiencing*, describing the world by means of poetic realism, as Belinsky first enunciated.

R. I. G. Hughes writes that by 1910, 'Stanislavsky had rejected a straightforwardly naturalistic aesthetic in favor of a Tolstoyan expressive

---

[49] *Ibid.* p. 141.

view',[50] as he changed from aiming primarily to create feeling in the audience to aiming to engender it by means of the actor's *experiencing*. His insistence on using naturalistic detail in set, costume, sound effects and so on was no longer to help the audience experience the feeling or mood, as in the first production of *The Seagull* in 1898, but to help the actors.

Eventually, in 1912, the First Studio was set up, where Stanislavsky and Suler were able to work with young actors more receptive to the ideas, including Michael Chekhov and Vakhtangov, who were to develop their own influential theories of training actors. Second, Third and Fourth Studios were set up at the MAT in 1916, 1920 and 1921. Edward Gordon Craig, Isadora Duncan and many other foreign artists visited and worked at MAT, though in the period of World War I this flow was interrupted. Meanwhile, Meyerhold was working for the Imperial theatres and had begun his studio in St Petersburg under the pseudonym of Dr Dapertutto.

The 'Salieri crisis' occurred in 1915. Stanislavsky was playing the part of Salieri in Pushkin's *Mozart and Salieri* and realised that he was 'not able to realise in external form the sincere internal feeling' (*MLIA*, p. 450). Again, he called this situation *dislocation* (*vyvikh*). Stanislavsky *experienced* the part and its internal life correctly,

while my feeling came from the heart to the moving centres of the body, to the voice and the tongue. But when what was experienced was expressed in movement and particularly in words and speech, there was dislocation and false declamation, against my will, and I was not able to realise in external form my sincere internal feeling (p. 450).

Again, tension and vocal strain resulted. He wrote that he realised that all his life he had spoken badly (p. 452). Stanislavsky continued to seek methods of vocal and physical training in order to achieve his ideal: 'all great artists...had bodily freedom and their physical apparatus was submitted to the will of the actor' (p. 376).

Nemirovich-Danchenko and Stanislavsky were at odds over a number of issues and worked increasingly separately within the MAT. In 1917 their disputes reached a peak during rehearsals of the *Village of Stepanchikovo*. After 156 rehearsals Nemirovich-Danchenko removed Stanislavsky from the cast, stating that he had 'failed to bring life to the part'

[50] R. I. G. Hughes, 'Tolstoy, Stanislavski and the Art of Acting', *The Journal of Aesthetics and Art Criticism*, 51:1 (Winter 1993), p. 41.

of Rostanev. After that, Stanislavsky never created a new role, playing only those he had created already.[51] He continued to develop the *system* over the next twenty years, but did not himself test out his ideas on the creation of a role.

In 1917, after the establishment of Bolshevik power, the Alekseev factory was taken into state ownership and dedicated to the manufacture of steel cables. Stanislavsky's private fortune was confiscated and for the first time he was dependent on his earnings from theatre work to survive. The MAT management asked the Moscow Soviet how they could best serve the people, and were told to open again as soon as possible. In 1919, during the civil war, a group from the company led by Vasily Ivanovich Kachalov was stranded in Kharkhov, and then toured the south of Russia, retreating with Denikin's White Army. They then toured Europe and did not return to Moscow until 1922. In 1919 Stanislavsky was arrested, though released on the same day. Despite terrible conditions, Stanislavsky continued to act, teach and direct and was active in discussions on the role of theatre in Soviet society and warned against the dangers of taking agit-prop theatre, which for many actors was now the main work, as genuine art. Worse still, for Stanislavsky, were the criticisms of *experiencing* and the psychological approach as bourgeois art, and the new emphasis in certain quarters on training the revolutionary actor based solely on physical culture. This was a debasement of avant-garde processes with their foundations laid before the revolution, as with Meyerhold's work. Stanislavsky criticised the idea of the new actor, who was an acrobat, singer, dancer, declaimer, an exponent of plastique, a lampoonist, wit, orator, compère and political agitator, popularised by some on the grounds that such an actor was dilettante in many of these skills. In fact 'the sharp external form of contemporary art is filled inside with the old rubbish of the actor's craft, which is being mistaken for something new' (*MLIA*, pp. 486–8).

The Bolshoi Opera Studio was formed in 1918 with Stanislavsky's involvement, with the aim of improving the acting skills of the young opera singers. Much of his important experimentation took place here, as with the other studios. The MAT (which from 1919, after the nationalisation of the theatres, was known as the Moscow Art Academic Theatre, MAAT) toured in Europe and America during 1922–4, to great acclaim, but received little financial reward. In this period Meyerhold was very

---

[51] Benedetti, *Stanislavski: His Life and Art*, p. 241. Stanislavsky took over the part of Shuiskii in *Tsar Fedor*, as there was no one else to play the part in a foreign tour in 1923/4.

much to the forefront of theatrical life in Russia. There was criticism of MAAT and a backlash against Stanislavsky's methods. In 1922 Stalin became secretary-general of the Central Committee of the Communist Party and in 1924 Lenin died. The New Economic Policy (NEP), 1921–8, saw the partial restoration of private business:

The Bolshevik or Communist Party controlled the mainsprings of the economy and kept a tight rein on political life. Its cultural code proscribed eroticism, mysticism, religion or upper-class fluff (except as objects of derision). As a counterweight it promoted a new proletarian morality based upon mutual respect and equality of the sexes; atheism rooted in science; a spirit of collective comradeship and a veritable cult of technology and the machine.[52]

Last period, 1926–38

Stanislavsky, like other directors, was under pressure to find a repertoire in keeping with the government's views of the purposes of art in Soviet society. A 1927 production of Vsevolod Viacheslavovich Ivanov's *Armoured Train No. 14–69* was a great success. However, in 1928 Stanislavsky performed for the last time when he collapsed with heart problems after playing the part of Vershinin in a gala performance for MAAT's thirty-year jubilee, including one act of *Three Sisters*. Bouts of illness, to which he had always been susceptible, occurred more frequently. As Stanislavsky's main practical work from then on was connected with what became the Stanislavsky Opera Studio (and later Theatre) the productions he worked on were operas and classics, a total of seven productions being mounted in the final period of his life. He gave practical and theoretical lessons to the studios. After ceasing to act, his practice of his theories and methods relied on observation of others. He wrote, as always, but as yet writing on his *system* had not been passed by the censor for publication, although a version of *MLIA* had been published in America in 1924 and then it was published in Russia in 1926.

In 1929 Stanislavsky was asked to collaborate with Lunacharsky and the magazine *Iskusstvo* (*Art*) in an attempt to resolve the problem of the development of a Marxist aesthetic that went beyond slogans, his contribution being knowledge of the past and the traditions of realism.[53] Benedetti describes how in 1931, when only *My Life in Art* of Stanislavsky's writings had been published in the Soviet Union, the *system*

[52] Richard Stites, *Russian Popular Culture* (Cambridge University Press, 1992), p. 40.
[53] Benedetti, *Stanislavski: His Life and Art*, p. 319.

came under attack from the far left in the Russian Association of Proletarian Writers (RAPP). The *system* was attacked for its 'idealism'. At that stage in the development of Soviet thought, the important aspect of human beings was their behaviour. There was a rejection of the idea of universal or transcendent truths and anything that sounded mystical. At the RAPP conference in 1931, Stanislavsky's *magic if* was one of several elements of the *system* that were pilloried. Stanislavsky replied that 'the actor's feeling did not derive from some abstract imaginary world but was rooted in human necessity' and all that was meant by the *magic* or *creative if* was: 'if this were the case, what would you do?'.[54] The explanation he gave, and the inability of his opponents to describe the actor's experience any more clearly, meant that his work carried on, with only some changes in terminology and apologia.

In the same year Meyerhold's work also came under attack, not for the first time. He was called a 'mechanist', lacking an understanding of art as a spiritual interaction between people; his *biomechanics* was said to treat human beings as if they were engines, leaving out the factor of psychology. Meyerhold replied that *biomechanics* was merely for training purposes, and had been developed in order to allow actors to escape from the influence of the 'vitalists' at MAAT, whose training system had prevailed before the revolution.[55]

In 1932, it was revealed that Josef Stalin liked MAAT's production of Bulgakov's *Days of the Turbins*, which had been in repertoire since 1926, directed by I. Sudakov under Stanislavsky's guidance. Generally, Stanislavsky's work, unlike Meyerhold's, was beginning to find favour with Stalin's government. It was said that Stanislavsky's method of work was in accordance with socialist realism as it placed no limits on the creative activity of actors and directors, nor did it espouse any one theatrical form.[56] It has been suggested that Stalin saw Stanislavsky as an ally in the sense of his 'artistic many-sidedness and versatility, even his inconsistency and the formal eclecticism of his system, whose guiding principle was style not craftsmanship. Of all these features Stalin could take advantage'.[57]

[54] *Ibid.* p. 337.
[55] Mel Gordon and Alma Law, *Meyerhold, Eisenstein and Biomechanics: Actor-Training in Revolutionary Russia* (North Carolina: McFarland, 1996), p. 57.
[56] I. V. Kostetskii, *Sovietskaia Teatral'naia Politika i Sistema Stanislavskogo* (Munich: Institut po Izucheniyu CCCP, 1956), p. 93.
[57] *Ibid.* p. 92.

Whatever was behind it, Stanislavsky's concepts of truth and realism were eventually translated into socialist realism. Lenin had in many ways been a traditionalist in terms of culture. The president of the State Academy of Artistic Science communicated to Stanislavsky the approval of Tolstoy,[58] whose concept of the brotherhood of man was adopted in socialist realism and espoused as the brotherhood of socialist man. It was the purpose of art to promote this. Later, under Stalin, Belinsky, Chernyshevsky, Pushkin and others who had influenced Stanislavsky were also celebrated. Artistic excellence was sought in the proponents of socialist art. There were emigrations and disappearances of people Stanislavsky knew whose work did not fit the parameters. These shifts in official policy and their frequently drastic personal consequences for artists explain why Stanislavsky and Meyerhold said their work was scientific at certain points in their career and later denied it, as, concomitantly, the definitions of what was acceptable in science narrowed.

In the 1930s Stanislavsky's writings included important statements about physical action and he continued to experiment with rehearsal methods, developing the concept of *active analysis* when working on *Three Sisters* in 1934 at the Opera Studio.[59] After reading the play he got the actors to work on their feet, exploring the play through action rather than the round-the-table analysis which had characterised rehearsals at an earlier period. One aspect of this was termed by others the *method of physical actions*. This is simply a rehearsal method where the actor develops a logical sequence of actions for his or her role in order to fulfil the *tasks* demanded by the given circumstances of the play. The idea is that by this means the emotional life of the character can be aroused and fixed for performance, more easily sometimes than through *emotional memory*. Although Stanislavsky maintained his beliefs about *emotion* he was under political pressure to emphasise *action* in his work after the revolution and to use terminology that was more concrete than many of the expressions he tended to use. His writings were scrutinised and criticised and Gurevich, his editor, frequently advised revisions on the basis of the unacceptable terminology he used.[60]

The key features of the later period of Stanislavsky's work indicate how he shifted over the course of his life from the idea of acting as representing states of being which he rejected early on, as it were, to movement; from

[58] Vinogradskaia, *Letopis*, vol. 4, p. 58.
[59] Benedetti, *Stanislavski: His Life and Art*, p. 356.
[60] See Benedetti, *Stanislavski: His Life and Art*, Chapter 27.

expressing something 'in general' (for example, being alarmed or angry), to *tasks*. To illustrate this, Kostia realises that the character of the husband in the 'Burning Money' étude does not need to act in a tragic way to express his despair and desperation at seeing a packet of money burning on the fire, but to perform the task of knocking his disabled brother-in-law out of the way in order to try to get the money out of the fire (*AWHE*, p. 239). Stanislavsky shifted from attempting to express something fixed either by habit (the *stencils* or the fixed representation of a role), to demanding that the actor is constantly *experiencing*, creating the *life of the human spirit of the role*. The emotion, mood or atmosphere of a scene is not sought directly but created as a by-product of the actor's *experiencing*, and having the *creative sense of self*, while in *communion* with other actors. Central to all this is action, and the idea is that the action of the actors is made up of the sequence of logical physical actions forming their roles. Action is internal and external, psychological and physical and the actor executing such an action is *active* (*aktivnyi*). Nevertheless, feeling and the communication of feeling remains in Stanislavsky's view the purpose of art.

In 1935, after various crises at MAAT, including a troubled production process of Bulgakov's *Molière*, Stanislavsky began a new Opera-dramatic Studio with his sister Zinaida. Over the next few years his illness worsened, but though more and more bedridden, he continued to work. In 1938 he invited Meyerhold to work at what was now called the Stanislavsky Opera Theatre, after Meyerhold's own theatre had been closed. Stanislavsky died that year while two productions he had worked on were being prepared: Verdi's *Rigoletto*, which Meyerhold completed, and Molière's *Tartuffe*, completed by Mikhail Kedrov. Stanislavsky's books were published after his death: *AWHE* in 1938 and, as part of the edited *Complete Works*, *AWHI* in 1955 and *AWR* in 1957.

Politics, science and Stanislavsky's truth

In summary, it is important to consider the ideas and forces that brought about changes in thought in the period framed by Stanislavsky's birth and death (1863–1938). In scientific terms, Darwinism, psychology and Pavlov's work could all be said to have introduced paradigmatic shifts in thought. The golden age of Russian art and philosophy was succeeded by modernism and the silver age. The revolution, midway through Stanislavsky's professional career, ushered in a period after which certain ideas in politics, philosophy, work, daily life and the arts began to be enforced. New ideas about acting and actor-training emerged and Stan-islavsky developed his own concepts. One was of nature's mysterious and creative power, a view popularised by romantic philosophy, which he affirmed in his reading of yoga. Darwinism, as it was understood in Russia and in Marxism, presented no conflict with this. His readings of pre-revolutionary psychology indicated that the human mechanism oper-ated in accordance with nature's laws, and could be studied empirically, by introspection and observation. Stanislavsky's notion of the beneficent influence of nature informed his aesthetic, as he viewed feelings as 'natural', and the proper subject of art. The perception that art ennobles both per-former and audience has a long tradition dating back to the Greeks, but Stanislavsky inherited it from golden age artists and thinkers. Stanislavsky sought to achieve naturalism in acting, in that it should be based in real, or natural experience. This search went through various stages, in which con-siderations of inner and outer technique were crucial but the goal remained the creation of life on stage. Chapter 2 will examine further how Stanislavsky went about this in an exploration of *experiencing*.

Experiencing: the emotional and spiritual actor

INTRODUCTION

Stanislavsky divides the training of the actor into work on *experiencing*, the inner emotional and spiritual work, work on *incarnation* or external expression and work on a role, as indicated by the titles of his three books, *The Actor's Work on Him/Herself Part 1 – in the Creative Process of Experiencing, Part 2 – in the Creative Process of Incarnation* and *The Actor's Work on a Role*. This chapter investigates of some of the sources of Stanislavsky's ideas on *experiencing*. Stanislavsky sought scientific corroboration for some of his theories and attempted to marry the development of the *system* with the new scientific paradigm of conditional reflexes, which emerged during the course of his career. This throws light on the question as to whether Stanislavsky adapted his training methods in the light of advances in science during his lifetime. In fact, Stanislavsky's ideas on the mechanisms of emotion are rooted in associationist psychology, as were many of the other ideas that found their way into the *system*, and throughout his lifetime he did not swerve from the views he held as a result of this. The reasons for changes of emphasis in the way he explained his methods were primarily practical, as finding new ways of describing techniques of acting was a way of keeping the work fresh, and also political. It was incumbent on him to find terminology to describe his work that was in keeping with the increasingly insistent Soviet methodologies. The establishment of the science of Sechenov and Pavlov and theories of reflex conditioning as the science of Soviet society involved a rejection of the vitalism of much associationist psychology, and a paradigm shift in beliefs about emotion. Although Stanislavsky tried to make the shift, he did not reject his earlier beliefs, and they held sway in practice.

The drawing by Stanislavsky of 'The Plan of Experiencing' (see figure 1), with its accompanying description, was included with manuscripts he was working on in 1935 and can be taken as the way he thought about the *system* in the last period of his life (*AWHI*, 1st edn, pp. 360–3; 2nd edn, pp. 308–11). The drawing is entitled 'The Plan of the System' in the text (*AWHI*, 1st edn, p. 347). This is the name it was given by Stanislavsky's editors, but it is in fact entitled 'The Plan of Experiencing' in his notes, indicating the importance of this concept for him. The diagram is in the shape of a pair of lungs, containing all the aspects of *experiencing* and *incarnation*, and a spine, which represents the *role*. The topics under discussion in this chapter are referred to on the left side of the diagram as *experiencing*, whereas the right side, *incarnation* (described by Stanislavsky in *AWHI*), will be covered in Chapter 3. These topics on the left-hand side are covered comprehensively by Stanislavsky in *AWHE*, but it is useful to look at his other writings, his diaries, notebooks and other primary materials as they display consistency in how he envisaged the mechanisms by means of which the actor can engender emotion and spiritual truth. For *AWHE* some changes in terminology in the first edition of Stanislavsky's works in particular were necessary to conceal Stanislavsky's use of yoga and references made to associationist psychology and, therefore, I will refer to a range of writings, some of which include unpublished material from the MAT archive. These include teaching materials.

Stanislavsky's main work in training others began when he introduced the system during rehearsals of *Hamlet* and Tolstoy's *Living Corpse* in 1911. By 1912, the First Studio was established with Sulerzhitsky as its leader, and Vakhtangov and Michael Chekhov engaged in various ways with the developing *system*.

The three bases of the system: *activeness, truth of passions and the subconscious*

The first base, *activeness*, is summarised by Stanislavsky thus: 'the art of the dramatic actor is the art of internal and external action'. In one of the appendices to *AWHI* a slogan draws the students' attention to the derivation of the Russian word for action to the Greek word, δράω, to do, from which comes also 'drama'.

AGO, ACTION
AKTER, AKT
DEISTVIE
ΔΡΑΩ-DEISTVUIU
DRAMA, DRAMATICHESKOE ISKUSSTVO

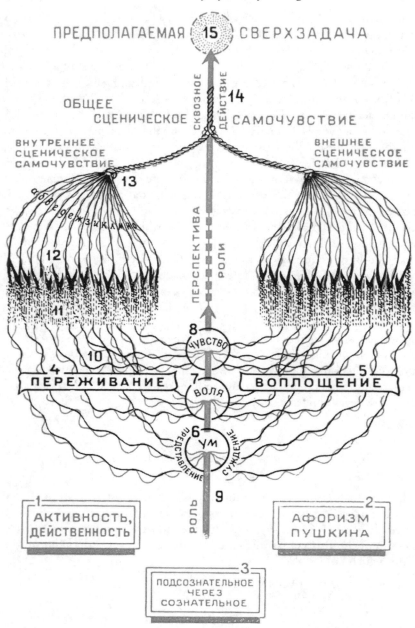

1. *The Plan of Experiencing* (see boxed text opposite).

The Plan of Experiencing (*AWHI* pp. 308–311).
The five bases of The System:[1]

1. Activeness: The art of the dramatic actor is the art of internal and external action.
2. Pushkin's Aphorism: the truth of passions, verisimilitude of feelings in proposed circumstances.
3. The subconscious creativity of nature itself – through the artist's conscious psycho-technique.
4. Experiencing.
5. Incarnation.
   The three motivators of psychic life (our current scientific definition) or "representation, judgment and will–feeling" (the former scientific definition):
6. Mind.
7. Will.
8. Feeling.
9. The Role: the new play and role permeate the motivators of the psychic life. They scatter seeds in them and evoke creative aspiration. Along the line: Perspective of the Role and Through Action.
10. The lines of aspiration of the motivators of psychic life, bringing with them the seeds of the play and the roles that have been sown in them. At the beginning these aspirations are scrappy, patchy, disordered and chaotic but through clarification of the basic aim of creativity they become continuous, straight and supple.
11. 'abcdefghijk' the internal region of the soul, our creative apparatus, with all its qualities, capacities, gifts, natural gifts, artistic skills, psycho-technical methods which we have earlier called 'elements'. They are necessary for the fulfilment of the process of experiencing.
    a. Imagination and its inventions ('if', the given circumstances of the role)
    b. Bits and tasks
    c. Attention and objects
    d. Action
    e. The feeling of truth and belief
    f. Internal tempo-rhythm
    g. Emotional memories
    h. Communion
    i. Adaptation
    j. Logic and consistency
    k. Internal characterisation

l.   Internal stage charm

m.   Ethics and discipline

n.   Control and finish.

These all live in that region of the soul where the motivators of psychic life … are buried together with the particles of the soul of the role which are implanted with them. See on the sketch how the lines of aspiration penetrate through this region and how they gradually take on the colour tones of the artist's 'elements'.[2]

12. These are the same lines of aspiration, already regenerated, of the motivators of the psychic life of the artist-role. Compare them to 10 and you will see the difference after they have passed through the psychical region. Now, gradually taking into themselves not only the 'elements' of the play but also the tones and colours of the 'elements' of the artist himself, the lines of aspiration of the mind, will and feeling, become unrecognisable.

13. This is that bundle in which all the lines of aspiration of the motivators of psychic life are entwined; this is that spiritual state which we call the 'internal sense of the self on stage'.

14. These are the lines of aspiration of the motivators of psychic life interwoven with each other like a plait, striving towards the supertask. Now, after their regenation and converging with the role, we call them 'the lines of through action'.

15. The as yet ghostly, not fully defined supertask.

[1] Note 11, *AWHE*, p. 87 explains that sometimes there are four bases, the other being: 'the aim of art is the creation of the life of the human spirit'.

[2] Stanislavsky's intention was for the different elements to be in different colours in the diagram.

'All these inscriptions bear witness to the fact that our art is active and it is best to speak of it in action' (*AWHI*, p. 430) (see figure 2). This connection with the origins of theatre in ancient Greece is important for Stanislavsky's view of acting and the other important connotation this has for him is that of 'real life' action. Stanislavsky tended not to use the most common word for acting in Russian (*igrat'*), which can have the connotation of 'play-acting' or pretending, but preferred the word (*deistvovat'*), which means to take action, to behave.[1] It is logical, purposive action as he described it in *MLIA* when he realised as a child the

[1] Sharon M. Carnicke, *Stanislavsky in Focus* (Amsterdam: Harwood Academic Publishers, 1998), pp. 147–8.

2. Action: Staging the programme. 'In our language to know means to be able to.'

difference between being on stage in a tableau, where he experienced 'unconsciously a feeling of awkwardness at this meaningless activity' (*bezdeistvie*), and then the point on stage where he put a stick into the real fire to see it burn – a purposeful activity (p. 55). Roach notes that Diderot said (of painting), 'every attitude is false and little; every action is beautiful and true'.[2] Action on stage must likewise be truthful for Stanislavsky; there can be no theatrical gesturing.

In his search for truthful emotional expression, Stanislavsky is commonly held to have moved from emotion to action, from reliance on *experiencing*, including the technique of *emotional memory* (which was a lynchpin of the developing *system* from 1908/9 onwards), to the *Method of Physical Actions* as the means of generating emotion in acting. Smeliansky, for example, writes that Stanislavsky 'evolved' from emotion to action, implying that he moved from a lower stage of understanding to a higher one (foreword to *AWHE*, p. 16). The term *method of physical actions* came into use from about 1934, and many commentators, Soviet ones influencing others, have taken it to be the culmination of the *system* and Stanislavsky's life's work, which is not in fact the case. It may be conjectured that it was politic for Stanislavsky to make action one of the bases of *experiencing* on his diagram, whereas the disputed term *emotional memory* is one among several *elements* in the *creative apparatus of the soul*, in view of the rejection of individual emotional experience as opposed to collective action after the revolution.

Whether that was the case or not, the second base is about emotion in general, or the passions, in Pushkin's aphorism, so emotion is on a par with action. Aleksander Pushkin (1799–1837), Russia's famous golden age poet, wrote part of an article in 1830 entitled 'Notes on popular drama and M. P. Pogodin's *Martha, the Governor's Wife*'.[3] Here he wrote of dramatic writing, 'The truth concerning the passions, a verisimilitude in the feelings experienced in given situations – that is what our intelligence demands of a dramatist.' Stanislavsky applied Pushkin's words to acting, as Tolstoy had to art in general, defining the truth of passions here as 'genuine, living human passion, feeling, experiencing of the artist himself' (*AWHE*, p. 105). Stanislavsky adopted the idea of *given circumstances*: 'the plot of the play, its facts, events, epoch, conditions of life, our actors' and directors' concept, additions from oneself, *mise-en-scène*, setting, set

[2] Joseph Roach, *The Player's Passion: Studies in the Science of Acting* (Newark: University of Michigen Press, 1993), p. 127.
[3] Tatiana Wolff (tr. and ed.), *Pushkin on Literature* (London: Methuen, 1971), p. 265.

and costume, props, lighting, sound and so on – what it is proposed the actor gives attention to during creativity' (*AWHE*, p. 104). *Given circumstances* are listed in the diagram under 'inventions of the imagination', part of the internal region of the soul.

The third base, 'the subconscious creativity of nature itself – through the artist's conscious psycho-technique', asserts the importance attached by Stanislavsky to the processes of the subconscious. The source of Stanislavsky's ideas of the *unconscious* was in particular the work of the philosopher Edouard von Hartmann. Some of these ideas are also found in the yogic philosophy that interested Stanislavsky and Sulerzhitsky, and also in associationist psychology, though by the time he drew the diagram, Stanislavsky had to take care how he wrote about this. Finally, elsewhere Stanislavsky explains that sometimes there are four bases, the other being as follows: 'the aim of art is the creation of the life of the human spirit' (*AWHI*, 1st edn, p. 487, n. 11). Stanislavsky borrowed this phrase from Chernyshevsky and used it frequently to assert that acting involves processes of *experiencing*, as in real life.

EXPERIENCING: THE MECHANISMS OF EMOTION AND ACTION

In *AHWE* Stanislavsky devoted a chapter to *action* (*deistvie*), and also one to *emotional memory* even though in the diagram of the scheme of *experiencing*, one of the bases is *action* and *emotional memory* is an element. Throughout his career, Stanislavsky sought a way to pin down the means of truthfully expressing emotion. His early experiences in amateur drama convinced him that any direct attempt to express emotion would result in 'the simple mechanical actor's stencil, trick or conventional external sign' and what he describes as 'actor's emotion'.

Actor's emotion is not a real emotion, real experiencing of the role on stage. It is an artistic irritation of the periphery of the body. For example, if you clench your fists, contract the muscles of the body strongly or breathe spasmodically, you can bring about in yourself great physical strain, which is often taken by the audience as the appearance of great temperament, violent passion. You can rush about and be excited mechanically with a cold soul, pointlessly – in general (*AWHE*, p. 77–8).

Hence the actor's emotion must be real, not pretended. In further defining his opinion and methods, Stanislavsky considered acting theory from the past. Famously, the problem of emotion and acting theory was raised in *Paradoxe sur le Comédien*, written c.1773 and rewritten in 1778 by French philosopher Denis Diderot (1713–1784). With Gurevich's help,

Stanislavsky studied this, and other works on theatre in French, when he was in Marienbad in 1914. Diderot asserted that the great actor should be devoid of sensibility, that is, he should not experience emotion when he is acting. The great actor 'must have in himself or herself an unmoved and disinterested onlooker'.[4] The *Paradoxe* was first translated into Russian in 1882 and Nikolai Efros translated it again in 1922 with a foreword by Lunacharsky. Stanislavsky's annotated copy indicates that he continued to work on it after the revolution, when Diderot's works found favour with such cultural leaders as Lunacharsky, and Lenin praised Diderot as a materialist, a realist and a naturalist.[5] Stanislavsky wrote that Diderot was misunderstood: 'he says that you cannot experience the same feelings as you do in life, he says that... you can live with actual born again feeling, he says what we say, that you can live with affective feelings. Diderot was not understood, in the same way that Tolstoy's wonderful book is not understood' (MAT, KS Archive 833, p. 24).[6]

The other works included *Réflexions historiques et critiques sur les différents théâtres de l'Europe, avec les pensées sur la déclamation* (1738), and also *Histoire du Théâtre Italien* (Volume 1: 1728, Volume 2: 1731), both by Luigi Riccoboni (c. 1675–1753), whose life spanned the last epoch of commedia dell'arte. Stanislavsky also studied Luigi Riccoboni's son Francesco's *L'Art du Théâtre* (1750). Typescripts and excerpts from these works are in the MAT archives, with annotations by Stanislavsky. Stanislavsky said that Riccoboni the father, 'directly says something like the system' whereas 'the son, a complete copy of Meyerhold, says completely the opposite' (MAT, KS Archive 834, p. 24). Gurevich states that Luigi Riccoboni's tract vindicated the type of acting that Stanislavsky named *experiencing*. She describes Stanislavsky's joyful expressions of affection towards the imaginary figure of the writer when he first read it. He also loved Francesco Riccoboni's 'demonstration that the actor should not rely on inspiration and improvise on stage; he should work and work',[7] although Francesco disagreed with his father's belief that the actor should experience emotion while performing.[8]

[4] Toby Cole and Helen Krich Chinoy, *Actors on Acting*, rev. edn (New York: Crown, 1970), p. 162.
[5] Denis Diderot, *Paradoks ob Aktere*, tr. into Russian by Nikolai Efros (Yaroslavl: 1923), foreword by A. V. Lunacharskii, pp. I–IV.
[6] See Christine Edwards, *The Stanislavski Heritage* (New York University Press, 1965), pp. 131–2 in support of Stanislavsky's view.
[7] Liubov' Gurevich (ed.), *O Stanislavskom, Sbornik Vospominanii* (Moscow: Vserossiskoe Teatral'noe Obshchestvo, 1948), p. 141.
[8] Pierre Remond de Sainte-Albine's *Le Comédien* (1749) concurs with Luigi Riccoboni that *sensibility* is the basis of the actor's art. (A typescript of de Sainte-Albine's work with Stanislavsky's marginalia

The discussion in the eighteenth century focussed on 'sensibility'. Stanislavsky studied the French actor François-Joseph Talma's preface to his predecessor Lekain's *Memoirs*, which states that

to impart a sort of reality to the fictions of the stage ... the actor should have received from nature an extreme sensibility and a profound intelligence ... sensibility is not only that faculty which an actor possesses of being moved himself and of affecting his being so far as to imprint on his features and especially his voice, that expression and those accents of sorrow which awake all the sympathies of the art and extort tears from the auditors.[9]

For Diderot, *sensibility* was a potentially dangerous force, which must be controlled.[10] Emotion and feeling (the Russian term for the latter is *chuvstvo* or *chuvstvovanie*, which I take to be the equivalent of the French *sensibilité*) were for Stanislavsky something that can be represented, falsified or engendered truthfully. For Stanislavsky, true sensibility is the capacity for emotional memory.

The debate was brought up to date by Alfred Binet (1857–1911), the French psychologist famous for his experimental investigations of intelligence, who wrote on Diderot's *Paradoxe* in 1897, and published *On Double Consciousness* in 1889, and whose work Stanislavsky studied. Binet conducted a surveying of nine leading French actors and using evidence gained from them, dismissed Diderot's argument that the great actor should not experience emotion when performing. The actors interviewed refuted what Binet refers to as Diderot's best argument, that it is not possible for actors to observe themselves and experience emotion sincerely. He cited Sarah Bernhardt as an example of 'tragedians who have attained such virtuosity in their art that they have become complete masters of their own organism'. Bernhardt, he writes, was able to cry at

---

is also in the MAT archive.) John Hill translated this into English, and then Hill's work was re-adapted into French by Antonio Fabio Sticotti in 1769 as *Garrick ou les Acteurs Anglais*. Diderot wrote a response, *Observations sur une brochure intitulée 'Garrick ou les acteurs anglais'* (1770), and notes were made for Stanislavsky on this by one of his assistants. Stanislavsky studied other works by Diderot. Gurevich wrote out an excerpt for him from Diderot's *Oeuvres de théâtre ... avec une discours sur la Poésie Dramatique*, 1759. In the archive there is a typescript of Alfred Binet's *Thoughts on Diderot's Paradoxe*, and another typescript with marginalia by Stanislavsky, of *Mademoiselle Dumesnil et Mademoiselle Clairon*. The former was Diderot's example of the actor who identified emotionally with the part, and the latter the conscious, unemotional actor. There is a manuscript and typescript in Russian and French entitled *M-elle Clairon* and a typescript of Talma's preface to Lekain's *Memoirs*. Other typescripts include *On the Art of Declamation*, compiled from C. J. Dorat's *La Déclamation Théâtrale* (1771) and Victor Fournel's *Curiosités Théâtrales* (1859).

[9] Cole and Chinoy, *Actors on Acting*, p. 181.
[10] Roach, *The Player's Passion*, p. 113.

will; this had become 'a natural function'.[11] Similarly, Stanislavsky wanted the actor to *experience* naturally and asserted the actor's capacity for self-observation while performing.

The French actor Benoît Constant Coquelin (1841–1909) had also kept alive the debate raised by Diderot. There are notes and excerpts in the archive in Stanislavsky's hand from Coquelin's *L'Art du Comédien* (1894). Coquelin adopted Diderot's model of the unemotional actor representing the role. Stanislavsky rejected this and often discoursed on the short-comings of the *representational* actor, however skilled this actor may be, citing Coquelin's school of acting as an example (particularly in *AWHE*, Chapter 2, 'Stage Art and Stage Craft'). Here he also quotes Shchepkin and the essay by the Italian tragic actor Tommaso Salvini (1829–1915), *Some Thoughts on the Art of the Stage* (published in Russian in 1891), as support for his response to Coquelin. In 1923 he stated that

The muscular memory is more developed in us than the affective one (we memorize gestures). What is typical of our actor is that he says: give me an image. According to us: a muscular image. Coquelin experiences according to the muscles (MAT, KS Archive 1293, '*Beseda o Gamlete*', 3 August 1911, p. 4).

Tortsov, the actor-teacher in Stanislavsky's books, states unequivocally, quoting Salvini,

every artist must actually feel what he is portraying. He must experience this emotion not once or twice while he is studying the role, but to a greater or lesser degree every time he performs it, whether it is for the first or the thousandth time (*AWHE*, p. 63).

Stanislavsky also refers to Coquelin when explaining the difference between the art of *experiencing* and the art of *representation* and also stagecraft. In stagecraft the actor reproduces *stencils*, the external results of the creative process. *Stencils*, as Stanislavsky explains in *MLIA* (pp. 183–4), are fixed ways of representing characters or emotions. For example, peasants always spat on the floor, aristocrats played with their lorgnettes; to express despair actors tore their hair and to express jealousy, rolled the whites of the eyes and showed their teeth (*AWHE*, p. 75). In the art of *representation*, the actor creates a model for himself in his imagination and then, 'like the painter he realises every feature and fixes the likeness not on canvas but on himself'.[12]

[11] Alfred Binet, 'Réflexions sur le Paradoxe de Diderot', *Année Psychologique*, 3 (1897), p. 286. My translation.
[12] Constant Coquelin, *The Art of the Actor*, tr. Elsie Fogerty (London: George Allen and Unwin, 1932), p. 26, quoted in *AWHE*, pp. 70–1.

What is significant is that in his research, Stanislavsky referred to texts on acting dating from the eighteenth century. Meyerhold also drew from traditions of acting but for different purposes, seeking inspiration from theatres of the past. Clearly Stanislavsky saw his research as a way of seeking validation for his own ideas of emotional truth in acting.[13] Sometimes the experience described verified his own, as with Luigi Riccoboni or Lekain, and if not, he thought that the theorists were simply wrong. He did not consider it important that actors of the previous century might have had different concepts of the mechanics of expressing emotion.[14] For him there were certain natural and immutable laws.

Experiencing

The word *experiencing* (*perezhivanie*) encapsulates what Stanislavsky prioritised in the actor's emotional expression. The Russian word means to experience, undergo or live through. Tolstoy wrote in *What is Art?* (Tolstoy's italics):

To call up in oneself a feeling once experienced and, having called it up, to convey it by means of movements, lines, colours, sounds, images expressed in words, so that others express the same feeling – in this consists the activity of art. Art is that human activity which consists in one man's consciously conveying to others, by certain external signs, the feelings he has experienced, and in others being infected by those feelings and also experiencing them.[15]

So the actor in performing must *experience* a feeling previously *experienced*. Stanislavsky writes in *The Art of Experiencing*, one of a number of manuscripts written and reworked between 1909 and the early 1920s, 'it is necessary to experience the role, that is to have the sensation (*oshchushchat'*) of its feelings, every time and on every repetition of creativity' (*Collected Works*, vol. 6, p. 80).

Tolstoy asserts that 'Feelings, the most diverse, very strong and very weak, very significant and very worthless, very bad and very good, if only they infect the reader, the spectator, the listener, constitute the subject of art.'[16] *Infecting* the audience might occur directly, when someone infects

---

[13] Gurevich mentions Lessing, Goethe, Schiller, August Wilhelm Iffland, Ludwig Tieck, Konrad Ekhof, Friedrich Ludwig Schroeder, Johann Friedrich Ferdinand Fleck and Edouard Devrient.

[14] See Joseph Roach, *The Player's Passion*, for a survey of the different conceptions of the human body in relation to acting from the seventeenth to the twentieth centuries.

[15] Leo Tolstoy, *What is Art?* tr. Richard Pevear and Larissa Volokhonsky (London: Penguin, 1995), pp. 39–40.

[16] *Ibid.* p. 39.

another by his look or the sounds he produces at the moment he experiences a feeling; for example, by making someone yawn when he feels like yawning, or laugh or cry or suffer when he laughs or cries or suffers, but this is not art. According to Tolstoy, 'Art begins when a man, with the purpose of communicating to other people a feeling he once experienced, calls it up again within himself and expresses it by certain external signs.'[17] In Stanislavsky's terminology, this expression is *incarnation*. An example is given of a boy telling a story about meeting a wolf and *infecting* others with his description. This is art (for Tolstoy) and it would also be art if the boy invented the story. Stanislavsky emphasises that actors must also *infect* themselves:

In order to infect myself with some feelings or other, I need to experience them. And as soon as a person begins to experience, there is truth. The aim is achieved. From here comes characterisation (*Beseda o Gamlete*, MAT, KS Archive 1293, 1911).

For Stanislavsky the expression and conveying of emotion is the creation of truth, of life. Tortsov tells the students (in *AWHE*, Chapter 2) that artists who do not have the inspiration of genius must create consciously and faithfully:

in the conditions of the life of the role and fully analogously with it, to think, desire, want, aspire, act correctly, logically, consistently, as a human being, while standing on stage. Only when artists achieve this do they approach the role and begin to feel identically with it . . . Experiencing helps the artist to fulfil the basic aim of stage art, which is contained in *the creation of 'the life of the human spirit of the role' and conveying this life on stage in artistic form* (p. 62).

Radishcheva cites Stanislavsky's explanation of the mechanism of 'the art of psychological *experiencing*' from a manuscript entitled *A Direction in Art. Experiencing* the role is the 'artistic arousal of . . . spiritual and bodily sensations and developing them with the help of repetition and habit into a natural state'.[18] As with Bernhardt, the ability to *experience* must become 'a natural function'. The philosopher I. I. Lapshin, with whom Stanislavsky was on close terms,[19] emphasised that this is a 'natural'

---

[17] *Ibid.* p. 38.
[18] O. A. Radishcheva, *Istoriia Teatral'nych Otnoshenii, 1909–1917* (Moscow: Artist Rezhisser Teatr, 1999), p. 14.
[19] Stanislavsky was well acquainted with Lapshin. He is mentioned several times in Stanislavsky's letters (Collected works, vol. 9, 1999, pp. 52, 53, 74, 281, 283). For example, in a letter to his son Igor, who had tuberculosis (from Moscow, dated 22 August 1922), Stanislavsky includes health advice from Lapshin, and refers to him again, in connection with his views on the family health problems in letters in 1923 and 1927. There is a reference to books sent by Lapshin.

process, and that Stanislavsky demonstrated it is possible to train oneself in the 'art of *experiencing*' and to 'get accustomed to a role' so that it is possible to perform it in a 'much more lifelike way thanks to the actor's constant experimentation on him/herself, and getting into the feelings of (*vchuvstvovanie*) the role'. (This is also a term used by Tolstoy.) This *experiencing*, Lapshin continues, has to become a constant quality of the actor. 'Stanislavsky has made it his task *to develop in the actor this ability for getting into the feelings of the role by voluntary exercises and moreover exercises which are not artificial but completely natural.*' In this way the actor will avoid the 'vocal and visual *stencils*' that are inevitable in the art of *representation*.[20] The manuscript where Stanislavsky makes this definition was begun in 1909, but Stanislavsky was still working on this theme in the 1930s, keeping the same definition.

Furthermore, Sulerzhitsky stated that *experiencing* involves thought and must be expressed beautifully. He noted this from a conversation with Stanislavsky in 1914:

Actors *have always understood* the dramatic theatre as an arena where they compete in the expression of feelings. And in this arena there were great actors who had the ability to feel beauty and the strength of feelings and to *use words* in so far as they gave the possibility of expressing feelings. Many can *experience feelings* – well or badly – but no one is yet able to experience thoughts together with feelings, feeling at the same time all the beauty of the language producing the beauty of the *word*. This is – I assert – still not touched upon, they do not yet live with the beauties of the thought itself.

This must be the next stage of the development of the dramatic theatre.[21]

Stanislavsky does not define emotion or feeling, which is problematic. He rarely uses the word emotion (*emotsiia*) except in discussing emotional memory, preferring feeling (*chuvstvo*), which includes for him atmospheres and sensory experiences, such as memories of sounds and so on, but he takes this as primary and universal, part of human nature. (He sometimes refers to the *kernel of feeling*, as if the feeling were an entity in itself, for example, *AWR*, p. 121.) It is because of this assumed common understanding and experience that *infection* is possible, in Stanislavsky's view. Meyerhold took a different view, treating emotion as something secondary or even incidental in theatrical communication, as Brecht did also in accordance with his own particular theatre system. Stanislavsky needed to find a way to put his Tolstoyan ideas, corroborated by the

[20] I. Lapshin, *Khudozhestvennoye Tvorchestvo* (Petrograd: Mysl', 1923), p. 45.
[21] E. Poliakova (ed.) *Sulerzhitsky* (Moscow: Iskusstvo, 1970), pp. 368–9.

eighteenth-century writers, into practice, to find methods that could be consciously used so that the actor could always *experience* in performance. He explored the work of Ribot as a source for the mechanism of *affective* or *emotional memory*, a means of *experiencing* the bodily sensations of a emotion required by a role.

Théodule Ribot

Théodule Ribot (1839–96) was a professor of experimental psychology at the Sorbonne, and then at the Collège de France. He is considered, along with Alfred Binet and Pierre Janet (1859–1947) to be one of the founders of modern French psychology. He was influenced by associationist philosophy, which claimed that all mental activity including rational thought was no more than the association of ideas or sensations. The philosopher John Locke coined the phrase 'association of ideas' in the fourth edition of his *Essay Concerning Human Understanding* (1700). Associationism was at its height in the mid-nineteenth century, with the British associationists James Mill (1773–1836), John Stuart Mill (1806–1873) and Alexander Bain (1818–1903) promoting the principle of associative learning. As such it was a major influence on developing experimental psychology. Associationist psychologists such as Ribot asserted that the mind is a system operating in accordance with discoverable physical laws.

Vinogradskaia quotes Stanislavsky's notes for *MLIA*. When in Homburg in the summer of 1908, he said,

I made the acquaintance of a most educated and well-read person, who in the course of conversation suddenly came out with the following: 'You know . . . that the experiencing and creativity of the artist are based on the recollections of affective feelings and memories?' . . . I became silent, but immediately wrote to ask them to send me literature on this question. Soon I received Ribot's pamphlets.[22]

According to Benedetti, what Stanislavsky received were the translations of *Les Maladies de la Memoire* (Paris 1881) and *Les Maladies de la Volonté* (Paris 1884), both published in Russian in 1900.[23] Between 1908 and the following summer, Stanislavsky studied these books and also *La Logique des Sentiments* (Paris 1905), which was published in Russian in 1906, 'La Memoire Affective', an article published in Paris in 1896 and

[22] I. Vinogradskaia, *Zhizn' i tvorchestvo K. S. Stanislavskogo, Letopis*, vol. 2 (Moscow: Moskovskii Khudozhestvennyi Teatr, 2003), p. 128.

[23] Jean Benedetti, *Stanislavski: His Life and Art*, 2nd edn (London: Methuen, 1999), p. 185.

published in Russian in the journal *Obrazovanie* in 1899, and *La Psychologie de l'Attention* (Paris 1889), published in Russian in 1897. His notes and copies of the books are extant in his library. The editors of the first edition of Stanislavsky's *Collected Works* also note that he read *L'Evolution des Idées Generales* (Paris 1909).

N. Abalkin, the Soviet author of *Stanislavsky's System and the Soviet Theatre*, quotes various contemporaries of Stanislavsky, who all asserted that Stanislavsky's *system* is rooted in French psychology, particularly that of the 'sensualist' Ribot. (This was used pejoratively in Soviet times for those propounding the origin of ideas in sensation.) One of these contemporaries was V. M. Volkenstein, who worked as dramaturg for MAAT, taught speech in the Opera Studio and became Stanislavsky's secretary in 1921.[24] Abalkin confidently asserts that Stanislavsky's contemporaries were exaggerating Ribot's importance, and that the emphasis on *emotional memory* was a passing phase before Stanislavsky found 'a materialistic resolution for the problem of inspiration in the creativity of the stage'.[25] The importance of Ribot to the development of Stanislavsky's ideas was obfuscated for political reasons in Russia, and has been neglected as a field of enquiry in the West.

Stanislavsky's copy of the pamphlet *Affective Memory*, published in Russian in St Petersburg in 1899, is heavily annotated. There are also two sets of notes from the pamphlet; one set is dated 'June–August 1909'. *AWHE*, Chapter 9, is devoted to the discussion of *emotional memory*, he says, 'as is it now called. Before we called it *affective memory*, after Ribot' (*AWHE*, p. 279). The term 'affect' refers to a wide range of concepts including feelings, emotions, moods, motivation, drives and instincts. Stanislavsky's Soviet editors say that Stanislavsky replaced the term 'affective memory' with 'emotional memory', which is 'a more complete and exact concept' (*AWHE*, 1st edn, p. 414), whereas in fact Stanislavsky was persuaded to change the name for political reasons.

Here is the central idea that Stanislavsky verified from his reading of Ribot – that *affective memory* gives veracity to acting because it is based in 'nature', that is, in 'real' experience. Stanislavsky adopts Ribot's thesis from *Affective Memory* (*AM*),[26] that emotional images as well as visual, auditory, tactile-motor, verbal images and images derived from smell, taste, internal sensations, pleasure and pain can be revived both

[24] *Ibid.* p. 267.
[25] N. A. Abalkin, *Sistema Stanislavskogo i Sovietski Teatr* (Moscow: Iskusstvo, 1954), p. 96.
[26] Théodule Ribot, *The Psychology of the Emotions*, 2nd edn (London: Walter Scott, 1911), Chapter XI, 'The Memory of Feelings', pp. 140–71.

spontaneously and voluntarily. Ribot's enquiry takes the form of a questionnaire issued to sixty people whom he asked to record their experiences of spontaneous sense memories, memories of pain and pleasure, and emotional memories, that is, recollections which occurred to them in association with other events or thoughts they were experiencing, and their voluntary recollections of sensory experiences and emotional events. As one of his conclusions, Ribot states that 'the emotional memory is *nil* in the majority of people' (p. 171), although it is necessarily of frequent occurrence in poets and artists (p. 154). Stanislavsky asserts that the actor can develop this voluntarily. Hence part of Stanislavsky's training for actors was the development of the *sense* and *emotional memory*.

In *AWHE*, Chapter 9, Tortsov tests the students on their capacity for spontaneous *emotional memory*:

If you are able to pale or blush at a memory of something you have experienced, if you fear to think about an unhappy event experienced long ago, you have a memory for feelings, or an emotional memory. But it is not developed enough to hold its own in the struggle with the difficulties of the conditions of creation in public (p. 281).

The implication is that if the actor has the capacity for spontaneous emotional memory, Stanislavsky can find ways for the actor to develop his ability for voluntary recall and control over its use in performance.

Tortsov tests the students' capacity for *sense memory*. Stanislavsky makes the equation that the capacity for emotional recall is the same or dependent on the ability to recall sensory experiences, smells and tastes. An example is given of two young men who after a drunken night out can remember the motif from a polka that they have heard, but cannot remember where or when. They go through a process of recollecting where they sat, what they ate, smelled, the music they heard, and then they remember that they had quarrelled. 'From this example', says Tortsov, 'you can see the close link and interaction between our five senses and their influence on the recollections of the emotional memory. So the artist needs not only an emotional memory but also the memory of our five senses' (*AWHE*, p. 285). Actors, for example, need to 'impress and resurrect in themselves memories of visual and aural images' – a person's face, expression, walk, mannerisms and voice. The students are instructed to do many exercises to develop their sense memories, such as imagining the taste of fresh caviar or the smell of salmon (*AWHE*, p. 168). These are also exercises in developing *attention*.

These exercises pave the way for the more sophisticated techniques of which the actors avail themselves in developing a role. In *AWR*, Stanislavsky writes that part of the analysis in the period of getting to know the role is in seeking for material contained within the artists themselves, that is, in self-analysis.

> This material . . . is composed of live personal living memories of all five senses, preserved in the affective memory of the artist him/herself, from knowledge acquired by learning preserved in the intellectual memory, from experience s/he has gained in life and so on . . . these memories must be absolutely analogous with the feelings of the play and the role (p. 55).

Stanislavsky concurred with Ribot that as there are people of different types so there are artists of a visual and of an aural type, notably, in Ribot's description, painters and musicians (*AM*, p. 141). Therefore, there are those who, in his opinion, want to be shown what they should do in action and those who wish to hear the sound of a voice or the speech or intonation of the character they are playing (*AWHE*, p. 283).

Stanislavsky asserted that the 'experiences which are analogous to the role belong to the artist, not the character . . . you cannot get away from yourself . . . you kill the character if you do not use your own feelings' (p. 294). These *experiencings* are analogous though none the less 'real'. Throughout his works, Stanislavsky gives examples of emotional experiences of his own that he has used in his roles; for example, his confusion and embarrassment in encountering a girl he liked as an adolescent (*AWR*, 1st edn, p. 146). For Stanislavsky, in rehearsals for Ostrovsky's *Snow Maiden* in 1900, the sight of painters suspended in baskets working on the ceiling somehow evoked the atmosphere he wanted for the play, although it was years later that he retrieved the memory of icon painters he had seen working on the ceiling in the cathedral in Kiev, which suggested the atmosphere and then, he says, he understood the connection.[27]

Of course, like Bernhardt, Stanislavsky's actors do not give way to their emotions: they are not possessed by their emotions in the way that Diderot attributes to actors of sensibility. One of the elements of the internal region of the soul (**11 n** on the diagram) is 'control and finish'. In the chapter with this title in *AWHI*, Tortsov (who says that in this he agrees with Salvini) relates how people undergoing an emotional crisis cannot describe it without their voice giving way, or crying, but in time they can speak calmly and logically about the past event, and it is those listening who cry. In the same way the stage artist, who has cried and suffered over the role in rehearsals, calms down from the superfluous

---

[27] David Magarshack, *Stanislavsky: A Life*, 2nd edn (Westport, Connecticut: Greenwood Press, 1975), pp. 208–10.

emotion that would get in the way of describing to the audience what has been *experienced* with his own feelings. 'Then the spectator is more upset than the artist and the artist preserves his powers to direct them where he most needs them to convey *the life of the human spirit*' (*AWHI*, 1st edn, p. 225). Although it can be controlled, nevertheless the emotion is still really *experienced* in Stanislavsky's view. Therefore, in essence he concurs with Ribot, who writes in the note to the second edition of *Affective Memory*, about the mechanism of memory:

every recollection must be a **reversion**, by virtue of which the past once more becoming a present, we live at present in the past. The recollection of an emotion as such does not escape the action of this law; it must become actual once more – must *be* a real emotion, whether acute or obtuse.[28]

Tolstoy held the same view. It is not clear at which point Stanislavsky clarified this in his own thinking. He does use the term 'repeated feelings' on occasion but this does not detract from the fact that there must be actual experiencing (*Collected Works*, vol. 6, p. 81). He may have taken the concept from Tolstoy or his own experience. His espousal of Ribot may have been confirmation of this or part of the formation of his views.

Intellectual *and* emotional memory

Stanislavsky drew from Ribot the distinction between the *intellectual* and the *emotional memory*, as above (*AWR*, p. 55). Stanislavsky underlined in red Ribot's conclusion, drawn from the reports of those he surveyed, when he asked them to recall a particular case of a particular emotion:

In the greater number of cases only the conditions, circumstances and accessories of the emotion can be recalled; there is only an *intellectual* memory. The past event comes back to them with a certain emotional colouring (and sometimes even this is absent), a vague affective trace of what once has been but cannot be recalled.[29]

On the other hand, a true *emotional memory* involves a change in bodily state. 'The recollection of a feeling, it will be said, has this special property, that it is associated with organic and physiological states which make of it a real emotion. I reply that it *must* be so, for an emotion which does not vibrate through the whole body is nothing but a purely intellectual state.'[30]

---

[28] Ribot, *The Psychology of the Emotions*, p. 171.
[29] *Ibid.* p. 152.
[30] *Ibid.* p. 163.

It is interesting that Stanislavsky distorts Ribot's example. Ribot in fact gives two unrelated stories of intellectual memories, one of C__'s and one of his own. C__ narrowly escaped being cut off by the tide, and can recall the sight of the waves rising and his rush for the shore, but not the emotion. Ribot himself nearly fell into a gorge.[31] When recalling it he can see the landscape, but experiences only a slight shiver in his back and legs. However, Stanislavsky writes that Ribot reported that two travellers were marooned on a cliff by sea tides. They were rescued and afterwards related their impressions. One remembered all his actions, the other his emotions (*AWHE*, p. 279). This distortion indicates Stanislavsky's thinking on the indivisibility of *action* and emotion, and the possibility of attaining emotion via *action*.

The purification of emotional memory

Emotion cannot be achieved directly, at will, but requires *lures*. A *lure* is anything that arouses feeling: the *magic if*, the sets and costumes, physical actions, *affective memories*. With the latter, it is not as simple as giving yourself an experience which you recall later. Stanislavsky had rejected this early on, describing in *MLIA* how he had himself been locked in a castle overnight in the attempt to find internal experience for the character of Pushkin's Miser Knight. He caught a cold and fell into despair (p. 162), later writing, 'We cannot use the memories of our feelings like books in our library' (*AWHE*, p. 290). Kostia explores the changes of his emotion over time on recollecting a street accident that he witnessed and how other emotional memories, such as that of a Serb musician crying over his dead monkey and trying to feed it orange peel, become mixed up with the other memory. Tortsov explains that *emotional memory* purifies the recollections in the furnace of time. Memory crystallises or synthesises and purifies feelings, providing a bank of repeated memories, which when refined forms material for the life of characters. These may change and the artist should seek to find new ones (pp. 290–1).

Memory is associative. Ribot's *Diseases of the Memory* states (in a passage marked by Stanislavsky) that 'each of us has in his consciousness a certain number of recollections; images of men, animals, cities, countries, facts of history or science or language. These recollections come back to us in the form of a more or less extended series.'[32]

---

[31] *Ibid.* pp. 152–3.
[32] Théodule Ribot, *Diseases of the Memory* (London: Kegan Paul, Trench, 1882), pp. 41–2.

False experiencing

However, Stanislavsky asserts that *experiencing* can be false, and this is when *emotional memory* is lacking; as Tortsov points out in *AWHE*, Chapter 9, Kostia and other students perform an étude – they are in a room where a madman is at the door, trying to get in. The first time the étude goes well and they are praised. They repeat it and Tortsov's criticism is that there is no doubt that they are *experiencing*, but it is false. The students can convince themselves that that they are reacting to the situation in the étude but unless their experience can be verified by *emotional memory* their *feeling* may be false: they are merely showing off to the audience. Elsewhere, Stanislavsky writes, emphasising this, 'everyone feels something, experiences something at every moment of his or her life, if he felt nothing he would be dead . . . but the question is *what* does the artist feel and experience' (*Collected Works*, vol. 6, p. 81).

In Stanislavsky's version of Ribot's example of the marooned travellers, one remembers his emotions spontaneously. If the students had been able to re-enact the étude, experiencing the emotions of the first time they did it, they would have had exceptional emotional memories. However, they pretended; they copied the external aspects of the emotions and exaggerated them. The implication is that they would have done better to recall exactly what they did, each action they undertook, like Ribot's first traveller, rather than falsify the emotion.

Hence Stanislavsky noted that

In Khaliutina's school at Mchedlov's the students experience for the sake of experiencing. They bathe in *experiencing* – there are pauses for two minutes, and then a quietly and indistinctly thrown-out muffled phrase. This is terrible. Consequently from this year on – 1912 – I shall not teach *experiencing*, but action, that is, fulfilling a task.[33]

Significantly, the alternative approaches to emotional truth, through *experiencing* and action, are posited as equally valid as early as 1912.

Emotion and action

Although Stanislavsky did not attempt to define emotion, he was certain that stage emotion was not something repeating external manifestations but it could be as 'real' or 'organic' as emotion experienced in life. Ribot

---

[33] Vinogradskaia, *Letopis*, vol. 2, p. 318.

thought that an emotion should 'vibrate through the body'. In the introduction to *The Psychology of the Emotions*, he draws a distinction between what he calls the 'intellectualist' thesis of emotion, and the 'physiological' one. He cites the German Johann Friedrich Herbart (1776–1841), whose school, according to Ribot, believed emotions to be secondary and derived from intelligence; they result from the 'co-existence in the mind of ideas that agree or disagree'. Ribot himself follows the physiological doctrine where all states of feeling are connected with biological, vegetative conditions. The publication of Darwin's *Expression of the Emotions in Man and Animals* in 1872 gave impetus to the development of the theory of emotions as organic processes. Ribot names Alexander Bain (1818–1903), Herbert Spencer (1820–1903),[34] Henry Maudsley (1835–1918), William James (1842–1910) and Carl Lange (1834–1900), as proponents of the 'physiological' theory. Feelings and emotions 'plunge into the individual's depths; they have their roots in the needs and instincts, that is to say, in movements'.[35] The so-called James-Lange theory, Ribot added, sparked off much discussion and further research. It had an impact in Russia as well as the West, in particular with regard to the idea of emotion as indivisible from movement or action.

James's *Principles of Psychology* (1890) describes the similarities between James's own views on emotion and those of the Danish physiologist Carl Lange. Both sought a physiological explanation of emotions such as fear, grief, rage and love in which 'strong organic reverberations' can be recognised, and also those where the reverberations are less strong, such as moral, intellectual and aesthetic feelings'.[36] The causes of emotions are assumed to be internal, physiological, nervous processes rather than mental or psychological processes. Other theories of emotion and, as James writes, common sense, would assert that a mental perception of a fact excites what is called the emotion, and this mental state evokes the bodily expression: 'We meet a bear, we are frightened and we run.' Instead, '*the bodily changes follow directly the PERCEPTION of the exciting fact and . . . our feeling of the same changes as they occur is the emotion*' (James's italics). Therefore, we meet a bear, and in James's view, we are afraid because we tremble.[37]

---

[34] According to Ribot's editor, Ribot was mistaken in thinking that Spencer held this view of emotion.
[35] Ribot, *The Psychology of the Emotions*, p. viii.
[36] William James, *Principles of Psychology*, vol. 2 (London: Macmillan, 1890), p. 449.
[37] *Ibid.* pp. 449–50.

The James-Lange theory, as such, did not exist. Lange and James had not worked together. James explained in *Principles* that there were similarities in their work, though they took different angles. Lange was more interested in the investigation of visceral changes in relation to a broad range of experience and James was trying to find a way of investigating emotion that would escape from the subjective descriptions with which he felt the issue had been saturated, and from over-simplified categorisations. For example, in *Physiognomy and Expression*, published in 1885, Paulo Mantegazza claimed to identify the universal language of expression.[38] However, the James-Lange theory was an idea that existed in popular perception and has often been stated in an over-simplified way. In reference to acting, it was purported to indicate that adopting the appropriate pose or taking the appropriate action would result in experiencing the appropriate emotion. James stressed that he was not necessarily writing from a materialist point of view, stating that the thesis was no more materialistic than any other thesis that says our emotions are conditioned by nervous processes.[39] Meyerhold took it to be a materialist theory and claimed it substantiated his actor-training method in biomechanics.

Stanislavsky also met the theory in Ribot's work that the root of feelings and emotions is in movement. Ribot wrote in *The Psychology of Attention* that 'there is no thought without expression, that is, a commencement of muscular activity'.[40] This was corroborated for Stanislavsky by his reading of Sechenov and there were also sources other than Ribot in which the new ideas about emotion were presented to Stanislavsky. A. P. Petrovsky, a fellow actor, director and trainer working in Moscow and St Petersburg, also recommended William James to Stanislavsky (*Iz Zapisnich Knizhek*, vol. 1, p. 231) and Lapshin, with whom Stanislavsky was on close terms, translated James's *Textbook of Psychology* into Russian, which was published in 1896.

The editors of the first edition of Stanislavsky's *Collected Works* state in a note that in his research on the nature of artistic creativity, he 'takes a false, idealistic position', and explain that although Stanislavsky uses Lapshin's theoretical terminology, this does not detract from Stanislavsky's correct understanding. As a metaphysical idealist, Lapshin had to leave Russia after the revolution and settled in Prague. Like

---

[38] *Ibid.* p. 447.
[39] *Ibid.* p. 453.
[40] Théodule Ribot, *The Psychology of Attention*, tr. from 6th edn (Chicago and London: Open Court, 1911), p. 12.

Stanislavsky, he believed the actor experienced emotion in a lifelike way (though Lapshin prefers to describe these as 'aesthetic' rather than 'genuine, everyday emotions' (*Iz Zapisnich Knizhek*, vol. 1, p. 45). Most importantly, it is likely that Stanislavsky would have learned of Jamesian views on emotion through him. Stanislavsky's library contains Bezpiatov's *Elements of Scientific Psychology in the Theatrical Art in Connection with General Questions of Theatre* (published in 1912). Bezpiatov aimed to establish the much-needed 'science of theatre', which would unite 'both the technical-material part of the theatre and its so-called "aesthetic philosophy" '.[41] Psychology is the scientific discipline most closely related to theatre, and he cites James's *Textbook on Psychology* and the *Essay on Elementary Psychology* by the American G. T. Ladd (1842–1920), which was published in Russian in 1900, to corroborate the view that 'psychology is a natural science concerning the description and interpretation of states of consciousness'. Empirical psychology is important for the theatre; empirical science studies the external manifestations of a person's mental activity and has at its basis this law: 'to each psychic manifestation corresponds a nervous-mechanical manifestation, which is inextricably linked with it'.[42]

Bezpiatov explains that emotions are everyday feelings such as fear, love and pride, and that they play a large part in the creativity of the actor but belong to the sphere of reactions of vital activity, not feelings. Here, he is drawing the distinction James drew between emotions, which have 'strong organic reverberations' and moral, intellectual or aesthetic feelings. Regarding the expression of emotion in acting, he writes, 'expressive gesture describes emotion', adding, 'the connection between the facial expression and spiritual experience is so close that not only does emotion evoke facial expression but often a facial expression evokes emotion'.[43] He states that the phrase 'we are sad, because we are crying' has as deep a meaning as the opposite. Bezpiatov, adopting the popular conception of the James-Lange theory, cites both James and Bain, among others, to corroborate this.

Stanislavsky does not make this crude equation but this is another indication that empirical psychology and its ensuing theories of emotion were dominant at the time he was forming his theory and practice of generating emotion, in his period of 'Artistic Maturity', and the idea that

---

[41] Evgenii Bezpiatov, *Elementi Nauchnoi Psikhologii v Teatral'nom' Iskusstvike* (St Petersburg: I. V. Leont'ev, 1912), p. 5.
[42] *Ibid.* p. 8.
[43] *Ibid.* p. 29.

theatre could be verified scientifically by psychology. The thesis that all thought is accompanied by muscular activity seemed incontrovertible in Stanislavsky's time and the materialist reduction of mental states to activity meant that Stanislavsky saw emotion and action as inextricably linked. This is to be taken into account in an assessment of any changes in his theories.

There was a practical reason for emphasising action: there is the rather bitter statement that 'the so-called Stanislavsky system . . . is not always correctly understood . . . in some theatres, for example, experiencing is seen as the "privilege" of certain people and enterprises of the capital city' (*AWHI*, p. 429). Again, it is apparent that for Stanislavsky the distinction between *experiencing* and *action* is a matter of choice, of how best to get over his meaning. There was also a political reason. Stanislavsky's replacement of the term *affective memory* with *emotional memory* distanced the concept from its origins in pre-revolutionary psychology. An editorial note to *AWR* in the first edition of Stanislavsky's *Collected Works* states that he defined *affective memory* as 'memory of feelings experienced in life'. In distinction from the visual, aural and other kinds of memory, it 'imprints not the facts and situation themselves, but the spiritual feelings and physical sensations accompanying them'. The editor states that

Stanislavsky, following Shchepkin demanded that the actor 'go from life' in work on the role . . . however, at the first stage of the development of the 'system' Stanislavsky strongly overestimated the significance of affective memory in the creativity of the actor. He considered it basic to the creativity of the actor, the main lure of feelings; thence he drew the mistaken conclusion that all the experiencings of the actor on stage have a repeated character. Whilst not denying the significance of affective memory as one of the elements of the 'system', Stanislavsky later revised the role of this element in the actor's creativity. He came to the conclusion that the logic of physical actions, directed along the implementation of the line of through action and the supertask of the play and the role was a more complete means of influencing feeling than affective memory. In contrast to affective memory which deals with capricious and elusive feeling, the logic of physical actions of the role is more defined, accessible, materially palpable, easily fixed and subject to the control and influence of consciousness. Together with that, it is closely linked to the internal life of the role (*AWR*, pp. 477–8, n3).

The view that Stanislavsky had 'moved' from emotional memory to the *method of physical actions* was perpetuated by Western practitioners and such writers as Sonia Moore,[44] while others cast doubt on it. Burnet

---

[44] Sonia Moore, *The Stanislavski System*, 2nd rev. edn (London: Penguin, 1984), p. 10.

Hobgood, for example, called the *method of physical actions* a 'red herring'.[45] Carnicke explains this dismissal as a rejection of Soviet propaganda around the *method of physical actions*, which Sonia Moore took up.[46] According to Carnicke, 'in the System "the life of the human spirit of the role" is continuous with "the life of the human body on stage." In short, inner content (emotion) is inextricably linked to outer form (action).'[47] She thinks, therefore, that although Stanislavsky did not reject the possibility of the actor finding a path from feeling to action, that the *method of physical actions* 'assumes that emotional life can be more easily aroused and fixed for performance through work on the physical life of the role than through emotional recall'.[48] She argues that it is essentially a rehearsal technique, rather than the culmination of Stanislavsky's work.

Stanislavsky's first written description of what became known as the *method of physical actions* was in a letter to his son Igor in 1936, though the term had been used in teaching before:

I am setting a new device in motion now, a new approach to the role. It involves reading the play today and tomorrow rehearsing it on stage . . . A character comes in, greets everybody, sits down, tells of events that have just taken place, expresses a series of thoughts. Everyone can act this, guided by their own life experience . . . and so we break the whole play, episode by episode into physical actions. When this is done exactly, correctly, so that it is true and it inspires our belief in what is happening on stage, then we can say that the line of the life of the human body has been created. This is no small thing, but half of the role. Can the physical line exist without the spiritual? No. So the internal line of experiencing is outlined (*Collected Works*, vol. 9, p. 665).

There is a transcript dating from 1936 outlining a plan for the use of this method in the rehearsal process (see Appendix). It was a device, a new approach, a form of *active analysis*. Stanislavsky emphasised further in the later period of his work that following the line of action in the role was a way into the emotion, but this did not contradict his earlier beliefs because for him the two things were inseparable. The increasing enforcement of ideas of materialism in the Soviet Union contributed to reasons for changes in description and emphasis, but, also, as an inventive director, Stanislavsky constantly sought fresh ways of getting actors to

[45] Burnet M. Hobgood, 'Central Conceptions in Stanislavsky's System', *Educational Theatre Journal*, 25: 2 (1973), pp. 147–59.
[46] Carnicke, *Stanislavsky in Focus*, p. 150.
[47] *Ibid.* p. 148.
[48] *Ibid.* p. 177.

think about what they were doing. Benedetti writes that Volkenstein's book *Stanislavsky*, published in 1922, is significant in its description of the *system* for the emphasis it places, even at this early period, on physical action rather than on the search for emotion.[49] This indicates that Stanislavsky knew that emotion could not be sought directly and *emotional memory* was as important a key as action. After all, as Hughes points out, 'both methods serve the same strategic and Tolstoyan end, to evoke within the actor the feeling proper to the character'.[50] As Carnicke notes, in *AWHE*, Dymkova performs an improvisation about a baby where she finds the appropriate emotional experience directly; she has no need of working through the physical actions (p. 451). Significantly, three months before his death, Stanislavsky said, 'One must give actors various paths. One of these is the path of action. There is also another path; you can move from feeling to action, arousing feeling first.'[51]

Action

Action was, therefore, always an important concept in Stanislavsky's theory and practice. Somewhat confusingly, action is not only a base of the *system*, but occurs at **11d** in Stanislavsky's diagram, as an element of the internal region of students at Tortsov's drama school are introduced to the concept of *action* in their first lesson with the director (*AWHE*, Chapter 3). As Tortsov himself demonstrates, stage *action* can mean inactivity, for example, sitting waiting for something. Stanislavsky sees this as internal, psychic *action*, expressed in outward immobility. The formula is: 'on stage it is necessary to act, internally and externally' (p. 89). In *action*, what is 'psychical' is linked with what is 'physical'. Tortsov states, 'the imagination must be linked not just with the psychical but the physical . . . Every movement and word on stage must be the result of the true life of the imagination' (*AWHE*, p. 142). Concentration is also 'inner action'.[52]

In Chapter VIII, 'The Sense of Truth and Belief' (**11e** on the diagram), the students are asked to perform a scene looking for a lost purse, which

[49] Benedetti, *Stanislavski: His Life and Art*, p. 268.
[50] R. I. G. Hughes, 'Tolstoy, Stanislavski, and the Art of Acting', *The Journal of Aesthetics and Art Criticism*, 51: 1 (Winter, 1993), p. 42.
[51] Stanislavskii, *Stanislavskii repetiruet: Zapisi i stenogrammy repetitsii*, ed. 1. Vinogradskaia, 2nd edn, Moscow: Moskovskii Khudozhestvennyi Teatr, 2000, p. 498. Quoted in Carnicke. *Stanislavsky in Focus*, p. 151.
[52] Stanislavsky, *Stanislavsky on the Art of the Stage*, tr. David Magarshack, 2nd edn. (London: Faber and Faber, 1967) p. 166.

they have just done in actuality. The scene does not work because they do not believe in their *tasks*. In the étude 'Burning Money' Kostia pretends to count money. Tortsov goes through the actions of counting money with him meticulously; 'As soon as I felt the real truth of the physical action, I immediately became comfortable on stage' (p. 235). He goes on to suggest that 'What is important is not just the physical actions themselves, but truth and belief in them, which these actions help us evoke and feel' (p. 237). Psychology, drama and tragedy, he further suggests, are hidden in simple physical actions (p. 240). It is the logic and consistency of physical actions, attention to the constituent parts of them, with truth and belief, that enables the actor to *experience* fully on stage' (p. 247). Tortsov concludes, 'In each physical action there is something psychological and in each psychological one there is something physical' (p. 258).

Action *and the* task

Stanislavsky often mentions *bits* and *tasks* together, as both are ways to analyse the play (**11b** on the diagram), probably first using this method in *Hamlet* in 1911.[53] *Bits* are sections of action in the play. The *task* (*zadacha*) is exemplified in a famous example in *AWHE*, Chapter 3. Maloletkova is asked to go on stage and at first is awkward, then tries to do something to entertain the audience. When Tortsov sits on stage, looking though his notebook, she sits waiting until he has finished. In his assessment, this is successful; she did not 'play act' but was *active*; she performed an *action*. The next step is to perform an *action* in the *given circumstances* of an improvisation. Her *task* is to look for a valuable brooch, which a friend has given her to pay her drama school fees, which is pinned to the stage curtain. At first, she overacts 'looking' so much that she forgets about the brooch. She pretends to experience despair and terror when she cannot find the brooch, in an exaggerated way, to the amusement of her fellow students. As Tortsov points out, she is not really looking for the brooch. Then Tortsov gives her new *given circumstances*. If she cannot find the brooch, she will have to leave the school. She begins her *task*; really looking among the folds of the stage curtain and her intensity this time impresses the audience (p. 90).

In a discussion with Suler, Nemirovich-Danchenko and others at the MAT (V. Kachalov, A. Stakhovich, V. Luzhsky and N. Massalitinov) in

---

[53] Laurence Senelick, *Gordon Craig's Moscow Hamlet* (Westport, Connecticut: Greenwood Press, 1982), p. 132.

August 1911, Stanislavsky said that if an actor defines a task, *experiencing* will result, and defined the difference between 'wanting' desire (*zhelanie*) and the task.

> If you are a monarchist by nature and you play the role of a monarchist you don't need a task, there is truth . . . If a republican plays a monarchist there is no faith and feeling of truth. Then wanting is replaced by a creative task. A series of tasks are created which are definitely natural (because they are from my affective feelings). If I perform this score many times, the feelings of another become mine (MAT, KS Archive, 1293, 'Beseda o Gamlete', 3 August 1911, p. 4).

To understand what Stanislavsky really meant by *task*, it is important to note the accretions it has developed through translation and transportation across cultures. Strasberg and the Method actors understood the term *zadacha* to mean 'objective', and it became for them embroiled with Freudian concepts of motivation. Freud's work was translated into Russian from 1910, and it was read by Michael Chekhov. It is possible that Stanislavsky was aware of it, but it is definitely the case that Stanislavsky's own view of the unconscious was pre-Freudian. Crohn Schmitt writes (using the word 'objective', where 'task' is more accurate and 'ruling-idea' for *supertask*),

> Freud saw the unconscious as a source of motives and desires. Stanislavsky was interested in unconscious objectives. Thus Freud would have sought the unconscious reasons for your hatred of your father while Stanislavsky was interested in your goal (as your character) to kill him (your character's father) . . . The problem for the actor was to define the character's *objective* in a way consistent with the 'ruling idea' and to act to achieve it – the nature of the action towards the end defining the nature of the character. The actor was to carry out the character's action as if it were his own.[54]

Confusion has resulted from the problems in translation and the *lure* inherited by the Method actors, as Carnicke terms the ideas transmitted by émigré Russian actors, some of whom, such as Richard Boleslavsky, were members of the First Studio. Reynolds Hapgood translated the Russian word *zadacha* as 'objective' (and *sverkhzadacha*, the task which the whole play aims to carry out, as 'ruling idea') but it can simply be a *task*. Stanislavsky was not so much interested in objectives but in the *tasks* the actor has to perform as the character in a way that combines the life of the spirit/body/emotions.

---

[54] Natalie Crohn Schmitt, 'Stanislavski, Creativity and the Unconscious', *New Theatre Quarterly*, 2:8 (1986), pp. 346–7.

In *AWHE* for example, one of the students suggests that Brand's *task* in the Ibsen play is 'to save humanity'. Tortsov encourages the students not to choose *tasks* like this, which are too grand. He points out that 'the psychology of Salieri when he has decided to kill Mozart is very complicated'. But what you have to do if you are playing Salieri is to carry out physical actions, which in fact have much of psychology in them, that is, 'taking the glass, pouring wine in it, putting in the poison and taking it to your friend, the genius whose music delights you'. He states that 'Truly fulfilling a physical task helps you to create the right psychological state' (p. 218).

In Stanislavsky's view, for an actor to portray killing his character's father would involve this process; what he or she does would be broken down into the appropriate *tasks* in the *given circumstances*, according to the *supertask* rather than, as Crohn Schmitt writes, the fulfilment of an objective. Crohn Schmitt understands this as 'action towards a fixed end', and therefore as teleological in an Aristotelian way. In fact, Stanislavsky's theory of action is not teleological in an Aristotelian sense because it involves *tasks* and not *objectives* (a term that became heavily laden with Freudian unconscious motivations). For Stanislavsky the *unconscious* is the source of inner *experiencing* and truth, not of hidden drives. *If* and the *given circumstances* are much simpler concepts than many commentators suggest. In practice, the actor performs *tasks* in *given circumstances* using the *magic if,* generating truthful acting.

Soviet science and reflexes

Stanislavsky had a set of ideas about emotion and *action* originating in associationist psychology. He then tried to make this fit with the paradigmatic shift to Pavlovian physiology after the revolution and the Soviets' increasingly equated Stanislavsky's work with that of Sechenov and Pavlov, distancing him from Ribot. The physiologist P. V. Simonov, writing in the sixties, wrote that Stanislavsky's work corroborated and even developed Pavlov's theory of conditional reflexes.[55]

In their different epochs Sechenov and Pavlov were the foremost Russian physiologists working on the study of behaviour from the point of view of reflex responses, leading the way for the work of the American behaviourists J. B. Watson and B. F. Skinner. Sechenov worked on the chemistry of respiration and was the first person to study the physiology

---

[55] P. V. Simonov, *Metod K. S. Stanislavskogo i Fiziologia Emotzii* (Moscow: AN SSSR, 1962), pp. 3–4.

of work in Russia. His work on central inhibition in the nervous system, though it was superseded by later work, was very important. Sechenov and Pavlov's theories were associationist but central to their research was the study of thought or mind or emotions from the point of view of their physiological manifestations. They asserted, as some of the associationist psychologists had done, that there is no thought without muscular activity.

Vinogradskaia writes that in 1930 Stanislavsky studied the history of philosophy and also read and made notes from Sechenov's *Reflexes of the Brain*.[56] This is a grand description of what amounts to half a page of notes but is in keeping with the Soviet emphasis. The excerpt made by Stanislavsky is noted below. Stanislavsky had come into contact with Sechenov's work much earlier. In 1884, F. P. Kommisarzhevsky (the famous opera singer who taught Stanislavsky and who was another performing artist with an interest in contemporary physiology) asked Stanislavsky to buy him some books he needed for his work, including Sechenov's *The Physiology of the Nervous System*.[57]

Sechenov (1829–1905) investigated central inhibition in the hope of finding 'a materialist, physiological explanation of the complex and apparently spontaneous behavior of human beings'.[58] In *Reflexes of the Brain*, as part of his thesis that what we call thought and emotion are both reflex in nature and that what we call voluntary movements are essentially mechanistic, reflex reactions, Sechenov propounded that all external expression of emotions and passions is the result of muscular movement.[59]

In Sechenov's epoch the centuries-old debate on the mind/body problem had progressed in the light of discoveries made in the nineteenth century about the physiology of the nervous system. These discoveries corroborated work on the idea of reflexes current since the time of Descartes. It was refined, here, to the view of the neuron, nerve impulse and reflex arc as the model for the way in which neurons combine to transform an incoming event or 'stimulus' into behaviour adapted to deal with that event or 'response'. The reflex arc is the term given to the circuit made in a reflex reaction where sensory nerve fibres transmit a stimulus to the brain or spinal cord, which then activates the afferent or motor nerve fibres, resulting in action.

---

[56] Vinogradskaia, *Letopis*, vol. 4, p. 125.
[57] *Ibid.* vol. 1, p. 65.
[58] Daniel Todes, 'Biological Psychology and the Tsarist Censor: The Dilemma of Scientific Development', *Bulletin of the History of Medicine*, 58 (1984), pp. 535–6.
[59] I. M. Sechenov, *Reflexes of the Brain*, tr. S. Belsky (Cambridge: Massachusetts, 1965) p. 3.

Sechenov published *Reflexes of the Brain* in 1863, the year of Stanislavsky's birth.[60] It was condemned as nihilistic and immoral. He had studied in Germany, but opposed the idealist philosophy of J. G. Fichte and F. W. Schelling, which dominated thinking in Germany of the mid-nineteenth century.[61] He asserted instead the reductivism of associationist philosophy, which then strongly influenced such nineteenth-century German thinkers as Herbart and Gustav T. Fechner (1801–1887), as well as French psychologists such as Ribot. However, Sechenov rejected the introspective approach adopted by Ribot, working in the laboratory instead, experimenting on frogs to explore the idea of reflex action.

Sechenov worked in Germany with Hermann von Helmholtz (1821–1894) and Emil Dubois-Reymond (1818–1896) asserting mechanism and opposing vitalism, and then went a step further in arguing that all human behaviour including thought and emotion could be analysed as reflex activity. Even our most complicated emotional or spiritual experiences result from the associative capacities of the brain, which has learned its responses since childhood. As Graham states, 'Thus, at the very birth of Russian physiology an explicit link to materialism was made and this tradition has remained a part of Russian and Soviet psychology to the present day.'[62]

In summary, he saw sensation (and what we call emotion) as a combination of the reception of reflex stimulation and muscle activity. External sensory experiences cause the beginning of reflexes and, in Sechenov's extrapolation, the whole of our psychical life. Stanislavsky noted from *Reflexes of the Brain* Sechenov's statement that the brain is an organ of the spirit and not vice versa; it is a mechanism, which if brought into action by a certain cause ultimately produces a series of external phenomena that are expressions of psychical activity.[63] These can be reduced to muscular movement. Examples are given of a child laughing, a girl trembling at the first thought of love, and Newton writing scientific laws (even intellectual work is expressed through muscular movement). Hence, all the characteristics of the external expression of the emotions and passions are the result of muscle contraction that is mechanical (Stanislavsky's notebook 1929–1932, MAT, KS Archive 544, p. 43).

---

[60] Sechenov is the name given to a teacher of the drama students in *AWHI* (p. 132). As many of the names given to teachers and students in Stanislavsky's writings are meaningful (see Preface) this is perhaps a homage to I. M. Sechenov.

[61] K. Kh. Kekcheev, *I. M. Sechenov* (Moscow: Zhurnalno-gazetnoe Obedinenie, 1933), p. 20.

[62] Loren Graham, *Science in Russia and the Soviet Union* (Cambridge University Press, 1993), p. 236.

[63] Sechenov, *Reflexes of the Brain*, p. 3.

Sechenov asserted that there is no thought without muscular activity and there is always an external stimulus for our behaviour. By the mechanism of association we analyse and synthesise our notions, so that our behaviour becomes increasingly complex as we develop, but essentially, he thought, it is all reflex. Memory, by the preservation of traces in the nervous system, is our capacity to reproduce sensations in the human consciousness. If we imagine circumstances from the past that made us experience gooseflesh, the effect is the same as the actual sensory stimulation and we experience gooseflesh again. Significantly then, for Stanislavsky, Sechenov wrote that the recreation in the imagination of past experiences produces the same effect as actual sensory stimulation, as Ribot had written.[64]

However, he differed from Ribot in saying that although thought is generally accepted as the cause of action, 'the initial cause of any action lies in external sensory stimulation because without this, thought is inconceivable'. Emotions too are, 'in origin, intensified reflexes'.[65] Sechenov writes that what he calls 'wishing' (*khotenie*) is the element of striving for the completion of a reflex (that is to satisfy an emotion): 'Life's necessities give birth to wishing and these draw action behind them'.[66] This view became significant in Soviet times.

Unlike Sechenov, Stanislavsky writes consistently of behaviour in terms of voluntary, willed action. However, Stanislavsky's reading of Sechenov confirmed some of the ideas he had encountered in Ribot and from James, such as the equation of thought and movement, and the idea that emotion cannot be divorced from its physical, that is, muscular expression, and also the idea that the recreation in the imagination of past experiences produces the same effect as an actual life experience. It confirmed that his *system* was in accordance with what he described as 'laws' and in the thirties he seemed to be attempting to reconcile his ideas with those of Sechenov and Pavlov.

Ivan Petrovich Pavlov (1849–1936), building on Sechenov's work, conducted his famed experiments on conditioned reflexes in the spectrum of his work on the higher nervous system between 1902 and 1936. Like Stanislavsky, he had a reputation abroad and was left to conduct his work in the Stalinist period without interference, and even with substantial support. Graham writes:

The greatest significance of Pavlov derives from his success in bringing psychic activity within the realm of phenomena to be studied and explained by the

---

[64] *Ibid.* p. 77.
[65] *Ibid.* pp. 88–9.
[66] *Ibid.* p. 101.

normal objective methods of natural science. In contrast to the introspective approach of many investigators of mental activity at the turn of the century, Pavlov's method was based on the assumption that psychic phenomena can be understood on the basis of evidence gathered entirely externally to the subject.[67]

Although his theories were found to have their limitations later, in the first third of the twentieth century (the period of Stanislavsky's most important work), Pavlov's work was well known and was generally presented as a vindication of the Marxist materialistic approach to the study of biology and human behaviour.

The aim of Pavlov's work was essentially to investigate the physiological laws of human psychical activity and to include psychology in the sphere of natural science. This would inevitably have had an impact on Stanislavsky, or anyone in the period around the Russian revolution working on any sphere of human behaviour. Pavlov had won the Nobel Prize in 1904 and the work of the revolutionary leaders ensured that his work was seen as of great importance. Small wonder that his theory of conditional reflexes became a scientific paradigm for Stanislavsky and his contemporaries, after the revolution. It was generally held to be an important breakthrough in science. Perhaps few people fully understood it, but it was held to be ideologically correct.

Unlike Sechenov, Pavlov was not a strict materialist. Horsley Gantt, the translator of *Lectures on Conditioned Reflexes* into English, wrote:

He explains that the teaching of conditioned reflexes is science, but that it has nothing to do with materialism. As long as the dualistic theory is accepted and mind and matter are considered separate entities, it is difficult to reconcile the new facts with this belief; but according to Pavlov, 'We are now coming to think of the mind, the soul and matter as one, and with this view there will be no necessity for a choice between them.' (Personal conversation, April 1928.) The dualistic theory in his opinion has kept physiologists from working with the higher nervous phenomena.[68]

Cuny writes that 'Pavlov's thinking revolutionised conventionally accepted ideas', adding that Pavlov did not reject psychology as a valid philosophical study of vital manifestations; he was simply reacting against the subjectivism of the psychologists of his day. His aim was to demonstrate the close interdependence of psychical activities and physiological reactions.[69]

---

[67] *Ibid*. p. 239.
[68] I. P. Pavlov, *Lectures on Conditioned Reflexes*, tr. W. Horsley Gantt, 1 (London: Lawrence and Wishart, 1963), pp. 24–5.
[69] Hilaire Cuny, *Ivan Pavlov: The Man and his Theories*, tr. Patrick Evans (London, Souvenir Press, 1964), pp. 13–14.

It was impossible to consider one without the other. Mental life was not a 'thing in itself' any more than are physiological or physiochemical phenomena. As Pavlov himself wrote:

I am convinced that an important stage in the development of human thought is approaching, a stage when the physiological and the psychological, the objective and the subjective, will really merge, when the painful contradictions between our mind and our body and their contraposition will either be actually solved or disappear in a natural way. ... when the physiologist is able to foresee with absolute exactitude the behaviour of the higher animals under any conditions ... will not the activity of any living thing, man included, be indispensably regarded by us as a single indivisible whole?[70]

The central thrust of the theory of the conditioned reflexes was the investigation of how an animal adjusts to a changing environment, in accordance with evolutionary theory. Although Pavlov's experiments were on dogs, he thought that his work would result in an understanding of human behaviour in terms of reflexes. He thought that reflexes were acquired through education, cultural association and personal experience, another way of describing these being 'habits'. Each thought causes us to create new reflexes. Our reactions to people are conditional reflexes. Memory, Pavlov believed, is formed of acquired and innate reflexes.[71]

Stanislavsky's approach was introspective, subjective and more in keeping with the psychologists Pavlov rejected but he was no doubt encouraged to believe that Pavlov's work would elucidate the theoretical basis of his *system*, as it was believed it would reveal the mainsprings of all human action. There is a set of correspondence in the MAT archive, written between October 1934 and January 1935, mostly between A. E. Ashanin, a representative of the All-Russian Theatrical Organisation (*Vserossiskoe Teatral'naia Organizatsia*, V.T.O.), N. A. Podkopaev who worked in Pavlov's laboratory, and V. I. Pavlov, Pavlov's son. It concerns the setting up of meetings in Leningrad and Moscow to discuss a collaboration between the school of Pavlov and the school of Stanislavsky (MAT, KS Archive 5361–5377).

The sole letter from Stanislavsky to Pavlov states:

A. E. Ashanin, a representative of V.T.O. ... has conveyed to me your delightful request to acquaint yourself with the materials of a book about the work of an

---

[70] I. P. Pavlov, *Experimental Psychology and other Essays*, tr. Kh. S. Koshtoyants (New York: Peter Owen, 1957), p. 286.
[71] Cuny, *Ivan Pavlov*, p. 40.

actor on himself that I am writing... I am touched that you, having heard about the agreement binding me to an American publisher, have proposed checking my materials personally (*Collected Works*, vol. 9, 543, p. 612).

Could it be that Stanislavsky, having secured a contract with an American publisher, was under pressure to ensure that his work conformed to the prevailing scientific paradigm? The proposal was that V.T.O. would set up a laboratory for the study of the actor's creativity. The themes of work were to be as follows:

General: 'Genesis', the actor's beginning; particularities of the actor's constitution.

    Particular: the analysis of how the actor can increase at will his possibilities – both psychic and physical; the role of conditional reflexes in the work of the actor; the problem of double consciousness in the actor's creativity; the results of the actor's constant exercise of artificial emotional arousal; the peculiarities of the affective state of the actor; the significance of eidetic capacity as a factor in the actor's creativity; the problem of synaesthesia in the work of the actor; the peculiarities of differentiation of the actor's attention; the peculiarities of the actor's memory; the problem of momentum in the actor's creativity; the analysis of physiological, psychological, sociological factors conducive to the actor's creativity; the problem of heredity and questions of anamnesis in relation to outstanding masters of the stage of the past (MAT, KS Archive 5371, pp. 1, 2).

A desire to explore these questions from a physiological point of view was expressed, with the participation of a psychologist, physiologist, psychiatrist, neurologist and theatre specialist, with members of Pavlov's school and under the occasional supervision of Pavlov himself. Pavlov died in 1936, Stanislavsky in 1938, the work later being carried forward by others.

Stanislavsky and reflexes

Stanislavsky dutifully tried to incorporate reflex theory into his own theoretical writing. In the chapter entitled 'Imagination' in *AWHE*, Stanislavsky writes, 'It is important to acknowledge that the disembodied dream which has no flesh and matter has the ability to evoke as a reflex the genuine action of our flesh and matter – the body. This ability plays a large role in our psycho-technique' (p. 142). Stanislavsky appears to be saying that thought produces reflex action, rather than, as Roach thinks, that thought is part of a reflex response to stimuli, as Sechenov would have asserted. The term 'disembodied dream' implies that Stanislavsky saw psychic acts as separate to bodily ones, unlike Pavlov or Sechenov, and the real problem with Stanislavsky's theory of *action* is that he sometimes thinks of physical and psychical/psychological as different things. Similarly, in discussing external expression – facial expression, speech, movement – Stanislavsky says this must be excellently developed but also subjugated to the internal order of the will: 'The connection with the internal side and the mutual action must be taken to a momentary, unconscious, instinctive reflex' (*AWHI*, p. 135). There are other instances, where he states that if what goes on internally (feeling and thought) is correct, and the means of expression (for example, the voice) are good, then 'intonation will come of itself, as a reflex' (*AWHI*, p. 135). Thought and its expression are seen as a reflex, and a reflex that can be learned, and maybe conditioned.

Moreover, the subconscious can also be evoked by reflex. 'Not knowing about the subconscious we have nevertheless sought a link with it, felt the reflex path to it and evoked the responses of the world, as yet unknown to us, of the subconscious' (*AWHI*, p. 378). However, Pavlov did not address the phenomenon of consciousness directly and conditioned reflexes can operate at an automatic level, even subconsciously, so the subject reacts mechanically. What is crucial is that Stanislavsky wants the actor to be responding on stage in a state of full attention. The actor must consciously train his attention on his actions on stage, his tasks and on his partners so that he avoids a fear response, which Stanislavsky sees as natural or inevitable (and maybe unconditional) in view of the stimulus of the audience.

Stanislavsky did not adopt the theory of conditioned reflexes and may not have known much about it or understood it. He uses the term 'reflex', seemingly, as in the examples above, as a way to describe the interface between physical and the psychical, although he himself often thinks of the two separately. Rather than action bringing about thought as part of the reflex chain, as Sechenov thought, Stanislavsky sometimes seems to reiterate the view he had encountered in Ribot that there is no thought without muscular expression.

Another crucially important difference between the post-revolutionary thought inspired by Pavlov and Stanislavsky's way of thinking is the extent to which our behaviour is conditioned by our environment. As Cuny states, citing Victor Lafitte, 'Pavlov has helped us to understand that in Marx's words, "if circumstances shape man, we must shape circumstances in a human way"'.[72] For Stanislavsky there is something innate and intrinsic to

---

[72] *Ibid.* p. 100.

the human being, which is not alterable by circumstances. He makes it clear in a letter to Gurevich written in 1931 that in his view the material for a role lay in the actor's personality and nowhere else.[73] This, of course, is a crucial difference between Stanislavsky and Brecht. As Thomson states, 'It is generally true that a Stanislavskian actor will locate in character the explanation for behaviour, whilst the Brechtian actor will look for it in circumstance.'[74]

Although the appeal of Sechenov and Pavlov was understandably enormous in Russia in the machine age and beyond, their theories as such hold little sway now. The assumption made by Pavlov that what he observed to be true in animal behaviour would hold true for humans is questionable and experiments in conditioning human behaviour are now seen as having limited value. Stanislavsky's inability to integrate reflex theory coherently into his own was for a good reason. The work of both Pavlov and Sechenov, promoted as it was by the revolutionary govern-ment, no doubt influenced Stanislavsky in his considerations on action and emotion, but his main influence in this remains Ribot and the associationist philosophers. He did not abandon the idea of *emotional memory* and the understanding of it gained from Ribot.

In 1931 Stanislavsky's system was criticised at the conference of the Russian Association of Proletarian Writers (RAPP). At a meeting later that year with Stanislavsky, N. Afigenogenov, one of his critics, records Stanislavsky saying,

Here they abuse me for idealistic terms in my book. You also abuse me here, but I can find no other words, they do not give me them. Affective memory – propose something else instead of this term and I will accept it. Art is a condition of the human spirit. The word 'spirit' is harmful. Propose something else instead and I will accept it. But only an understandable word, one that immediately penetrates the essence. In my whole life I have only read five books on psychology and I don't understand complicated questions.[75]

Also, in a letter to E. Hapgood, dated 11 January 1937, he wrote:

As regards affective memory – this appellation belongs to Ribot. He was criti-cised for such terminology, as there is confusion with affect. Ribot's appellation has been abolished and not replaced with a new, definite one. But it is necessary

---

[73] Benedetti, *Stanislavski: His Life and Art*, p. 355. See Stanislavsky, *Collected Works*, vol. 9, pp. 449–53.

[74] Peter Thomson, 'Brecht and Actor Training' in Alison Hodge (ed.), *Twentieth Century Actor-training* (London: Routledge, 2000), p. 107.

[75] Vinogradskaia, *Letopis*, vol. 4, pp. 159–60.

for me to name the main memory on which almost all our art is based. I have called this memory emotional, that is, the memory of feeling (*chuvstva*).

It is untrue and a complete nonsense that I have renounced memory of feelings (*chuvstvovanie*). I repeat that it is the main element in our creativity. I only had to renounce the appellation (affective) and to attach significance to memory suggested to us by feeling, that is, that on which our art is founded, more than I had previously. (*Collected Works*, vol. 9, p. 665).

Far from a materialistic analysis of emotion, Stanislavsky has recourse to the unconscious.

SPIRITUAL MECHANISMS: THE SOUL AND THE UNCONSCIOUS

The emotional life of the character, which in some way cannot be dissociated from its external side or from action, cannot be sought directly, but is dependent on the workings of what Stanislavsky variously termed the *spirit* or the *soul*, or the *unconscious* or *subconscious*. The third base of the *system*, on his diagram, is the 'subconscious creativity of nature itself – through the artist's conscious psycho-technique'. Something that he called the *superconscious* also comes into play. From 1906 Stanislavsky recognised that the actor, in seeking *fusion* (*slianie*) with the character, needed to avoid falling into the trap of mechanical, habitual acting, by means of a spiritual preparation. He also calls this spiritual preparation the actor's *toilette* (see figure 3). He developed exercises on *freeing the muscles, attention, belief, magic if,* and the *radiation of creative will and feeling,* and work on the role as well as the self and voice. Working in this way should become the actors' habit or second nature. As well as overcoming the problem of mechanical acting, that will enable the actor both to overcome the problems presented by standing in front of an audience and to achieve the *creative sense of the self.*

Ever since the late-nineteenth century it had been recognised that 'by his work on the physiology of the brain, Sechenov . . . dealt a blow to the old clerical view of the soul – with a boldness such as Descartes could not boast of',[76] so by Stanislavsky's time the word for spirit (*dukh*) in 'spiritual preparation' could mean 'spirit' without religious connotation. However, there are religious or spiritual connotations to the way Stanislavsky talks about acting. At the beginning of the MAT, Stanislavsky led the actors

---

[76] Y. P. Frolov, *Pavlov and his School: The Theory of Conditioned Reflexes*, tr. C. P. Dutt (London: Kegan Paul, Trench, Trubner, 1937), p. 4.

3. The actor's *toilette*: thinking through the line of the role, Opera-dramatic Studio.

in prayer and the Metropolitan blessed the enterprise.[77] Perhaps he maintained Russian Orthodox faith throughout his life, secretly, as many Russians did after the revolution, or perhaps his spiritual beliefs changed. Rayner describes how Stanislavsky's religious vocabulary indicates his belief in the transcendental power of art. She explains that for Stanislavsky 'the outside of the actor is mere appearance, the truth is within, in his soul'.[78] She comments on the religious tone of his language, in which art is the god and actors the priests; there is the true path (of *experiencing*) and the false path (of mechanical acting). As Carnicke writes, the phrase *Ia esm'* is in fact from church Slavonic, the language used in Russian Orthodox liturgy since the Middle Ages. She suggests that *Ia esm'* is a synonym for *experiencing*, for being fully present in the dramatic moment, but it also suggests Stanislavsky's interest in the spirituality of yoga.[79] Khersonsky attributes the formulation of the term to Sulerzhitsky:[80] 'The state of *Ia esm'* is "I exist, I live, I feel and I think identically with the role" '(*AWHE*, p. 266). Furthermore, Antarova's notes of Stanislavsky's lectures discuss how the exercises of the *system* enable the actor to 'renounce the self' in order to achieve the truth of passions in the given circumstances.[81] Whatever Stanislavsky's beliefs about spirituality and acting he saw the location of the spiritual in the *unconscious* and needed to develop mechanisms to enable the actor to convey spiritual truth, via unconscious mechanisms.

Yoga

Carnicke believes that Stanislavsky sought these mechanisms via yoga. She sees the *system* as a sort of fusion of Russian materialism and eastern mysticism, attributing to yoga Stanislavsky's understanding of the indivisibility of mind and body and of the *unconscious*, which, as she states, Stanislavsky divided into *superconscious* and *subconscious*.[82] There were indubitably a variety of influences from the East at various periods in the work of MAT. Tolstoy, always a great influence on Stanislavsky, corresponded with Gandhi in the early years of the twentieth century. Russian symbolism demonstrated an interest in the East and the MAT

---

[77] Vinogradskaia, *Letopis*, vol. 1, p. 263.
[78] Alice Rayner, 'Soul in the System: On Meaning and Mystique in Stanislavski and A. C. Bradley', *New Theatre Quarterly*, 1:4 (1985), p. 340.
[79] Carnicke, *Stanislavsky in Focus*, p. 175.
[80] Kh. Khersonskii, *Vakhtangov* (Moscow: Molodaia Gvardia, 1940), p. 68.
[81] K. S. Stanislavsky, *Stanislavsky on the Art of the Stage*, p. 115.
[82] Carnicke, *Stanislavsky in Focus*, p. 181.

produced plays by symbolist writers. Sulerzhitsky, Stanislavsky's assistant, was influenced by Tolstoy. He lived among the peasants, was a pacifist and had been imprisoned and exiled for refusing military service. Tolstoy asked him to help with relocating the Dukhobors (spirit wrestlers), who were a religious sect prominent in Russia from the eighteenth to nineteenth centuries. There is a theory that the Dukhobors originated from a Quaker who lived in Russia in about the middle of the eighteenth century. Like the Quakers, they rejected the priesthood and sacraments. They promoted equality, democracy and communal living. The tsars persecuted them for their refusal to be conscripted, and in 1898 to 1899 Tolstoy helped them to emigrate from the Caucasus to Canada. There is a possibility that the religion was influenced by eastern religious practice (aspects of Buddhism, for example), but they were against written traditions and so little is known about them. There is no corroboration for the idea that Sulerzhitsky brought yoga to the developing *system*, which he had learned from them.[83] Carnicke and Wegner claim that Stanislavsky was interested in yoga from 1906, the time of the Stockmann crisis, when Sulerzhitsky became his assistant, working on the *Drama of Life*. Nemirovich-Danchenko organised lectures on Hindu philosophy in 1913 when directing a play for the MAT by Rabindranath Tagore. Huntly Carter asserts that Vakhtangov was interested in Tibetan mysteries and yoga.[84]

Stanislavsky employed terms and concepts from yoga to some extent in his writings, despite Gurevich's fears of censorship. Many references were excised when the books were originally published in Russia.[85] Those that remain include the story in 'Stage Attention', (*AWHE*, Chapter 5), a Hindu maharaja's test of potential ministers. He challenged them each to walk around the city on top of the city wall, carrying a vessel full to the brim with milk, without spilling a drop despite attempts to distract and frighten them. In 'Freeing the Muscles', the next chapter, lying on the back for ten minutes is recommended and cited as a technique used by leaders of caravans in the desert. In the chapter on 'Communion' in *AWHE*, Stanislavsky discusses the idea of centres in the body, although not explicitly. Stanislavsky read Ramacharaka's *Hatha Yoga*, which discusses the solar plexus as 'an important part of the nervous system; in fact

---

[83] See Mel Gordon, *The Stanislavsky Technique: Russia* (New York: Applause Theatre Books, 1987), pp. 31–2.
[84] Huntly Carter, *The New Spirit in the Russian Theatre 1917–28*, (New York: Brentano, 1929), p. 10.
[85] Carnicke, *Stanislavsky in Focus*, pp. 144–5.

"a form of brain" and the "great central storehouse of prana"'.[86] He hopes
that western science will soon recognise its true importance. Stanislavsky
talks about *centres* when discussing *self-communion*:

As well as the centre of our nervous psychic life, the brain, there is another centre
near the heart where the solar plexus is. I tried to establish communication
between the two centres I have mentioned . . . the head centre seemed to me to be
the representative of consciousness and the nerve centre of the solar plexus the
representative of emotion. So, it felt to me that my mind communicated with my
feeling . . . subject and object (*AWHE*, pp. 323–4).

In March 1912 Stanislavsky wrote in his diary that he played well in the
sixth performance of Turgenev's *A Provincial Lady*, because of 'communion with the solar plexus'.[87]

  Gordon asserts that Sulerzhitsky introduced Stanislavsky to a morning
meditation on daily activities, where the Dukhobors would sit in a relaxed
position and visualise in detail how they would carry out each work task
in front of them. Such a meditation need not be related to yogic practice,
however. In *AWR*, Stanislavsky describes the actor visualising the tasks of
his role in this way (pp. 72–85). As regards yoga itself, Hatha yoga is
certainly listed in Stanislavsky's diary of 1919/20 among the kinds of
exercises being carried out in the Bolshoi Opera Studio, the MAT, and
the First and Second Studios, along with rhythmic exercises, freeing the
muscles, Duncan's dance and Swedish gymnastics, speech exercises, exercises on affective feelings and crowd scenes, (MAT, KS Archive 833, p. 19).
In the lectures to the Opera Studio noted by Antarova between 1918 and
1922 there is a comparison made by a Hindu sage of undisciplined man's
mind to the movements of a drunken monkey stung by a scorpion.[88] She
also noted the yogic idea of

creative repose, that is to say a state of mind in which all personal perceptions of
the passing moment have disappeared and in which, life – the whole of life – is
concentrated, clearly, forcefully and definitely, on the circumstances given in
your play and only on the given piece of the scene.[89]

Wegner quotes Antarova's notes, inserting what he believes to be the
equivalent yoga terms: 'To teach the student the art of self-observation,

---

[86] Yogi Ramacharaka, *Hatha Yoga, or the Yogi Philosophy of Physical Well-being* (London: L. N. Fowler, 1917), pp. 164–5.
[87] Vinogradskaia, *Letopis*, vol. 2, p. 332.
[88] Stanislavsky, *Stanislavsky on the Art of the Stage*, p. 164.
[89] *Ibid.* pp. 191–2.

the studio must teach him the laws of correct breathing [*pranayama?*], the correct position of the body [*asana?*], concentration and watchful discrimination [*dharana?*]'.[90] Antarova quotes Stanislavsky, adding, 'My whole system is based on this.'[91]

The question is whether yoga was as strong an influence on the development of the *system* as claimed, or whether it was one among many. In 1919 Stanislavsky wrote:

At the time when the so-called system was being brought to life, the fashion for the yogis appeared. Someone brought a book on the yogis to a rehearsal for me. It turns out that a thousand years ago they were seeking the same thing as us, only we extend into creativity and they into their half-detached world... on the boundary of our consciousness. (MAT, KS Archive 833, p. 20)

The MAT archive reveals only one book on yoga and another to which Stanislavsky made reference. In 1920 he made a summary of Yogi Olga Lobanova's book *Breathe Properly*,[92] and stated that the first lessons in breathing must become the foundation of the development of that introspective attention, on which all the work in the art of the stage must be built.[93] The only book extant in the MAT archive on yoga is Ramacharaka's *Hatha Yoga, or the Yogi Philosophy of Physical Well-being*, which was translated into Russian and published in 1909. It was written by American occultist author William Walter Atkinson, an influential figure in the New Thought movement. His publishers, the Yogi Publication Society, claimed that a series of books on yoga had been written collaboratively by Atkinson with Brahmin Baba Barata and attributed to Baba Barata's guru, Yogi Ramacharaka. There is no evidence that Baba Barata or Ramacharaka actually existed. *Hatha Yoga* includes a description of 'the Vital Force', a description of bodily systems and recommendations on healthy eating, relaxation, breathing, exercise, sleep and bathing, from the point of view of yogic principles of respect for the body and non-indulgence of its appetites. There are some pencil marks by Stanislavsky. He also marks in his copy of the book warnings against those who view yoga as a set of physical tricks, or see it as an oriental form of 'physical culture'.[94] It is possible that Stanislavsky was acquainted with the other aspects of yoga. The purpose of the practice of Hatha yoga is to

[90] William H. Wegner, 'The Creative Circle: Stanislavski and Yoga', *Educational Theatre Journal*, 28:1 (1976), pp. 86–7.
[91] Stanislavsky, *Stanislavsky on the Art of the Stage*, p. 116.
[92] Vinogradskaia, *Letopis*, vol. 3, p. 135.
[93] Stanislavsky, *Stanislavsky on the Art of the Stage*, p. 117.
[94] Ramacharaka, *Hatha Yoga*, pp. 11, 16.

attain mastery of the body to facilitate the meditative practice of Raja yoga. Karma yoga is the study of the actions and thoughts of humans; Bakthi yoga is the study of yoga by devotion and love; Gnani yoga is the study of wisdom and Raja yoga is the practice of these four aspects of yoga in a course of spiritual exercise. He seems to have been interested in Ramacharaka's interpretation of yogic philosophy and the breathing exercises, but there is no indication that the *asanas* (yoga postures) were practiced.

That ideas from yoga were part of the episteme is confirmed by Michael Chekhov, who describes an insight into the foundation of Hindu philosophy arising from the work he had done in his studio:

I succeeded in understanding that the keynote of yoga is the *creativity of life*. The creativity of life! This was the new keynote, which gradually imbued my soul. I began carefully to look back over my past and consider the present. Did not the process of founding and leading the Chekhov Studio have something in it of the *creativity of life*? Had the First Studio not been created by Konstantin Stanislavsky, Leopold Sulerzhitsky, and by us ourselves? But why had I hitherto understood by *creative work* only what was enacted on the stage?[95]

A very important concept that Stanislavsky took from yoga was that of *prana*. Carnicke states that '*prana* becomes the vehicle for infecting the spectator with the artist's emotion'.[96] *Prana* as defined by Ramacharaka is,

a universal principle, which principle is the essence of all motion, force or energy, whether manifested in gravitation, electricity, the revolution of the planets and all forms of life, from the highest to the lowest. It may be called the soul of Force and Energy in all their forms, and that principle which, operating in a certain way causes that form of activity, which accompanies Life. This great principle is in all forms of matter, and yet it is not matter...air... food...water...sunlight...it is the 'energy' in all these things – the things acting merely as a carrier.[97]

Prana rays are that which is emitted and received in spiritual or non-verbal *communion* – on Stanislavsky's diagram this is the internal region of the soul (**11h**). In the chapter on communion in *AWHE* Tortsov explains that we are always in communion with something: other people, ourselves, imaginary objects in our own thoughts. It is stressed, however, that even the most spiritual or internal types of *communion* are still active, or types of action.

---

[95] Michael Chekhov, *The Path of the Actor*, (eds) Andrei Kirillov and Bella Merlin (London: Routledge, 2005), p. 86
[96] Carnicke, *Stanislavsky in Focus*, p. 141.
[97] Ramacharaka, *Hatha Yoga*, p. 158.

Although the word *prana* is not used, the idea of *rays* also occurs in Ribot's *The Psychology of Attention*: 'Mental life consists in perpetual coming and going of inward events, in a marching by of sensations, feelings, ideas and images which associate with or repel each other according to certain laws. It is not a chain, a series but an irradiation in various directions.'[98] Stanislavsky's ideas of *sending rays out* (*lucheispuskanie*) and *receiving rays* (*luchevospriatie*), essential to his ideas of *communion*, have a basis in Ribot's idea of *irradiation*, as his editors confirm (*AWR*, 1st edn, p. 490, n27) and *prana* is another way of describing the phenomenon. *Sending rays out* and *receiving rays* is what conveys *experiencing*; it is what grips and *infects* an audience (*AWHE*, pp. 340–52).

Stanislavsky's notebook entry for 13 October 1919 for a lesson at the MAAT forms a brief unacknowledged synopsis of *Hatha Yoga*, in context, including a couple of the few references to *prana* that were not excised by the editors of the first edition of Stanislavsky's notebooks. I note the corresponding passages in *Hatha Yoga* in double brackets.

We shall begin with the art of experiencing . . . the elements of the creative sense of the self are a) freedom of the body (the muscles), b) concentration, c) activeness. I will begin with freeing the muscles.

A study of prana. a) Prana, the life energy is taken from the air ((This is the subject of *Hatha Yoga*, Chapter XX)), food ((Chapter X)), the sun ((Chapter XXVII)), water ((Chapter XII)), human rayings out. b) When a person dies, the prana goes into the ground with the worms, into micro-organisms ((Chapter XVIII)). c) I, I am (*Ia esm'*) is not prana. It is that which unites all pranas into one. d) How prana goes into the blood and the nerves through the teeth, chewing the food. How to breathe, how to take unboiled water, the sun's rays. How to chew and to breathe in order to absorb the prana (chew up the food so you can drink it rather than swallow it). ((Chapter X)) To breathe: six heartbeats – breathe in: three heart beats – hold the breath; six heartbeats, breathe out. Go up to fifteen heartbeats . . . ((*Hatha Yoga*, Chapter XXI)).

He also introduces the idea of *prana* into exercises in *freeing the muscles*:

Sitting exercises. a) Sit and identify the place which is tense. b) Free up to the point where you can freely turn with the neck and so on. c) Don't stiffen into immobility. Pay attention to the movement of the prana. d) The prana moves, flows like mercury, like a snake from the beginning of the hands to the fingertips, from the hips to the toes . . .

---

[98] Ribot, *The Psychology of Attention*, p. 3.

Other exercises are detailed, with this addition: 'The movement of prana creates, in my opinion, an internal rhythm' (*Iz zapisnich knizhek*, vol. 2, pp. 220–1). In *Hatha Yoga*, Chapter XXI, the importance of rhythmic breathing and the rhythm of the body is described. Stanislavsky believed his method to be the same as that of the yogis, 'first, removing what is harmful and then the ground on which it is possible to create the necessary mood will appear' (MAT, KS Archive 833, p. 20).

Discussing *prana*, Stanislavsky writes in *AWHI*, 'artists must *sense* their movements, will, emotions, thought so that the will makes them do some movements or others (prana) so that they are not meaningless movements'. Actors such as Tommaso Salvini, Eleanora Duse and Anna Judic are cited as able to transmit their will by movement in a thrilling and startling way (*AWHI*, pp. 423–4). In *AWR*, describing the 'artists' toilette', in an incomplete section (p. 448), he wrote the heading '*Plastique*' and put underneath it 'the feeling of movement (*prana*)'. *Prana* is therefore the quality, subject to the will, which distinguishes mechanical movements from *justified* ones. The *justification* of poses, a very important exercise in the *system* (*AWHE*, pp. 195–6), is one of *three moments* in any pose or position on stage. The actor first notes the superfluous tension which comes from adopting a new pose and the excitement of appearing in public; secondly, they let this tension go with the help of the *muscle controller* (also described as 'an inspector of prana') and, thirdly, the actor *justifies* the pose if necessary, for example, by thinking of *given circumstances*. Thus, I put my hand up, noting and letting go of any excess tension created and then find a *justification* for this pose, such as, if there was a peach above, what would I do to pick it? The *prana* transforms the movement from a mechanical action to a meaningful one. *Prana* is the mechanism for linking 'external movements . . . with the internal movements of emotion' (MAT, KS Archive 834, 1919, p. 37).

As the term *prana* became less ideologically acceptable, Stanislavsky began to replace it with 'energy'. His notebook from 1919 contains a series of lectures for the Opera Studio. In the first one, he states that 'it is to the liking of the Hindus to call 'energy' *prana* (*Notebook* 834, p. 37). However, Stanislavsky still used the term, especially in practical work, as recorded by Pavel Rumyantsev when working on a production of *Boris Godunov* at the Opera Studio in 1928.[99]

[99] P. I. Rumyantsev, *Stanislavski on Opera*, tr. Elizabeth Reynolds Hapgood (New York, Theatre Arts Books, 1975), p. 327.

Yoga and the subconscious

In *AWR* Stanislavsky describes the yogis' advice on the *subconscious*, as described in Ramacharaka's *Raja Yoga*.[100] Ramacharaka's concept also appears to draw on pre-Freudian ideas of the subconscious. He writes that yogis approach the unconscious through conscious, preparatory methods, from the bodily to the spiritual, the unreal from the real, from naturalism to the abstract. In order to access the *superconscious*, which Stanislavsky claims is a yogic concept, the yogis' advice is to take a bundle of thoughts and throw them into a subconscious sack. Then you go for a walk and when you come back you ask 'ready?' The answer might be no at first but eventually the subconscious will say 'ready' and return to you what was entrusted to it (*AWR*, p. 143).[101]

The authors of *Raja Yoga* cite William James as stating that 'effort of attention is the essential phenomenon of the will' and discuss voluntary and spontaneous attention in a way that is strongly reminiscent of Ribot.[102] In *Hatha Yoga*, again, the authors cite 'the axiom of psychology, "thought takes form in action"'.[103] Similar ideas relating to the *subconscious* seem to occur in both yoga and psychology.

Ramacharaka's plea for western science to recognise the importance of the solar plexus indicates that yoga and science were not so far apart. This indicates that the same ideas were being circulated in the body of knowledge of the epoch, in science, philosophy and art, rather than the *system* being a fusion of Russian materialism and eastern mysticism as Carnicke believes. When Stanislavsky came across similar ideas from different sources, he would have seen them as corroborating what he already thought to be true. Stanislavsky wrote in 1919, 'Everything I am to say is taken and proved by both psychology and physiology and proved and affirmed by the yogis' (MAT, KS Archive 833, p. 25). In the modernist period ideas from East and West crossed domains and were reshaped in both eastern and western traditions.

Theosophy, occultism and grasp

It is possible that other ideas from occult thought also in circulation found their way into Stanislavsky's thinking, despite the insistence by the Stalinist

---

[100] Yogi Ramacharaka, *Series of Lessons in Raja Yoga* (Illinois: Yogi Publication Society, 1906), pp. 223–46.
[101] See also, Stanislavsky, *Stanislavsky on the Art of the Stage*, pp. 207–8.
[102] Ramacharaka, *Raja Yoga*, pp. 92–4.
[103] Ramacharaka, *Hatha Yoga*, p. 178.

authorities that Stanislavsky's *system* was essentially materialistic and endorsed reflex theory. There were links between occultism, spiritualism and theosophy and the symbolist movement in pre-revolutionary Russia; the influence of Helena Blavatsky, the Russian proponent of theosophy, was considerable. Rudolf Steiner's Anthroposophical Society, to which Michael Chekhov belonged, was formed in 1913. In fact, Stanislavsky introduced Chekhov to Steiner when he was, as Chekhov says, inaccurately describing Steiner's speech system, although it was later that Chekhov's own interest in Steiner was sparked.[104] Stanislavsky was well acquainted with Prince Sergei Volkonsky, who taught at the MAT from 1911. As well as being an expert on Delsarte and Dalcroze, Volkonsky had made a study of Steiner's ideas and lectured on them outside Russia at Dartington, England, in 1935.[105] In 1912 Stanislavsky read Lapshin's *Mystic Knowledge and the Universal Feeling* (1905), and his 1911 essay, *The Universal Feeling* (*Collected Works*, vol. 8, pp. 525–6). He read and annotated *Concentration*, by the theosophist Ernest Wood, which was published in Russian in Petersburg by *Vestnik Teosofii* in 1917. Vinogradskaia writes that in 1917 Stanislavsky marked exercises in the book that he used in the *system*, relating to the *superconscious*, the *circle of attention* and *creative or stage attention*.[106] From this he drew some of his ideas about attention and objects, and the concept of *grasp* (*khvatka*). *Grasp* is necessary on stage,

in the eyes, the ears, in all the organs of the five senses. If you are listening, then you must listen and hear. If you smell something, then smell it. If you are watching something, then watch and see, don't glance across the object without catching on to it, but only running your vision over it. You need to catch on to the object, so to speak, with your teeth. Of course, this doesn't mean that you should strain (*AWHE*, p. 345).

Ernest Wood refers to his exercises in *grasp* also as an 'expansion of concentration'. They are exercises in giving one's whole to an object, taking in all its details.[107]

The unconscious, superconscious *and* subconscious

In Stanislavsky's Russian these terms are *bessoznanie, sverkhsoznanie,* and *podsoznanie*. Eastern philosophies may have made some contribution to

[104] Chekhov, *The Path of the Actor*, p. 133.
[105] Deirdre Hurst du Prey, 'Chekhov in England and America', in Laurence Senelick (ed.), *Wandering Stars: Russian Emigré Theatre, 1905–1940* (University of Iowa Press, 1992), p. 162.
[106] Vinogradskaia, *Letopis*, vol. 2, p. 550.
[107] Ernest Wood, *Concentration: A Practical Course with a Supplement on Meditation* (India: The Theosophical Publishing House, 1979), pp. 87–9.

Stanislavsky's ideas of the spiritual mechanisms of acting but there were other sources. For example, he was interested in the idea of hypnosis as a way of accessing the unconscious and appears to have gone for hypnosis himself, or at least considered it.[108] L. L. Whyte writes:

The idea of unconscious mental processes was in many aspects conceivable in 1700, copied around 1800 and became effective around 1900 . . . flowering among romantic, idealistic writers in nineteenth century Germany. But it was through hypnosis that the influence of unconscious factors in behaviour became clearly demonstrated and the idea of the unconscious mind ceased to be merely a philosophical abstraction.[109]

Stanislavsky refers to the *unconscious, the superconscious* and *the subconscious*. Carnicke's suggestion is that Stanislavsky saw the *unconscious* as divided into *superconscious* and *subconscious*, after yoga. This division is found in the nineteenth-century philosophy of Edouard von Hartmann. However, Stanislavsky also referred to late-nineteenth and early-twentieth century psychologists.

In discussing *analysis* in the *period of getting to know the role* in *AWR*, Stanislavsky writes that getting to know by feeling (*chuvstvennoe poznavanie*, Lapshin's phrase) is most important in the creative process because 'only with its help is it possible to penetrate into the region of the unconscious, which, as is known, comprises nine-tenths of the whole life of a person, or the role, and besides that, the most important part' (*AWR*, p. 54). Later, in *AWR* in a section entitled *The Superconscious*, Stanislavsky writes in one of the few actual citations, that Professor Helmar Gates, the American professor of experimental psychology (1859–1923) claims, 'at least 90 per cent of our mental life is subconscious,' and Henry Maudsley (psychologist and psychiatrist 1835–1918, author of *Philosophy of the Mind* and *Pathology of the Soul*) asserts that 'consciousness does not have even the tenth part of the functions which are usually ascribed to it' (p. 140). These statistics are of doubtful accuracy but they serve to indicate the importance of the unconscious for Stanislavsky.

How Stanislavsky envisaged consciousness in general is hard to say. He marked in Bezpiatov's pamphlet, 'everything leads to the interaction between the internal world ('I', consciousness, self-consciousness, the consciousness of my 'I' and the external 'not-I'). According to James and Spencer consciousness is identified with the life of movement and is interpreted as the sensation of life in all its daily changes.'[110] This could

---

[108] Benedetti, *Stanislavski: His Life and Art*, p. 228.
[109] L. L. Whyte, *The Unconscious Before Freud* (London: Tavistock Publications, 1967), p. 63.
[110] Bezpiatov, *Elementi*, p. 12.

be compared with Stanislavsky's idea of the *feeling of movement*, which he equates with *prana*, describing the difference between mechanical or subconscious movements and ones which are consciously executed, or *justified*.

Stanislavsky begins to discuss the *superconscious* in relation to symbolism and impressionism in *My Life in Art*. This period, at the beginning of the twentieth century, was when Stanislavsky was pre-occupied with the creation of *mood* in Chekhov's plays, before his encounters with yoga. He writes that this was an expression of the *superconscious* and helped the group of actors with the problem of being on stage:

The superconscious begins where the ultra natural ends. But only when the spiritual and physical life of the artist on stage develops genuinely, naturally, normally, according to the laws of nature itself, does the superconscious come out of its hiding place. The least force over nature and the superconscious hides in the depths of the soul, saving itself from the coarse anarchy of the muscles (*MLIA*, p. 287).

Von Hartmann

Crohn Schmitt states that the term *unconscious* has different psychological connotations to *subconscious* but that they were both the same for Stanislavsky. She equates his concept with that of von Hartmann who predicated the existence of the unconscious in 1860.[111] Edouard von Hartmann (1842–1906) was a German philosopher in some ways inspired by Darwinism, but whose main thesis was the attempt to reconcile Schopenhauer with Hegel, Schelling and Leibniz. 'Will' and 'idea' are interrelated and are an expression of an absolute – the unconscious.[112] The unconscious is the fundamental active principle in the universe, the creative force upon which depends the meaning of all creation. Instinct is action that embodies a purpose, although without knowledge of that purpose. It is a mysterious hidden power and the unconscious of the individual has contact with the powers of nature. Memory serves as a storehouse of the unconscious. Von Hartmann defended vitalism, called himself a transcendentalist and attacked mechanistic materialism. The book outlining these ideas, *Philosophy of the Unconscious*, was published in

---

[111] Crohn Schmitt, 'Stanislavski, Creativity', p. 346.
[112] Robert Audi, *The Cambridge Dictionary of Philosophy* (Cambridge University Press, 1999), p. 363.

1869 and was enormously influential in Russia over the next decades. According to Ellenberger,

Von Hartmann described three layers of the unconscious: (1) the absolute unconscious which constitutes the substance of the universe and is the source of the other forms of the unconscious; (2) the physiological unconscious, which, like Carus' unconscious, is at work in the origin, development and evolution of living beings, including man; (3) the relative or psychological unconscious, which lies at the source of our conscious mental life.[113]

Here is the source of Stanislavsky's tri-partite idea, although perhaps it is indirect. Carnicke writes that Stanislavsky took the term *superconscious* from yoga,[114] but the same idea exists in von Hartmann and clearly the writers of Ramacharaka's books mixed yogic traditions with more contemporary ideas. Stanislavsky's *superconscious* equates to von Hartmann's absolute unconscious; Stanislavsky's *unconscious* to von Hartmann's physiological unconscious; and Stanislavsky's *subconscious* to von Hartmann's psychological unconscious. The situation has been obscured, of course, because von Hartmann's ideas of the unconscious were no more acceptable than those of yoga to the editors of the first edition of Stanislavsky's *Collected Works*. They state that the *superconscious* was a term Stanislavsky took from bourgeois idealistic psychology, and that he later used the term *subconscious* which was more in keeping with contemporary scientific terminology (*MLIA*, p. 479, note).

It is Stanislavsky's aim to access the creative *subconscious* through the *system*:

It is necessary to create with inspiration, but only the subconscious knows how to do this and we are not in control of it ... the way out is not by the direct, but oblique influence of consciousness on the subconscious. The fact is that there are certain aspects of the human soul, which are subject to consciousness and the will. These aspects are capable of influencing our involuntary psychic processes ... this demands complicated creative work which takes place under the control and direct influence of consciousness only in part. To a significant extent this work is subconscious and involuntary. It is our genius ... organic nature, which is able to accomplish this, with psycho-technique (*AWHE*, pp. 60–1).

Crohn-Schmitt holds that the central difference between Freud and Stanislavsky in the understanding of the subconscious is that for Freud the subconscious was irrational, whereas for Stanislavsky it was logical,

---

[113] Carl Gustav Carus (1789–1869) wrote *Psyche*, the first attempt to give a complete and objective theory on unconscious psychological life. Henri F. Ellenberger, *The Discovery of the Unconscious* (New York: Basic Books, 1970), p. 210.

[114] Carnicke, *Stanislavsky in Focus*, p. 180.

closer to the faculties of will and feeling than to the faculty of mind. The subconscious for Stanislavsky is a mystery, but not irrational. One of the elements of the internal region of the soul is logic and consistency (**11j** on Stanislavsky's diagram). She attributes this view to 'nineteenth century faculty psychology'.[115] This was the theory, associated with phrenology, in vogue in the second half of the eighteenth and the first half of the nineteenth centuries, that the mind is divided into separate inherent powers of 'faculties' such as 'memory', 'intelligence', 'perception', 'will'.

Like Von Hartmann, Stanislavsky sees memory as a storehouse of the unconscious, and like Sechenov sees memory as receiving traces or impressions of stimuli from the outside world, which we receive through the sense organs in our nervous system.[116] For example, Stanislavsky describes impressions of the performances of Italian opera that he heard as a child, receiving them 'organically, unconsciously, not just spiritually but physically' (*MLIA*, p. 70).

One of the items in Stanislavsky's personal library is an excerpt from an article by Sukhanov entitled 'The Subconscious and its Pathology', which was published in 1915. V. G. Gaidarov, a MAT actor from 1915 to 1920 copied out the excerpt. Sukhanov's article discusses the relationship between the conscious 'I' and the subconscious in the context of information that can be gained from the study of pathological states such as hysteria:

If you eliminate from the consciousness as far as possible at a given moment all willed-voluntary effort and observe what floats into the field of consciousness, then it could turn out that in the midst of the apparent chaos of thoughts and ideas, which are as if unguided and arising one after another without order, there is an influence which is recognisable and, besides, goes in a different direction; it comes in these conditions from the subconscious, with its colossal store of nervous energy, but organised and somehow united. The first things to float into the field of consciousness, when voluntary efforts are eliminated are those thoughts and ideas which are combined with the brightest desires and ideas, now unfulfilled, now consciously suppressed under the influence of education, culture and the voice of moral feeling. Besides this, the content of these thoughts and ideas that float into the field of consciousness, when voluntary efforts are eliminated, will be infinitely varied in different situations; it will not be identical in one and the same individual at different moments of his conscious life, when his personality is considered more or less formed.[117]

---

[115] Crohn Schmitt, 'Stanislavski, Creativity', p. 346.
[116] Sechenov, *Reflexes of the Brain*, pp. 67–8.
[117] S. Sukhanov, 'The Subconscious and its Pathology', *Voprosi filosofii i psikhologii*, 26: 128 (1915), pp. 368–9.

The same idea as that of the 'subconscious sack' encountered by Stanislavsky in *Hatha Yoga* occurs here. The 'bundles of thought' or the 'floating thoughts and ideas', as far as the artist is concerned, consist of knowledge, information, experience and memories – material which is, according to Stanislavsky, preserved in the 'intellectual, affective, visual, aural, muscle memory.' This store must be constantly replenished by the artist.

Stanislavsky recommends thinking of the basic tasks when acting which show what he calls the creative path of the landmarks (the 'what'). The rest (the 'how') comes of itself, unconsciously. In not thinking of 'how', but directing all our attention onto 'what', we divert our consciousness from that region of the role that demands the participation of the unconscious in creativity (*AWR*, p. 263). Ribot discusses this in *Diseases of the Memory*. He writes that unconscious activity is not mysterious, citing 'spontaneous acts of memory which appear to be incited by no association, and which are experienced daily by everyone'. Stanislavsky has underlined Ribot's example of 'problems long pondered over, whose solution suddenly flashes on the consciousness'. Ribot argues that questions of the unconscious are vague and contradictory if it is considered a fundamental property of the mind and rather it should be considered a phenomenon with its own conditions of existence.[118]

Stanislavsky's ideas of the subconscious are rooted in the philosophy of the mid-nineteenth century, with an admixture of ideas from Sechenov and Ribot and confirmed by his readings on yoga. His practical experience led him to believe that problems can be solved if the actor stops trying to think about them consciously and allows answers to emerge. Examples of this are when characterisations such as that of Stockmann emerge, or when Kostia initially gets his ideas for the character he calls 'the critic' from a coat and then develops it when ideas flow as a result of accidentally smudging his make-up (*AWHI*, Chapter 8). This process is described in different ways by various people, such as Sukhanov, Ribot and Ramacharaka. Stanislavsky does not offer a definition of the subconscious or a theory of its mechanisms, seeing it essentially as a mystery, governed by nature, but accessible through the artist's conscious psycho-technique.

PSYCHIC MOTIVATORS: *MIND, WILL* AND *FEELING*

In the artist's use of conscious psycho-technique in order to access the *unconscious*, there is a role to be played by the three *motivators of psychic*

---

[118] Théodule Ribot, *Diseases of the Memory* (London: Kegan Paul, Trench, 1882), pp. 36–7.

life, which Stanislavsky refers to at **6**, **7** and **8** on the spine of the diagram of *experiencing* as mind, will and feeling – 'our current scientific definition' or 'representation, judgement and will-feeling – the former scientific definition' – as he writes, without naming his sources. Bezpiatov also discusses mind, will and feeling as functions of the psyche.[119] Stanislavsky, according to the diagram, sees them somewhere between the 'internal elements of the soul', linking with the perspective of the role, and the external incarnation of the role.

Stanislavsky's concept of these *motivators*, according to Crohn Schmitt, originates from the 'faculties' of nineteenth-century psychology and it is hard to square their appearance on the 1935 diagram with Soviet commentators' insistence that Stanislavsky had embraced the science of Sechenov and Pavlov. In nineteenth-century psychology, feeling, mind and will have a hierarchical order, as they do for Stanislavsky. Sullivan, in a discussion entitled 'Stanislavski and Freud' notes that Stanislavsky, unlike Freud, used the term *subconscious*, in the French psychiatric tradition, where it was based on an analogy with the organisation of the central nervous system, where 'the higher mental processes are presumed to be located in the cerebrum and the emotions located in the brain stem. The location of the emotional source of behavior is topographically below the 'higher' centres, is more basic in evolutionary terms.'[120] Stanislavsky often suggests that feeling is more accurate than the mind or intellect and often denigrates the mind. For example, he distinguished between knowing something intellectually and really knowing and feeling it (*MLIA*, p. 373). He goes so far as to say that for the creative artist *to know means to be able to feel.*[121] Ribot, too, writes in *The Psychology of Attention* that

True causes of emotional life must be sought lower down in organic, vegetative activity – heart, digestion, respiratory, sexual organs are the subject matter of sensibility, whereas everything that comes from the external senses constitutes the primal matter of intelligence and just as physiologically, vegetative life precedes animal life which rests upon it, so also psychologically, emotional life precedes intellectual life which rests upon it.[122]

[119] Bezpiatov, *Elementi*, pp. 12–14.
[120] John J. Sullivan, 'Stanislavski and Freud', in Erika Munk (ed.), *Stanislavski and America* (New York: Hill and Wang, 1966), pp. 103–4.
[121] Stanislavsky, *Stanislavsky On the Art of the Stage*, p. 121.
[122] Ribot, *The Psychology of Attention*, p. 106.

Again, in *Diseases of Memory*, Ribot states:

Emotional faculties are effaced much more slowly than intellectual. Feelings are the most profound, common and tenacious of all phases of mental activity. While knowledge is acquired and objective, feelings are innate . . . the immediate and permanent expression of organic life. Viscera, muscles, bones all contribute to their formation. Feelings form the self; amnesia of the feelings is the destruction of the self.[123]

In this connection we may note Stanislavsky's frequent use of the word 'organic' to describe *feeling*. The Russian word 'feeling', as in English, includes emotion, but can also refer to sensory experience and intuition. Here is further validation for Stanislavsky of the Tolstoyan precept that the subject of art is *feeling*, in that it expresses the self, is shared in *communion*, and the actor's self-expression must involve real, organic *experiencing*. Further, Bezpiatov distinguishes the second function of our psyche *feeling* or sensibility (*chuvstvovanie*), from those affective states (in Ribot's terminology) that are generally called feelings or emotions and this seems also to be Stanislavsky's concept.

Moreover, there is *logic* and *consistency of feeling*. Stanislavsky drew this idea from Ribot's *La Logique des Sentiments* and stated in 1912 that L. M. Lopatin, professor of philosophy at Moscow University, also accepted the term 'the logic of feelings' (*Collected Works*, vol. 8, p. 301). Ribot asserts that there is a logic of feeling, as there is of reason, and that judgement under the influence of passion can be superior to that of reason.[124] Faddeev's assertion of 'logical feeling' may also be drawn from Ribot. Hence, *feeling* although it is capricious, is the most important in the hierarchy.

The second is the mind, which begins and directs creativity (on the basis of imagination, *if* and *the given circumstances*, **11a** on the diagram). Stanislavsky's editors explain that his note on the diagram indicates that he saw the mind as having two operations: representation and judgement (*AWHE*, 1st edn, p. 417, n50). The first describes the emergence of a more or less generalised image-representation of a subject. This is particularly characteristic of artistic thought and involves what is called the imagination. The second operation, judgement, leads to the establishment of a definite relationship towards the subject of thought.

The third motivator is the will (*volia*) which is the capacity to will, want or desire (*khotenie*) (*AWHE*, pp. 371–9). Carnicke explains Stanislavsky's view of the actor's will in relation to a task. Willing or wanting

---

[123] Ribot, *Diseases of the Memory*, pp. 120–1.
[124] Théodule Ribot, *La Logique des Sentiments* (Paris: Felix Alcan, 1905), pp. viii–ix.

to fulfil a *task* results in the actor's taking *action*. Stanislavsky's note-book from 1905 to 1908 (MAT, KS Archive 762) makes several references to Ribot (excised from the published notebooks *Iz Zapisnich Knizhek*, p. 297), in a plan for a description of the nature of the *will*. Stanislavsky's marginalia on Ribot's *Diseases of the Will* includes the comment, 'a weak desire (*khotenie*) does not produce action, which should be the desire of the actor'.

Stanislavsky's view of the will (and willing or desiring), like mind and feeling, is that of Ribot. Ribot writes in *The Diseases of the Will* that in every voluntary act there are two elements: the state of consciousness, 'I will', and a complex psycho-physiological mechanism that has the power to act or restrain. Desire is a stage between the two, between voluntary conditions and reflexes.[125] Therefore, desire must be stimulated in the healthy person: diseases of the will result in people being inactive. Sta-nislavsky writes, 'The will is the nervous sensitivity and the spiritual and physical excitability for the stimulation of nervous desires (*khotenii*); motor, visual, aural' (*Iz Zapisnich Knizhek*, vol. 1, 762, p. 210). The way for actors to stimulate the will is to 'put yourselves in the position of the character and ask the questions: what would I do in this position, what do I now want, where will I go? Attract your will. Answer with verbs expressing actions and not nouns expressing concepts and ideas,'[126] that is, the *magic if*. Stanislavsky says that the actor's will is not the same thing as their will as a person, and can in fact be trained (*MLIA*, p. 429).

Furthermore, he writes that each of the three motivators draws the others into action; in fact, they are inseparable especially *will* and *feeling*. Military similes are used to describe the three marching into action together (*AWHE*, pp. 371–4). Either the *mind* or *emotion* can initiate the creative process (*AWHE*, p. 380). There is also a discussion in *AWHI* of how some actors are led by the intellect and others by feeling (p. 318). Neither is more or less valid than the other, as long as the actor is aware of this.

The diagram of *experiencing* shows how the new role (**9** on the dia-gram) and the play permeate the *motivators of psychic life*, evoking creative aspiration (*stremlenie*): Whatever the initiator has been, a line of aspir-ation is created, keeping the attention of the actor on the role unbroken (*AWHE*, p. 393). Stanislavsky states, 'at every moment of his life a person

---

[125] Théodule Ribot, *The Diseases of the Will*, tr. Merwin-Marie Snell, 8th edn (Chicago and London: Open Court, 1896), p. 2.
[126] Vinogradskaia, *Letopis*, vol. 2, p. 498.

wants something, is striving (*stremitsia*) for something, to overcome something... if the aim is significant he will not be able to complete what he has begun in his whole life' (*AWHE*, p. 213). This concept of *aspiration* is found in Ribot and James who said that 'An emotion is a tendency to feel.'[127] The word 'tendency' was translated into Russian as *stremlenie*.

The important thing is that *aspirations*, whether a result of *mind*, *will* or *feeling* enable the actor to have *a through line of action* in the role (**14** on the diagram). These lines of *aspiration* are initially disordered (**10**) but they penetrate through the region of the internal elements of the soul, as the actors' aspirations are deepened by work. For example, on the bits and tasks of the role and so on, they become entwined in a bundle (**13**), which is the spiritual state called the 'internal sense of the self on stage'. At **14** they are interwoven with each other like a plait, striving towards the supertask. Now, after their regeneration and converging with the role, we call them 'the lines of through action' proceeding towards the as yet ghostly, not fully defined *supertask* (**15**).

In *Actors and Onlookers*, Crohn Schmitt quotes Stanislavsky's description of action involving one running into the strivings of other people or conflicting events or obstacles.[128] She concludes from this that in Stanislavsky's view the human environment and human identity do not interact, and certainly they are not interpenetrating; instead the self is largely autonomous, identifying the same entity from beginning to end.

Stanislavsky's view of action can involve a conflict of wills, a well-known description of drama.[129] In one of his later rehearsal periods Stanislavsky chose to focus on the action of the play as the clashing of wills of the characters, as Irina and Igor Levin describe in *The Stanislavski Secret*.[130] Stanislavsky's aim was for the actor to engage with the environment as he saw it, in life. For Sechenov the human being responds to the environment simply in a series of mechanical reflexes. Stanislavsky's problem lies in determining how the actor engages as in life with the stage environment; what, in performance, evokes his mind, will, feeling, *aspirations* and what, in fact, these are and how he keeps his attention on

---

[127] William James, *Textbook of Psychology* (London: Macmillan, 1892), p. 373.
[128] Natalie Crohn Schmitt, *Actors and Onlookers* (Illinois: Northwestern University Press, 1990), p. 97.
[129] See, for example, Ferdinand Brunetière, *The Law of the Drama*, tr. Philip Hayden (New York: Dramatic Museum of Columbia University, 1914), p. 13.
[130] Irina Levin and Igor Levin, *The Stanislavski Secret* (Colorado: Meriwether Publishing, 2002), pp. 13–15.

the *through line* of the role. Crohn Schmitt rightly asserts that Stanislavsky espouses nineteenth-century concepts here.

ELEMENTS OF THE INTERNAL REGION OF THE SOUL

The elements of the internal region of the soul 'live with the motivators of psychic life'. Some have been mentioned already.[131] One of the most important is attention and its *objects* (**11c** on the diagram) where, once again, what Stanislavsky says coincides with what Ribot has to say. As part of the actor's *toilette*, the students do many exercises on observation, *circles* and *objects* of attention and are told about the capacity for *multi-layered attention*, which enables them to develop the actor's *sense of him/herself on stage*.

Attention is divided into intellectual attention and attention of the senses (*chuvstvennoe*), the latter being Lapshin's term (*AWHE*, p. 174). Attention is always linked with the work of mind, will or feeling. The first problem of attention is that stiffening the muscles reduces the capacity to pay attention. Stanislavsky annotated and made notes from what Ribot has to say on this topic in *The Psychology of Attention*. Ribot quotes Maudsley: 'The person who is unable to control his own muscles is incapable of attention.'[132] There were other influential ideas, such as the assertion that excessive muscular tension can be controlled by habit. Stanislavsky gives as an example that people lifting a piano are unable to recite a multiplication table. He says you cannot reflect while running. While exerting effort, it is impossible to give attention to anything else (*AWHE*, pp. 185–6).

Stanislavsky's exercises on freeing the muscles are described in *AWHE* (see figure 4). The students do isolation exercises, thinking of a part of the body and freeing the muscles. This is essential because

you cannot imagine what an evil for the creative process muscular spasms and bodily contractions are. When they happen in the vocal organ, people born with a good sound begin to be hoarse or even lose their voice. When the contractions become fixed in the legs the actor walks like a paralytic; when it is in the hands the hands stiffen and turn to sticks and move like a road barrier . . . but worst of

---

[131] *Stage charm* and *ethics*, two of the elements of the *internal region of the soul* are outside the scope of this discussion. This is not to say that they are not important. For an interesting discussion of the ethics of Stanislavsky's system, see Klaus Lazarowicz, Spontaneität oder "Training und Drill" in Günter Ahrends (ed.), *Konstantin Stanislawski, Neue Aspekte und Perspektiven*, (Tübingen: Forum Modernes Theater, 1992), pp. 39–50.

[132] Ribot, *The Psychology of Attention*, p. 1.

4. Exercises in the Opera-dramatic Studio on 'freeing the muscles'.

all when the contraction is fixed in the face and distorts it, it paralyses or makes the facial expression turn to stone... The contraction can appear in the diaphragm and in other muscles which participate in breathing, destroy the rightness of the process and cause shortness of breath (p. 185).

The actor must develop a *controller*, the role of which is to check for, and get rid of, superfluous tension (*AWHI*, p. 189). There are exercises in letting the tension go from parts of the body. These could be compared with Delsarte's decomposing exercises, as described by Genevieve Stebbins in *Delsarte System of Expression* (pp. 83–6), which she describes as 'withdrawing the will-power'. There are also the *exercises* in 'three moments'. Stanislavsky may well have been confident of what he says about the controller, because Ribot describes the plurality of states of consciousness[133] affirming Stanislavsky's statement that we have the capacity of multi-layered attention (*AWHE*, p. 175), which resolves, for him, Diderot's paradox of dual consciousness. The actor can pay attention to several *objects* at once: the role, the stage partner, psycho-technique including the *controller*, the prompter and even to an extent the audience. Here is Stanislavsky's reply to Diderot's paradox: the actors can *experience* and observe themselves at the same time.

The second problem is keeping the *attention* from drifting. Ribot, after James, discussed *spontaneous* and *voluntary attention*, the *object of attention* and *adaptations*. There are things that engage our interest spontaneously, especially as children. When older, we must learn how to give our attention to subjects such as study, which may not engage our interest spontaneously. The problem for actors is that they must learn to sustain their interest in a role, often for long periods of time, which may not happen spontaneously. Ribot writes that 'attention adapts itself to what is without, reflection to what is within'.[134] Therefore, Stanislavsky developed exercises for the actors to focus on *objects* outside themselves. In the chapter on *attention* in *AWHE*, Tortsov uses lamps to illustrate points and circles of attention. The students have to practise sustaining their attention on close objects, such as the stage partner, or ones in the wider circle, such as the whole stage.

Stanislavsky also used the concept of *adaptation*, with which Chekhov and Vakhtangov experimented:

We shall use this word adaptation (*prisposoblenie*) in future to name the inner and outer devices by means of which people accommodate themselves to each

---

[133] *Ibid.* p. 4.
[134] *Ibid.* p. 15.

other in communion and by means of which they help to influence an object (*AWHE*, p. 354).

Examples of *adaptations* are given in Chapter 9, such as closing the door for different reasons – to keep out a draft, or to keep out a murderer. The topic is elaborated upon (in MAT, KS Archive 1293, 'Beseda o Gamlete', 1911, p. 6):

> If an actor defines an adaptation, a stencil results.
> If an actor defines a task, experiencing results.
> I come on stage to fulfil some task.

It is necessary to assign desire not from reason but from the soul.

It is necessary to learn how to be alone in public. Only here can you feel the truth. When a large monologue is performed with desire only, it becomes singsong. Here it is necessary to call adaptation to our aid.

'To be or not to be' is one desire. Here is self-communion. In self-communion there are almost adaptations alone.

In poetic turns of speech it is necessary to find a living adaptation, in order to grasp them quicker and make one's task easier.

If you have got used to standing up in a particular place, this will remain with you – (you don't erase anything from the memory).

The idea of adaptation comes again from Ribot who writes in *The Psychology of Attention*:

Attention has an object . . . to distinguish it from similar states like fixed ideas, we must take account of the adaptation that accompanies it, which to a large extent constitutes its character . . . physical and external adaptation is a sign of psychic and inward adaptation, spontaneous or artificial.[135]

He goes on to say that attention depends on emotional states, and that emotional states are reducible to tendencies, that is, *aspirations* (*stremlenia*). These tendencies are fundamentally movements (or arrested movements) and may be conscious or unconscious. Attention, both spontaneous and voluntary, is from its origin bound in motor conditions. He writes that Maudsley and Lewes say it is a series of reflexes, and essentially, motion (*PA*, p. 14).

Attention, according to Ribot, is intellectual, although it is not a pure act of spirit (*PA*, p. 5). If it also depends on emotional states or feelings, which are reducible to *aspirations*, and can be either willed or spontaneous, it is easy to see why Stanislavsky saw the mind, will and feeling as inseparable. Attention, like emotion, is reducible to motion. The question is whether this theory was useful to Stanislavsky's development of the *system* or whether it overloaded it with complicated concepts.

---

[135] *Ibid.* pp. 5–6.

The internal sense of the self on stage (13 on diagram)

The *general sense* (literally feeling) *of the self on stage* is divided into internal and external. This may well be a borrowing from James who discusses 'self-feeling', our idea of who we are, which can be changed.[136] Carnicke defines it as 'the state of mind and body necessary to create a performance'.[137] The internal sense of the self is achieved by means of the training in inner, psycho-technique. It is the state on stage when the actor experiences *public solitude* (*AWHE*, p. 159), a state of muscular relaxation in spite of the presence of the audience:

The stronger the actor's circle of public solitude and the more intent his attention and thoughts on discovering the beautiful in himself and those around him, the greater his charm, the stronger the vibrations of his creative work and the more powerful his influence on the auditorium.[138]

It can be equated with *Ia esm'*:

This formula signifies such a stage sense of the self of the actor that in the actor, or more accurately, in the creative act is expressed both the everyday character of the hero and the character of the artist himself.[139]

The *external sense of the self on stage* is gained by training in the processes of *incarnation*.

SUPERTASK

Nikolai Gogol (1809–1852) wrote in 1846 in his 'Notes on how to act *The Inspector General*', that the actor should

observe the main, chief concern of each character, on which his life is supported, which is the constant subject of his thoughts, the eternal nail sitting in his head. Having grasped this main concern of the character, the actor must perform such that the thoughts and aspirations of the character have been assimilated by him and remain in his head continuously during the performance of the play.[140]

Stanislavsky took from this the term 'nail', which occurs frequently in his writings and becomes transformed into the *supertask* of the character. Again it emphasises that the actor must seek truth, performing as if the thoughts and aspirations of the character were his own. In *MLIA*

---

[136] James, *Principles*, vol. 1, p. 310.
[137] Carnicke, *Stanislavsky in Focus*, p. 179.
[138] Stanislavsky, *Stanislavsky on the Art of the Stage*, p. 123.
[139] Khersonskii, *Vakhtangov*, p. 68.
[140] Nikolai Gogol, *Polnoe Sobranie Sochinenii*, vol. 4 (Leningrad: AN SSR, 1951), pp. 112–13.

Stanislavsky gives examples of the *supertask*, which is also the *kernel* or main idea of the play, or character, from Gogol. It is the main aim of the writer, the expression of the writer's thoughts and feelings, to which are linked all the *tasks, motivators of psychic life*, and elements of the *sense of the self* of the artist. For example, Tolstoy struggled all his life for self-perfection and Chekhov against triviality and these are the *supertasks* of their work. The search for God is the *supertask* of Dostoevsky's *Brother's Karamazov* (*AWHE*, p. 412). The director can interpret the *supertask* of the play and the actors the *supertasks* of individual characters, and define the *through action* or unified line of the character's action in accordance with the *supertask*. The *supertask* of the play exercises a pull on the *unconscious*, or the *logic of feelings* of the character. The *supertask* is an example of the amalgamation of Stanislavsky's ideas from the nineteenth century with those of Ribot and then Pavlov.

Remez writes that at different stages of the system Stanislavsky answered the question of how to enter the *logic of passions* of the character in different ways, starting with *desire*, as defined by Sechenov, from which the *supertask* emerged. This provoked the *desire* or need of the character but, he argues, resulted in a circularity of *desire* and *supertask*. The *method of physical actions* is meant to resolve this:

I. M. Sechenov wrote in *Reflexes of the Brain*, 'If there is an almost passionless psychic reflex in the consciousness, in the form of a thought then I shall name "desire" (*khotenie*) the side of it which is passionate and aspiring (*stremitsia*) towards an end, that is the satisfaction of the passion. "I want to do something or other." ... Desire is the aspirational side of some thought or other.'

'I want' was a device of the system for a long time, and the task and the bit, were the components that defined it. Desire was the conductor of feeling. On the soil of the new methodology arose the supertask – the sign of the dominant role, leading the need of the stage hero, the means of transformation into the living need of the performer.

But this was not enough. Bits and tasks subdivide the centripetal power of the movement of the role. Another link was needed even more accessible to the consciousness and sensibility of the actor.

'Living need gives birth to desire' Sechenov established, and 'these draw actions behind them'.

Shouldn't they be the beginning, in fact? Shouldn't the task be interpreted with the help of the chain of acts and the supertask fulfilled with through action? It seems that in this discovery there is no discovery.[141]

---

[141] O. Remez, 'Istoki Teorii Stanislavskogo', *Voprosi Teatra, Sbornik Statei i Publikatsii* (Moscow: Soiuz Teatral'nykh deiatelei, 1990), p. 92.

Remez writes that action then came into the system, at first divided into internal and external action, but in the thirties Stanislavsky followed Pavlov in establishing the *method of physical actions*, in which the psychological and physiological merged, resolving the problem of the 'discovery in which there is no discovery'. He also states that 'the supertask fulfilled with through action and the task with the chain of acts is surely the best translation of Aristotle's rules of 'unity of action' in the language of stage art'.[142]

Vladimir Mikhailovich Volkenstein, who worked as a dramaturg from 1911 to 1921 at the MAT, wrote an article entitled 'Drama as a Reflection of the Reflex of Purpose', published in 1936. In it he abjures metaphysics and psychology, which treat the soul and spiritual experience as something self-sufficient, cut off from the external world, and hails Pavlov's work on conditional reflexes as the way forward, although it was still at an early stage of development. In later life Pavlov worked to define the reflex of purpose, which he believed to exist in humans and animals – an innate reflex to seek a goal. Volkenstein claims that Stanislavsky's *supertask* of the role or the play is a prime example of the reflex of purpose, without which a play lacks life and meaning.[143] The idea of the *supertask* is an example of how ideas spread and transform. Stanislavsky adopted Gogol's simple idea, and began to describe the *supertask* in Ribot's terms of the *logic of feelings* and his idea of the *unconscious*. It was then linked with the work of Sechenov and Pavlov so the *supertask* is the stimulus that will set into action all the reflex mechanisms enabling the actor to develop the role purposefully. These scientific accretions may serve only to complicate an essentially simple concept.

In summary, in studying historical accounts of emotion and acting, Stanislavsky took the side of Lekain and Riccoboni against Diderot and Coquelin in that, for him, the actor should undergo an emotional experience while performing. He found support for this in the Tolstoyan aesthetic and the work of such pre-revolutionary psychologists as Binet and primarily Ribot. Ribot distinguished *intellectual* and *emotional memory* and the latter, involving a change in bodily state, provided a mechanism for the actor's *experiencing*.

Stanislavsky did not define emotion/spiritual but was certain throughout his career that *affective memory* is an important key to the expression of

---

[142] *Ibid.* p. 93.
[143] Vladimir Volkenstein, 'Drama, kak izobrazhenie refleksa tseli', *Vestnik Kommunisticheskoi 'Akademii'*, 14 (1926), p. 166.

emotion in acting. The view that emotion is indivisible from action or movement was supported by various sources and the theory of conditional reflexes supplied the theoretical basis for the Soviet materialist view. Stanislavsky tried to express himself in keeping with this and at the same time disguised the ideas he had adopted from yoga and his ideas of the *unconscious*. In practice, his views on acting did not change: *experiencing* was essential, whether it was achieved via *emotional memory* or action. His attempts to incorporate current knowledge after the revolution, and the fact that this knowledge was attributed to him by others, resulted in the interesting fact that many of the concepts of the system are amalgams of ideas from the nineteenth century with materialism, and ideas purportedly from eastern philosophy.

CHAPTER 3

Incarnation: the actor as machine

STANISLAVSKY'S CONCEPT OF *INCARNATION*

The right-hand side of the diagram from *AWHI* discussed in Chapter 2 is labelled *Incarnation* (5). The methods used by Stanislavsky to *incarnate the life of the human spirit* of the role, that is, methods of physical and vocal training, were to develop what he saw as the external means for the expression of the actor's *experiencing* in the characterisation overall. The paradigmatic concepts and theoretical bases of these methodologies include, firstly, the concept of the human being as a machine, governed nonetheless by nature (and the inherent contradictions within this) and, secondly, the belief in the necessity for exercises and drills to develop physical expressiveness. The latter is dependent theoretically on a Jamesian concept of habit, which is not necessarily upheld by the physiology of today.

The development of Stanislavsky's thinking was prompted by reactions against his work, and the popularisation by Prince Sergei Volkonsky and others of the work of Delsarte and Dalcroze. This was seized upon in the theatre world in Russia as offering possibilities for alternative approaches to that of Stanislavsky. Stanislavsky investigated and made use of the work of Delsarte and Dalcroze, but was not swayed by the reaction against his work. He maintained his earlier beliefs about truth and emotion in acting. Vakhtangov, Meyerhold and Michael Chekhov each offered challenges to the *system* in different ways as they moved away from their mentor and developed their own ideas.

It is important to question from today's perspective the scientific validity of the training exercises developed as part of the *system*, and other aspects of the training work at MAT and in the studios. The sources of these exercises are to be considered, as are the manuals consulted by Stanislavsky, particularly in his work on voice and breathing. Stanislavsky's ideas on *incarnation* (*voploshchenie*) are outlined in connection with the development of the *external sense of the self on stage*. In Stanislavsky's view, the actor needs to be able to convey *experiencing* to the audience by the proper external means, or *incarnation* of the character: 'In order to reflect subtle and often subconscious life, it is necessary to possess exceptionally responsive and excellently developed vocal and bodily apparatus' (*AWHE*, p. 64).

The second volume of the *AWHI* acting manual, therefore, concentrates on methods of achieving this development. Stanislavsky acknowledges in the two books the artificiality of the division of the *Actor's Work on Him/Herself* into two areas. This is the reason why, he says, *Freeing the Muscles* comes into *AWHE*, although as external work it properly belongs in *AWHI*. Nevertheless, he makes this division, claiming that 'the *life of the body* is fixed more easily than the *life of the spirit*' (*AWHI*, p. 329). The implication is that working with the vocal and bodily mechanisms will facilitate the expression of emotion and spirit; this preparation is valuable, as the right inner content may not be immediately accessible. Also, as the spiritual and emotional aspects of acting are of primary importance, the technical aspects must not impede their expression.

In *AWHI*, Tortsov's training programme is described under the chapter headings:

I.   Approach to Incarnation
II.   Physical Culture (Development of the Expressiveness of the Body)
      1. Gymnastics, Acrobatics, Dance, et cetera
      2. Plastique
III. Singing and Diction
IV.   Speech and its Laws
V.   The Perspective of the Artist and the Role
VI.   Tempo-rhythm
VII. Logic and Consistency
VIII. Characterisation
IX.   Control and Finish
X.   Stage Charm and Allure
XI.   Ethics and Discipline
XII. The External Sense of the Self on Stage
XIII. The General Sense of the Self on Stage

There is additional material in both the old and new editions of Stanislavsky's *Collected Works*. These terms will be discussed and defined throughout this chapter.

The machine and the system

The fact that Stanislavsky often uses mechanical metaphors in his descriptions of training gives an indication of his idea of *incarnation*, the external aspects of the human organism. For example, in *AWHE*, Kostia says of Tortsov, 'Like a mechanic, Arkady Nikolaevich unscrewed us, took us apart, each bone, each joint and muscle, washed, cleaned and oiled them, then put them back together in the old place and screwed them up' (pp. 199–200). When learning new movement skills, the way the students perform the movements is compared with that of a car; 'At the first movement it makes infrequent, abrupt bursts, then they become continuous, like the movement itself' (*AWHI*, p. 34–5). In speech lessons Kostia's lips are described as 'not compressed together tightly enough, like the valves of a cheap instrument from a bad factory' (*AWHI*, p. 65). Tortsov states that 'It is necessary not just to be an actor but also an engineer and a mechanic' (*AWHI*, p. 39). In discussing his perform-ance as *Petr* in Ostrovsky's *Don't Live as You Wish*, for the Society of Art and Literature in 1890, Stanislavsky writes that

From the first steps I went along the surface of the part not reaching its core. It was like a free-running transmission, which keeps on working powerfully while the car itself is not moving. So I worked as if free-running with the superficial nerves and peripheries of the body, not touching the soul itself, which remained cold and inactive. Words, gestures, movements flew past feeling like a passenger train past stations where it does not need to stop, like an empty steamer which has broken loose from its anchor without a navigator, passengers or cargo (*MLIA*, p. 182).

Firstly, this reflects the thematic interest in the machine in general in his time, and secondly, throws light on Stanislavsky's paradigmatic concept of the human organism. In one sense this organism is for him a set of mechanisms and the teacher of acting must therefore be, among other things, a physiologist (*AWR*, 1st edn, p. 390–1). However, it is a 'natural machine'. It has been suggested that Stanislavsky followed Pavlov in beli-eving that 'The human being is a system (more crudely a machine) which like any other in nature, is governed by laws inevitable and single for nature as a whole.'[1] The word 'system', in its Greek origin, means the parts which make up a whole, and Stanislavsky views the human being as having an external part which is a mechanical system, and possessing an inner part indicated by the words 'spirit' and 'feeling', which system as a

---

[1] K. S. Stanislavsky, *Konstantin Stanislavski 1863–1963, Man and Actor, Stanislavski and the World Theatre, Stanislavski's Letters*, tr. Victor Schneierson (Moscow: Progress, 1963), p. 151.

whole is governed by nature and is not mechanical. Elsewhere, in contradiction, he states, 'A person is not a machine, he cannot feel the role
identically each time and on each repetition of the role; he cannot be
aroused by the same creative stimuli' (*AWR*, p. 94). However, he believes
that the two parts can be described independently and trained in different
ways. Stanislavsky's paradigm of the *emotional and spiritual machine* is
problematic because of the division he creates: the inner aspects, which
are more mysterious and the province of nature, which can be trained by
the methods described in *AWHE*, and the outer, more mechanical aspects
which should be trained by specific exercises, as discussed in *AWHI*.

Stanislavsky inherited ideas regarding exercises from the late-nineteenth
century when physical culture began to be in vogue. His own education
had included instruction in Swedish gymnastics and fencing, among
other exercise forms. In addition, he, Meyerhold and their contemporaries were influenced (in different ways) by what Segel calls 'the extra-
ordinary modernist preoccupation with physicality', which, he says,
'developed in the context of widespread disenchantment with intellectual
culture in the late-nineteenth and early-twentieth centuries'.[2] Stanislavsky
prioritised feeling, for example, over intellect. Physical culture movements
such as the German Turnverein, the Slavic Sokol movement, and the Boy
Scouts of America, the stated aim of which was to combat degeneracy
and promote physical regeneration, all influenced the development of
physical culture in Russia. Prevalent were ideas of the body as machine,
and the making of the new man and these took on particular significance
in the period of the revolution. Stanislavsky was a pioneer of actor-training
at the time when 'exercises' for the actor began to be devised. Eugenio
Barba states that 'the revolution of the invisible', as he terms the twentieth
century's discoveries of hidden structures in physics, sociology and
psychology, marked 'the age of exercises' in the theatre.[3] That which is
invisible gives life to acting; the key to it is in acting exercises.

What Stanislavsky meant by calling his training method for actors a
system, is debatable. In 1907, Stanislavsky read J. P. Muller's *My System*,
a book given to him by A. P. Petrovsky, a fellow actor, director and trainer,
working in Moscow and St Petersburg.[4] The book, which he annotated,

---

[2] Harold B. Segel, *Body Ascendant: Modernism and the Physical Imperative* (London: Johns Hopkins
University Press, 1998), p. 1.

[3] Eugenio Barba, 'An Amulet Made of Memory: The Significance of Exercises in the Actor's
Dramaturgy', *The Drama Review* 41:4 (1997), p. 128.

[4] I. N. Vinogradskaia, *Zhizn' i Tvorchestvo K. S. Stanislavskovo: Letopis*, 2nd edn (Moscow:
Moskovskii Khudozhestvennyi Teatr, 2003), vol. 2, p. 78.

includes a series of stretching and bending exercises to be practised daily, and other recommendations for health and fitness. Stanislavsky worked through the exercises, adapting them as he saw fit, and appears to have worked them into his daily routine. At this time he was developing the actor's *toilette* and his initial idea was that his *system* would be the actor's daily warm-up exercises. He began referring to his own *system* in 1909, planning a programme of essays under the heading '*My System*'.[5] Other 'systems' were in existence; for example, Volkonsky refers to Delsarte's 'system'.[6] The term developed other meanings in the popular understanding until in 1931 Stanislavsky tried to issue a disclaimer in a new foreword to *AWHE* in response to an article about his and Vakhtangov's disagreements:

In the approach to my so-called system there exists among almost all those criticising it (with some exceptions) a number of identical misunderstandings, bearing witness to the fact that my approach to the question is not understood at its basis . . . The first radical misunderstanding is in the very name of the Stanislavsky system. In spite of the fact that it is preserved in the very name of the book, the name is wrong. In saying 'my system' it is supposed that a person has invented and thought up something, he has found before some sort of basic theses, which he has developed and made into an entire well-put together system. How many such systems passed before us before and during the revolution! I never thought anything up, did not compose any theses. I simply honestly and attentively observed my own and others' natures at the moment of their creative work.

   Much that I worked on and pursued, which did not receive real confirmation in living practice . . . on the stage itself, was not allowed into this book and will remain in the period of research until that moment when it gives a palpable practical result in the technique and creativity of the actor.[7]

He reiterated on many occasions that he did not create the *system*, nature did,[8] and he urged people to create their own systems, although 'there is much that is general and necessary for all in the system because we are all subject to the general laws of nature'. He states that the ability to create the *system* is inside us, but we lose what nature has given us when we go on stage and begin to pretend, so the components of the *system*, such as its *magic if*, *given circumstances*, *creative ideas* and *lures* are there to help the actor (*AWHI*, p. 366).

   Although it can be argued that Stanislavsky set out to develop a systematic daily exercise routine as training for the actor, this began to be

[5] *Ibid.*, p. 193.
[6] Prince Sergei Volkonsky, *Vyrazitel'nyi Chelovek"* (St Petersburg: Apollon, 1913), p. 5.
[7] Vinogradskaia, *Letopis*, vol. 4, p. 189.
[8] *Ibid.* p. 120. See also K. S. Stanislavsky, *Stanislavsky on the Art of the Stage*, tr. David Magarshack 2nd edn (London: Faber and Faber, 1967), p. 136.

construed into a body of theory about acting as well, which could be validated scientifically. Also, Stanislavsky's claim that he did not invent anything is not precisely true; his acting exercises are often inventions based in a priori assumptions about the human organism that are not surprising for someone of his time. The *system* may not be coherent as a theoretical system, even if the exercises work in practice. In his later years, Stanislavsky noted the 'Communist dictum: daily life defines (thought)... My system answers the dictum, that is, I go from life, from practice to a theoretical rule.'[9] Stanislavsky trained himself from an early age, as described in *MLIA* (p. 131), going from practice to theory. The method, as ever, was one that Stanislavsky was confident he could develop by himself and refine by means of observation.

Other exercises were added to the basic premises of physical exercise and relaxation. He invented and adopted exercises as part of the *system* in order to achieve specific ends and because there were concepts underlying these methods of training of which he approved. Various reasons for the actor to exercise are indicated: correcting posture, freeing oneself from tension, as part of the actor-training process and working with the *life of the body* as a means of accessing the *spirit*.[10] Firstly, regarding correcting posture, Stanislavsky's description of himself as a youth is that he was 'tall, clumsy, graceless and mispronounced many letters'. He therefore set himself a programme of work to train the body in front of a mirror. He would return in the evening from his office work as director of the Russian Musical Society and work, it is claimed, from 7 p.m. until 3 or 4 a.m. He had some success, he writes, in developing skills in *plastique*, or bodily expressiveness, in getting to know his body (*MLIA*, p. 131). (The Russian word *plastika* or bodily expression is the counterpart of *mimika*, facial expression.) In *AWHI*, Stanislavsky explains how many people have bodies that are ill-proportioned, which could be corrected by exercises. He believes it is crucial that the actor does this, as shortcomings that pass unnoticed in daily life are magnified on stage:

People do not know how to use the physical apparatus given them by nature. Moreover they do not even know how to keep it in order, how to develop it. Flabby muscles, a bent spine, incorrect breathing are normal phenomena in our

---

[9] I. N. Vinogradskaia, *Zhizn i tvorchestvo K. S. Stanislauskovo, Letopis*, 2nd edn, vols. 1–4 (Moscow: Moskovski; Khudozhest vennyi Teatr, 2003), p. 213.

[10] Lazarovich argues convincingly that Stanislavsky's purpose in promoting training and drill is a moral one, to enable the students to develop self-control and fight against dilettantism. See Gunter Ahrends (ed.) Spontaneität oder "Training und Drill" in *Konstantin Stanislawski, Neue Aspekte und Perspektiven* (Tübingen: Forum Modernes Theater, 1992), pp. 39–50.

life. All this is a result of unskilful training and use of our bodily apparatus. It is not surprising because the work intended for it by nature is not being done satisfactorily (p. 18).

Stanislavsky does not explain how these shortcomings have come about. In his view, nature needs some improvement, and exercise systems, particularly (Swedish) gymnastics, will perform this function resulting in 'the body on display being healthy, beautiful, its movements plastic and harmonised' (p. 18). He believes that dance (in Isadora Duncan's style, but also ballet, sports and acrobatics) can help the actor improve his or her shape and adds that posture can be corrected by methods favoured by nineteenth-century governesses, such as lying on hard floors, and that 'children's posture can be corrected by a stick between the arms behind the back' (p. 24). Gutta-percha balls placed in the armpit can correct problems with the arms, ensuring that the elbows do not turn in towards the body, and sharp angles of the elbows can be remedied by blows with a ruler, teaching the student to 'instinctively watch out for this shortcoming'[11] (*AWHI*, p. 454). When all possible correction has been achieved, the rest is up to the designer, costumier, a good tailor and cobbler (*AWHI*, p. 20). Stanislavsky asserts that the exercise forms he discusses will achieve the purpose of improving posture, which argument he would no doubt support by his own experience. Postural correction of the kind Stanislavsky describes is not widely practised now, and possibly he simply outgrew a clumsiness that was to do with adolescence.

Secondly, he wished to be free from tension, having noticed at an early stage of his work with great actors and dancers, 'the freedom and lack of tension in the muscles at emotional high points . . . whereas I was always tense on stage and my imagination was sluggish because I was using others as models' (*MLIA*, p. 145). Fedotova told him he had 'No training, no restraint, no discipline' (*MLIA*, p. 149). Ribot stated that there is a connection between muscle tension and the ability to pay attention which Stanislavsky verified for himself. The experiment of lifting a piano and attempting to do mental arithmetic is described in Chapter 2. His answer to this is that the actor must develop a *controller*, a system of checking where there is muscular tension and releasing it, and this has to become a

---

[11] As Roach describes in *The Player's Passion: Studies in the Science of Acting* (Newark: University of Michigan Press, 1985), p. 167), Goethe's *Rules for Actors* contains strictures about the actor's elbows and Stanislavsky may have got the idea from there.

mechanical habit (*AWHE*, p. 188). Stanislavsky's concept of habit here is problematic – he does not explain how the control can be established below the level of consciousness.

Stanislavsky viewed the voice and body of the actor as their apparatus or instrument, which is undeveloped initially and must be trained, in the same way as musicians must train to use their instruments, by means of exercises (*MLIA*, p. 432; *AWHI*, p. 423). This equation with other art forms is one used by Stanislavsky many times to justify the need for practice. As Roach points out, Diderot had asked the question why the actor's art should differ from that of the sculptor, painter, orator or musician in 'Observations sur une brochure intitulée Garrick'.[12] As Stanislavsky posed this question early on in his career, and studied Diderot later, it is likely that it was an idea that had gained general currency. Acting was being seen as an art form, no longer a craft. However, thinking of the actors' voice and body as their instrument is a dichotomous way of thinking that brings about problems for Stanislavsky and his contemporaries.

Although Stanislavsky is aware that more than mechanics is involved, whatever he thinks about the spirit/soul or superconscious, he thinks that the mechanics are easier to work with. His statement, 'the life of the body is fixed more easily than the life of the human spirit of the role', could be compared with Pavlov's assertion that an understanding and explanation of psychic phenomena could be gained from the evidence of external behaviour. However, Stanislavsky's thinking tends to be more dualistic and finding a way to access the spiritual is of great importance to him. Stanislavsky sees the body as the surface, the spirit the depths. The aim of the psycho-technique is the *superconscious* through the conscious, but the training begins with the work of the actors on themselves. The source of Stanislavsky's tri-partite view of the *unconscious* is, of course, von Hartmann.

Physiology and anatomy

Stanislavsky states, 'It is necessary to cultivate the voice and body of the artist on the basis of nature itself' (*AWHI*, p. 14). However, the exercises taught by Stanislavsky are underpinned by concepts of the physiology and anatomy of the human organism particular to his epoch, because he

---

[12] *Ibid.* p. 133.

believed that the laws of nature were being revealed by science. Apart from his reading of Sechenov, it does not appear that Stanislavsky directly studied very much anatomy or physiology. Some of the voice manuals to which he refers discuss respiration, and at his House Museum are N. E. Shirokova's *Deep Breathing and Muscle Strain in Singing* (1910), and also Razumovsky's *The Foundations of Physical Development and Stregthening of the Organism* (1926). There are also copies of N. Kabanov's *Essays on the Physiology of the Healthy and Unhealthy Human Organism* (1910), of which the pages are not cut, and M. Duval's *Anatomie Artistique* (c.1891) which contains, drawings of the human body for visual artists. In Stanislavsky's discussions of how the human mechanism works he often makes up his own terms, rather than using physiological or anatomical ones, or uses terms inherited from the movement forms he borrows. For example, he often speaks of 'centres' in the body, such as 'gross movement centres' (*AWHI*, p. 19) the head centre and the centre of the solar plexus (AWHE, pp. 323–4), a term from yoga.

Also, Stanislavsky took the concept of *prana* from yoga and then equated it with 'energy'. He says of energy that it 'flows down the network of the muscular system and arouses the internal movement centres; this energy evokes external action'. He adds that 'the basis of plastic movement is not what is visible externally but the internal movement of energy. This internal sense of energy passing through the body we call the feeling of movement' (*AWHI*, pp. 29–37). There is more understanding now of how energy is produced than there was in Stanislavsky's day and his idea could not be substantiated by physiology now.[13] However, this idea of *prana* or energy flowing was of great importance to him. Furthermore, he described the lowest vertebra as like a screw, which is fixed in, securing the flexible spine (*AWHI*, p. 24). This is anatomically inaccurate; maybe he is thinking of the fusion of vertebrae to form the sacrum. In his description of walking, 'Tortsov explained the structure of the leg and the basis of walking correctly.' This explanation is of a spring mechanism: 'Human legs, from the pelvis to the foot remind me of the good movement of a Pullman carriage, thanks to its many springs' (*AWHI*, p. 39). This is a descriptive simile – the Pullman carriage was noted for smooth travel – but is anatomically incorrect, as the action of the leg and foot in walking involves the mechanism of rotation around axes, but not a

[13] Mitochondria, the cells which take in oxygen and emit Adenosine Triphosphate (ATP) in the formation of energy, were discovered by 1890, but their function was not known until the mid-1920s and the way the process worked was not really understood until the 1940s, when the fact that energy is produced locally and does not travel through the body was made clear.

spring mechanism.[14] It is interesting to note that Meyerhold also described walking in terms of spring mechanisms, according to Mikhail Korenov, who wrote 'The biomechanical movement of the actor on the stage platform is a half-run, half-walk, and always on springs'.[15]

Although Stanislavsky declares himself unsure about what artistic inspiration is, he quotes a theory that:

genius or inspiration lives in our brain, that the super- and unconscious are in fact conscious. They compare consciousness with a light which is directed on a definite spot in our brain, on it all our attention is concentrated. The remainder of the brain cells remain in darkness or reflexly receive a weak reflection. But there are moments when the whole surface of the brain cortex is illuminated for a moment by the light of consciousness and then for a short time the whole area of consciousness and the subconscious is illuminated by the light and seizes everything that was in darkness before. These are moments of insights of genius (*AWHI*, p. 377).

This reads like Stanislavsky's amalgam of ideas from von Hartmann with Sechenov and Pavlov. Some of these concepts would be unacceptable today in terms of scientific understandings of the workings of the human organism and, indeed, some of the descriptions would not have been in accordance with the anatomy and physiology of Stanislavsky's day. They are artistic metaphors and this must be taken into account in the assessment of Stanislavsky's theory of acting as a whole.

HABIT: MECHANICAL ACTING OR *SECOND NATURE*?

A further paradigmatic concept in Stanislavsky's training methods is the idea that repetition and practice are needed. Stanislavsky thought it was necessary for actors to establish habits, by means of repetition of exercises and approaches to work. His campaign, therefore, was to get performers to recognise the importance of daily work on the self and preparation for performance by means of the actors' *toilette*. In a description of rehearsals for *Woe from Wit* in 1914, Sulerzhitsky describes Konstantin Sergeevich's dream of the whole troupe doing exercises, such as freeing the muscles and taking oneself into the circle, for half an hour before rehearsal, as

---

[14] M. A. MacConaill and J. V. Basmajian, *Muscles and Movements* (New York: Robert E. Krieger, 1977), p. 14. See also Tristan M. Roberts, *Understanding Balance: The Mechanics of Posture and Locomotion*, (London: Chapman and Hall, 1995), Chapter 3.

[15] Mel Gordon and Alma Law, *Meyerhold, Eisenstein and Biomechanics: Actor-Training in Revolutionary Russia* (North Carolina: McFarland, 1996), p. 136.

singers do vocal exercises without regard to what parts they are singing.[16] Stanislavsky kept arguing for this throughout his career, as a result of which, no doubt, the 'warm up' has become established. In 1931, he stated to the Artistic Council of the Opera Theatre that the teaching of plastic disciplines to young singers was not taken seriously enough as one or two lessons a week had no meaning: daily exercises, if only for half an hour, were what was necessary.[17]

In *MLIA* he criticises people who made use of the terminology of the *system* without recognising the fact that the system as such was only a theory which the artist, by means of 'working for a long time, habit and struggle, had to turn into second nature and turn into practice'. He states that it is possible to only know the *system*, that is, to be acquainted with it intellectually to a degree, but what is necessary is to make it *second nature*. He also states that when what has been learned has become habitual the artist can cease thinking about it and wait for it to manifest itself naturally (*MLIA*, p. 431).

Stanislavsky's understanding of *habit* and *second nature*, and the underpinning scientific theory for these concepts (though perhaps via an indirect route), is based in the ideas on habit put forward by William James in his theory of psychology. It was James who popularised the term *second nature*, writing in *Talks to Teachers on Psychology: And to Students on Some of Life's Ideals* (1899), 'Habit is thus a second nature, or rather, as the Duke of Wellington said, it is "ten times nature"'.[18] Also, James writes in the *Textbook of Psychology*, ' "Habit a second nature! Habit is ten times nature", the Duke of Wellington is said to have exclaimed ... the daily drill and years of discipline end by fashioning a man completely over again."[19] This sentiment would have been applauded in post-revolutionary Russia with the interest in physical culture. It may also have been confirmed for Stanislavsky by the idea that he came across in his reading on yoga: the body should be mastered in order to meditate, to practise Raja yoga.

Stanislavsky sees good habit or *second nature* as the actor's salvation. The recognition of this came from the crisis that prompted the development of the *system*. By 1906, Stanislavsky recognised that in his acclaimed role as Stockmann in Ibsen's *An Enemy of the People*, his performance had

---

[16] Vinogradskaia, *Letopis*, vol. 2, p. 444.
[17] *Ibid.* vol. 4, p. 149.
[18] William James, *Talks to Teachers on Psychology: And to Students on Some of Life's Ideals* (London: Longmans, Green, 1927), p. 65.
[19] William James, *Textbook of Psychology* (London: Macmillan, 1892), p. 142.

become mechanical. He writes in *MLIA* that 'mechanical acting forestalls inner experiencing', explaining this with the example that, as the actor, he copied Stockmann's naivety by making his eyes look childlike and innocent, but was not naive himself; he did not *experience* naivety internally, as he had discarded the affective memories on which the role was based. There was, therefore, a dislocation (*vyvikh*), a split between internal and external. He expands on this:

I repeated mechanically exactly those developed and established tricks of the role, the mechanical signs of the absence of feeling ... from performance to performance I ingrained in myself the mechanical habit of going through this technical gymnastics that I had once laid down, and muscle memory which is so strong in actors had firmly fixed the actor's habit (*MLIA*, pp. 371–2).

He attempted to apply the results of his experimentation in acting after the 1906 Stockmann crisis, to a production of Hamsun's *The Drama of Life*, in 1907. The symbolic drama was successful with audiences seeking a departure from realism, but in Stanislavsky's view this was because of the *mise-en-scène* rather than the acting. He had implemented the internal techniques he was developing, and had stopped the actors using any external means of *incarnation*, that is, gestures, movements and action, because the actor's gesture and movement was too ordinary and insufficiently expressive. This did not work either, because there was no internal *justification* for the absence of gesture, and muscle strain resulted from the attempt to force the actors to be internally impassioned:

There were many days and months of tormenting doubt until I understood the long-known truth that in our business everything must be done through habit, which turns what is new into something that is my own, organic, into second nature. Only after this was it possible to use what is new, not thinking about the mechanics of it (*MLIA*, p. 388).

What he meant by this is elucidated by Volkonsky's aphorism, which Stanislavsky quotes on a number of occasions: 'What is difficult becomes habitual, the habitual easy and the easy beautiful' (*AWHI*, p. 456) (see figure 5). This is the case, in Stanislavsky's view, because despite the fact that creative work should not become mechanical, habit can 'unburden attention' (p. 457), freeing the performers from having to think about certain aspects of what they are doing in order to give their attention to the more important aspects of performance. On stage, the artist has to be consciously aware of the inner or spiritual processes of attention, imagination, the *feeling of truth and faith, emotional memory, communion* and *adaptation*. At the same time the actors must take care of their body and the

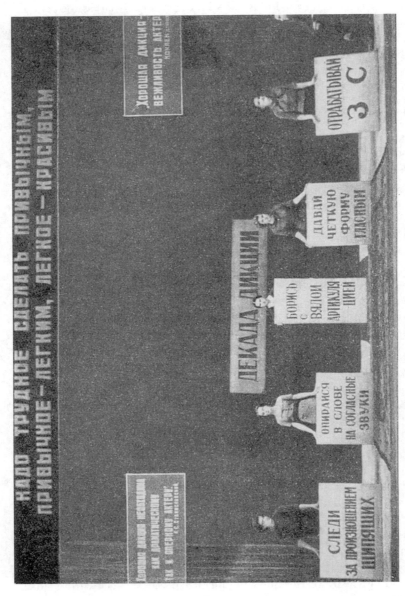

5. Placards of the week; staging the programme. Slogan at top: 'It is necessary to make what is difficult habitual, the habitual easy and the easy beautiful.'

movements made with different parts of the body – how they are walking, their physical expression or *plastique*. Attention must also be given to regulating breathing, placing the voice, diction and the process of speaking, and to the internal line of the role, its score, the *supertask* of the play, the demands of the director, the acoustics of the theatre, the lighting, the noises from offstage and the auditorium. But some of the 'burden of attention' can be taken by training the actor to respond automatically to the conditions of the auditorium, and to performing in public. If this work is done consciously at first, Stanislavsky says, in time it will become the artist's *second nature*.

What might be the sources, in the science of Stanislavsky's day, for some of his ideas? There is no direct evidence that Stanislavsky read William James, although he was certainly aware of his work. Stanislavsky's concept of the mechanism of *habit* and its role in learning is close to James's theories as described in the *Textbook of Psychology*. James was an influence on Ribot, who also discusses habit. The same two ideas found in Stanislavsky are articulated by James, who writes, 'first, habit simplifies our movements, making them accurate and diminishes fatigue' and 'secondly, *habit diminishes the conscious attention with which our acts are performed*'.[20] He adds:

The great thing then in all education is to make our nervous system our ally instead of our enemy... For this we must make automatic and habitual as early as possible, as many useful actions as we can ... the more we can hand over to the effortless custody of automatism, the more our higher powers of mind will be set free for their own proper work.[21]

This can clearly be equated with Stanislavsky's ideas of the need to 'unburden the attention' by training the actor to respond automatically to performance conditions and to develop the sense of the self on stage, so the actor can consciously attend to the higher, 'spiritual' aspects of performing. Stanislavsky's application of the ideas to actor training becomes problematic, however. He writes, 'The actor's belief in what he is doing, his ability to use his imagination in a role can also be acquired as a *habit*' (*AWR*, p. 95). 'Daily, systematic work in imagining the given circumstances of a role can create *habit* in the imaginary life which becomes second nature, a "second imaginary actuality"' (*AWR*, p. 79). Antarova records Stanislavsky as saying 'It is absolutely wrong to do any of the

[20] *Ibid.* pp. 138–9.
[21] *Ibid.* pp. 144–5.

exercises laid down in my system mechanically and unthinkingly. It is absolutely wrong to speak your words to no purpose. You must acquire the habit of putting the greatest possible meaning into every word you utter.'[22] As with the discussion of the *controller* checking for muscle tension, Stanislavsky's way of thinking about this embodies a contradiction. If the actor stops giving attention to aspects of their acting, it will then become mechanical, and so the creation of a habitual imaginary life is likely to result in repeating the role habitually.

In 1916 in a speech to the actors working on an adaptation of Dostoevsky's *The Village of Stepanchikovo*, Stanislavsky speaks about his mission as a director, part of which is to 'save nature from actor's habits and conventions of acting which are against nature and pernicious to it. I, like a doctor will resort to an operation, which regrettably cannot be anything but painful.'[23] In the same period he makes a note of the 'blind alleys' in which actors can find themselves. These are firstly, 'playing the image', secondly 'playing passion', or thirdly 'giving oneself up to the habitual mould of the role. This transforms actors into performing dogs and stops forever the internal life of the role'.[24]

There are a variety of ways in which the actor can fall into the trap of habit. As well as the fact that a role once created well can become mechanical, the actor can produce a characterisation which is stereotyped from the beginning, that is, a *stencil*. Stanislavsky describes the 'bogatyr', the Russian warrior hero of folk tales, where actors adopt a particular walk and mannerism, as the worst *stencil*, a 'banality that is fixed so strongly in the ears, eyes, body and muscles of actors that there is no possibility of getting rid of it' (*MLIA*, p. 184). These 'ready-made mechanical methods of acting', he writes, are easily produced in the *craft* school of acting. 'The muscles of actors trained in this way turn into habit and become their second nature, which replaces human nature on stage' (*AWHE*, p. 75; also *AWHI*, p. 468).

As well as producing stereotyped characterisations (from maintaining a habitual, unexamined way of thinking about the character), the actor can have other problematic habits. Stanislavsky mentions his own habit of stooping as a young man, which he was determined to overcome (*MLIA*, p. 81). From the photographs of the statuesque Stanislavsky as an actor and in portraits, it appears that he did overcome this habit, which no

---

[22] Stanislavsky, *Stanislavsky on the Art of the Stage*, p. 128.
[23] Vinogradskaia, *Letopis*, vol. 2, p. 496.
[24] *Ibid.* vol. 2, p. 512. The comment on image perhaps relates to Meyerhold and Michael Chekhov's emphasis on *image* rather than character (see Chapters 4 and 5).

doubt gave him faith that it was possible to improve postural problems by his methods. He names the habit, common to many actors of 'gabbling the words' (*MLIA*, p. 117). Stanislavsky does not analyse the different types of bad habits himself, but says this must be a result of bad training, lack of understanding or control. Also, there are warnings against the habit of lying, of being false in acting (*AWHI*, p. 391). For example, the actor should not look into the stalls where the director or his admirer habitually sits, when in accordance with the role they should be looking somewhere else (*AWHE*, p. 175). There are warnings to the actor not to drill oneself in the words of the role but recreate its feelings and thoughts.

Stanislavsky sees that habit, therefore, is a double-edged sword: the result of repeating the external aspects of a characterisation, or working with uncorrected physical or speech habits, becomes by dint of what Stanislavsky calls *muscle memory* so deeply part of the whole actor's approach, so much his or her *second nature*, that the result can only be mechanical acting, espoused by the schools of *craft* and *representation*, which goes against nature and brings about 'spiritual death' (*MLIA*, p. 373). Again, 'muscle memory' is metaphor, though widely used, as habitual ways of acting can only be generated by the brain and, literally speaking, muscles cannot remember anything. In his view the other kind of habit, the other type of *second nature*, must be developed in acting.

Stanislavsky believes that you have to correct constantly the 'organic ailment' whether it is a speech problem or a bodily shortcoming until the correction becomes *second nature* (*AWHI*, p. 459). Also, the performer must cultivate the *habit of the controller*, which enables the actor to free the muscles. For these *habits* to become *second nature* for the artist takes a lot of work (*AWHE*, pp. 187–9). The problem is that insufficient time is devoted to this work. For example, students have only two lessons in diction a week, each of a quarter of an hour. This means that the student talks properly for half an hour a week and then for the rest of the week it is not required. But Stanislavsky says that you cannot devote all your time and attention to this; it is better to 'train the attention itself' to make corrections subconsciously, automatically and constantly'. Only *habit* can organise constant, subconscious, automatic self-observation, which is developed by constant reminders over the course of years (*AWHI*, p. 459). Again, there is a contradiction here between habit and attention.

In 1908 Stanislavsky wrote various sketches in his notebook about preparation for performance and on 'the manifestation of the will in the repetition of creativity in a show', where, according to Vinogradskaia, he writes for the first time about 'unity and the link between physical and psychological principles in the creative process'. In referring to *through action* Stanislavsky wrote, 'the physiological habit of the role arouses its psychology in the soul of the artist and the psychological *experiencing* of the feelings of the role engender the physiological state of the body of the artist which is habitual for the role'.[25] In the same way as he uses the term *reflex*, Stanislavsky is here using the term habit to explain the relationship between 'psychology' and 'physiology'. The problem lies with his conceptualisation of 'psychology' and 'physiology' as in some way split and needing to be connected and, again, there is a contradiction here between habit, which is below the level of consciousness and attention, which is not.

In 1916 Stanislavsky wrote that when belief has been engendered and the artist is living the life of the role, 'unconsciously choosing his feelings and the events, facts known to him through life experience . . . he unconsciously weaves feeling with the soul and life of the role. From habit and time the artist . . . receives features of feeling cultivated and born with the role.'[26] Stanislavsky does not explain the difference between the occasions when, as he sees it, habit works for the performer and occasions, as in the Stockmann crisis, when the unconscious process works against him and the notion of an 'unconscious choice' is not explained, although it demonstrates Stanislavsky's faith in the unconscious process.

On the positive aspects of habit he is clear, as is James, that habit enables skill development: 'Children learn to walk or speak with great difficulty and effort of attention at first but we learn to consider all these 'mechanical motor tasks' easy and we don't need to think of them. In the same way the artist can develop skills, made easy by habit. Unconscious mechanical muscle control memory remembers the most complicated combinations of steps in dances' (*AWR*, p. 105). He further believed that also it enables veracity and accuracy in acting. In exercises with real objects many of the moments constituting the action slide past the conscious attention of the creator, because they are taking place habitually (*AWHE*, p. 476; and *AWHI*, p. 215). For example, he states that in taking a drink from a carafe in real life we do not think about the actions we are performing but they are logical and consistent, in accordance with motor habit and the necessary subconscious feeling. Again, however, Stanislavsky does not explain how it is that these actions when performed on stage do not become habitual in the bad sense, that is, mechanical. In view of

[25] *Ibid.* vol. 2, p. 149.
[26] *Ibid.* vol. 2, p. 499.

Stanislavsky's pronouncements on how physical actions should be imbued with psychological meaning this view of habit is again problematic.

Part of the problem may be that Stanislavsky is attempting to make a practical application of a term that James and others were discussing from a philosophical as well as a practical perspective. James asserted that habit has a physical basis; it is an aspect of the intrinsic nature of all things, inanimate as well as animate. He cites from M. Léon Dumont's article in *Revue Philosophique* (1875), on acquired habit:

Everyone knows how a garment, after having been worn a certain time, clings to the shape of the body better than when new; there has been a change in the tissue, and this change is a new habit of cohesion.[27]

He gives further examples such as the fact that it is less trouble to fold a paper once it has been folded. He states:

habit has a physical basis. The laws of Nature are nothing but the immutable habits, which the different elementary sorts of matter follow in their actions and reactions upon each other.'[28]

Habit for James is as much a characteristic of how animate beings function as it is characteristic of inanimate objects.

Stanislavsky, it seems, concurs with James in his ideas on habit and nature. Stanislavsky writes that when a person who has been drowning is made to breathe air mechanically, although the heart and breath have stopped, because of habit the other organs of the body begin to function again. If Stanislavsky believed with James that habit was part of the essential nature of all things, it clarifies why he would think it necessary to describe it in explaining the actor's art. He goes on to say, 'The same organic habit of our nature, the same habitual consistency and logic of tasks, actions and experiences are used in our art in giving birth to the process of *experiencing*' (*AWR*, p. 110). Stanislavsky does not make any distinction between automatic responses of the nervous system and habits, which are learned and, therefore, could be changed. James's philosophical argument does not translate easily into the explanation of acting that Stanislavsky is trying to give, although the fact that these ideas were being discussed by such an authority as James perhaps explains Stanislavsky's adherence to the idea.

---

[27] James, *Textbook*, p. 135.
[28] *Ibid.*, p. 134.

James emphasised the ethical and pedagogical importance of the principle of habit.[29] He writes, 'habit is thus the enormous fly-wheel of society, its most precious conservative agent', and gives examples of how habitual modes of life keep different social strata from mixing, preserving social stability. He stressed the need to cultivate moral habits, to determine how much to smoke during the day by only smoking at set times, to regulate the day by getting up and going to bed at set times, to develop one's moral character by cultivating the habit of applying oneself to unpleasant tasks that need to be done, in order to get them out of the way each day. Although he is speaking of establishing moral habits rather than performance, like Stanislavsky, James recommends daily work to establish them, and issues dire warnings to those who allow habit to fashion their characters in the wrong way.[30] For both James and Stanislavsky, habit can be good or bad – what is important is to continue to work at inculcating good habits.

Stanislavsky clearly wishes to urge the actors to make it their practice to do daily work, to develop a controller, and all the other habits that are beneficial for the performer. He refers to the scientific ideas of his time. Unfortunately, there was then insufficient understanding of the nature of learning for him to be able to develop his theories in the best way possible. As a result, his recommendations can be confusing and mean that he is unable to deal with the problem of *dislocation*, where the performer may be going through the motions of the role habitually and mechanically except by means of the circular argument already mentioned, where the establishment of habits enables the actor to pay less attention to certain aspects of performance but the only solution when the role becomes habitual is for the actor to pay more attention to what he or she is doing.

VOLKONSKY, DELSARTE AND DALCROZE

While Stanislavsky was refining his methods of training in the second decade of the twentieth century, as Iampolsky states, 'there was at that time in Russia an active reaction against the method of Stanislavsky's Moscow Art Theatre. The principle of the transformation and embodiment of the actor in the character was being criticised from all sides.'[31]

[29] *Ibid.* pp. 142–3.
[30] *Ibid.* p. 149.
[31] Mikhail Yampolsky, 'Kuleshov's Experiments and the New Anthropology of the Actor' in Richard Taylor and Ian Christie (eds), *Inside the Film Factory: New approaches to Russian and Soviet Cinema* (London: Routledge, 1991), p. 31.

Some of the proponents of alternative approaches were Meyerhold, Chekhov and Vakhtangov. The methods of Delsarte and Dalcroze were important in this, though Stanislavsky also drew from them. This reaction was in the context of ideas about signs and gesture. The importance of the publication of the *Course in General Linguistics* by Swiss linguist Ferdinand de Saussure in 1916 is noted by Nicholas Worrall:

the existence of a general science of signs or semiology, of which linguistics would form a part, was important in going beyond language to incorporate any system of signs which form the content of ritual, convention or public entertainment.[32]

Nietszche also derided the idea that truth could be expressed by language and the modernist period was a time of the rejection or deconstruction of the word. In the wake of Darwin's assertion of a universal expression of emotions, similar claims were made for all gesture. As early as 1886, Professor Moses True Brown of Tufts College described the Delsarte system as 'semiotics', and said 'give the sign and you suggest the mood'.[33] By the time of modernism, many theatre artists asserted the supremacy of the sign over the word. Harold Segel quotes American academic and psychologist G. Stanley Hall, writing in 1911, 'Mien, mimesis and pantomime can together express every one of the feelings and emotions more graphically and forcibly than words can do.'[34] These ideas were eagerly embraced in Russia, although individual practitioners such as Stanislavsky and Meyerhold interpreted the concept of the universal language of signs quite differently. Then Bolshevism brought with it another view, and there was the desire to reassert the written or spoken word but in a more 'scientific' way. As a result of this Stanislavsky was forced to alter some of his terminology when his writing began to be published in the late twenties.

A key figure was Prince Sergei Volkonsky (1860–1937), who had been in charge of the Imperial theatres from 1899 to 1901, and was a patron of the arts in Russia, with contacts in the West. He taught speech and gesture throughout the revolution until his emigration in 1921, popularising the work of both Delsarte and Dalcroze. The gestural and vocal training of Francois Delsarte (1811–1871) owes much to J. J. Engel's *Practical Illustrations of Rhetorical Gesture and Acting*, originally published

[32] Nicholas Worrall, 'Meyerhold's Production of *The Magnificent Cuckold*', *The Drama Review*, 17:1 (1973), p. 16.
[33] George Taylor, *Players and Performances in the Victorian Theatre* (Manchester University Press, 1989), p. 150.
[34] Segel, *Body Ascendant*, p. 14.

in the late-eighteenth century, a lexicon of gestures which were purported
to have a direct correlation with the inner states of man – the passions.
Engel proposed a 'science' of expressive gesture, modelled on the Linnaean
system of botanical classification for the 'study of natural history'.[35]
Volkonsky wrote that Delsarte's work, which was drawn from his observations of people, was confirmed by Darwin, Mantegazza and others.[36]
Paolo Mantegazza's work on physiognomy and expression was popular in
the nineteenth century. He aimed to categorise and record 'the phenomena
of spontaneous automatic expression, which are almost the same in every
country in the world, and which constitute a veritable universal language'.[37]
Delsarte also studied art and statues, as actors and directors have done since
ancient times, and saw universal meaning in the classical poses.

As a musician, Delsarte emphasised the rhythmic aspects of gesture and
developed 'Laws of Motion', considering position or attitude, strength,
pace, direction, rhythm and balance of gestures. He sought a precise record
of gesture, its segmentation like musical notation, and the detailing of the
inner content of each gesture. There was a triadic division throughout
the theory: 'the psyche was defined as Body, Soul and Mind, and its functions as Vital, Emotional and Intellectual. From this triad he developed a
highly complex system, which correlated psychological impulses with particular zones of the body.'[38] The Delsarte system was widely known in the
1880s and had an influence in nineteenth-century European theatre, but its
main impact in Russia, owing to Volkonsky's efforts, was from the beginning of the twentieth century.

In 1913 Volkonsky published *The Expressive Person: A Stage Training
in Gesture According to Delsarte*. The bibliography notes comprehensively
the treatises on both Engel and Delsarte published in a variety of languages, but Volkonsky asserts that his book is guidance for the actor
according to Delsarte rather than an exposition of Delsarte's system. It is
a practical book and there is little theory, but sufficient, he hopes, to
convince the reader that 'the whole practical side of the system is based on
a scientific foundation . . . on laws'.[39] These laws, as he describes, include
the law that there is a correct gesture, which corresponds with the feeling

[35] Roach, *The Player's Passion*, p. 76. Carl Linnaeus (1707–1778) was a Swedish botanist who invented
    a system for defining living things according to 'genus' and 'species'.
[36] Volkonsky, *Vyrazitel'nyi Chelovek"*, p. 48.
[37] Paolo Mantegazza, *Physiognomy and Expression* (London: Walter Scott, 1885), p. 81.
[38] Taylor, *Players and Performances*, p. 149.
[39] Volkonsky, *Vyrazitel'nyi Chelovekii'*, p. 5.

that suggests it, a simple example being nodding the head to express agreement.

Volkonsky describes the system as 'semiotics': 'Art is the knowledge of those external methods by which life, the soul and the mind are opened up for the person – the ability to possess them and to direct them freely. Art is finding a sign corresponding to the essence.' He goes on to suggest that 'Signs of feeling, received by the external organs of hearing and sight must be classified if we wish to use them as the material of art.'[40]

The correct gesture embodies all aspects of expression:

1. Gesture can be studied from the point of view of expression as an external sign corresponding to a spiritual state; this is Semiotics.
2. It can be studied from the point of view of those laws governing the balance of the human body: this is Statics.
3. It can be studied from the point of view of those laws governing the sequence and alternation of movement: this is Dynamics.[41]

The book categorises different positions and movements of parts of the body and what these express, and various other laws such as Laws of Combination of individual movements, and the Law of Succession, which determines the organic development of movement and is constructed according to natural laws, or the laws of mechanics, such as gravity. As Iampolsky indicates, the equation of Laws of Movement with Laws of Nature, and the 'combination of mechanics and feeling . . . seems strange to us now' but in the developing ideas of the time provided a 'path from the old physiognomy of ballet and pantomime to the machine ethic of the twenties'.[42]

Volkonsky's Delsartism was open to different interpretations and was used by theatre trainers in different ways: some, like Meyerhold, Chekhov and film-maker Lev Kuleshov embraced the idea of the language of gesture. For Stanislavsky there were aspects of Volkonsky's Delsartism that he could applaud, such as the recommendation, 'On stage do not think of these laws and rules, they must sit in you, they will have value only on condition that they turn into something unconscious.' In a love scene the actors are not thinking how to hold out their hands, they are just holding them out: 'You should think during the time of preparation and in the time of performance you should feel. While you are studying the role you should think how to act, and during the show you should

---

[40] *Ibid.* p. 1, 8.
[41] *Ibid.* pp. 61–2.
[42] Yampolsky, 'Kuleshov's Experiments', in Taylor and Christie (eds), *Film Factory*, p. 35.

act. And the more you have thought while doing the exercises the less you will have to think while performing.' Again, it is *second nature* that will enable the actor to employ 'consciously the law in art with the naturalness with which you obey it unconsciously in life'.[43] In fact the Delsarte system claimed to encapsulate emotion in a way that was too direct for Stanislavsky, who spent so much time devising *lures* to bring out emotion from its 'secret hiding places in the soul' (*AWHE*, p. 315). Volkonsky recognised this, writing to Stanislavsky in 1913 about *The Expressive Person*;

I admit that I am giving it to you with some caution: the system I discuss 'approaches' the matter in the opposite way to your approach. But what is ultimately sought is the same thing – the truth of life in representation. If it is indicated that it places mechanics higher than feeling, then that is only something being indicated and in fact it is not so.[44]

Others, such as Meyerhold and Chekhov, thought with Delsarte that the routes to emotional expression need not be so complicated or have such priority, and this was part of Stanislavsky's disagreement with them. An important rule for Stanislavsky, Meyerhold, Chekhov and Vakhtangov was the idea of *justification*. Delsarte's notebook, quoted in *The Expressive Person*, states 'there is nothing worse than a gesture which has not been justified'.[45] This may be the source of Stanislavsky, Vakhtangov and Chekhov's exercises in *justifying* a pose. Dalcroze (1865–1950), was born Emile Henri Jaques in Vienna, adding 'Dalcroze' to his surname later. He studied music, at one time attended lectures by Delsarte in Paris, and from 1892 was a professor of harmony at the Geneva Conservatory. Dalcroze developed a system of rhythmic gymnastics on which he based an aesthetic theory. He had found that students could have a level of technical competence without having a trained 'ear' for music and also that many students had problems with time and rhythm. He asserted that 'musical sensations of a rhythmic nature call for the muscular and nervous response of the *whole organism*'.[46] He also explored ways of attaining economy of movement, making his work public from 1903, as 'eurhythmics'. The Swiss theatre designer Adolphe Appia and French

[43] Volkonsky, *Vyrazitel'nyi Cheloveky"*, pp. 9–10.
[44] Letter from Volkonsky to Stanislavsky, Petersburg, 18 February 1913, MAT Archive 7628.
[45] Volkonsky, *Vyrazitel'nyi Chelovek"*, p. 31.
[46] Emile Jaques-Dalcroze, *Rhythm, Music and Education*, tr. Harold F. Rubenstein, 2nd edn (London and Whitstable: The Dalcroze Society, 1967), p. viii.

director Jacques Copeau were among Dalcroze's supporters and in 1909 he collaborated with Appia at Hellerau. Hellerau was a 'garden city' financed by German magnates, the Dohrn brothers.[47] As Beacham describes it, the goal of its founders was 'the establishment of eurhythmics as the defining and motivating spirit of the Hellerau experiment'.[48] Volkonsky brought Wolf Dohrn, the director of the Hellerau Institute, to meet Stanislavsky in Moscow in 1912.[49] Stanislavsky, among many other luminaries from the arts world, visited the second festival of Hellerau in 1913, at which there was a production of Gluck's *Orpheus*, utilising eurhythmics and Appia's innovatory design.

In 1911/12 Volkonsky published *Iskusstvo i Zhest*, a translation of *L'Art et le Geste* (published in Paris in 1910) by Jean d'Udine, a disciple of Dalcroze. As Iampolsky describes, d'Udine was a propagandist of 'synaesthesia', where a sensation of one kind can be suggested by experiencing another; a certain musical note may provoke the image of a colour, for example. This was of importance to such artists of the period as Kandinsky. D'Udine compared man to a dynamo through which rhythmic synaesthetic inductive impulses pass. Human emotion, he asserted, is expressed in external movement and the sensation of movement can 'inductively' provoke in man that emotion that gave rise to the movement: 'For every emotion of whatever kind there is a corresponding body movement of some sort: it is through that movement that the complex synaesthetic transfer that accompanies any work of art is accomplished.' No doubt d'Udine was influenced by the popular ideas about James and Lange's work on emotion.

He goes on to explain that movement must be made rhythmical and that music is the synaesthetic effect of body movement: 'the ability to express feelings through musical combinations consists in nothing other than finding sound movements whose subtle rhythm corresponds to the body movement of someone experiencing enjoyment or suffering'.[50] Music imitates the internal rhythms that accompany the phenomena that exist in life. Rhythmicised body movements must be segmentary, that is, fixed in certain poses, crystallised in an immutable form and thus human expressive movement is analogous with musical notation that records a

---

[47] Garden Cities were built to combine the best elements of country and town life according to ideas outlined in Ebenezer Howard's *Tomorrow: A Peaceful Path to Real Reform* (1898).

[48] Richard C. Beacham, 'Appia, Jaques-Dalcroze, and Hellerau', Part One: 'Music Made Visible', *New Theatre Quarterly*, 2:1, 2 (1985), p. 159.

[49] Letter from Volkonsky to Stanislavsky, Petersburg 11 November 1913, MAT KS Archive 7626.

[50] Yampolskii, 'Kuleshov's Experiments' in Taylor and Christie (eds), *Film Factory*, p. 32.

melody. Therefore, art is the transmission of an emotion by means of stylised natural rhythm. These ideas had a widespread impact, including on Stanislavsky's *tempo-rhythm* and Meyerhold's *biomechanics*. Volkonsky refined these ideas in 'Man as Material for Art. Music. Body. Dance.' and 'Man and Rhythm: The System and School of Jacques-Dalcroze' (published in *The Person on the Stage – Chelovek na Stsene*) written in 1912. He describes how Dalcroze inculcated in his students an automatism of rhythmic movements: twelve-year-olds could beat out a 2/4 rhythm with their heads, 3/4 with one hand, 4/4 with the other and 5/4 with the feet.[51] Volkonsky, encapsulating the thinking of the time, wrote:

the most important thing in the human being is *the ability to receive impressions and to give expression*. Rhythmic Gymnastics teaches this…rhythm teaches impressionableness and gymnastics expressiveness…And expressiveness acts on impressionableness: movement which expresses music exactly and in this forming a true *picture* of feeling, arouses the *feeling itself*.[52]

Hence, a first condition for creation in art is the adoption of a different rhythm, whether in the voice, the movements of the body or in the soul's emotions and this different rhythm must be assimilated by the actor to the point where it becomes an unconscious automatism: 'Only by complete automatism of movements can the will and the mind return to themselves that independence and freedom of which they are deprived while the spiritual person is occupied with the bodily.'[53] Volkonsky gives an example of how our minds can be free while we are occupied with the most automatic of all our movements, that is, walking. He cites James to corroborate this, making several references to the *Textbook of Psychology*: 'habit simplifies and improves movements and reduces tiredness', and 'habit diminishes conscious attention'. Also, 'the most important thing is to make of the nervous system an ally and not an enemy.'[54]

The influence of Delsarte and Dalcroze in Russia

Yuri Erastovich Ozarovsky (1869–1924), actor, director and creator of a theory of stage speech, lectured on Delsarte from 1903, but Delsarte's ideas gained real popularity from 1910 to 1913, when Volkonsky published

---

[51] Prince Sergei Volkonskii, *Chelovek" na Stsene* (St Petersburg: Apollon, 1912), p. 153.
[52] *Ibid.* p. 175.
[53] *Ibid.* p. 151.
[54] *Ibid.* p. 151.

a series of articles on Delsarte and Dalcroze in the journal *Apollon*, and then published the books already mentioned. Centres for Dalcrozian eurhythmics were set up in Russia in the second decade of the twentieth century and Volkonsky started to publish the periodical *Papers of Rhythmic Gymnastics Courses (Listi kursov ritmicheskoi gimnastiki)* from 1913 to 1914. He also gave hundreds of lectures. In St Petersburg, D. M. Musina-Ozarovskaia founded a School for Stage Expressiveness, then the One Art Society, which set itself the aim of promoting a future synthesis of the arts based on Delsarte's system. The upsurge in interest in voice and the art of declamation or expressive reading resulted in the publication by Ozarovsky of the Delsartean journal *Voice and Speech*, which appeared monthly for several years from 1912. In 1913, V. K. Serezhnikov set up an establishment in Moscow to deliver courses in diction and declamation (including Delsartean gesture and Dalcroze's eurhythmics). From this the State Institute of Declamation (GID), which existed from 1919 to 1920, and the State Institute of the Word (GIS), from 1920 to 1922, were developed with the support of Lunacharsky. There was a proliferation of manuals on all aspects of voice and speech, written by members of these institutes, many of whom also published in *Voice and Speech*. Stanislavsky studied and drew ideas from some of these manuals, as detailed below, including those by Volkonsky, V. K. Serezhnikov, D. N. Ushakov and N. M. Safonov who taught 'orthophonics' and diction in singing at the Opera Studio. Volkonsky and Stanislavsky met in Rome in 1911 and discussed Stanislavsky's developing *system* and Volkonsky's work on voice. Stanislavsky invited him to the MAT later that year to lecture on Dalcroze's rhythmic gymnastics and he taught at the MAT and in the Opera Studio from after the revolution until his emigration. He organised a tour in 1912 and eurhythmics was taught in the First Studio from 1912. Volkonsky himself was still teaching there in 1919.[55] Stanislavsky's editors note that Stanislavsky's brother, V. S. Alekseev, taught Dalcroze's rhythmic gymnastics in the studios in the twenties and thirties (*AWHI*, p. 491, n4). Although it seems that Stanislavsky did not ultimately embrace the methods of Delsarte and Dalcroze with the fervour that others did, he was willing to experiment with them, as with other ways of developing the expressiveness of the body.

---

[55] Moscow Art Theatre, KS Archive 71. A timetable of studies for the young actors at MAT in November 1919 shows Volkonsky taking a number of sessions, classes in Rhythmic Gymnastics and Vakhtangov leading sessions on the *system*.

DEVELOPMENT OF THE EXPRESSIVENESS OF THE BODY

The training course described in *AWHE* and *AWHI*, with training first in the *psycho-technique* and then *incarnation*, was carried out in its fullest form late in Stanislavsky's life. A training school was set up from the beginnings of the MAT, where Nemirovich-Danchenko taught with others such as MAT actor Ioasaf Aleksandrovich Tikhomirov but, apparently, Stanislavsky's input was limited. Later, he worked in the studios with students on elements of the *system*. In 1919 he was doing so with the four studios, and then in 1920, with the Habimah studio on stage movement and rhythm. In 1922 he proposed organising physical training for young MAT actors under his general leadership; that is, courses of dances, *plastique*, rhythmics, declamation, for which other teachers would be invited as necessary. Later that year he made a statement on his work with nine studios: 'Concerning the technique in art, in these last years much has been done in the area of rhythm, phonetics, musicality, both from the point of view of diction and movement.'[56]

Gymnastics and acrobatics

In order to develop expressiveness, the students learnt gymnastics (including Swedish gymnastics, which Stanislavsky learned as a child), acrobatics, physical culture, stage fighting, fencing, and acrobatics for decisiveness (*AWHI*, p. 20). [See pictures 6 and 7]. Stanislavsky believed that 'gymnastics helps to correct the external apparatus of incarnation in a healthy way' (*AWHI*, p. 18). Russia followed Germany in the development of physical education. In the eighteenth century there had been Knight Schools in Europe, where young gentlemen were taught skills such as fencing, riding and dancing. These died out but Johann C. F. GutsMuths (1759–1839) re-established this training in Germany in the first part of the nineteenth century. The German national physical training movement, the Turnverein, which had begun in 1811, incorporated gymnastics, fencing and military exercises. Swedish gymnastics was developed in the early nineteenth century by Per Henrich Ling, who both studied anatomy and physiology and 'built up his practice empirically, proceeding by experience and observation of the effects of his exercises'.[57]

---

[56] Vinogradskaia, *Letopis*, vol. 3, p. 247.
[57] P. C. MacIntosh, et al., *Landmarks in the History of Physical Education* (London: Routledge and Kegan Paul, 1957), p. 92.

6. Exercises in acrobatics in the Opera-dramatic Studio.

7. Exercises in the Opera-dramatic Studio: methods of stage fighting.

Stanislavsky may have approved of fencing as actor-training because it had formed part of his own education. There would then be no scientific justification for its inclusion in a training programme except that which exists for fencing, other than if needed for a scene in a play. The idea, as with acrobatics, was that it enabled the actor to develop decisiveness, although this is questionable; why should the ability to respond quickly in acrobatics or fencing equate with the ability to respond quickly on stage? Although Stanislavsky questions the inclusion of certain elements into his training, he does not always examine them fully and sometimes brings in ideas a priori. Such exercise forms may have been originally in scientific theory, such as Ling gymnastics, but this was the science and anatomy of a century or more previous to Stanislavsky's time and based, therefore, on information that might be outdated. The same applies to his inclusion of ballet and dance in the training curriculum.

Ballet and dance

Stanislavsky writes that ballet corrects the body, opening up movements, giving them definition and finish, and corrects hands, legs and the spine and puts them in place (*AWHE*, p. 22). Ballet had long been included in actor-training in dramatic schools and many nineteenth-century actors undertook ballet training. However, Stanislavsky also suggests that ballet can result in movement that is too mannered, and that many ballet dancers have hands and fingers that are dead or stiff (p. 23). Isadora Duncan's school provided a better training for the actor's hands. In summary, Stanislavsky says here, 'we need only to borrow from [ballet] the amazing capacity for work and the knowledge of how to work on one's body'. The question is why it is included at all as training for the non-dancing actor. Ballet had survived the revolution, partly perhaps because of the fame of Sergei Diaghilev and the Ballets Russes, whose work was 'intended to make the cultural world of Western Europe marvel at the theatrical secrets of Russia',[58] despite the fact that the company was in exile after the revolution. As Iampolsky writes, the 'spread of the new anthropology was facilitated by the flowering of Russian ballet, which with Duncan's work, seemed to be the principal expression of a new model of actor and man.'[59] The Delsarte system had been taken up in America in the early-twentieth century by

---

[58] A. Adamson, 'The Russian Imperial Ballet', in Robert Leach and Victor Borovsky (eds), *A History of Russian Theatre* (Cambridge University Press, 1999), p. 197.
[59] Yampolsky, 'Kuleshov's Experiments', in Taylor and Christie (eds), *Film Factory*, p. 36.

actors and dancers, including Isadora Duncan, who in turn was in great vogue in Russia and was respected by Stanislavsky. Meyerhold mentions her frequently, though often disparagingly, in his writings. Stanislavsky, as he writes in *MLIA*, was a balletomane (p. 140), and he was a great admirer of Duncan's dramatic expressiveness in her dance. The reasons for the inclusion of these art forms in his training may have been tradition, and his enjoyment of them as art forms.

Stanislavsky introduced classes in Dalcroze's eurhythmics in 1911, at the same time as he introduced some elements of yoga to the MAT actors, but the reception was hostile. As well as the classes taught by Stanislavsky's brother, V. S. Alekseev, from 1919 there were lessons in stage movement according to Dalcroze led by Kholevinskaia in the Opera Studio.[60] In *AWHI* the students learn that they are to have classes in Dalcroze's rhythmic gymnastics alongside classes in *plastique*, but here Stanislavsky states that what is more important is the latter (p. 28).

In general, Stanislavsky had problems with developing the actor's capacity for physical expression or *plastique*. He stated in 1919 that 'studies of plastique in the form that they now take are able to bring little benefit to our art'. (He is referring to ballet and dance.) He added that what was needed was a 'gymnastics which can make all the muscles of the body mobile'.[61] In the chapter on *plastique* in *AWHI* Tortsov states that 'what we need are simple, expressive, sincere movements with internal content. Where can we find them?' (p. 29). The rest of the section is devoted firstly to a discussion of walking, and an attempt to get the students to adopt a 'soaring gait' instead of a 'crawling' one. The basic premise of this is the technically incorrect notion that the legs work as springs. The second part of the chapter focuses on a description of the mercury exercise, where the students move parts of their limbs as if a drop of mercury were travelling through them, in turn, for example, shoulder, upper arm, lower arm, wrist, hand, fingers, to an increasingly faster rhythm until the entire movement acquires smoothness and plasticity. According to Tortsov, the feeling of this inner line of the movement of energy is the secret of external *plastique* (p. 37).

Stanislavsky was seeking to resolve the problem of teaching actors to move with the freedom he so admired in great actors. He always maintained that this freedom of movement was crucial for the performers even when teaching singers. Antarova, one of Stanislavsky's students at the

---

[60] Vinogradskaia, *Letopis*, vol. 3, p. 104.
[61] *Ibid.* p. 46.

Opera Studio, noted from one of Stanislavsky's lectures, 'the first signpost which helps to set free the whole man for his creative stage problems is, of course, the function of the body – movement'.[62] However, in the period when he was working, his knowledge of the workings of the human organism were limited. His other problem was that there were few opportunities for him to fully test his ideas. In April 1933 he was still arguing at general meetings that the programme for training actors should be supplemented by movement disciplines, that is, gymnastics, acrobatics, dance, fencing, rhythmics, deportment, *plastique* and work on speech (placing voice, diction, singing, expressive reading, laws of speech).[63] The Opera Studio was where he had the freest hand in implementing his training methods.

VOICE: SINGING, PLACING THE VOICE, DICTION, LAWS OF SPEECH

The Opera Studio

Towards the end of 1918, E. K. Malinovskaia, the manager of the academic theatres in Moscow, approached the MAT to see whether there was a way to help improve the standard of acting at the Bolshoi Theatre. Benedetti reports that in 1919 when Stanislavsky began teaching a small group of singers from the Bolshoi, he initially had reservations; he had not worked in the musical sphere since his youth and was aware that established singers might well be resistant to further training. The Opera Studio of the Bolshoi Theatre was founded with young singers from the Bolshoi and students from the Conservatoire under the direction of Stanislavsky.[64] Three performances were mounted, Massenet's *Werther* (1921), Tchaikovsky's *Evgeny Onegin* (1922) and Cimarosa's *The Secret Marriage* (1924), all to great acclaim. Thirty-two lectures on the *system* as it was taught at that time, and the rehearsals of *Werther*, were recorded between 1919 and 1922 by Konkordia Antarova, a singer who became one of Stanislavsky's assistants.

The studio was later separated from the Bolshoi, from 1924 it was called the Stanislavsky Opera Studio, from 1926 the Opera Studio-Theatre and from 1928 the Stanislavsky Opera Theatre. Stanislavsky continued to direct operas here until his death. A new Opera-dramatic

---

[62] Stanislavsky, *Stanislavsky on the Art of the Stage*, p. 215.
[63] Vinogradskaia, *Letopis*, vol. 4, p. 249.
[64] Jean Benedetti, *Stanislavski: His Life in Art*, 2nd edn (London: Methuen, 1999). pp. 255–6.

Studio was formed in 1935. The studio members were working on a production of Verdi's *Rigoletto* when Stanislavsky died in 1938. The production was completed by Meyerhold. In 1935 Stanislavsky began a project working with a group of assistants at the new Opera-dramatic Studio to run a four-year training course with a particular emphasis on the *method of physical actions*. Novitskaia, one of the assistants, recorded the training in *Uroki Vdokhnovenii (Inspiring Lessons)*:

Stanislavsky proposed organising not a usual drama studio but an opera-drama studio to study the method of physical actions . . . Konstantin Sergeevich gave particular attention to musical theatre in the Soviet period. KS thought that uniting future dramatic and opera students in a studio would enrich both; the drama students would approach voice work, intonation, tempo-rhythm more seriously and would understand the importance of music in art: and the opera students would appreciate the necessity of learning about true communion with the partner, action on stage.'[65]

He died before the end of the course, so the assistants completed it. This course of training was the most complete implementation of the exercises described in Stanislavsky's books.

Various manuscripts describing aspects of the training programme of the Opera-dramatic Studio are included in *AWHI* including 'Staging the programme', the text for a presentation where a master of ceremonies takes an audience through the training programme with the aid of placards and by demonstrating études (pp. 429–89). In addition, Pavel Rumyantsev joined the Opera Studio at the age of twenty, in 1920. He wrote an account of the three operas produced between 1921 and 1924 and Stanislavsky's methods of working, including some details of Stanislavsky's training of the young singers, published as *Stanislavski on Opera*:

The theory of the Stanislavski acting 'system', daily exercises to music, sketches acted out for the purpose of giving a basis to the most varied kind of body positions, movements in space, the freeing of muscular tenseness and finally the principal and most interesting work, the singing of arias and lyrical ballads (in the execution of which the students synthesized all the component parts of the 'system') – all this preparatory work was done by the students before they began to put on any Studio productions.[66]

---

[65] L. P. Novitskaia, *Uroki Vdokhnoveniya: sistema K. S. Stanislavskogo v deistvii* (Moscow: Vserossiskaia Teatral'naia Organizatsia, 1984), pp. 13–14.

[66] P. I. Rumiantsev, *Stanislavski on Opera*, tr. Elizabeth Reynolds Hapgood (New York: Theatre Arts Books, 1975), p. 2. By 'sketches' Rumiantsev is referring to 'études'.

Stanislavsky also gave lectures. The training lasted from 1921 to 1926, with half of each day being devoted to class activities and half to rehearsing for performance. Stanislavsky's assistants included his sister Zinaida Sokolova and his brother Vladimir Alekseev. Stanislavsky set two goals for the students, the first being to achieve expressive and incisive diction as 'not a single word must fail to reach the audience'. The second goal was to free themselves from tension, especially in the arms, wrists and fingers, 'for the purpose of achieving easy, simple, handling of themselves onstage'. Rumiantsev explains that all these exercises were done to music 'in order to make every movement consonant with musical rhythms' (see figure 8).

The students stood in a semicircle and while music was played they went through various forms of gymnastics, such as eight quarter notes for the raising of the arms, elbows, hands and fingers, and eight quarter notes for their relaxation and return to position. Relaxing the hands, they swung them, and then did the same with the forearm. Standing on one leg, they were to relax the foot and rotate it, then the lower leg, rotating the knee. The neck was relaxed by throwing the head forward and rolling it from side to side, then sitting, throwing the head backwards. Relaxing the muscles of the torso and chest was also required and these exercises were seen as just as important as *vocalisi*, which are wordless exercises sung on vowels.

Smooth walking was practised to slow music. Then the tempo was increased but the smoothness had to be maintained. Arms and hands were exercised as in ballet training except each movement had to be *justified*. Dancing was included: all students had to be able to dance mazurkas, waltzes, polonaises, schottisches. The students were required to do fencing, as it was claimed that it prepared the actor to execute all sorts of actions on stage. According to Rumyantsev, duelling with rapiers obliges an actor

to combine the working tensions of his legs and whole body with an extremely flexible lightness in the use of his arms, especially his hands and this can be accomplished only by sharp attention to the condition of his entire physical apparatus. But the main point . . . was that each duel was the best possible training for concentration of willpower and attention, for the development of an inner interrelationship with a partner, for the always necessary study of one's opponent.

Furthermore, Rumyantsev writes that it was always stressed that movement without *justification*, or the establishing of some *given circumstances*, is just 'ballet'; that is to say they are beautiful poses that lack inner meaning.[67]

[67] *Ibid.* pp. 4–7.

8. Exercises in rhythm in the Opera-dramatic Studio.

One of the ideas that Stanislavsky brought to the training of opera singers was that this movement training was as essential for them as it was for actors. He also had ideas about voice that dated back to his youth. Stanislavsky intended as a young man to be an opera singer and worked in the 1880s with Fedor Kommisarzhevsky, professor at the Moscow Conservatoire. He did not pursue this career because of vocal problems.[68] However, this early training as a singer and his lifelong interest in opera is significant. He mentions many opera singers in his writing and acknowledges the influence of Fiodor Chaliapin, who was famous as an exponent of bel canto, the term for singing as practised by the great Italian singers of the eighteenth and early-nineteenth centuries. This was characterised by its lyrical rather than declamatory style, its beauty of tone, legato phrasing and the faultless technique of the singers.

Stanislavsky believed that voice in itself could affect the hearer profoundly. He wrote that his early experiences of Italian opera made an impression not just on his 'aural and visual memory, but physically, that is I sensed them not just with my feeling but my whole body' (*MLIA*, p. 70). He relates a story of walking up an alley in Rome in 1911, thirty-five years after hearing Cotogni sing in Moscow. He heard someone singing a note in a house on the street and immediately recognised (that is, 'felt', as he puts it), that it was Cotogni (p. 72). It is not just a sound but the word or *word-thought*, which *infects* the hearer (for example, 'I love' – *liubliu* – one word in Russian). Stanislavsky and Sulerzhitsky used the term *word-thought* to emphasise the word's inner content. Stanislavsky is keen to stress that this is also action. 'The Greek word – ἄγω – I act – already tells you of the great force of the word-thought flung into the crowd from the stage. The power of an actor's thought bursts like a high-explosive shell among the people.'[69]

If this is conveyed rather than the word just being pronounced mechanically, Stanislavsky believed a word can arouse all five senses. Another example is given of someone reading about toothache in *MLIA* and getting toothache as a result (*AWHI*, p. 81). Moreover, *feeling-thought-word*, the spiritual image of thought, must always bear the stamp of truth; it must be the law that enables every man to communicate facts as man sees them.[70] For this, the actor's attention is essential: 'Thought-feeling-word – everything is rolled around the familiar cylinder, round

---

[68] Benedetti, *Stanislavski: His Life in Art*, p. 20.
[69] Stanislavsky, *Stanislavsky on the Art of the Stage*, p. 225.
[70] *Ibid.* p. 116.

the attention you have to devote to the man whom you are now concerned to depict.'[71] Antarova quotes Stanislavsky: 'There must be some object to attract a man's attention to itself as well as time for the attention to assume the form of thought, which, communicated through the brain centres, finds expression in word and action.'[72]

True to Tolstoy, Stanislavsky thought that his speaking of a text should communicate artistic truth to the hearer, as well as the content of the text itself. Like Vakhtangov and Michael Chekhov,[73] Stanislavsky believed that the actor should be able to communicate with an audience when speaking in a foreign language (*AWHI*, p. 105). He is fond of quoting Salvini, who, when asked what was needed in an actor in order to play tragedy, replied, 'Voice, voice and more voice!' (*MLIA*, p. 455). What is communicated is the actor's *experiencing*, but the way the actor does this, his vocal means of communication, is important. In a speech given at MAAT in 1919, Stanislavsky quotes Chaliapin saying, 'every word has a soul', and adds 'when the word has ceased to be a simple external sign and has begun to express the life of the human soul we can talk about real diction'.[74]

Development of the vocal training programme

From the beginning of Stanislavsky's training work for actors there is an emphasis on voice. In 1900 he wrote about *vocalisi*, and the importance of rhythm for the actor.[75] He rejected the traditional techniques of drama schools where students were taught to imitate the teacher technically, for example, in diction classes the students imitated the teacher's style, which might, Stanislavsky says, have been that of false pathos. Also, singing teachers 'placed' the voices of drama students (*MLIA*, pp. 124–5). Stanislavsky often speaks of 'placing the voice', which involves the discovery of one's natural pitch in speech and other aspects of training. He discusses whether there are different considerations for speaking and singing. In vocal work he was also seeking 'the sense of true measure': 'The most difficult thing on the stage is to speak neither more quietly nor loudly than necessary and to be simple and natural' (p. 100). He later writes, 'let us learn to speak simply, in an elevated way, beautifully, musically but without any vocal flourishes, actorly pathos and tricks of stage speech. We

---

[71] *Ibid.* p. 124.
[72] *Ibid.* p. 141.
[73] Mikhail Chekhov, *Vospominania, Pisma* (Moscow: Lokid-Press, 2001), p. 137–8.
[74] Vinogradskaia, *Letopis*, vol. 3, p. 46.
[75] *Ibid.* vol. 1, p. 293.

want the same thing in movements and actions. Let them be simple ...
We have theatricality in the theatre' (p. 214). And the challenge for the
actor is to discover how can the sound of this 'human organ, which is so
material and coarse, express that which is abstract, elevated, noble?' (p. 356).

Again for Stanislavsky, the answer is in a 'secret of nature'. Stanislavsky
relates an anecdote (on more than one occasion and in various versions)
where he is with a companion who has a weak voice which training has
not helped. In a situation of danger, however (where he and the companion are set upon by sheepdogs or robbers), the companion cries out
for help with a loud and resonant voice: 'That means that the whole
thing is in whether you feel the role, then everything will come by itself.'
Stanislavsky recollects that in 'Artistic Youth' he attempted to achieve this
directly, but discovered that trying to 'feel', to be 'inspired', results only
in muscle spasms and 'the heavy speech of a dimwit' (*MLIA*, p. 357).

In *AWHI* the students are taught to place their voices, to use the facial
mask and resonators. These techniques may owe something to bel canto,
but Stanislavsky claimed his own system for placing the voice since
rehearsing *Othello* in 1895, when he again had problems with hoarseness,
because his voice had been placed for singing; it had been 'forced inwards
and I tensed my diaphragm and throat so much that it could not res-
onate'. His voice grew and it became easier to speak so he could get
through the play, though with difficulty (*MLIA*, pp. 230–1).

In 1909 he was instrumental in changing the programme at the Art
Theatre School. There were to be no classes in diction and declamation
until a new programme was developed. Speech on stage was no longer to be
taught through students learning to recite poetry.[76] He held that singing
for the actor developed breathing and intonation. He asserted that declamation is a *stencil* (p. 356), and that declamatory and poetic speech is the
opposite to simple, strong, noble speech (p. 453). The *craft* actor's voice is
sugary-sounding in lyrical places, a boring monotone when reciting epic
poetry, with sonorous and actorly speech when expressing hatred, and false
tears in the voice in the expression of sorrow (*AWHE*, p. 76).

His search continued. In 1915, while playing the part of Salieri, he
realised that all his life he had spoken badly on stage and he did not know
how to express 'what was inside' (*MLIA*, p. 452). He decided that he
needed to look at voice in life as well as on the stage. The search continued
for the rest of his life, working with voice trainers such as Volkonsky and
consulting manuals.

---

[76] Vinogradskaia, *Letopis*, vol. 2, p. 189.

Volkonsky

The Expressive Word was published in 1913 and Stanislavsky made notes from it in 1920. As a foreword, Volkonsky quotes Goethe,[77] 'every art must be preceded by some mechanical knowledge'.[78] The book, as well as comprising a plea for training includes a description of the breathing mechanism, three kinds of breathing, breathing exercises, exercises on vowels and consonants, pitch intervals in questions, intonation, stress, and the logical and psychological pause. In the MAT archive there is also a copy of Volkonsky's *Laws of Living Speech and Rules of Reading: intonation, intervals, stress and logical and psychological pauses*. There are also notes from a manuscript entitled *Laws of Speech*, which cover the same topics in more detail.

Volkonsky, as mentioned, taught classes on diction at the Opera Studio from 1919 and in the other studios. In 1922 Stanislavsky wrote, 'Volkonsky's mistake is that he always seeks a result and it is necessary to create it. But Volkonsky is necessary.'[79] Stanislavsky was no doubt referring to the emphasis in Volkonsky's writings on achieving the results of good diction, intonation and pauses, which could be done without the inner content so important to Stanislavsky. Benedetti writes that in the thirties, 'Having used methods of voice training based on the work of Volkonsky for many years he abandoned them as too rigid and liable to mechanical repetition without thought or inner justification.'[80] At this point Stanislavsky was collating his work for publication of his books, and he still refers to Volkonsky in the books, although he may have stopped using the exercises in practice.

The problems Stanislavsky sought to solve were, firstly, the balance between inner content and outer technique, which had presented itself so vividly to him in the Salieri crisis. He complained in a draft of a letter in 1923 about the acting of tragedy, that 'Rhythm, phonetics and vocal graphics, as well as the correct placing and good diction is one of the most powerful and least known methods in our art' (*Collected Works*, vol. 8, 1st

---

[77] Stanislavsky referred to Goethe's *Rules for Actors*, published in 1803, there is a typescript of it in the MAT archive. It enumerates rules of diction, which Goethe insists must be pure and clear, and also positions, gestures and behaviour on stage. It describes the rhythm and musicality of speech. He noted however that Goethe had come up with ninety-two rules for the theatre, about how the actor should stand and so on, but then 'wrote in despair to Schiller and asked him to find the internal side of the theatre' (KS Archive 833, p. 23).

[78] Prince Sergei Volkonskii, *Vyrazitel'noe Slovo* (St. Petersburg: Apollon, 1913), p. 6.

[79] Vinogradskaia, *Letopis*, vol. 3, p. 205.

[80] Jean Benedetti, *Stanislavski: An Introduction* (London: Methuen, 1989), p. 50.

edn, p. 62). Rumyantsev notes Stanislavsky saying (Reynolds Hapgood's italics):

When you are learning the text and music of a role, be extremely careful not ever to go over it by rote, but always combine it with the inner course of your part. Relate the enunciation, the text, the music all to the through-line of action that goes through your whole role. This is how I interpret this thing. A role is not made interesting by words alone but by what the actor puts into them.[81]

The other problem was that Stanislavsky on more than one occasion suffered from vocal strain. He had been unable to pursue his career as a singer. He mentions vocal strain in relation to *Othello*, produced in 1896 (*MLIA*, p. 230). In 1922 Stanislavsky was touring with the Art Theatre in America. He once again began to have problems; his voice was hoarse and weak, and so he did daily the exercises he had learned from Kommi-sarzhevsky, M. G. Gukova and A. V. Bogdanovich from the Bolshoi Opera Studio. His neighbour complained about the noise, so Stanislavsky practised these exercises at half-volume and after two years of daily work, he reports, got his voice strong enough for singing; according to Novitskaia he got inside a wardrobe and sang so as not to disturb anyone and the result was that when he returned home Nemirovich-Danchenko did not recognise his voice on the telephone.[82] Precisely what these exercises were is not known and whether they were efficacious or whether he got better for other reasons is questionable.

Voice and speech in AWHI

AWHI divides the subject *Voice and Speech* into two: *Singing and Diction* and *Speech and its Laws*. There are additional sections from incomplete manuscripts entitled, 'On the Musicality of Speech', 'From the Manuscript "Laws of Speech"', and 'On the Perspective of Speech'. When writing about the voice Stanislavsky, unusually, gives references to some texts from which he draws ideas about voice work, rather than just citing his own experience and experiments.

On 'Singing and Diction', in a section entitled 'Placing the Voice for Singing', he describes how he trained himself to sing opera; he understood the importance of placing the voice in the facial mask, that is, in the front part of the face where the hard palate, nasal cavities, antrum

---

[81] Rumyantsev, *Stanislavski on Opera*, p. 293.
[82] Novitskaya, *Uroki Vdokhnoveniya*, p. 123.

of Highmore and other resonators are situated (p. 53). (The antrum of Highmore is the cavity of the upper jaw.)

He practised this at a quarter voice, also making 'mooing' sounds (p. 55). This gave a nasal quality to his voice, but he found that by identifying and releasing tension within his nose he could achieve resonant, ringing tones. He then found that lowering his head and chin allowed the note to come as far forward as possible, a strategy, he states, which is endorsed by singers (p. 56). However, he believed that there was an unpleasant 'gypsy twang' to his voice. By exploring the resonators of the hard palate, soft palate, the top and back of the head, he was able to overcome this and add new colours to his voice (p. 57). He discovered another secret, which was the 'yawn' on the high notes. He was told by a singing teacher that tension will be released when singing on a high note if the throat and pharynx are placed as if one is yawning (p. 58).

He also consulted Serezhnikov's *The Technique of Speech* (1924). Professor Vasily Serezhnikov had conducted scientific experiments into the difference between spoken and sung sounds, looking at overtones and pitch.[83] Stanislavsky asserts, with Sereznikov, that speech is musical. Chaliapin, according to Stanislavsky's editors, is the opera singer he is referring to when he says that when the voice is correctly placed, one should speak as one sings (*AWHI*, 1st edn, p. 462, n16). It took some time for Stanislavsky to learn what this meant because it was not simply a question of placing his voice in the facial mask in speaking. The problem was that he had spoken incorrectly all his life and had to learn to pay constant attention to the placing of his voice (p. 68). The result of this was the *'same unbroken line of sound as I had developed in singing and without which there cannot be any genuine art of the word'* (p. 69).

Excerpts in the MAT archive from *The Art of Declamation* (1919), by V. V. Sladkopevtsev, an actor from the Suvorin Theatre and one of Michael Chekhov's teachers, include the statement, by Salvini, underlined by Stanislavsky that 'soon I realised that singing and declamation are incompatible, as the methods of placing the voice are completely different in both cases and must harm one another'.[84] Stanislavsky does not make a definitive statement on the issue of placing the voice, but asserts as his main argument that it is as essential to train the voice of the actor as the singer (*MLIA*, pp. 449–56) and uses methods taken from traditions of singing, his own experiments and what he has read.

---

[83] V. Serezhnikov, Iskusstvo Khudozhestvennoe Chtenia: tom 2, *Tekhnika Rechi*, 2nd edn (Moscow-Petrograd: Makiz, 1924), pp. 45–6.

[84] V. V. Sladkopevtsev, *Iskusstvo Dekcamatsii* (St Petersburg, Teatr i Iskusstvo, 1910).

In the section in *AWHI* on diction, Tortsov makes impassioned speeches about the importance of good diction, and states that it took him many years to arrive at the realisation that the actor must 'feel' each syllable and every letter as well as the word and phrase (*AWHI*, p. 59). The students are taught technically about producing sounds of vowels and consonants. Here Stanislavsky cites Volkonsky's *The Expressive Word*: 'consonants are the riverbanks which contain the flow of the vowels'.[85] The students do exercises to practise each letter. The exercises are not just in diction to improve their articulation, as each letter is examined for its expressive potential; for example, a joyous 'a', an ominous 'a', a ponderous 'a' and so on: 'All sounds that words are formed from have their soul, nature, content. If the word is not connected with life and is pronounced formally, mechanically, insipidly, soullessly, then it is like a corpse. The living word is saturated internally' (*AWHI*, p. 61).

Serezhnikov's books, *The Music of the Word* and *The Technique of Speech*, both published in 1924, assert that the external production of sound cannot be divorced from inner content. Ozarovsky's distinction between *psychological* and *physical timbre* is quoted in an excerpt written out for Stanislavsky by an assistant:

The usual 'physical' timbre of a person's voice depends on these additional sounds. On the other hand, the usual timbre undergoes changes dependent on the changes in feelings. A certain psychological feeling which seizes a person evokes mimic changes in his organs in general and the vocal apparatus in particular chest, neck, head. This physiological process gives its reflection in the facial expression, and the facial expression is reflected in the timbre aspect of the voice. From hence comes the rule: tone is born in facial expression. Compare the colourations of voice of the same person in resting and excited states, and you will hear a difference in timbre. Such a particular colour of the voice, as distinct from the usual, habitual, physical one, Ozarovsky calls 'psychological timbre'.[86]

There are excerpts written out by Gurevich for Stanislavsky in the MAT archive from *The Music of Speech*, *Aesthetic Research*, by Leonid Sabaneev, published in 1924. Sabaneev taught in the Opera Studio. The excerpts include a discussion of the fact that the range of intonation, the diapason, in human speech is comparatively narrow, usually less than an octave, and 'only strong emotions (anger, joy, fright), take the speech melody beyond

---

[85] Volkonsky, *Vyrazitel'noe Slovo*, p. 57.
[86] V. Serezhnikov, *Iskusstvo Khudozhestvennogo Chtenia: tom 1, Muzika Slova* (Moscow-Petrograd: Gosudarstvennoe Izdatelstvo, 1923), pp. 127–8.

these boundaries'.[87] This confirms Stanislavsky's view that nature holds the secrets of voice. In the *Singing and Diction* section there is a reference to D. N. Ushakov's *Short Introduction to the Science of Language* (1923). This is one of the earliest works on linguistics in Russian by an academic (who later became a foremost lexicographer). There are sections on morphology, language and dialect developments, and also 'the psychology of speech' and the physiology of speech and phonetics. The sections on the psychology of speech emphasise the fact that the external production of sound should not be divorced from its inner content, a point Stanislavsky is very anxious to make.

In the section 'Speech and its Laws' Stanislavsky recommends again *The Expressive Word*, which draws on Dr Rush's *Philosophy of the Human Voice* (one of the earliest books on voice, written in 1833), Oscar Guttman's *Gymnastics of the Voice* and Genevieve Stebbins's *Dynamic Breathing and Harmonic Gymnastics*. Like Volkonsky, Stebbins and Guttman were Delsarteans. Volkonsky states that in his mission to establish the need for speech training for the actor he consulted many texts:

The bibliography for our question is . . . wide, but . . . mostly one-sided. There is more interest in research than instructions. In the research there is more interest in the anatomy of the speech apparatus than its relationship with the logic and psychology of speech. Only some American works . . . have satisfied me . . . with practical instructions . . . which aim to give a meaning to the complicated mechanism of speech, which are interested in speech not only as an articulate emission of sound but as expressive of our thoughts and feelings. Dr Rush's work is particularly valuable. Those principles are at the basis of this book. The breathing exercises are partly from Oscar Guttman 'Gymnastics of the Voice' and Stebbins's 'Dynamic Breathing and Harmonic Gymnastics'.[88]

Stanislavsky took from Volkonsky the concept of *pauses* (*logical and psychological*) and *stress* and *intonation*, including *intervals* in speech on stage.

Stress, pauses and intonation

Stanislavsky quotes rules from *The Expressive Word* about stressed and unstressed adjectives (p. 120). There is a need for *perspective* in speech as in painting so that the important word stands out against less important ones (p. 123): 'Stress can be combined with intonation . . . among all the

---

[87] Leonid Sabaneev, *Muzika Rechi* (Moscow: Rabotnik Prosveshchenie, 1923), p. 47.
[88] Volkonsky, *Vyrazitel'noe Slovo*, p. 12.

demarcated and undemarcated words it is necessary to find the correspondence, the gradation of power, the quality of stress and to create from
them sound planes and perspective giving movement and life to the
phrase' (p. 124–5). A reference is made to I. L. Smolensky's *A Manual for
the Study of Declamation*, 1907: 'It is self-evident that the general picture
of logical perspective will also be achieved with **distributive** stresses,
which will always be weaker than logical ones' (*AWHI*, p. 147). Stanislavsky's editors note that the term 'distributive' means additional stresses
in a phrase defining the quantity of clauses in its composition (p. 494,
n16). These degrees of stress are 'felt by reflex' in music. Stanislavsky gives an
example he attributes to Smolensky from Mussorgsky's *Boris Godunov*;
'There call the people to a feast, *all* from boyars to the beggarly blind man, *all*
are free to come, *all* the guests are dear' (*AWHI*, p. 147).

TOP (logical or psychological pause)

Intonation is exemplified by Volkonsky's diagram (p. 99). There are
also exercises in *intonation* in contrasting high and low sounds and in
transitions from *piano* to *forte* and so on.

Intonation, pausing, stress and perspective should all be studied, but
Stanislavsky also emphasises the necessity for deep penetration into the
internal essence of words (p. 139–40). He writes that *intonations* and
pauses by themselves can have a power of emotional influence on the
audience (p. 105). Elsewhere, he states, to the *logical* pause (of the mind)
you can add the *psychological pauses* (of feeling) that are creative nature,
intuition, imagination and the subconscious (p. 128). Logical pauses

unite words into groups or measures of speech (read according to the punctuation marks), and divide groups from each other. *Psychological pauses* involve the gaze, facial expression, *sending out rays*, hints, scarcely perceptible movements and subconscious means of communication (p. 103). They also reveal the *subtext* (p. 94).[89]

Subtext

Stanislavsky contrasts mechanical speech, which can result from our speaking text written by the author that is in conflict with our own needs and desires, with speaking for a purpose as we do in life. The former is an example of *dislocation*. Also, when actors speak mechanically, it can mean that they are not listening to each other or that they are 'consciously giving the words of the role an incorrect designation . . . using the text to show the quality of their vocal material, diction, manner of declamation and technique . . . putting vocal cadences and figures in their voices' (pp. 78–9).

What is needed, he says, is the notion of the *subtext*:

This is not apparent, but it is the internally perceived 'life of the human spirit of the role', which flows unbroken under the words of the text, all the time justifying and enlivening them. In the subtext there are many varied lines of the role and the play, woven from the magic 'ifs', from various inventions of the imagination, from given circumstances, internal action, objects of attention, small and large truths and belief in them, adaptations and other elements. It is that which makes us pronounce the words of the role . . . leading to the superobjective . . . that which in the region of action we call through-action, we call the subtext . . . in the domain of speech (p. 80).

The actors must work on their speech, vocal and other apparatuses of incarnation to make them sensitive, because we use them to convey our internal feelings, thoughts and visions, which are stirred by nature, the subconscious or intuition (p. 83).

The word is not just a sound, but arouses images, which speak to the eye as much as the ear (p. 84). Tortsov says that he 'doesn't believe'[90] Shustov's improvised story because he is not creating pictures in his imagination internally (p. 89). One of the main elements of the *subtext* is

---

[89] Stites writes that the Moscow Cabaret *The Bat* (which name was a jibe at the MAT seagull logo) parodied 'the portentous Moscow Art Theatre and its famous Stanislavsky pauses'. Richard Stites, *Russian Popular Culture* (Cambridge University Press, 1992), p. 22. It developed from MAT's cabbage parties, which Stanislavsky describes in the last part of *MLIA* where MAT's actors parodied themselves.

[90] Stanislavsky's famous phrase, which caused consternation to many an actor, though Suler is said to have turned the tables on Stanislavsky with it. It was ridiculed in Bulgakov's *Theatrical Novel* (translated as *Black Snow*) and used by Grotowski in his work with actors.

the capricious *memory of experienced emotions* (p. 90). The *subtext* may be conscious, but in *pauses* there is often that part of the subtext that comes from the *subconscious*, which does not give itself to concrete verbal expression (p. 103). Shustov is given an *object*, that is, Maloletkova. He must tell his story to her and make her perceive the *subtext*. The task of making others see our visions gives us activeness (*aktivnost'*) (pp. 87–9). It appears that the *subtext* is synonymous with *experiencing*.

Perspective

Tortsov gives a rendition of a speech from *Othello* and after each phrase gives an account of his thought processes on the technical use of stress, intonation and the other laws of speech. Kostia is confused and upset. He does not understand how there can be such technical and professional calculation where he expected inspiration (p. 148). Tortsov explains that this does not mean performing mechanically. He resolves Kostia's dismay at his professional calculation in the speech from *Othello*, by explaining to him about the difference between the *perspective of the role*, and the *perspective of the actor*, the stream of *psycho-technique*. He quotes from Salvini to explain the double life of the actor (p. 150), which is the same, in effect, as Diderot's actor and onlooker (the difference being that Stanislavsky's actor *experiences*.

Breathing

Stanislavsky's House Museum contains D. Koroviakov's *Studies in Expressive Reading* (1900), S. D. Robezh's, *The Technique of Singing* (1925), N. E. Shirokova's, *Deep Breathing and Muscle Strain in Singing* (2nd edn, 1910), and Iu. Ozarovsky's *Music of the Living Word* (1914), but there are no direct references in Stanislavsky's work to these texts.

Novitskaia describes Stanislavsky's work on preparing the apparatus of speech. As well as exercises in placing the voice and diction, there was work on the development of 'correct breathing'.[91] Neither she nor Stanislavsky describe what this work was, but in 1920 he made extensive notes on Yogi Olga Lobanova's *Breathe Properly or the Teaching of the Indian Yogis about Breathing Altered by the West* (1915). Lobanova acknowledges a debt to Leo Kofler, who published *Art of Breathing as the Basis of Tone-Production*, published in America in 1887, which had widespread impact. Kofler sang as a young man, but suffered vocal strain

---

[91] Novitskaia, *Uroki Vdokhnoveniia*, p. 122.

and began to investigate why this might be. He studied physiology, particularly of voice, respiration and works on voice, including those by Guttman. He developed a system of 'breathing gymnastics', which, he claimed, enabled him to cure himself of consumption. He identified different sorts of breathing: clavicular, rib and diaphagm breathing, a classification which twenty-first century physiology rejects.[92] *Breathe Properly* contains sections on 'everyday breathing', 'breathing and singing', 'breathing during speech', and 'the gymnastics of breathing'. There is a distinction between types of breathing: high breathing, rib breathing and diaphragmatic/abdominal breathing, which is the same as Kofler's distinction. Correct breathing, it is stated, is diaphragmatic breathing.[93] Kofler also recommends that inhalation must be involuntary and through the nose. In singing the performer must take in the greatest quantity of air with the least strain. There is attention to the position of the head and relaxing neck muscles. Lobanova adopted Kofler's exercises. They are similar to the breathing exercises of both Ramacharaka and Muller. They consist of adopting different positions, inhaling holding the breath and exhaling to a count, with the aim of increasing the elasticity of the lungs, expanding the rib cage, gaining control of the breathing apparatus and improving vocal tone and duration. Their efficacy would now be questionable.

Antarova notes that Stanislavsky drew a connection between attention and breathing: 'What happens to you when you are distressed, cross, irritated or when you fly into a rage? All the functions of your breathing are upset.' He goes on to say that this means that the development of the powers on which creative work depends, which include attention and respiration, must be placed under control. Calm breathing means healthy thought, a healthy body, healthy feelings, easily controllable attention.[94] This is the axiom of the yogis, and both Lobanova and Ramacharaka make similar statements. For Stanislavsky this is crucial: 'And the first lessons in breathing must become the foundation of the development of that introspective attention, on which all the work in the art of the stage must be built.'[95] Later he says, 'Til you realise that the whole basis of your life – respiration – is not only the basis of your physical existence, but that

---

[92] Leo Kofler, *Art of Breathing as the Basis of Tone-Production* (Montana: Kessinger, 1887).

[93] Delsarte also described diaphragmatic breathing, according to Volkonsky. There are interesting comparisons to be made between Kofler and Delsarte, both contemporaries, and both singers who had vocal problems.

[94] Stanislavsky, *Stanislavsky on the Art of the Stage*, p. 143.

[95] *Ibid.* p. 117.

respiration plus rhythm forms the foundation of all your creative work, your work on rhythm and breathing will never be carried out in full consciousness.'[96]

Tempo-rhythm

Chapter 5 in its entirety is devoted to *tempo-rhythm*, reflecting the interest Stanislavsky showed in this topic in the last years of his career. Vasily Osipovich Toporkov describes his application of *tempo-rhythm* to work on Valentin Petrovich Kataev's *The Embezzlers*, which opened in 1928, in *Stanislavski in Rehearsal*. In *AWHI*, Tortsov explains to the students that there is internal and external *tempo-rhythm*, the external being visible to the spectator in physical actions, the internal being an important element of *the sense of the self on stage* (p. 158). *Tempo-rhythm* applies to movement and speech. Tortsov defines tempo as 'the speed of alternation of identical durations which are agreed as a unit within a fixed measure ((a bar)). Rhythm is the quantitative relationship of effective durations of movement or sound to durations, which have been agreed as a unit in a defined tempo and bar. A bar is the repeated (or proposed to be repeated) sum of identical durations which are taken as a unit and marked by the stress on one of the units (the duration of the movement or sound' (p. 159). The students are baffled by the complexity and no doubt the verbosity of the definition and begin to explore the concept with some practical work. The fictional students, such as the Bolshoi Theatre-Studio students, listen to and do exercises with a metronome.[97] They then understand what tempo is, what a beat is, and how there may be variable rhythms within a bar. They listen to a number of different metronomes at the same time, all on different settings, and Tortsov draws an analogy with the situation on stage where action and speech take place within time, alternating with pauses. In collective stage action the individual actors must find their particular tempo and measure for the speech, movement and experiencing of the role.

They go on to do clapping games, getting excited when the beat is fast, lethargic when it is slow, and Tortsov tells them that *tempo-rhythm* has the power to affect what is inner; it can be an influence on *emotional memory* and imagination.

They beat out the *tempo-rhythm* of events such as storms, of emotions such as grief, but in listening to each other they cannot guess the meaning of what is being beaten out. Tortsov says this is not important, the idea of

[96] *Ibid.* p. 168.
[97] Vinogradskaia, *Letopis*, vol. 4, p. 334.

the tempo-rhythm of a situation is for themselves, and others gain a general impression of what is going on. He demonstrates buying a newspaper in different *tempo-rhythms*. The students do exercises to explore the influence music can have on *experiencing* (p. 175), and perform detailed études focussing on the *tempo-rhythm* of a train journey, an execution and so on. Speech *tempo-rhythm* is explored using Smolensky's technique of *tatir-ovanie* (p. 199), or speaking the text in syllables of 'ta ta', instead of the words, in order to explore its rhythm. There can be a contradiction between inner and outer *tempo-rhythm* for an individual actor, they can be *experiencing* a heightened emotion while being outwardly calm.

Stanislavsky was clearly influenced by Dalcroze's idea that every person has his or her own rhythm.[98] This idea was expounded by d'Udine and popularised by Volkonsky. Antarova noted Stanislavsky's statement that in his creative work every man is a unique individuality, an individual rhythmic entity, and that he made a connection between this rhythm and breathing.[99] Also, he writes that each person has their own *tempo-rhythm*, as do groups, and in the theatre, moments, scenes and whole plays and performances can have their own *tempo-rhythm* (p. 184). It is even important to pay attention to standing in the correct rhythm for a scene.[100] Toporkov writes that the old-fashioned and nebulous idea of finding the right 'tone' for a play has now been replaced by *tempo-rhythm* – the intensity and rhythm of scene.

Again, Stanislavsky's ideas are those of a particular epoch and need re-examination. His view of inner and outer again indicates his view that the correct inner state can be achieved by external means.

The sense of the self on stage

In summary, training and exercises are seen as necessary to develop the *external sense of the self on stage*: the body and voice have been warmed up so that 'order, discipline, suppleness and harmony is established in your physical nature. Now all the parts of your physical apparatus of incarnation have become supple . . . like a well-oiled and regulated machine' (*AWHI*, pp. 306–7). This is a preparation for the internal elements of the *sense of the self*:

on stage, the artist had to be consciously aware of the spiritual elements of the sense of the self: of attention, imagination, the feeling of truth and faith, emotional memory, communion and adaptation (*AWHI*, p. 455).

---

[98] Volkonskii, *Chelovek" na Stsene*, p. 150.
[99] Magarshack, *Stanislavsky on the Art of the Stage*, p. 94, 142.
[100] V. O. Toporkov, *Stanislavski in Rehearsal: The Final Years*, tr. Christine Edwards (New York: Theatre Arts Books, 1979), p. 62.

This had been studied in the first part of the training course, preparing the actor for working in front of the public. What is significant here is the division between internal *experiencing*, feeling and external *incarnation*, the machine.

The 'natural machine' does not always work in the way that is necessary for the actor if left to nature alone; it needs training and correction. Training takes the form of repetition and practice, repetition and re-learning with regard to body and voice: 'Each person who goes on stage has to learn how to watch, walk, act, communicate and finally speak. The vast majority of people use speech badly, vulgarly in life and don't notice this because they have got used to their own shortcomings' (*AWHI*, p. 77).

A first-class artist cannot play on an instrument that is out of tune. Artists must get to know what their shortcomings are, so that they can break the habit. While writing the chapter on *Speech and its Laws* in 1933, Stanislavsky noted, 'it is very difficult, as I do not teach the laws of speech myself, but only allude to them and want to make the students understand clearly why they need this science. In a word, the aim is to evoke a conscious attitude to this subject, as to others (gymnastics, dance and so on)' (*Collected Works*, vol. 9, p. 547). He concluded that good habit or second nature is necessary. He wrote that drilling is also necessary so that actors do not have to pay attention to diction when they step on stage (*AWHI*, p. 68), not explaining how the actor can avoid the trap of mechanical habit.

Stanislavsky's work drew on the scientific thinking of his time, whether from the manuals he consulted, all of which are written methodically with lists of anatomical and physiological references, or from scientific ideas in circulation, such as those of William James. Although science has made vast advances since Stanislavsky's time, he claimed that 'Specialists will criticise ... but my methods have been taken from living practice, from experience and the results are available and may be tested' (*AWHI*, 1st edn, p. 80). His invitation remains to be carried out.

CHAPTER 4

Challenges to the system: *Vakhtangov and Michael Chekhov*

THE CONTEXT FOR TRAINING

It is clear from the previous two chapters that Stanislavsky's essential views about acting did not change in the light of new scientific information, and despite apparent changes in his approach to training and theatre production and his conflicts with the proponents of methods based in other theories, Stanislavsky steadfastly maintained his own theoretical base. A consideration in this chapter of the divergence of views held by Evgeny Vakhtangov and Michael Chekhov (those held by Meyerhold will be discussed in Chapter 5), and Stanislavsky's reactions to these divergences, will illuminate later developments in Stanislavsky's work and the dispute over his views on emotion and action. Vakhtangov and Chekhov began developing their own ideas about acting over the time when they were when working at MAT in the context of changing views in the revolutionary period.

There were a variety of approaches to training actors when theatrical production proliferated in post-revolutionary Russia, as well as those of Meyerhold, Chekhov and Vakhtangov. Aleksandr Tairov, founder of the Kamerny Theatre in Moscow, which opened in 1914, rejected both Stanislavsky's and Meyerhold's approaches, and called for the *synthetic* actor, who could act in plays of all genres, sing, dance and perform acrobatics. Nikolai Evreinov, director of the Distorting Mirror Theatre, St Petersburg, 1910–1917, and creator of the mass spectacle *The Storming of the Winter Palace* (1920), also opposed Stanislavsky, demanding the revitalisation of theatre by examining its origins in children's play, again with an expressive acting style, stating that the true aim of theatre is 'the theatricalisation of life'. Nikolai Foregger created the Theatre of the Four Masks in Moscow after the revolution, then a workshop entitled Mastfor, and developed a training system for actors that he called *TePhysTrenage* (*Teatral'no-Phyzicheskii Trenazh*), based on acrobatics and other forms of movement. Boris Ferdinandov left the Kamerny Theatre to establish the Experimental-Heroic Theatre, where actors were schooled in rhythm and gymnastics according to Ferdinandov's laws of theatrical presentation. Sergei Eisenstein and Sergei Tretiakov developed their ideas of *Expressive Movement* from 1922 onwards, which Eisenstein transferred into film acting. The film-maker Lev Kuleshov, also working in the early twenties, posited that stage training was wholly unsuitable for film actors and set up his own studio, at which Vsevolod Pudovkin studied. Interestingly, in his later film-making, Pudovkin asserted that Stanislavsky's *system* was in fact of use to film actors.[1] Of course, his writings about Stanislavsky in the 1940s and 1950s were in the period when the *system* had become the canonical actor-training method for socialist realism.

Gorchakov describes how between 1918 and 1925 many studio theatres apart from those connected to the MAT emerged.[2] Many young people who worked in factories and offices in Moscow would rehearse late into the night to stage performances for small audiences of like-minded people, family and friends. Volkonsky, decrying the lack of proper actor training in all this, stated that 'at all opening ceremonies, assemblies and meetings, Lunacharsky always said, "We shall create the new actor."' He continues with some irony: 'the whole of Russia acted . . . there was not a village (I speak of the first two years after the revolution), where some barn had not been turned into a theatre; the hairdressers received 10,000 roubles for an evening'.[3] There were, however, hundreds of studios under the auspices of Proletkult which were led by theatre professionals (one of these being the Kursk Studio led by Chekhov's assistant Viktor Gromov). Despite the apparent variety of approaches, Stanislavsky's influence was all-pervasive, whether received positively or negatively. As Gorchakov states, 'One must study Konstantin Stanislavsky's Theater to be able to evaluate correctly such innovators as Meyerhold, Tairov, and Evreinov; they arose in opposition to the revolution of Stanislavsky and Nemirovich-Danchenko.'[4] Vakhtangov and Chekhov's innovations in the years when the *system* was still relatively new were of crucial importance. Worrall writes that Stanislavsky's theories

came to figure centrally in the ideological struggle between an actor-centred and a director-centred theatre, between a 'realistic' theatre and a 'theatre of convention';

---

[1] Amy Sargeant, *Vsevolod Pudovkin: Classic Films of the Soviet Avant-garde* (London: I. B. Tauris, 2000), p. xvii.
[2] N. A. Gorchakov, *The Theater in Soviet Russia*, tr. Edgar Lehrman (New York: Columbia University Press, 1957), p. 244.
[3] Prince Sergei Volkonsky, *My Reminiscences*, vol. 2, tr. A. E. Chamot (London: 1924), pp. 219–20.
[4] Gorchakov, *The Theater in Soviet Russia*, p. x.

between 'humanist' and 'formalist' conceptions of theatre art and even between apparent acceptance or apparent rejection of the political 'status-quo' – of 'reality' itself.[5]

It has been suggested that Stanislavsky incorporated into his own work ideas put forward by his critical former students, at a later date, without attributing them.[6] Others have asserted that Stanislavsky at some periods in fact developed faster than some of these innovators. Worrall writes that Stanislavsky was dismayed by the excessive naturalism in the First Studio's production of *The Deluge* in 1915 and started to change it to make it more theatrical. Vakhtangov protested, as he was 'still a vehement disciple of a Stanislavsky who had moved on creatively from the point where Vakhtangov thought him to be'. Worrall quotes actor Boris Sushkevich: 'we all believed in the Stanislavsky system to the limit, to the point of fanaticism. Vakhtangov most of all of us . . . He considered that Suler should fight with Konstantin Sergeievich to defend the new laws which Stanislavsky himself had created.'[7] Vakhtangov had a considerable influence on Chekhov's development and both sought to find a way out of what they saw as the limitations of Stanislavsky's views on *experiencing*.

EVGENY VAKHTANGOV AND THE SEARCH FOR NEW FORMS

Evgeny Bagrationovich Vakhtangov was born in Armenia in 1883 and died young in 1922, just as his work as a director was gaining acclaim. In 1909 he joined a drama school run by MAT actor Alexander I. Adashev (1871–1934), where Suler taught. His abilities were soon recognised and after six months he was transferred to the second year, graduating in 1911. In 1910 Vakhtangov accompanied Suler to Paris as his assistant in a production of *The Blue Bird* for the Réjane Theatre. After what he saw of theatre in Paris, Vakhtangov wrote, 'My thinking that Stanislavsky's 'system' is a great thing has been conclusively confirmed.'[8] In March 1911

[5] Nicholas Worrall, *Modernism to Realism on the Soviet Stage* (Cambridge University Press, 1989), p. 2. The Russian word 'uslovnyi', translated here as 'conventional', was also used in this period to mean 'theatrical' or 'stylised'. J. B. Woodward, quoted in Senelick, points out that it can also mean conditionalism, a conditioned reality, that is the reality conditioned by the subjective viewpoint of the artist (Laurence Senelick (tr. and ed.), *Russian Dramatic Theory from Pushkin to the Symbolists*, Austin: University of Texas Press, 1981), p. 171. It is of course the word also used for conditioned or conditional reflexes.

[6] Michael Chekhov, *Lessons for the Professional Actor* ed. Deirdre Hurst du Prey (New York: Performing Arts Publications, 1985), Introduction by Mel Gordon, p. 12.

[7] Worrall, *Modernism to Realism*, p. 94.

[8] Kh. Khersonskii, *Vakhtangov* (Moscow: Molodaia Gvardia, 1940), p. 72.

Nemirovich-Danchenko and Stanislavsky accepted him at the MAT and later that year Stanislavsky asked Vakhtangov to compose *tasks* for exercises with actors involved in the production of *Hamlet* on which Edward Gordon Craig was working. At one point he was given a mandate for his work at the MAT by Stanislavsky: 'Stanislavsky said to me: "Work. If anyone interferes, I'll tell them to leave. I need a new theatre. Go on working quietly. Don't mention my name".[9] Sushkevich said Vakhtangov was fanatical about the *system* but this did not mean he was a blind adherent; he wrote in 1911 about the need for a studio where 'We would test Stanislavsky's system on ourselves. We would either accept or refute it, correct it, add to it, or take what is false out of it.'[10] Vakhtangov was, therefore, one of the founder members of the First Studio, under Sulerzhitsky's leadership, in 1912. He also taught at Sofia Khaliutina's drama school until 1915. Despite his talents as an actor and Stanislavsky's protests he was only ever given small parts at the MAT.[11] He performed in some of the First Studio productions, for example, in 1914 as Tackleton in *The Cricket on the Hearth*, with Michael Chekhov as Caleb.

The MAT that Vakhtangov joined had 'returned to realism' as Stanislavsky proclaimed in 1910 and was developing 'spiritual naturalism'. The First Studio aimed for theatrical truth to be as true to life as possible, for the provision of

psychological, intimate theatre like that pioneered by Strindberg... and Reinhardt... Stanislavsky and Sulerzhitsky needed... experimental work on the developing 'system' and training of the new breed of actor capable of filling the stage with the life of the human soul.[12]

From 1912 to 1914 the studio staged plays and excerpts from plays, with the work focussing on training – on facilitating *experiencing* and improvisational work. In 1913, Sulerzhitsky wrote to Gorky about experiments in the Studio. He was using improvisation to help the students develop concentration, temperament and communion, and used stories or episodes that the students acted in their own words, arranging the order of the scenes.[13] This way of working, so familiar now, was very new at that time.

[9] Evgenii Vakhtangov, *Evgeny Vakhtangov*, (eds) L. D. Vendrovskaia and G. P. Kaptereva, tr. Doris Bradbury (Moscow: Progress, 1982), p. 15.
[10] Evgenii Vakhtangov, *Sbornik*, (eds) L. D Vendrovskaia and G. P. Kaptereva, tr. Doris Bradbury (Moscow: Vserossiskoe Teatral'noe Obshchestvo, 1984), p. 88.
[11] Serafima Birman, 'Life's Gift of Encounters', *Soviet Literature*, 3 (1975), p. 81.
[12] Worrall, *Modernism to Realism*, p. 84.
[13] I. N. Vinogradskaia, *Zhizn'i tvorchestvo K. S. Stanislavskogo, Letopis*, 2nd, edn. vols 1–4 (Moscow: Moskovskii Khudozhestvennyi Teatr, 2003), vol. 2, p. 374.

Vakhtangov was influenced by Sulerzhitsky's humanist worldview, writing that 'the purpose of art is to force people to be more attentive to each other, soften their hearts and ennoble their actions'.[14] Stanislavsky and Sulerzhitsky wanted to form a spiritual community of actors and there were summer retreats, the first in 1913 near to Kanevo in Kievski province, and then in 1915 and 1916 to Eupatoria on the Black Sea, where Stanislavsky had bought land. Khersonsky writes that Vakhtangov was also inspired by what Sulerzhitsky had to say about the significance for the actor of fantasy and intuition.[15]

Vakhtangov used the *system* in the first play he directed in the Studio, Hauptmann's *Festival of Peace*, in 1913, in which Chekhov played the role of Fribe. Vakhtangov had emphasised internal technique at the expense of external technique and led the actors into inwardly focussed emotional states lacking external clarity and expression. This was a problem Stanislavsky himself had encountered but he did not spare Vakhtangov. S. V. Giantsintova, one of the Studio members noted, 'I have never seen K. S. so angry. He was literally in a fury and cursed us, cursed Vakhtangov, saying that it was some sort of illness, hysteria.'[16] However, Boris Zakhava wrote:

People said that the show created a great impression because of the unusual truth of the actors' performance. It was asserted that such a fusion of the actor with the image, such faith in the truth of fantasy, such commitment from the actor to the life on stage had never been known, even at the Art Theatre.[17]

Vakhtangov began his own studio, the Students' Dramatic Studio (which Zakhava joined), using Stanislavsky's methods but the premiere on 26 March 1914 of *The Lanin Estate* by Boris Zaitsev was criticised. Again, the raw young actors were moved by their own *experiencing*, and used Stanislavsky's teaching of naivety, faith and 'going into the circle' (of attention) to induce in themselves a state of self-hypnosis, which in no way communicated with the audience.[18]

Vakhtangov wrote sadly about Stanislavsky and Sulerzhitsky's interference in his second directorial attempt for the First Studio (Henning

[14] Evgenii Vakhtangov, *Zapiski, Pis'ma, Stat'i*, (eds) N. M. Vakhtangova, L. D. Vendrovskaia, B. E. Zakhava (Moscow: Iskusstvo, 1939), p. 93.
[15] Khersonskii, *Vakhtangov*, p. 69.
[16] K. S. Stanislavskii, *O Stanislavskom: Sbornik vospominanii* (Moscow: Vserossiiskoe Teatral'noe Obshchestvo, 1948), p. 367.
[17] Boris Zakhava, *Vospominania. Spektakli i. Roli. Stat'i.* (Moscow: Vserossiiskoe Teatral'noe Obshchestvo, 1982), p. 40.
[18] Khersonskii, *Vakhtangov*, p. 112.

Berger's *The Deluge* in 1915), where he and Chekhov were double cast in the role of Fraser: 'They came, they rudely involved themselves in the play, trampled over me insensitively, threw their weight about without asking me, cut and axed. Now I am indifferent to *The Deluge*.'[19] They objected to the extreme naturalism of the acting. It was said, however, that with this play Vakhtangov mastered the *system* in practice as a director. After this Vakhtangov desired more creative freedom and independence, working in his own studio, now called the Mansurov Studio. He was not alone in the need to look beyond what he had been taught. Vera Soloveva, a member of the First Studio, wrote,

Sometimes we thought that all we got from Stanislavsky was not enough. Michael Chekhov and Vakhtangov, who were the most devoted and favourite actors of Stanislavsky, started experiments in abstract forms.[20]

Conflicts between Stanislavsky and Sulerzhitsky and such pupils as Vakhtangov and Chekhov became ever more apparent. Rudnitsky writes:

'Relatively quickly,' recalled Alexei Popov, 'in the course of something like two or three years of vertiginous fame, in the Studio were sown the seeds of an ironic attitude to the 'system' and to the ethical foundation of Stanislavsky's teaching.' These conflicts came to full light after the Revolution and finally led to a dramatic split between the MAT and the First Studio.[21]

Nevertheless, in the beginnings of his own studio work, Vakhtangov stated 'I am a pupil of Stanislavsky. I see the purpose of my work with you as propagandising and disseminating the teaching of Konstantin Sergeevich.'[22]

The beginning of Vakhtangov's methods of acting

Zakhava writes that right at the meeting to set up his own studio, Vakhtangov, wearing his best suit, stated his credo: 'theatre is a holiday'. He said that his speciality was not the external technique of the actor but the internal one. The essence of internal technique was the ability to understand and produce the feelings of the image, to live its internal life on stage. The main source for stage *experiencings* was the *emotional memory* of the actor and the task of the actor was to lure the imprint of the necessary

---

[19] *Ibid.* p. 122.
[20] Vera Soloveva, 'Memories of the Moscow Art Theatre' (unpublished manuscript), p. 55, quoted in Christine Edwards, *The Stanislavski Heritage* (New York University Press, 1965), p. 122.
[21] Konstantin Rudnitsky, *Russian and Soviet Theatre, 1905–1932: Tradition and the Avant-garde*, tr. Roxanne Permar (New York: Harry N. Abrams, 1988), p. 22.
[22] Zakhava, *Vospomininania*, p. 42.

feelings from the actor's emotional storeroom and put them in the order required by the logic of the life of the image that has been created.[23] In the Mansurov Studio in 1914 to 1915, Vakhtangov taught attention (*the circle*), repeating *experiencings* from life and the development of fantasy. Creativity is the fulfilment of a series of tasks and the image appears as a result of fulfilling them. Each task consists of an action (what I do), wanting (why I do this – *khotenie*), and an *adaptation* (how).[24] Scenes from the life of the characters in the play were played through in an improvised way. Although this work did not depart far from the way in which Vakhtangov had been taught the *system* there was a strong emphasis on the imaginative work of the actor, creating the image of the character and the new idea of the actor as improviser.

His early experiments taught Vakhtangov that form must be taken into account, or *experiencing* will not be conveyed:

Vagueness of form, absorption in acting in inexpressive, inconsequential and superfluous details, 'everyday rubbish', lack of responsibility in one's external behaviour on stage, the absence of an exact, clearly delineated drawing – all these negative qualities of the amorphous theatre of experiencing were declared illegal.[25]

The members of the Studio searched for new forms on the principle that creativity is always 'unconscious'. Vakhtangov's embrace of some of Stanislavsky's beliefs about the unconscious, from his reading of Sukhanov and the yogis, is apparent.

The conscious mind never creates anything. It is the subconscious mind that is creative. Apart from the subconscious mind's independent ability to make selections without the conscious mind being aware of it, it can receive material for creation through the conscious mind. In this sense, no rehearsal can be productive unless it seeks or provides material for the next rehearsal; it is in the intervals between rehearsals that the creative work of processing the material received is carried out in the subconscious. Nothing can be created from nothing, which is why no role can be played simply 'by inspiration', without work being put in.

Inspiration is the moment when the subconscious mind has combined the material from previous work and, without the participation of the conscious mind – simply when called upon to do so by the latter – moulds everything into a form.[26]

Zakhava noted Vakhtangov's aphorism based on this concept of unconscious processing, that is, 'today's rehearsal is not for its own sake

[23] *Ibid.* pp. 42–3.
[24] Khersonskii, *Vakhtangov*, p. 131.
[25] *Ibid.* p. 128.
[26] Vakhtangov, *Evgeny Vakhtangov*, p. 120.

but for the sake of tomorrow's', which he said took away panic and strain in young actors.[27] Vakhtangov's interest in yoga for health is implied by his instruction in a letter to buy a copy of Ramacharaka's *Hatha Yoga* for Ekzempliarskaia, an actress who was ill. His instruction was for her to read it attentively and to perform the exercises in the section on breathing and *prana* that summer.[28]

Zakhava writes that no one was able to teach the *system* with such clarity, simplicity and exactness as Vakhtangov in the early work at the Mansurov Studio and that he in fact resolved contradictions within the *system* that Stanislavsky himself struggled with. An important example is the contradiction 'between the stage attention of the actor and his creative attitude to the object of his attention'.[29] Zakhava gives examples: the actor has to express delight at a landscape when in fact he is looking at a prop window, beyond which is the rubbish in the wings. What should be the object of his attention? Again, if he is playing Romeo with an actress he finds unattractive, 'what must he *see* on stage, the actress who is unattractive to him who is before him, or some sort of beauty, whom he can create in his imagination? Or perhaps, even a real girl who in life is the subject of the tender feelings of the actor?'

To propose, as some people do, that the actor sees not what is there but what is in his creative imagination is to encourage the actor to hallucinate. Instead, Vakhtangov came up with a formula: '*I apprehend (see, hear, smell, etc.) everything as it is given, I relate to everything as it is set.*' This, according to Zakhava (writing retrospectively after the revolution) expresses precisely the dialectic of the actor's creativity, which is a dia-lectical unity of contradictions: the actor-creator and the actor-image. The actor sees what is given but the image behaves according to what is set. Apprehending everything as it is, the actor, relying on life experience, *transforms* everything he has been given into something completely dif-ferent with the power of his fantasy. Here, Vakhtangov embraces Stan-islavsky's *magic if*, but develops the concept of *transformation*, which was important for Chekhov and his method of imitating the image.

Vakhtangov's interpretation of Stanislavsky's *tasks* was similarly very clear and consisted of the three elements mentioned: action (*what* I do), the aim (*why* I do it) and the *adaptation* (*how* I do it). The answers to these questions had to be short, clear and exact. Vakhtangov used Stanislavsky's formula

[27] Zakhava, *Vospomininania*, p. 53.
[28] Vakhtangov, *Zapiski, Pis'ma, Stat'i*, p. 211.
[29] Zakhava, *Vospomininania*, pp. 51–2.

'I need'. This formula expresses the internal sense of the self of the actor on stage so that they can say of every step of stage behaviour, of their every word or movement: *I need* to make this movement, *I need* to say these words. Zakhava writes that Vakhtangov taught that there were two stages of *I need*, the first being where the actor has recognised the necessity for the defined actions and words of the given character. The actor could describe this in the third person, that is s/he wishes, s/he speaks, s/he does, s/he needs. Secondly, the actor must feel the necessity of the given words, action and behaviour not only for the character but also for him/herself as the character. There must be an internal identification with the character through 'I need'. Zakhava explains that he fully understood this when playing the role of Chichikov in Gogol's *Dead Souls*. Vakhtangov told him he was 'acting' whereas it was necessary to 'become' Chichikov. Zakhava could understand that Chichikov needed to become rich and important but was only able to achieve the second stage of *I need* when he had a vision of himself as Chichikov in a carriage, riding through a crowd which was acclaiming him, and he was able to connect this with a memory of riding a horse-drawn carriage on an estate and the sense of importance this gave him. This point of contact, made through the Stanislavskian process of *emotional memory*, meant that he was then able to react fully as Chichikov to the character of Korobochka who was preventing his plans from going forward. Then Vakhtangov said to him, 'Now it's not "general" temperament but "emotion from the essence." '[30] Vakhtangov continued to work with the formula of *I need*, noting for his production of Ibsen's *Rosmersholm* in 1918,

I want actors to be serious in their strivings, not to pretend that they are striving towards something. I want them to feel that what their characters need *they* also *need inherently.*[31]

Vakhtangov continued teaching and lecturing on the themes to do with the *system* in the First Studio but in his own studio during the 1917 season he began to branch out, ironically revisiting a method Stanislavsky had discarded. Vakhtangov worked on P. Antokolsky's play *The Doll of the Infanta* and suggested that the actors take as their foundation the imaginary psychology of a doll, or a doll's soul. Khersonsky writes,

Thus there was a paradoxical application of Stanislavsky's 'system', which moreover had been found earlier by K. S. Stanislavsky and L. A. Sulerzhitsky in *The Blue Bird*, for such roles as Sugar, Milk, Bread, et cetera. The reality of any story is not in its subject but in a realistic internal justification of the conventionality of its characters.[32]

---

[30] *Ibid*. pp. 54–6.
[31] Vakhtangov, *Evgeny Vakhtangov*, p. 46.
[32] Khersonskii, *Vakhtangov*, p. 151.

But this solution to symbolist plays for Vakhtangov still meant a rejection of external theatricality – he wanted a 'holiday of the most real human feelings' where everything came from the inner depths of the actor, while setting up a situation demanding that the actor stretch the imagination. It was in this period, when Stanislavsky was guiding Sushkievich as director in the studio's *Twelfth Night*, that Vakhtangov protested against Stanislavsky's approach in a letter to the studio member A. I. Cheban. Vakhtangov found the sets too opulent and the production focussed on externals, 'making no step forward in the internal sense. And the system does not stand to gain.'[33] He himself took the opposite approach with *Rosmersholm* after the revolution.

Vakhtangov and the revolution

Vakhtangov welcomed the 1917 Revolution although he did not join the Bolsheviks, unlike Meyerhold. Despite his ill health he worked intensely. Anatoly Gunst (1859–1919), an artist and actor, opened a studio in 1917 and invited Vakhtangov to work there in 1918. In the same year the Jewish Habimah studio opened, where Vakhtangov worked and he was also invited to work in the second MAAT studio to teach the *system*. In 1918 he wanted to form the Peoples Art Theatre from his studio work but was not allowed to do so by MAAT, so it became The People's Theatre. In 1919 the Gunst Studio merged with Vakhtangov's Studio and Lunacharsky, head of the Theatrical Department of the People's Commissariat for Education and the Arts, offered Vakhtangov the management of its Directors' Section, an appointment he was unable to maintain because of his health. In 1920 Vakhtangov's studio became the Third Studio of MAAT.

In 1918, now running it on his own after Suler's death in 1916, Vakhtangov directed *Rosmersholm* at the First Studio and Maeterlinck's *The Miracle of St Anthony* at the Mansurov Studio. In Ibsen's *Rosmersholm* Vakhtangov strove for *fusion* of the actor with the *image* of the character. Stanislavsky had discussed the *fusion* of the actor and the character particularly early in the development of the *system*. Stanislavsky's training had been based on enabling the actor to overcome the unnatural sense of the self on stage by *fusion* of the personality of the actor with the personality of the character. Vakhtangov's aim in *Rosmersholm* was to encourage the actors to live in the image of the character but not to be the character. He asserted that the 'abnormal' condition of the actor on stage

[33] Vakhtangov, *Sbornik*, p. 158.

that caused Stanislavsky so many problems is indeed abnormal but natural for the theatre and, moreover, it is necessary for creativity. Without this 'contradictory state there would be no art. It was not about *fusion*, not about the identification of the actor with the character but about the originality of the contradiction between the unity of the actor and the image of the character'.[34] But Vakhtangov carried certain principles of the theatre of *experiencing* to extremes, in an attempt to create a situation where theatre ceased to be 'theatre' and became truth itself. *Rosmersholm* was Vakhtangov's last production for the First Studio using the framework of the *system*. Worrall writes of Vakhtangov's own studio as follows:

The immediate consequence of the revolution was a crisis within the Studio and a creative crisis in Vakhtangov's own mind. The Mansurov Studio fell apart during 1918 and 1919.

He explains that during Vakhtangov's illness discipline had lapsed there and in the First Studio the production of *Rosmersholm* was a last attempt to save the values of the 'Studio idea'.[35] The fact that Vakhtangov had been influenced by the psychological intensity typical of the work of Nemirovich-Danchenko, who had also directed *Rosmersholm* at the MAT in 1908, was evident in this production. According to Freidkina, in Vakhtangov's production there was a subtle textual analysis, disclosure of the main idea of the play and methods of character analysis typical of Nemirovich-Danchenko.[36] In 1922 Vakhtangov wrote to Nemirovich-Danchenko acknowledging his influence in particular with regard to *experiencing*:

I learned to join what is yours and Stanislavsky's together. You revealed the meaning of 'theatricality' and 'acting skill' to me. I saw that in addition to 'experiencing' (you don't like this term) you demanded something else from the actor. I learned to understand what it means to 'speak about feeling' on stage and what it means to feel.[37]

Popov describes how Nemirovich-Danchenko, unlike Stanislavsky, often began with study of the author and the work's style, guiding the actor to an understanding of the nature of the role. The logic of behaviour and actions is determined by the nature of the character, therefore, rather than by personality, as with the *system*. This idea was espoused by Michael Chekhov as well as Vakhtangov. Alexei Popov wrote,

---

[34] Khersonskii, *Vakhtangov*, pp. 208–9.
[35] Worrall, *Modernism to Realism*, p. 97.
[36] Vakhtangov, *Evgeny Vakhtangov*, p. 211.
[37] Vakhtangov, *Sbornik*, p. 428.

He liked to rehearse with *one actor* by tracing his role throughout the entire play. This gave rise to an entirely different directing terminology, 'the kernel' of the role, the 'temperament' of the character, the 'secondary level' and the 'physical sense' of a role . . . Vakhtangov observed the work of . . . directors who had studied with Stanislavsky and Nemirovich-Danchenko, ardently seeking but rarely finding a balance *between the inner essence and the image on stage.* The inner self does not come across on the stage, and what comes across on the stage is not necessarily internally motivated.[38]

Finding the balance between inner essence and justified outer expression became Vakhtangov's goal, but taking his cue from Nemirovich-Danchento he insisted that the actor should

desire and behave as indicated by the author (we have already explained that the actor accepts these desires and actions as the only possible and logical ones for the given character).[39]

Vakhtangov stepped over Stanislavsky's theatre of *experiencing* and real life to assert the life of the image and art – the imaginative creation of the director, actor and writer. Khersonsky claims that *Rosmersholm* was the first time in the history of the MAT that the actors had been made to think so intensely:

The reality of spiritual life is at its utmost and precision of form is utterly clear, natural . . . a living . . . but particularly theatrical world. This is already far from realism. This is one of the basic qualities of the style arising in post-war Europe, particularly Germany, which was to become known as expressionism.[40]

Vakhtangov believed that

The thing to aim for is to awaken temperament without any external stimuli; to this end, at rehearsals the actor needs to work mainly to make everything that surrounds him in the play his own atmosphere, to make the tasks of the character his own tasks, then temperament will speak 'from the essence'. This temperament 'from the essence' is the most valuable, being the only convincing and genuine sort.[41]

In his move away from Stanislavsky, Vakhtangov continued to assert the Tolstoyan idea that 'acting without an emotional or human basis could never make a true (or subconscious) contact with the spectator'.[42] He wrote in his notebook in 1917 that 'It is infectiousness, i.e. the unconscious enthusiasm of the subconscious mind of the perceiver, that is the sign of talent.'[43]

---

[38] Vakhtangov, *Evgeny Vakhtangov*, p. 170.
[39] Vakhtangov, Sbornik, p. 168.
[40] Khersonskii, *Vakhtangov*, p. 162.
[41] Vakhtangov, *Sbornik*, p. 275.
[42] Mel Gordon, *The Stanislavsky Technique: Russia* (New York: Applause Theatre Books, 1987), p. 80.
[43] Vakhtangov, *Evgeny Vakhtangov*, p. 121.

But theatre had a social and political purpose as well as a humanistic one. Vakhtangov thought that naturalism blocked the active expression of one's attitude to life and that revolution and naturalism in art are incompatible. Stanislavsky and Nemirovich-Danchenko's copying of life in theatre resulted in the presentation of

an unmediated experience of feeling without a deep analysis of social manifestations . . . a defence by artistic means of philosophical and political ideas . . . not the revelation of individual features but their social nature, in real social connections.[44]

He wished, therefore, to create an acting technique that was externally stylised and internally truthful – *imaginative realism*, as it became known.[45] Markov writes that this was in fact prompted by the revolution:

He wanted to create a theatre of temperament and emotional intensity . . . he rejected the Art Theatre's . . . delay in coming to terms with the new reality, although he was in agreement with its acting principles . . . [He] demanded sharply-focused, fiery stage productions on the basis of the Art Theatre's acting methods.[46]

His experiments were not always well received. In 1918 he wrote a letter to the council of the First Moscow Art Theatre-Studio, which was not completed because at this point a crisis occurred when twelve people left his own Mansurov Studio. The letter stated that he had endured reproaches for years from Sulerzhitsky, Stanislavsky and the council members, including Sushkievich. They said he had neglected the First Studio for his own studio, which Vakhtangov denied, also asserting that though they were not willing to admit it, they had recognised something in the acting of his students that they themselves sought in theatre.[47] He remained loyal to Stanislavsky in many ways, however. His article, 'To those who write about Stanislavsky's System', appeared in *Vestnik Teatra* comprising a spirited defence of the *system* in response to Kommisarzhevsky's 'The creativity of the actor and Stanislavsky's theory', which had seriously criticised the *system*'s subjective approach. Vakhtangov also criticised Michael Chekhov's article 'On the System of Stanislavsky', which had appeared in *Gorn* (*The Bugle*), and which Vakhtangov thought inaccurate. In 1919 Stanislavsky proposed that Vakhtangov and O. V. Gzovskaia help him to lead exercises on the system with the artists of the Bolshoi

---

[44] Khersonskii, *Vakhtangov*, p. 206.
[45] Ruben Simonov, *Stanislavsky's Protégé: Eugene Vakhtangov*, tr. Miriam Goldina (New York: DBS Publications, 1969), p. 146.
[46] Vakhtangov, *Evgeny Vakhtangov*, p. 6.
[47] *Ibid.*, p. 239.

Opera Theatre-Studio. Stanislavsky continued to teach lessons in the *system* himself, with the students from the MAAT Studios, the Habimah and Armenian Studios and Vakhtangov and Chekhov's Studios.

Imaginative realism

The solution to the problem of the actor's belief in what they are doing on stage was not to be solved by Stanislavskian *given circumstances*, which enables them to overcome the unnatural state induced by performance by the creation of the fourth wall, and making believe that the audience does not exist, but in what Vakhtangov called *justification*. The actor must justify everything he does on stage, but not necessarily in a way that fits with the logic of the play or the character. Vakhtangov's adaptation of this aspect of the *system* was to privilege the actor's art over the director's intentions. A summary of a series of lectures given in 1914 states:

Justification is the path to belief.

On the stage there should be no object, no action or event that is not justified. If you are playing an aristocrat and the assistant director has left a cigarette butt on your table – you need to justify this; your partner is laughing in the wings – you need to justify this. If your partner is late for his entrance, this does not mean that your comrade-partner has missed the moment but means perhaps that the person whose arrival you are awaiting and who will come soon has for some reason not yet arrived and this makes you come up with something, evoke some new sense of self but in no way should it mean you come out of role and get embarrassed. Justification is a cause about which I have no doubt. In order to learn quickly how to find justification you need to develop your imagination, as sometimes we find justification in the author but no less frequently we must find it in ourselves. Consequently, it is necessary to develop the imagination with the help of exercises, which consist in your justifying 1) the pose, 2) the place, 3) the action, 4) the state, 5) a series of unconnected propositions, et cetera. However, here it is necessary to raise a caution. It is easy to mix up justification with hallucination and so you must sense the border between them.[48]

The actor must believe in the importance of what he is doing every moment he is on stage.

Zavadsky comments on the improvisational quality of Vakhtangov's rehearsals, his new and unexpected solutions for the actors, such as 'here, now, today' – the thought they must keep in mind for every performance.[49]

---

[48] Vakhtangov, *Zapiski, Pisma, Stati*, p. 281.
[49] Vakhtangov, *Evgeny Vakhtangov*, p. 243.

Stanislavsky applied different methods at different stages and also sought fresh ways into the role. Interestingly, a technique he introduced late in his career was *here, today, now*, which Benedetti describes as asking the actor a question: 'What would you do, as a private individual, if such and such happened?'[50] He gives an example of Stanislavsky acting Lunacharsky arriving unexpectedly at a MAT rehearsal of *The Armoured Train No. 14–69*, and galvanising the extras, which then transformed the way they acted the scene.

Vakhtangov experimented particularly on external expression, running classes in plasticity of movement and 'sculpturalness', writing to the Gunst studio:

You must learn to feel the sculptural quality of a role, a scene, and a play, and you won't be able to do this if you don't know how to move. It is almost impossible to acquire this ability without the *correct* study of movement.

He goes on to recommend Volkonsky's *The Person on the Stage*.[51] It has been asserted that Vakhtangov drew his ideas for this particular form of stylisation from Stanislavsky. Gorchakov goes so far as to state that Stanislavsky's amateur staging of Gilbert and Sullivan's *The Mikado* preceded Meyerhold's experiments with stylisation by twenty years, and notes Stanislavsky's sculptural groupings in Stanislavsky's *Cain* in 1921 and his earlier symbolist productions of *The Blue Bird* and *The Life of Man*.[52] But Vakhtangov asserted that his particular way of working was original:

In my own strenuous attempts to escape from Stanislavsky's nets, a year before Stanislavski began to speak about rhythm and plasticity of movement, I myself achieved a sense of rhythm, realised what expressive movement is, what the audience's attention means and what stage quality, sculptural quality, statu- esqueness, dynamics, gestures, theatricality and stage space were.[53]

The theatre Vakhtangov envisaged 'demanded a more elaborate and pre- cise plastic expression of gesture. It called for large, clear, graphic, but above all, theatrical motion. Nevertheless, Vakhtangov still insisted on its naturalness and sincerity.'[54] The first objective was to be achieved by training the performers in rhythm. Gorchakov describes Vakhtangov's experiments to find the right inner rhythm for Chekhov's characters in *The*

---

[50] Jean Benedetti, *Stanislavski: His Life and Art*, 2nd edn (London: Methuen, 1999), p. 313.
[51] Vakhtangov, *Evgeny Vakhtangov*, pp. 96–7.
[52] Edwards, *Stanislavski Heritage*, p. 97.
[53] Vakhtangov, *Evgeny Vakhtangov*, p. 142.
[54] Aviv Orani, 'Realism in Vakhtangov's Theatre of Fantasy', *Theatre Journal*, 36 (1984), p. 460.

Wedding, in 1920. The characters dance and pause, finding different reasons to justify the pauses and they also dance while sitting.[55] For the second, Vakhtangov stated that 'one must always start from the essentially lifelike situation', so he used *affective memory* techniques with his actors to enable them to justify their character's behaviour, but then encouraged the performers to exaggerate their characterisations to achieve a certain grotesque.[56] The grotesque was an essential element of *fantastic/imaginative realism* and, according to Worrall, Vakhtangov developed his ideas of it under Meyerhold's influence.[57] Both saw it as an appropriate form in which to express the actuality of the revolutionary period, both tragic and comic, and an antidote to slice-of-life theatre.

In the last years of his life Vakhtangov directed a number of productions including Chekhov's *The Wedding* in 1920, a second version of Maeterlinck's *The Miracle of St Anthony* in 1921 (a previous version had been in 1918) and another version of *The Wedding* in 1921. All were produced at the Third Studio. He also directed Strindberg's *Erik XIV* for the First Studio in 1921, S. Ansky's *The Dybbuk* at the Habimah studio in 1922 and Gozzi's *Princess Turandot* at the Third Studio. It was said of him in his search for new forms that his imagination was inexhaustible and 'that he could make an actor from a table and a show from a matchbox'.[58] He also had the reputation of being able to explain the *system* with a myriad of concrete examples.

Like Meyerhold, Vakhtangov began to emphasise the actor's conscious mastery of skill:

Vakhtangov was striving in the second variant of *Miracle* for a stunning rhythmicity and plasticity of the actors' performance. It was already impossible to manifest the content of internal life as it manifests itself – unconsciously and elementally. Now consciousness guides everything, in everything mastery, precision, clear form is demanded. Only when this is done can the actor improvise (movement, gesture, intonation) in exact correspondence with the found form of the given show.[59]

As well as 'temperament from the essence', Vakhtangov now demanded from the actors absolute precision in gesture, movement and speech. Everything had to be fixed but at the same time improvised in the sense that the actors were to react to each other, the stage situation and the

[55] N. M. Gorchakov, *The Vakhtangov School of Stage Art*, tr. G. Ivanov-Mumjiev (Moscow: Foreign Languages Publishing House, 1960), pp. 38–45.
[56] *Ibid.* p. 471.
[57] Worrall, *Modernism to Realism*, p. 77.
[58] Khersonskii, *Vakhtangov*, p. 272.
[59] *Ibid.* p. 226.

audience, afresh every time. What was seen as essentially theatrical was to be returned to the theatre. Musicality was very important, as it was for Stanislavsky, Chekhov and Meyerhold. Vakhtangov's students attended weekly music classes and many of his actors played instruments. Fishman writes that

The Habimah Theatre became a laboratory where Vakhtangov experimented with the idea of unity of gesture, rhythm, costume, scenery and lighting. He elucidated each role so that the actors might capture the essence of each character; he removed superficial realism and replaced it with theatrical freezes, silences, chanting, singing, ghostly make-up, and grotesque formalized movements.[60]

Drawing from images by Goya, Daumier and Chagall, Vakhtangov adapted *The Dybbuk*, which tells the story of a bride believed to be possessed by a *dybbuk* or spirit, on the eve of her wedding, expanding the second act Beggar's Dance to dominate the entire act. It was said that he gave the play an abstract interpretation apposite to the revolution where the beggars represented the revolutionaries and the events of the play stand for the break with the established regime. Others found nightmarish the worlds of both beggars and the rich, with the only positive force that of the love of two individuals.

Similarly, Vakhtangov gave *Erik XIV* (where Michael Chekhov played the title role and Serafima Birman the Dowager Queen) a slant of opposition to tyranny, which was well received by audiences. In an article in *Theatrical Culture* he declared that this was an experiment in theatrical form, which was nevertheless true to Stanislavsky's teaching of the 'art of feeling' – an experiment which the Studio had been prompted to take by the revolutionary times. But like Meyerhold, Vakhtangov began to emphasise the conscious work of the actor and the self-consciously theatrical style of the productions. In Gozzi's *Princess Turandot*, Vakhtangov's swansong, mask, music, movement and gesture contributed to the theatricalism, and the actors appeared on stage as themselves, then put on the costumes of characters in front of the audience in a stylised sequence in the commedia dell'arte tradition. Vakhtangov said that of all other theatre productions perhaps Blok's *The Fairground Booth* as Meyerhold staged it was most like *Turandot*. 'But the actors did not play actors there.'[61] They played the image and the relationship to it simultaneously. Unlike Stanislavsky, who tended to use the word *deistvie*, or

[60] Pearl Fishman, 'Vakhtangov's *The Dybbuk*', *The Drama Review*, 3 (1980), pp. 44–5.
[61] Vakhtangov, *Evgeny Vakhtangov*, p. 156.

purposive action, Vakhtangov liked *igra* or 'play-acting' and emphasised this. The actors had a sense of 'self as an actor creating, with other actors, a tableau, vision, image or symbol'.[62]

Nemirovich-Danchenko saw the justification for *Turandot*'s improvisations and jokes not only in their ease, infectious sense of fun, and pertinence; he pointed out that 'these external effects do not disturb in the slightest the inner psychological process of the actor who plays the prince, but they do free the theatre from a stage method that has become a dead-end routine.[63]

Krivitsky writes that Vakhtangov as a director was a direct follower of Stanislavsky in that for him 'the external must only be reached through the internal', that is, the external form of the actor's role should arise naturally as the expression of inner content.[64]

   For this reason, Vakhtangov has been described as synthesising the art of *experiencing* and the art of *representation* and represented as a

point of intersection between two artistic extremes which have always been at odds with each other . . . the 'realism' of Stanislavsky at one end of the scale and the 'conventionalised theatre' represented by Meyerhold at the other.[65]

As Vakhtangov died at an early stage in his career his work can be difficult to assess. It seems that he may have concurred with the idea of this synthesis. When he was ill in Vsekhsviatsky sanatorium, Vakhtangov was anxious to leave some of his final thoughts about theatre to posterity. He noted in his journal,

I am thinking about Meyerhold. What a brilliant director, the greatest of all those who have lived until now. Each play of his is a new form of theatre. Each of his productions is capable of starting a whole new tendency. Of course, Stanislavsky is a less talented director than Meyerhold. Stanislavsky has no individuality. All his stage productions are banal.

He goes on to write that the first stage in Stanislavsky's directing career was an imitation of the Meiningen concept of theatre. The second stage was Chekhovian theatre where Stanislavsky transferred the Meiningen principle to the inner essence of roles, to emotion, and this was in fact the same naturalism. Although this was the correct form for the time

---

[62] Vera Gottlieb, 'Vakhtangov's Musicality: Reassessing Yevgeny Vakhtangov (1883–1922), *Contemporary Theatre Review*, 15: 2 (2005), p. 266.
[63] Vakhtangov, *Evgeny Vakhtangov*, p. 217.
[64] *Ibid.* p. 258.
[65] Zakhava, *Vospomininania*, p. 346 and Worrall, *Modernism to Realism*, pp. 76, 78–9.

and the plays, in this, he says, all naturalists are alike whereas Meyer-hold is original. He adds, however, that Nemirovich-Danchenko and Stanislavsky work better with actors than Meyerhold. Nemirovich-Danchenko, he wrote, knows how to analyse the role and the play psychologically and produce various emotions in the actor. Stanislavsky, he believes, has very little knowledge of psychology and structures it intuitively (often better and more subtly than Nemirovich-Danchenko).[66]

He carried on his critique in discussions with some of his students who came to sit at his bedside on 10 April 1922, shortly before he died, asserting that Stanislavsky, in his desire to do away with theatrical banality had done away with genuine theatricality as well, and of all the Russian directors the only one who had a sense of theatricality was Meyerhold. However, he adds,

> Conventionalised theatre was necessary in order to break down and do away with theatrical vulgarity. Using conventionalised means to do away with theatrical vulgarity, Meyerhold arrived at an understanding of genuine theatre. Carried away by real truth, Stanislavsky brought naturalist truth to the stage. He sought for theatrical truth in life's truth. Meyerhold arrived at genuine theatre through conventionalised theatre, which he now rejects. But in his enthusiasm for theatrical truth, Meyerhold did away with the truth of feeling, and there should be truth in both Meyerhold's theatre and in Stanislavsky's theatre.[67]

Vakhtangov always subscribed to the concept of *emotional memory* and wanted a theatre which combined Stanislavsky's emotional truth and Meyerhold's theatricalism, though Meyerhold's approach may have been reinforced by ideological beliefs about emotion in the way that Brecht's was and Vakhtangov's was not.

Obviously these ideas impact on training the actor. Gottlieb asserts that Vakhtangov needed a different kind of actor from the majority of the MAT actors, the exception being Michael Chekhov, and this was the sort of actor that Meyerhold was training, an actor who had physical, musical and improvisational skills, the the ability to change tempo and tone rapidly, and to move from tragedy to comedy in an instant.

The actor of the new theatre also needed a value system, not a 'system' in Stanislavsky's sense but rather a value system of morality, of 'truth' in a given

[66] Vakhtangov, *Evgeny Vakhtangov*, pp. 140–1.
[67] *Ibid.* p. 152.
[68] Gottlieb, 'Vakhtangov's Musicality', p. 266.

situation, of shared 'reality' in a mass grotesque whilst contributing as an individual – as, for example, in several scenes in *The Dybbuk*.[68]

Stanislavsky was resolute in his condemnation of the actor-acrobat, and although he was extremely warm in his praise of *Princess Turandot* to the dying Vakhtangov, he also said to Vakhtangov about his actors:

I am puzzled when you begin to tell me that such a super-conscious, supremely perfect creation of a genuine artist, the thing that you choose to call grotesque can be achieved by your students, who are completely untried, who do not have any notion how to speak so that one can sense the inner significance of a phrase or word which rises from the depths to express universal thought and feeling, your students who are still incapable of feeling what is inside them, who have only achieved a certain external ease through their lessons of dance and plastic movement – they are adorable 'puppies', their eyes are not even open yet and they are prattling on about the grotesque.[69]

But Vakhtangov wrote in a letter to Serafima Birman in 1921, gloriously mixing his metaphors,

While we followed the path set out by the Art Theatre, we walked calmly and surely, without any sense of what it meant to stage and perform a play. We made everything out of the same dough – rolls, muffins, cookies and bread – and their taste was identical, too. We followed this road and came to a luxurious cemetery.[70]

Whatever their differences, both Stanislavsky and Vakhtangov admired Chekhov:

Vakhtangov told us about Mikhail Chekhov, who was able to split his personality in an amazing way; he stunned the other actors in his performance as Caleb, making them cry along with him, not to mention the effect on the audience, and then winked at the people backstage, whispered witty remarks to his partners, fooled around and had a good time on stage. How was this possible?[71]

Vera Soloveva wrote that

The thing was that Chekhov never had to worry about emotions. He only needed to imagine a character he was to play to see him. He used to say he could find in himself, without any trouble, all the feelings of the character. Not everybody had that ability.[72]

[69] K. S. Stanislavski, *Stanislavski's Legacy*, ed. and tr. Elizabeth Reynolds Hapgood, 2nd edn (London: Methuen 1981), pp. 153–4.
[70] Vakhtangov, *Evgeny Vakhtangov*, p. 143.
[71] *Ibid.* p. 241.
[72] Soloveva, 'Memories' quoted in Edwards, *The Stanislavski Heritage*, p. 122.

ACTING AND THE SPIRITUAL SEARCH:
MICHAEL CHEKHOV

Mikhail Aleksandrovich Chekhov was Anton Pavlovich Chekhov's nephew.[73] He was born in 1891 in Russia and died in Los Angeles in America in 1955, where he had become known as Michael Chekhov. He attended the Alexei Suvorin dramatic school in St Petersburg where he excelled in comic roles where, among others, he was taught by Maria Savina (1854–1915) an actress from the Imperial Alexandrinsky Theatre, Vladimir Sladkopevtsev (1876–1957) and Boris Glagolin (1879–1948), actors at the Suvorin theatre. Chekhov said that he learned little from the classes in the school and far more from observing the performances of his teachers.[74] Graduating in 1910, he was then employed by the Suvorin theatre.

Chekhov's father, Alexander (Anton Chekhov's eldest brother, who was gifted, eccentric and alcoholic), taught Chekhov about the development of human consciousness 'from the epoch of Ancient Greece onwards and fostered his interest in philosophy'.[75] Chekhov describes Darwin, Freud and Schopenhauer as his mentors in the period before he joined the MAT in 1912. In a phase of atheism and nervous anguish he writes that he took from Darwin the idea that 'I, in the final analysis, am only *my body* with everything I have inherited from my parents.' His reading of Freud persuaded him that the human soul, if it could be said to exist, could only be studied objectively and scientifically and 'revealed the subconscious soul with all its impurity and sexual impulses'.[76] Under Schopenhauer's influence he studied the development of psychology and was particularly interested in Kant's philosophy. Chekhov's preoccupations with questions of identity were later reflected in his theory of acting.

Chekhov worked in the First Studio from 1912 enjoying great success as an actor. He worked with Vakhtangov and others and, like Vakhtangov, developed ideas that departed from the *system*. The period from 1918 to

---

[73] Michael Chekhov's first wife was also called Olga Knipper – she was the niece of Anton Chekhov's wife, Olga Knipper. In *Zhizn' i Vstrechi*, Chekhov describes how he wished to fulfil Schopenhauer's behest 'If you really consider your life to be nothing, consciously commit some act of folly which will have repercussions throughout your whole life.' Chekhov considered that for him to marry was such an act and so proposed to one of Olga Knipper's nieces. She left him some years later. See Antony Beevor's *The Mystery of Olga Chekhova* (London: Penguin, 2005).

[74] Andrei Kirillov, 'Teatral'naia Sistema Mikhaila Chekhova', *Mnemozina*, 3 (Moscow: Editorial URSS, 2004), p. 498.

[75] Lendley C. Black, *Mikhail Chekhov as Actor, Director and Teacher* (Michigan: Ann Arbor, 1994), p. 5.

[76] Mikhail Chekhov, from *Zhizn' i Vstrechi*, in *Vospominania, Pisma* (Moscow: Lokid-Press 2001), p. 133–4.

1928 after his 'spiritual crisis' is important as it consists of Chekhov's studio experiments with his own new technique of the actor's art, with major roles in the productions of Stanislavsky and Vakhtangov, and his leadership of the First Studio from 1922, which became MAAT-2 in 1924. This is also the period when he rejected some of his earlier beliefs, ceased to be an atheist, and became an anthroposophist, leaving Russia in 1928.

In April 1912 Chekhov auditioned before Stanislavsky, performing a scene from *Tsar Fedor Ioannovich* and Marmeladov's monologue from *Crime and Punishment*. He was accepted into the Art Theatre for the First Studio's opening season.[77] Despite their later differences on style and methods of acting, Stanislavsky was apparently always convinced of Chekhov's ability. Apparently Sulerzhitsky raised a doubt about him in his assessment of the new intake of actors at the end of the 1912/13 season, but Stanislavsky noted he was 'without doubt, talented and charming. One of the real hopes for the future . . . It is necessary to encourage him. He got depressed.'[78]

In this period it appears that Chekhov had no doubts about Stanislavsky. On 7 May 1915 the newspaper *Birzhevie Vedomosti* published an interview with Chekhov:

'We', said the talented actor Mikhail A. Chekhov, 'are a gathering of people who believe in the religion of Stanislavsky, and this is not blind faith, as amongst us you will not find one fanatic, but faith underpinned by strong principles of mutuality and agreement.'[79]

In September 1917 he signed a promise not to drink, adding, 'Not keeping this promise is an offence to K. S., as this would show contempt for him.'[80] But there were conflicts in their work together.

He drew attention in the role of Cobe in *The Wreck of the Good Hope* by Dutch writer Herman Heijermans, directed by Richard Boleslavsky in 1913 in the First Studio. His acting as Caleb Plummer in a version of Charles Dickens's *Cricket on the Hearth*, directed by Sushkievich in 1914, was highly praised, as was his creation of Fraser in *The Deluge* in 1915. Then Chekhov's nervous illness was sparked off by family problems and his feelings about the revolution. He lost his feeling of 'artistic

[77] I. N. Vinogradskaia, *Letopis*, 2nd edn. vols. 1–4, (Moscow: Moskovskii Khudozhestvennyi Teatr, 2003), vol. 2, p. 336.
[78] *Ibid*. p. 360.
[79] *Ibid*. p. 474.
[80] *Ibid*. pp. 552–3.

wholeness ... I lived mechanically and like a machine onstage and off.'[81]
He also wrote that he found Darwin's ideas terrifying, because (in his
interpretation) it meant that the universe was governed by 'meaningless
chance' and that Marx's historical materialism, despite its orderliness, only
confirmed this for him. His readings of Nietszche and Vladimir Solovev
brought him no solution to his existential crisis.[82] The interest of Stanislavsky and fellow studio members in yoga and Hindu philosophy offered
no solutions for Chekhov. Stanislavsky did not approve of what Chekhov
was doing and, according to Valentin Smyshlaev, reproached him:

K. S. Stanislavsky cursed Misha for all he was worth for his inertia in his attitude
to the theatre: K. S. literally cried, 'I know you are studying philosophy; all
the same you won't get a chair. Your business is the theatre, at twenty-six you are
already a celebrity.'[83]

Undeterred, Chekhov kept seeking.

Chekhov's psychological problems reached crisis point in December
1917. Stanislavsky sent a team of the best known Moscow psychiatrists
to see Chekhov, who also underwent hypnotic treatments.[84] In 1918 he
opened a studio at his home on Gazetny Pereulok. According to Gorchakov
it was while he was running his studio that he began to develop his own
theory and practice, although others assert that the basis for this studio's
work was the *system*.[85] Ultimately, the results of Chekhov's spiritual search
were fed into his artistic practice.

Chekhov wrote in *Life and Encounters* about Stanislavsky's alienation
from the First Studio:

I can't judge whether he was jealous of our independence or whether he disagreed
with the direction in which Vakhtangov was taking us but he, and behind him all
the 'old men' of the MAT distanced themselves more and more from us ...
I inclined to Vakhtangov's position. Stanislavsky didn't like this and he called
me several times to chat about the 'direction' I was drawn in ... Officially
acknowledging Vakhtangov's productions such as *The Dybbuk* and *Turandot*, he
all the same criticised them in private conversations.[86]

Nevertheless, their working relationship continued to be successful,
although their working methods were diverging. In April 1921, when
rehearsing Gogol's *Government Inspector*, Stanislavsky gave Chekhov
various keys to his role: he advised him to be more mischievous in the

---

[81] Michael Chekhov, *The Path of the Actor* (eds) Andrei Kirillov and Bella Merlin (London: Routledge, 2005), p. 74.
[82] *Ibid.* p. 72.
[83] Vinogradskaia, *Letopis*, vol. 3, p. 571–2.
[84] Chekhov, *The Path of the Actor*, p. 76.
[85] Gorchakov, *The Theater*, p. 247.
[86] Vinogradskaia, *Letopis*, vol. 3, p. 136.

role of Khlestakov and demonstrated aspects of the role for him. *The Government Inspector,* and Chekhov's acting in particular, was hugely successful. There was an enthusiastic discussion in the press on Chekhov's performance as Khlestakov and its directorial treatment:

Is Chekhov's Khlestakov realistic or 'conventionalised', true to life or fantastic; was the character decided by means of the 'placard', 'masks' or grotesque, by caricature or methods of naturalism; is he acutely contemporary or archaic? These are the questions which were asked and were being discussed by the critics and activists of the theatre on the pages of newspapers and journals.[87]

And despite their differences, in 1922 Vakhtangov wrote diplomatically to Stanislavsky, 'I have been told several times that you accuse Misha and me of separatism. Dear K. S., this is a mistake. Let my studio comrades tell you how fiercely I defend the project of unification for the sake of pantheon shows.'[88]

In 1921 Chekhov left his own Studio, which closed some time afterwards in 1922. After Vakhtangov's death Chekhov became the leader of the First Studio. After the MAAT tour of western Europe and America in 1924, the First Studio became the MAAT-2. He was at that period developing his own particular exercises in rhythmic movement and in *communion*, exploring archetype and working on *Hamlet* with techniques such as getting the actors to throw balls at each other, enabling the actors to explore the meaning of the text without the stimulus of speaking the words and exploring the connection of movement with words.[89] By the 1926/27 season Chekhov was teaching his theatrical-pedagogical system to the actors at the MAAT-2.

Stanislavsky did not approve of the direction of the work, but there were differences of opinion as to whether this was for personal or artistic reasons. Vinogradskaia quotes various sources as follows: first, there is a description of Stanislavsky at the dress rehearsal of *Hamlet* at the MAAT-2 in 1924 with Chekhov in the main role. Giantsintova said, 'The old men behaved all right but Konstantin! It's Salieri! He did not even call in to see Misha, he did not stand up when the whole theatre was standing, he was all twisted up, miserable, malicious and vile with it.' Stanislavsky himself gave other reasons for his viewpoint:

A real tragic actor is a great rarity, and not everyone possesses those qualities that are necessary. And Misha does not possess them. Here is Khlestakov – that's his forte, in that role he is of course, unparalleled. In *Hamlet*, instead of real tragedy

---

[87] *Ibid.* p. 170.
[88] Vakhtangov is referring to the Pantheon shows which were to be productions involving MAT and its studios working together – a project which never took place. *Ibid.* p. 184.
[89] Chekhov, *The Path of the Actor*, p. 107.

he is hysterical . . . And then, this playing with what is contemporary, this leather jacket. In a word, I went away in distress after the show.[90]

Stanislavsky had a problem in acting tragedy; his attempts to play tragic roles were generally seen as unsuccessful but whether any of this reaction was due to jealousy or not is impossible to ascertain. What can be said is that he was certain, throughout his career, that he knew what good acting was. The production was highly controversial: Alma Law writes that its eclectic stylisation was criticised but Chekhov's performance was celebrated by many.[91] Ivanov describes Chekhov's 'theatrical existentialism', a unique quality of Chekhov's acting that in Ivanov's opinion disappeared later when anthroposophy supplanted it as a way of thinking.[92]

Vinogradskaia adds another description of Stanislavsky's 'distress', written ten years later by N. N. Chushkin.

I myself heard a sharp and destructive review of this *Hamlet* and the 'grotesque of MAAT-2' from Stanislavsky in May 1935, sharp to the point of cruelty. In it could be felt his pain and insult at his former pupils, for their 'betrayal of realism', for their departure from the organic laws of creativity. Though Stanislavsky did not approve of Chekhov's treatment of *Hamlet*, he considered all the same that Chekhov was the only person who was *alive* and palpitating in this 'false spectacle of masks and symbols' and somehow could really move the spectator. In general Stanislavsky spoke of Mikhail Alexandrovich Chekhov with great warmth and love as of a talented artist, who had 'gone astray, tragically lost within his searching'.

There is a note by Stanislavsky about the First Studio from the preparatory materials for the book *My Life in Art:*

Very many of my once close followers and students in the last two years have completely and with great ease renounced what we prayed for together. Moreover, what they are doing is exactly the reverse of what I taught them and they have surrendered to the current fashion, taking it for a new art. The further you go into the subtlety of our business, the less the followers follow the searcher, the more he is alone and in this aloneness is his strength.

Interestingly, in speaking about his 'aloneness' and 'his strength', Stanislavsky is using a line from his role as Dr Stockmann. He went on to write, 'The further I go into the subtlety of art, the less followers I have. The old ones (First Studio) have given up.'[93]

[90] Vinogradskaia, *Letopis*, vol. 3, p. 356.
[91] Alma Law, 'Chekhov's Russian *Hamlet* (1924)', *The Drama* Review, 27: 3 (1983), pp. 34, 45.
[92] Vladislav Ivanov, 'Michael Chekhov and Russian Existentialism', in Laurence Senelick (ed.) *Wandering Stars: Russian Emigré Theatre 1905–1940*, (University of Iowa Press, 1992), p. 156.
[93] Vinogradskaia, *Letopis*, vol. 3, pp. 356–7.

Meanwhile, Chekhov's work was drawing disapproval not only from Stanislavsky, but from some officials and critics on ideological grounds, though Lunacharsky, as head of Narkompros (the Peoples' Commissariat for Education), supported Chekhov's work. The 1925 production of *St Petersburg* – about the 1905 Revolution – received severe criticism, though Chekhov's performance as Ableukhov was recognised. He had been working with Andrei Bely, the symbolist poet and anthroposophist whom Chekhov met in 1921. His 1927 portrayal of Muromsky in *The Case* by Sukhovo-Kobylin was praised by many; the critic Markov described how transforming the rhythm of his acting enabled Chekhov to play a whole register of genres.[94] Rudnitsky writes that Chekhov went from comedy to tragedy in the role 'with the apparent artlessness that only genius can achieve'.[95] Others at the time were not so positive. Steiner's work had been suppressed since 1923 and Chekhov's connection with it was held in suspicion. The actor-director, Alexei Diky, and six other members of MAAT-2, after an unsuccessful takeover bid, left the theatre denouncing Chekhov in the newspapers as an idealist and mystic. Chekhov's own account is that he did not attend the meetings of Moscow City Council (at which he was expected as director of MAAT-2) and his talks on art to workers, like his teachings, 'were highly coloured by the spiritual element in my worldview'.[96] He received a letter from Narkompros pointing out where his ideas sounded the same as Steiner's and where they were, therefore, suspect. Byckling writes that Party members advised Chekhov to grow fond of 'the machine' and become more acquainted with workers' jobs to gain a new approach to life.[97] Despite all this, Chekhov's work in film at the time was celebrated and the publication of his 1928 autobiography, *The Path of the Actor* (*Put Aktera*), gained him further acclaim. In the same year he moved to Berlin with his second wife Xenia and worked with director Max Reinhardt.

His last meeting with Stanislavsky also took place in Berlin in September 1928. Here, they had their significant discussion on the differences in their training systems. Stanislavsky recorded in a letter that he met Chekhov twice and that he tried to persuade him to return to the Soviet Union: 'I influence him bit by bit, that is, I hold him back from false steps. My impression is that if they allowed him to fulfil his dream

[94] Chekhov, *The Path of the Actor*, p. 216, n60.
[95] Rudnitsky, *Russian and Soviet Theatre*, p. 194.
[96] Chekhov, *The Path of the Actor*, p. 136.
[97] Liisa Byckling, 'Mikhail Chekhov i Antroposophia; iz Istorii MKHAT Vtorogo', *Studia Russica Helsingiensia et Tartuensia*, 4 (1995), p. 264.

about classical theatre, he would return straightaway, but from his own theatre he acknowledges only a small group.'[98] Stanislavsky is referring to Chekhov's discussions with the authorities just after his emigration, about the possibility of his returning to work in Russia if he were allowed to put on a repertoire of classical plays, his 'own theatre' being MAAT-2.

Also in Berlin, in 1930, Meyerhold tried to persuade Chekhov to return. Chekhov wisely refused, though no one could have known what was in store for Russia in the thirties. At that time he was attending Steiner centres and as well as his work in Germany he was directing a production with the Habima theatre (then on a visit to Germany). After this, Chekhov worked in various places, including Dartington, England, and eventually moved to America in 1939. But officially in the Soviet Union, as Vertman puts it, 'From 1929, the great actor Mikhail Chekhov ceased to exist.'[99]

The beginning of Chekhov's method of acting and his differences with Stanislavsky

Chekhov worked with closely with Stanislavsky from 1912 to 1921; it was a period of change and development of the *system*, after it was initiated by the Stockmann crisis in 1906. Stanislavsky's four books were published after 1928 and in them Stanislavsky is writing retrospectively about his process, and no doubt with the benefit of hindsight. Chekhov's writings, therefore, are an important source of information on the development of the *system* in this time. For example, Chekhov describes the round-the-table work that characterised the approach at MAT in the early part of this period, where they sat at the table for months discussing their parts and the play, and when they began to work they saw that nothing had come from all the analysis.[100]

Significantly he states, similarly to Vakhtangov,

During our first period of work with Stanislavsky, he stressed very much, in the first period of creating his method, that everything was from inside and we must forget how we looked. It was a lop-sided thing, we were very rich inside, but nothing came out because we didn't know how we looked. Then it was discovered that both things had to be developed; you are sure that you are inwardly rich, and you know how you look from the outside.[101]

---

[98] Vinogradskaia, *Letopis*, vol. 4, pp. 50–1.
[99] Yu. Vertman, 'Teatral'no-pedagogicheskie Iskania Mikhaila Chekhova', *Teatr*, 11, (1969), p. 92.
[100] Chekhov, *Lessons for the Professional Actor*, p. 95.
[101] *Ibid.* p. 152.

In *My Life In Art*, Stanislavsky describes his experiments in such symbolic drama as Hamsun's *The Drama of Life*, where he 'removed from the actor any external means of incarnation... because they seemed too physical, realistic, material, when what I wanted was incorporeal passion... straight from the soul of the actor' (*MLIA*, p. 386). This was in 1907. It proved unsuccessful (as did the technique of forcing an actor to emote, encapsulated by the anecdote of Sulerzhitsky sitting on an actor and shouting at him to get him to experience the required emotion), although Vakhtangov returned to these experiments when working on *The Doll of the Infanta* in 1917. But it was the beginning of Stanislavsky's experiments with the inner work of the actor employing the concepts of *radiation, the creative sense of the self on stage* and *experiencing*. In 1915, however, playing Salieri in Pushkin's *Mozart and Salieri*, Stanislavsky realised that, despite the experiments of the past years, he still had not solved the problem of how to 'realise in external form his sincere internal feeling' (*MLIA*, p. 450). Obviously, Chekhov and others would seek their own solutions to the problem.

Chekhov's articles on Stanislavsky's system

Chekhov's articles in *Gorn* in 1919 were some of the first publications on the *system*. He summarises the *system* and divides it, as Stanislavsky did, into the actors' work on themselves and the actors' work on a role. Chekhov then cuts across these, leaving out Stanislavsky's division of the first phase into *experiencing* and *incarnation*, by describing what he calls *The Process of Sowing Seeds* and secondly, *The Act of Incarnation. The Process of Sowing Seeds* has three parts: *reading the play, becoming delighted with the play* and *anatomy*. Stanislavsky's diagram of *experiencing*, discussed in Chapter 2, uses the metaphor of seeds being sown during the development of work on a role. *Delighting in the play* involves affective feelings and necessitates finding an object for these affective feelings (preferably your fellow actor), but Chekhov indicates a different view of *emotional memory* than that practised by Stanislavsky at this time. He writes, 'Affective life in the soul of the actor can begin in various ways, either by means of remembering feelings as such, or by remembering the circumstances in which one feeling or another has been experienced, or finally, by stirring external feelings, et cetera.'[102] The distinction between remembering feelings or the circumstances for the feelings is Ribot's, adopted by Stanislavsky, but the latter,

---

[102] Mikhail Chekhov, *Literaturnoe Nasledie* (Moscow: Iskusstvo, 1986), vol. 2, pp. 40–1.

rather vague phrase is a departure from Stanislavsky. *Anatomising the part* means defining the *through action* by finding out what the character wants (*khotenie*) at each point in the role. This is explored through études.

The Act of Incarnation means seeking the appropriate external forms, getting rid of stencils and finding *today's character*, that is, allowing events from daily life to help rather than hinder spontaneity in the character-isation. This article also includes a discussion of *tasks* and *justification*, but as an alternative to defining the given circumstances needed for the character, the actors find reasons as to why they are performing the task in the environment of the theatre. An example is given of a character taking care of a sick friend; in order for the actors to explain to themselves why they are doing this in a theatre as opposed to a house, they imagine that they have been thrown out of their home and a local theatre manager has taken pity on them. This is an extreme example the idea of *justification* with which Vakhtangov experimented. It replaced Stanislavsky's idea of the actor's *sense of the self on stage* or *public solitude* where the actors are able to forget that the audience is there because their belief in the *given circumstances* is so strong.

In a second article Chekhov discusses attention and fantasy, a term Steiner also preferred to use for imagination. In this period, therefore, it is clear that Chekhov based his ideas on Stanislavsky's work but is beginning to alter some concepts in accordance with ideas developed with Vakh-tangov. Although he valued attention as much as Stanislavsky, he did not think Stanislavsky's methods for the development of concentration were foolproof. In his later writings he includes the story of Stanislavsky expecting an honoured guest at a preview performance. Stanislavsky was so greatly concentrated on the performance that when a stranger appeared he grabbed him and guided him to the seat kept for the honoured guest, forgetting that the guest was a woman and not realising that the man was in fact her bemused chauffeur.[103] Chekhov saw this lapse as the price Stan-islavsky had to pay for his concentration on the performance.

Chekhov always states that his methods are a development of Stan-islavsky's work. He writes,

I have to confess – with all sincerity – that I was never one of Stanislavsky's best pupils, but I must say with equal sincerity that I made much of what Stanislavsky gave us my own forever and placed it as the foundation of my subsequent and, to some extent, independent experiments in the art of drama.[104]

---

[103] Michael Chekhov, *On the Technique of Acting*, (ed.) Mel Gordon (New York: Harper Perennial, 1991), p. 12.
[104] Chekhov, *The Path of the Actor*, p. 78.

Many of Chekhov's assertions in his writings for actors are echoes of Stanislavsky. For example, his starting point for the development of an actor-training technique is that the actor needs training, just as musicians, painters and dancers need to learn their technique, an assertion made by Stanislavsky many times in his writings.[105] Like Stanislavsky, and unlike Meyerhold, his approach is from the standpoint of the actor, not the director. Like Stanislavsky he denigrates the intellect; 'The body and the psychology find each other in the subconscious regions of our creative soul . . . It is our dry intellect which tries to interfere.'[106] Both sought high art rather than craft in acting and the methods of both men are intended to be a means to the same end (i.e. a technique to achieve inspiration).[107] He shared Stanislavsky and Sulerzhitsky's view of the spiritual purpose of theatre and their Tolstoyan belief in the transformational power of art. However, he wanted to go further, spiritualising theatre in terms of Steiner's anthroposophical Christianity, going in the opposite direction to Meyerhold, who sought the brilliance of technical skill.

Chekhov's studio, 1918–1922

Chekhov set up his studio in 1918, working with the actor Smyshlaev who had also been a member of the First Studio. Chekhov, like Stanislavsky, was interested in the problem of *psycho-technique* and the work was based largely on Stanislavsky's *system*, or, as Chekhov says, on his interpretation of it, and what he had learned from Suler and Vakhtangov.[108] Chekhov found working with students inspiring, setting up a situation where there was no 'boss' and the studio represented 'the ideal theatre of the future, a theatre of freedom but disciplined creativity, trust, a collective where friendship and trust reigned, a living organism, where each person served others and worked for common ends . . . a dream of the 'living theatre' as opposed to the theatre-machine'.[109] He was guided by what he calls *the sense of the whole*, which had deserted him in the time of his nervous crisis. This *sense of the whole* of a part he was to play or, in this case, the whole enterprise of the Chekhov Studio, gave him confidence in the undertaking and so the details of what should be done would emerge, as it were, of their own accord. Kirillov writes that the *sense of the whole* later gave

[105] Chekhov, *Lessons for the Professional Actor*, p. 23.
[106] *Ibid.* p. 25.
[107] Chekhov, *On the Technique of Acting*, p. xxxvi.
[108] Chekhov, *The Path of the Actor*, p. 77.
[109] Liisa Byckling, *Mikhail Chekhov v Zapadnom Teatre i Kino* (St Petersburg: Kikimora Publications, 2000), p. 39.

rise to the main principles of Chekhov's method of acting, such as atmosphere and rhythm.[110]

They worked mostly on études, spending days on some of them and did performance work, much of which was based on improvisation. A lot of work was done using fairy tales as a basis and Chekhov's overriding emphasis was to stimulate his own and his students' imaginations. As for the rest of the training he was dissatisfied with the technical teaching going on at MAAT and work on placing the voice, diction, declamation and plastique. He experimented with different systems for placing the voice and diction, but found them unsatisfactory.

A distinctive feature of the programme of the lessons in our studio was the minimal quantity of 'technical' subjects: voice training, articulation, declamation, movement and the acrobatics that were so fashionable during those years – all these subjects were either completely absent from our schedule of lessons or they occupied a secondary place in it. My attitude to all these subjects was almost negative . . . the Chekhov Studio played host to many of the best teachers of the time. We tried three or four different systems of voice training and made similar efforts with systems of articulation and so forth, but never without both myself personally and my students being left with a feeling of dissatisfaction. The dissatisfaction was all the greater the more zealously we undertook to study voice training or articulation, movement or rhythm. This unresolved question was always very difficult, since at the same time as not finding satisfaction in any of the 'technical' subjects, I also felt with my whole soul the immense importance of 'technique' on the stage. Only later did persistent work and research in this direction enable me to gain an understanding of this dilemma and resolve it.

He wrote that it was incorrect to approach the living word from the perspective of anatomy and physiology, as in studies of articulation and voice training:

the true path lies in the opposite direction: from living language, from *living* speech, from the sounding of each of the letters and sound combinations to the so-called resonators, vocal chords, lungs, diaphragm . . . No outward methods can teach the actor to speak truly artistically and expressively if he had not first penetrated into the deep and rich content of every individual letter, each syllable, if he does not first understand and feel the living soul of each letter as a sound.[111]

This interest in the elements of theatre (that is, sound, gesture and movement) typified the modernist preoccupation but he was not to find a solution to his training problems until later. Mala Powers states that from

---

[110] Chekhov, *The Path of the Actor*, pp. 26, 77, 204, n6.
[111] *Ibid.* pp. 78–9.

1922 Chekhov 'began to incorporate some of Rudolf Steiner's artistic innovations into his own acting technique',[112] and the combination of Steiner's eurhythmy with ideas developed with Vakhtangov enabled Chekhov to develop his own method.

The Studio received the title of State Academic Studio from Narkompros after Lunacharsky and others saw performances based on Leo Tolstoy's *The First Distiller*. However, Chekhov left the Studio in 1921; not only was he preoccupied with his performances in *Erik XIV* and *The Government Inspector* but also the work as it was, based on the *system*, held no future for him.[113]

ANTHROPOSOPHY AND ACTING

In 'Michael Chekhov – Problems of Study', Kirillov discusses the problem that much of the study on Chekhov has focussed on separating elements of his work, such as his performance technique from his philosophy: 'Thus one of the most important and treasured features of the actor himself, of his personal and creative perception of the world is being broken – perception and pre-perception of the whole.'[114] Indeed, Chekhov's work cannot be understood and assessed without looking at the anthroposophical concepts that underpin it, just as it is essential to examine the scientific and philosophical bases of the methods of Stanislavsky and Meyerhold.

Mysticism was a strong feature of modernist, pre-revolutionary Russia. The popularity of spiritualism, theosophy and other occult movements was an expression of discontent with materialism in Russia as in other western countries. Secret societies based on Rosicrucian and Templar traditions were also in existence.[115]

Interest in theosophy began to grow after Helena Blavatsky's death in 1891, despite the fact that she had been personally discredited in Russia by the spiritualist and novelist Vsevolod Solovev for her allegedly immoral behaviour, in 1901 the Russian Theosophical Society was founded. Its leader was Anna Alekseevna Kamenskaia, who maintained close contacts with Annie Besant, the dominant figure in theosophy after Blavatsky. The

---

[112] Mala Powers, *Michael Chekhov and the Art of Acting: A Guide to Discovery with Exercises* (New York: Applause Theatre Book Publishers, 1992), p. 15 (Booklet accompanying tapes).
[113] Michael Chekhov, *The Path of the Actor*, p. 211, n44.
[114] Andrei Kirillov, 'Michael Chekhov – Problems of Study', *Eye of the World*, I (St Petersburg, 1994).
[115] The Knights Templar were an association of warrior monks, initially founded in 1188. Their history since the seventeenth century has been associated with the Freemasons.

interests of the Russian symbolists are well known: Aleksandr Blok, Valeri Briusov and Andrei Bely were all influenced by spiritualism and Bely, later Chekhov's close collaborator, became a theosophist in 1908.

On 2 February 1913, the Austrian theosophist Rudolf Steiner (1861–1925) founded the Anthroposophical Society, and the Russian branch was founded the same year. Steiner had originally trained as a scientist and had written on Nietzsche and Goethe. His spiritualism postulated a form of knowledge that transcended sensory experience, which could be attained by the *higher self.* He held that human beings had the capacity to be attuned to spiritual processes by means of a dream-like state of consciousness but that a preoccupation with material things precluded this. People could be trained to recover this capacity. Bely and his wife K. N. Vasileva, and the painter and author Margarita Voloshchin, also an associate of Chekhov's, joined the society. From 1913 Voloshchin learned the movement form eurhythmy from Lory Smits, who had been developing it with Steiner's tuition and guidance since 1912.[116] Eurhythmy, or the 'science of visible speech', in which colour and sound were translated into movement, with spiritual significance, was performed as dance or in Steiner's Mystery dramas.

Chekhov and anthroposophy

Stanislavsky first mentioned Steiner to Chekhov, who later saw Steiner's *Knowledge of the Higher Worlds* in a bookshop.[117] Stanislavsky's spirituality did not go far enough for Chekhov. Yoga had led him to investigate theosophy but, after visiting Moscow priests, Chekhov began to be drawn to anthroposophy's expression of Christianity.[118] He had found that yoga 'put him to sleep and lulled him, bringing egoistic joy'.[119] Chekhov became a member of the Russian Anthroposophical Society at the beginning of the 1920s, having met Bely in 1921. Steiner's work was published in Russia in 1917 and in 1918, and Chekhov heard him lecture in the Netherlands in 1922 and met him in Berlin in 1922.

Theosophical, anthroposophical and other occult societies in the Soviet Union were suppressed and censored from the time of the revolution onwards. Chekhov was aware of the interest of the GPU (the security

---

[116] Magdalene Siegloch, *How the New Art of Eurhythmy Began* (London: Temple Lodge Publishing, 1997), p. 87.

[117] Chekhov, *The Path of the Actor*, p. 133.

[118] Michael Chekhov, *Vospimania, Pisma* (Moscow: Lokid-Press, 2007), pp. 149–50.

[119] Byckling, 'Mikhail Chekhov i Antroposofia', p. 247.

police) in his mystical pursuits.[120] This suppression continued and intensified but, despite it, Chekhov worked with Bely to stage *Petersburg*, based on Bely's novel, a symbolist work that expresses theosophical world view. It tells the story over twenty-four hours of a young revolutionary ordered to place a time bomb in the study of his father, Ableukov, a tsarist official.[121] Unfortunately, the adaptation did not draw such audience numbers as *The Flea*, an adaptation by Evgeny Zamyatin of Nikolai Leskov's story, also staged in 1925 by Chekhov's rival, Diky, at MAAT-2. Nadezhda Nikolaevna Bromley (1884–1966), an anthroposophist, writer and actress at MAAT, wrote *Archangel Mikhail* in 1922 and *The King of the Square Republic* (*Korol' Kvadratnoi Respubliki*) in 1925, which reflected anthroposophical interests. The Russian Anthroposophical Society closed in 1923 and thereafter Chekhov could not reveal the source of his exercises to his actors. Bely continued to work with him, however. It was in Paris, Chekhov says, where what he had known as anthroposophy, a system of ideas, became an *independent, living being* within him.[122] Chekhov borrowed general concepts from anthroposophy for his acting method. In his training he hoped he was enabling people to rediscover their higher selves, as Steiner had posited, although particularly in his later career, he also presented his work as valid simply as an actor-training theory for those who wanted only that. It was not necessary to subscribe to anthroposophy to learn from it as an actor.

The 'higher ego', which Steiner adopted from theosophy, appears in Chekhov's theory of acting:

Theosophical doctrine ... distinguishes between a lower and a higher human Ego; the Ego it defines simply as man's sense of 'I am'. The lower, mortal, personal Ego, incorporated in the three lower bodies, is associated with a particular historical incarnation, and is called 'personality'. The higher, immortal, impersonal Ego, associated with the higher bodies, remains unchanged through the reincarnation sequence and is called 'individuality'.[123]

In this regard Christ, in Steiner's system, is a 'cultural symbol of man's emerging sense of individuality, of the ego-consciousness' (I AM).[124] Chekhov had long been interested in philosophical questions of identity and Kant's idea of the *transcendental ego*. Kant contrasted the *empirical ego* (the self), as it is known through experience, with the *transcendental ego*,

[120] Chekhov, *The Path of the Actor*, p. 136.
[121] Maria Carlson, *No Religion Higher than Truth* (Princeton University Press, 1993), p. 204.
[122] Chekhov, *The Path of the Actor*, pp. 172–3.
[123] Carlson, *No Religion*, p. 121.
[124] *Ibid.* p. 132.

which was the subject of organising principles of thought and intuition that come from something other than individual experience. Chekhov not only found spiritual solace in embracing the concept of the *higher ego* but also believed that it could enable the actor to portray spiritual truth beyond the limitations of his own *lower ego*. In a questionnaire on the psychology of acting set by the State Academy of Artistic Sciences, Chekhov answered a question on the joy of performing by stating, 'I always experience a sense of joy when absorbed in a creative process and it is derived from the following: 1) a release from my own personality and 2) the enactment of the creative idea which would otherwise remain out of the grasp of my everyday consciousness.'[125] On being asked about the relationship between stage emotions and personal feelings he denied that creative emotions could be transformed into real-life ones and stated that what the audience wanted was creative emotion, 'not egotistic and an everyday life experience'.[126] Clearly for Chekhov, any emotions based in experience, as prescribed by Stanislavsky's system, limit the actor to the expression of his own personality, or the *lower ego*.

Transformation
In his youth Chekhov saw the well-known Petersburg actor Boris Glagolin perform in the role of Khlestakov. He experienced a kind of revelation as the quality of his acting, as Chekhov defined it was *not like everyone else*'s, though he had not seen anyone else in the role, meaning that there was a freedom and originality which Chekhov sought to emulate.[127] Chekhov described his own performance as Cobe in *The Wreck of the Good Hope* as '*going beyond* the playwright or the play' to find Cobe's 'true' character, and to express what he later termed his own 'creative individuality'. Kirillov notes the duality in Chekhov's early characters, which were both funny and pitiful; 'by concentrating intensely on the characters' comic aspects, he simultaneously expressed the characters' miserable features, and it was this paradox which provided the comic-tragic effect of Chekhov's acting'.[128]

While Stanislavsky sought 'truth' of characterisation based in his own human experience, Chekhov sought something deeper through imagination and intuition. By applying Chekhov's methods and accessing the higher ego and creative individuality, the actors can express what is beyond their own experience and by creating the character in their imagination, they can then imitate the character. Although there is an objective distance between the

---

[125] Mel Gordon (ed), 'Chekhov's Academy of Arts Questionnaire', *The Drama Review*, 27: 3 (1983), p. 32.
[126] *Ibid.* p. 31.
[127] Chekhov, *The Path of the Actor*, pp. 39–40.
[128] *Ibid.* p. 208.

actor and character, there is a kind of *transformation*. He writes of the actor Zhilinsky, contrasting him with actors who can only play themselves, 'for me, the ability to transform oneself totally has always been the hallmark of talent and the divine spark within the actor'.[129] A concept of trans-formation (*perevoploshchenie*) was also employed by Vakhtangov.[130]

Mind, will and feelings

In his later writings, after his emigration, Chekhov refers directly to Steiner. In *On the Technique of Acting*, he states that some of his ideas concerning the body are extracted from Steiner's teaching in the fields of art and *eurhythmy*. Like Stanislavsky, he describes the actor's mind, will and feel-ings. He writes that the actor should think of the human body in terms of its three forms and functions; mind, feeling and will, and in doing so will 'acquire a kind of aesthetic consciousness' that will tell him how to use his body's various parts. As for mind, unlike animals, humans walk upright. Thus the head is connected with thought, ideas and spiritual activity, reflecting the universe and crowning the human body.

Chekhov writes further that the sphere of the feelings is the chest, arms and hands, where there is the connection with the beating of the heart and rhythmical breathing. However, we know little about the expressiveness of the hands and arms. Also we neglect rhythm, which transforms and increases all the human feelings. The will is in the legs and feet. Their form expresses their function, which is to move the human body through space, according to man's ideas and feelings. He cites examples of different wills cited by Dr Friedrich Rittelmeyer, who wrote a biography of Steiner called *Rudolf Steiner Enters My Life*, published in 1963.

There is a strong Will, which easily becomes lame, and there is a prolonged Will that grows on obstacles. There is a flexible, a stiff, a conscious Will, a sleepy Will, a contrary Will, which always wishes things different than they are and so on.

As an example, Chekhov compared the walk of the actor when playing Othello, which revealed the subtleties of Othello's will, and the actor's ordinary walk, which revealed the pettiness of the actor's own character, particularly in dealing with women.[131] This example is clearly intended to verify the idea of the higher and lower ego in acting, and the idea that

---

[129] Chekhov, *The Path of the Actor*, p. 183.

[130] *Perevoploshchenie* means 'transformation' or 'reincarnation'. It would be worth further investi-gation of the work of P. D. Uspensky (1878–1947), a Russian who became a theosophist in 1907, but later developed his own influential esoteric system. His syncretism strove to unite western philosophy and eastern mysticism, grafting together Nietzschean concepts with Buddhism and the philosophy of Vladimir Solovov. He discussed reincarnation as 'evolution of the spirit', and Darwinism of the soul, rather than of the organism. These ideas, fashionable in early-twentieth-century Russia, could have contributed to ideas of *transformation* in acting.

[131] Chekhov, *On the Technique of Acting*, pp. 52–4.

there is something finer than one's self to inspire acting. These are artistic concepts, intended to develop in the actor an 'aesthetic consciousness' rather than the scientific, psychological ideas behind Stanislavsky's descriptions of mind, will and feeling, which did not interest Chekhov at all. Chekhov's work on *centres*, where the actor can work on a characterisation by imagining the 'centre' of the character in a specific part of the body (or separate from the body but connected to it), is again an artistic way of working with no considerations of anatomy or physiology.[132]

Imagination and atmospheres

Stanislavsky's 'truth as in life' can be contrasted with the actor's being true to the creation of the imagination, which was all-important for Chekhov. In his view, of the mind's three active phases (dreaming, thinking/remembering and imagining), only the imagination is truly effective in the creation of art.[133] Stanislavsky's notion of truth in acting was validated by the reality of personal experience, whereas Chekhov's *feeling of the truth* was validated by what was generated by his imagination, which was the route to 'other worlds'. Chekhov believed in otherworldly forces as the source for creativity and food for the imagination, and wished to harness their power through anthroposophy: 'Marrying the inner truth and emotional depth of Stanislavski's system with the beauty and spiritual impact of Steiner's work became Chekhov's obsession.'[134] An example of this attempted synthesis was Chekhov's work on atmospheres. Byckling asserts that 'the central concept of atmosphere in Chekhov's method in fact comes from the mood of the Chekhovian productions'.[135] Stanislavsky dispensed with mood after a certain period, but others, including Chekhov, did not. These others included Meyerhold, as according to Chamberlain, he was 'inspired by the Symbolist plays and theories of Maeterlinck and Briusov [and] was interested in the idea of a stylised theatre which emphasised 'atmosphere' or 'mood' over naturalistic detail.'[136] Kirillov notes that it was in the role of Fraser in *The Deluge* in 1915 that Chekhov first noted acting within the *atmosphere*, which became one of the main principles of his method.[137] For Chekhov, the actors' imagining the space around them filled with a certain atmosphere (e.g. of a street scene), generated an atmosphere. Chekhov's esotericism is evident here.

---

[132] *Ibid.* pp. 99–106.
[133] Chekhov, *On the Technique of Acting*, Introduction by Mel Gordon, p. xxiii.
[134] Byckling, *Mikhail Chekhov v Zapadnom Teatre*, p. 13, n5.
[135] Byckling, *Mikhail Chekhov v Zapadnom Teatre*, p. 13, n5.
[136] Franc Chamberlain, 'Michael Chekhov on the Technique of Acting: Was Don Quixote true to life?' in Alison Hodge (ed.), *Twentieth Century Actor-training* (London: Routledge, 2000), p. 79.
[137] Chekhov, *The Path of the Actor*, p. 209, n34.

There are influences around us in the world, which cannot be found out by analysis or any psychological means. Certain influences on which we depend more than we think, and the atmosphere is just an instance of these influences being strong enough for us to realise them, without being able to say what it is or where it comes from . . . These influences are longing to come to us and if we call them by means of creating the atmosphere consciously, 'they' are here.[138]

Atmospheres and other worlds were the verification for Chekhov's work as the regeneration of previous human experience was for Stanislavsky. In his description of his work with the Habimah group on *Twelfth Night* in Berlin in 1929 Chekhov writes about his discussions about Palestine and the Old Testament with the group after rehearsals.

At precisely this time I was interested in the esoteric side of Bible stories and once risked speaking about Elohim and Jehovah, but such kind, uncomprehending eyes were turned on me from all sides that I quickly sought to hide the uninvited guests whom I had almost brought into the society of my dear friends.[139]

They would also sing traditional songs and Chekhov writes that

It thrilled me to listen to these contemporary Jews who conveyed in their songs so deeply, so utterly unconsciously the hopes and few joys of their people. I heard them and marvelled: someone *was calling* them in that moment and was singing through them and speaking and crying, as though wanting to wake the singers, but they had fallen asleep long ago, nineteen and a half centuries ago and the singing would no longer rouse them. And the more joyful the song, the more the tears came to my eyes and I could not keep them back.[140]

Incidentally, with reference to *atmospheres*, Chekhov, like Stanislavsky, took the concept of *radiation* from yogic *prana* but whereas Stanislavsky's use of it was in *communion* with the actor's stage partners and the audience, for Chekhov *radiating* and *receiving* were linked not just with communicating with stage partners and the audience but also in communicating with other worlds through *atmospheres*.[141]

In giving free rein to his imagination Chekhov sometimes felt he went too far, perhaps into the realms of overacting. He said of himself in the production of *Twelfth Night* (in which he began to perform in 1920) 'my portrayal of Malvolio offended the audiences with its frank and at times indecent expression of lechery'.[142] On one occasion he got so carried away with improvising that he lost sight of both the improvisational tasks and his fellow actors, during work with Stanislavsky on *The Inspector General.*

[138] Chekhov, *Lessons for the Professional Actor*, p. 37.
[139] Elohim is a Hebrew name for God.
[140] Chekhov, *Vospominania, Pisma*, p. 194. Also, *The Path of the Actor*, p. 158.
[141] Chekhov, *On the Technique of Acting*, Introduction, p. xli.
[142] Gordon, 'Chekhov's Academy of Arts Questionnaire', p. 32.

Deirdre Hurst du Prey relates how he continued to make bridges and transitions from one improvised moment to another, in a scene involving an apple, until Stanislavsky said, 'All right now, Misha, we will go back and rehearse the scene, but this time there will be no apple.'[143]

Concentration

The actor needs powers of concentration in order to enter into an atmosphere or to work with an object. Chekhov's discussions on concentration and attention in a variety of writings from 1919 to 1941 deal with both spontaneous and forced attention and the link between attention and interest, and as such differ little from what he learned from Stanislavsky, drawing from Ribot.[144]

Eurhythmy and voice

Maria Knebel' a member of Chekhov's studio (and later of the Second Studio), states that Chekhov learned about eurhythmy and was using it in his teaching from 1923 without naming it.[145] Eurhythmy aims 'to express in movement and gesture the actual sounds which form the words we use in speech and the actual notes and intervals which compose the melody we hear in music'.[146] This correlated with other ideas current at the time about the primacy of movement and gesture. Steiner is reported to have said:

anyone who wants ... to acquire a pure conception of the quality of movement should study the sounds of *speech*, for speech is one of the greatest human mysteries. It is the human microcosm of the macrocosmic Logos or Creative Word – the speaking of the divine powers in the act of creation to which all religions refer. *Eurhythmy* begins, then, with the more difficult task of interpreting speech in movement – and then passes over to the more traditional and accepted task of doing the same with music.[147]

Bely's wife, Vasileva, probably brought back Steiner's Dramatische Kurs from Berlin soon after Steiner delivered it as a lecture course in about

---

[143] Deirdre Hurst du Prey, 'Working with Chekhov', *The Drama Review*, 27: 3 (1983), pp. 88–9.
[144] Michael Chekhov, 'Chekhov on Acting: A Collection of Unpublished Materials', *The Drama Review*, 27:3 (1983), pp. 46–83.
[145] Liisa Byckling, 'Michael Chekhov and Anthroposophy From the History of the Second Moscow Art Theatre', *Nordic Theatre Research*, (2006), pp. 64–5.
[146] Leaflet on Eurhythmy published by Steiner House.
[147] Marjorie Raffé, Cecil Harwood and Marguerite Lundgren, *Eurythmy and the Impulse of Dance* (London: Rudolph Steiner Press, 1974), p. 14.

1924. Chekhov read this and other works in German, and in 1926 abstracted and commented on Steiner's lectures on eurhythmy to his assistant Viktor Gromov.[148] He attended some classes at Steiner School in Berlin in 1931 but while in Russia ideas from eurhythmy inspired him.[149]

He discusses the 'soul content' of letters such as 'b's' 'closedness', or defensiveness, whereas 'l' means growth or sprouting. The actor should get to know the soul content of all the letters and will find the form the tongue and lips must take when the letter is seeking to express its soul through them: 'The actor must deeply feel the plasticity and musicality of speech.' Similarly, he writes, in movement there is a need to develop an aesthetic conscience. The actor must know that each of his movements not only has one or another kind of colouring but also has a particular sound.[150] In *AWHI* Tortsov teaches the students that 'all sounds that words are formed from have their soul, nature, content . . . if the word is not connected with life and is pronounced formally, mechanically . . . it is like a corpse' (p. 61). The students experiment with joyous 'A's and ponderous 'A's and so on. This is Steiner's idea – teaching sounds as gestures, as it were.

In *Life and Encounters* Chekhov describes how rhythm became even more important for him, after a period of being in hospital when he was in Latvia in 1934. He perceived rhythm in all the phenomena in the world, from the movement of plants to the rotation of the planets, and called this invisible movement or play of forces 'gesture', which, moreover, manifested 'will and feeling'.[151]

Psychological gesture

The notion of *psychological gesture* became important in Chekhov's method. It relies on the precept that 'everything which is going on while we are rehearsing on stage' can be interpreted as '*gesture* or *action* or *movement.* Everything can be turned into a gesture with qualities and through this an entire characterisation can be developed.'[152] Visible movement or gesture includes sound and is primary in acting. Chekhov's process in developing this idea, influenced as it was by Steiner, can be compared to Stanislavsky's development of the concepts of action and the *task* as well as Chekhov's

---

[148] Byckling, *Mikhail Chekhov v Zapadnom Teatre*, p. 42. See also letter to Gromov in Chekhov, *Literaturnoe Nasledie*, 1, pp. 331–2.
[149] Chekhov, *The Path of the Actor*, p. 160.
[150] *Ibid.* p. 80.
[151] *Ibid.* p. 187.
[152] Chekhov, *Lessons for the Professional Actor*, p. 107.

work with Vakhtangov. In explaining the flexibility that the *psychological gesture* brings to the actor, he gives several examples from his work at MAT:

If you have prepared your part so that you are able to change everything and not fix anything, you will have the pleasure of changing your part, or the archetype, or the gesture through the whole period of acting. I will give you an example from my own life. When Vakhtangov was directing me in the play *Eric XIV*, neither of us knew about these things, but somehow we were both driving towards the archetype or gesture. We found a complicated thing which was almost a gesture – we didn't know that it could be simplified to the point of gesture. Vakhtangov told me that if I had an imaginary circle on the floor and tried to go through it but could not, then it would be something of Eric. From this we found a certain form of gesture and shouting for the whole play.[153]

Again, he writes (and this gives an insight into Stanislavsky's methods when he was producing *The Government Inspector* in 1921):

When Stanislavsky was producing *The Inspector General* he did not ever speak to me about gestures or archetypes, but he suggested the following psychological trick which later was the key to the part. He suggested that I start to catch things, and to drop them suddenly. So he gave me the key to the psychology of the Inspector General – he is nothing actually, but that is the whole beauty of the character. Something goes on senselessly. Just the same, one simple gesture can be found for the character of the Inspector General which includes everything.[154]

A third example is given from the period of work on *The Deluge*:

again it was before we knew of the psychological gesture or the archetype. Vakhtangov and I tried to find the most characteristic thing for Fraser. We found that the character always had to look or search for something he had lost. That was the whole psychology. He was lost inside of himself, but it could be simplified to the degree of the gesture. The gesture has to grow and develop, and you change it always.[155]

Although Chekhov is describing here the *psychological gesture* of the character, it is also possible to work with *psychological gesture* so that the character develops a series of gestures expressing what he or she wants at each point in the play, and also to develop the *psychological gesture* of the play, which could be compared with Stanislavsky's *supertask*. In describing how using the *psychological gesture* makes it harder for the actor to speak a text for its meaning only, for its 'dry intellectual content', Chekhov quotes Steiner: 'If speech is to be made plastic on the one hand, musical on the other,' wrote Rudolf Steiner, 'then this is first of all a

---

[153] *Ibid.* p. 118.
[154] *Ibid.* pp. 118–19, see also *On the Technique of Acting*, p. 89.
[155] *Ibid.* p. 119.

matter of bringing gesture into the speech.'[156] Kirillov and Merlin point out that gesture integrates speech, movement and psychology in Chekhov's method.[157] It was an important part of a method that would allow the actor to express spiritual content without recourse to personal experience.

In summary, Chekhov states that 'through strong concentration and a vivid imagination, together with the use of the Psychological Gesture behind the acting, Rudolf Steiner's Eurhythmy and Speech Formation, the Objective and the Atmosphere, the actor will experience something resembling a process of awakening'. This inner activity, constantly seeking an outlet, is the impulse for creative work, by which the actor can perform easily and reach his audience.[158] This could be compared with Stanislavsky's *aktivnost'*. However, though Chekhov clearly made use of anthroposophical ideas and experimented with eurhythmy, he did not fully espouse Steiner's own dramatic method. The lack of conflict in productions based on eurhythmy did not result, in Chekhov's opinion, in good drama.

Chekhov's argument with Stanislavsky

Chekhov describes his meeting with Stanislavsky when the latter was in Berlin:

When Stanislavsky called me to talk about his 'system', in 1928, when I was already abroad (this was our last meeting), we talked (though we did not agree) about two points which evoked a difference of opinion . . . Both points of our conversation, in essence were one thing: *should an actor separate from or bring in to creative work, his personal, unworked-through feelings?* This discussion, which clarified such a lot for me, took place in a Berlin café.[159]

According to Gordon, at this meeting Chekhov espoused the 'dual awareness of performing before an audience while following his character's guidance . . . obeying the Higher Ego, or stepping outside oneself to comply with the character's demands', and admonished Stanislavsky for the harmfulness of his system, contending that its reliance on *emotional memory* led actors into uncontrolled hysteria.[160] He told him to replace it with imagination. Stanislavsky disagreed. Stanislavsky of course did not deny, but prized the imagination, though he had a different view of it. A whole chapter in *AWHE* is entitled 'Imagination', in which the *magic if*

---

[156] *Ibid.* p. 67.
[157] Chekhov, *The Path of the Actor*, p. 227.
[158] Chekhov, *On the Technique of Acting*, pp. 112–3.
[159] Vinogradskaia, *Letopis*, vol. 4, p. 51.
[160] Chekhov, *On the Technique of Acting*, p. xxiii. See also letter to Podgornii, *Literaturnoe Nasledie*, I, pp. 82–3.

is instrumental: '*All our movements on stage, every word must be the result of the true life of the imagination*' (p. 142). Chekhov used Stanislavsky's methods of work on études and exercises on the *internal object*. He also borrowed Stanislavsky's term *bodiless rehearsal* in his own studio work. The process of rehearsing whole scenes, by oneself and with partners before actually enacting them was very fruitful.[161] However, as Chekhov discusses in *Lessons for the Professional Actor*, the source for the work of our imagination should not be personal experience, as it is for Stanislavsky. Chekhov writes, 'If we take the real image of our real grandfather, it becomes too personal in the wrong sense.'[162] It will detract from the performance and, Chekhov asserts, possibly induce psychological illness in the actor who works this way.

We can compare this with Stanislavsky's view of working with *emotional memory*. In *AWHE*, Kostia discusses with Tortsov his memories; first of all, he saw a fatal street accident, and then an elderly Serb street entertainer in tears trying to feed orange peel to his dead monkey, unable to accept that his pet is dead. What is described is a process of distillation and crystallisation of these memories so that not one incident is recalled, but the memories of all similar ones are synthesised. Time 'not only purifies but can poeticise the recollections' (*AWHE*, p. 290). Tortsov adds, contradicting Chekhov, 'Always act in your own person as an artist. You cannot get away from yourself . . . You lose yourself on stage at the moment when experiencing ends and overacting begins . . . breaking this law means the artist kills the character' (*AWHE*, p. 294).

The *Encyclopaedia Britannica*, 14th edn, 1929, published an inaccurate translation of a 1928 article by Stanislavsky entitled 'The Art of the Actor and Director' (*Collected Works*, vol. 6). In the following (retranslated) excerpt, Stanislavsky describes the role of the imagination (which is subject to the influence of consciousness) in opening up the way to the feelings of the role.

It is impossible to influence feelings directly, but it is possible to stir creative fantasy in oneself in the right direction and fantasy, as the observations of scientific psychology indicate, will excite our *affective memory* and, luring the elements of feelings experienced at some time from its hidden stores beyond the boundaries of consciousness, organises them again to correspond with the images which arise in us. In this way the images of our fantasy, flaring up in us without any effort on our part, find a response in our affective memory and evoke in it the sounds of corresponding feelings. This is why creative fantasy is the fundamental gift the actor needs . . .

[161] Byckling, *Mikhail Chekhov*, p. 22.
[162] Chekhov, *Lessons for the Professional Actor*, p. 40.

There is widespread published opinion that the method I practise in the artistic training of the actor, as it appeals to the stores of his/her affective memory; that is, his personal emotional experience, via the imagination, will by the same token result in reducing the range of his/her creativity to the limits of his/her personal experience and will not allow him/her to play roles which are dissimilar to him/her in terms of psychological mould. This opinion is based on a very simple misunderstanding, since those elements of actuality from which our fantasy shapes its imaginary creations are also drawn by it from our limited experience and the wealth and variety of these creations is achieved only through *combinations* of the elements drawn from experience. The musical scale has only seven basic tones; the spectrum of sunlight only seven basic colours but the combination of sounds in music and colours in art is infinite. The same thing must be said about the basic feelings which are preserved in our affective memory, just as the way in which images we apprehend from the outside world are preserved in our intellectual memory; the number of these basic feelings in the internal experience of each of us is limited, but the shades and combinations are as numerous as the combinations created from the elements of the external experience of the activity of the imagination (pp. 280–1).

In an explanation of the higher ego, in a lecture demonstration to members of the Group Theatre in September 1935,[163] Chekhov observed that the Stanislavskian actor has been taught to build his role on the similarities between his personal history and that of the character in the play. But this constant 'repetition of the actor's own nature', in Chekhov's view, in creating different parts over the years, causes a progressive 'degeneration of talent'. Creative means are used less and less. Eventually the actor will begin to imitate himself, relying for the most part on repeated personal mannerisms and stage clichés. Elsewhere Chekhov refers to this process as 'degeneration', and attacks Stanislavsky's concept of *Ia esm*', this perception of the self as 'the condensed and closed "I Am"'[164] – very different from Steiner's 'I AM', which is individuality, or ego-consciousness, or man's symbolic connection with Christ. The higher ego is, firstly, the source of actors' creative individuality and therefore enables them to act one role differently from another; secondly, it has an ethical sense enabling the actor to sense the conflict between good and evil in the play; thirdly, it brings sensitivity to the audience's perspective of the play in performance; and fourthly, a sense of detachment, compassion and humour which the lower, selfish ego cannot bring.[165] By means of the anthroposophical

---

[163] Chekhov, *On the Technique of Acting*, Introduction by Gordon, pp. xxvi–xxvii.
[164] Chekhov, *Lessons for the Professional Actor*, pp. 26, 29.
[165] Chekhov, *On the Technique of Acting*, p. 155.

concept of the higher ego, Chekhov sought to solve the problems Stanislavsky aimed to solve by appealing to 'laws of human behaviour'.

Thus, imitation of the image is a central concept in Chekhov's method.[166] Chekhov, like Vakhtangov and Meyerhold, preferred to use the word *obraz*, or image, instead of the words for character or role, preferred by Stanislavsky. Chekhov's idea is that as the character is developed in the actor's imagination rather than from previous experience of the actor, the actor then imitates the image in order to begin the process of *transformation*. 'At the beginning the actor constructs his/her character/image exclusively in the imagination and then tries to imitate its internal and external qualities.'[167] In Chekhov's view the actor is objective, not reliant, like Stanislavsky's actor, on his personal feelings. Stanislavsky's actor 'goes from himself' but it is possible for the Chekhovian actor to 'go beyond' not just the playwright and the play but his own poverty-stricken soul, his lower ego into the realms of the *higher ego*, another consciousness. The *system*, according to Chekhov, limits the character to the personality of the actor.[168] As the excerpt from *Encyclopaedia Britannica* shows, in Stanislavsky's view this was not a limitation, but Chekhov was insistent on the separation of the actor from the role. He quotes Steiner: 'the actor must not be possessed by his role. He must stand facing it so that his part becomes objective. He experiences it as his own creation.'[169]

Therefore, the actor possesses a divided consciousness; the actor's consciousness is irrelevant to the image's consciousness. It is the image's *experiencing* that is important, not that of the actor.[170] Liisa Byckling relates this to Vakhtangov's concept of alienation, comparing it with Stanislavsky's discussion of 'self-control'.[171] Indeed, Stanislavsky describes the *controller* and writes of 'multi-layered attention'. But for Chekhov this discovery had a mystical significance. In *Artists* by Watters and Hopkins, the first play in which Chekhov participated with Reinhardt in Vienna in 1928, Chekhov struggled with problems of a short and sloppy rehearsal process, lack of direction and his own uninspired characterisation. But he saw a vision of his character Skid from which he was somehow separate and was able to conduct Skid's acting: 'I was in the auditorium and standing beside myself and in each of my fellow actors on stage and I

---

[166] See notes 56 and 62, pp. 214, 216 in Chekhov, *The Path of the Actor*.
[167] Byckling, 'Mikhail Chekhov i Antroposofia', p. 261.
[168] Chamberlain, 'Was Don Quixote true to life?' in Hodge, *Twentieth Century Actor-training*, p. 81.
[169] Chekhov, *On the Technique of Acting*, pp. 155–6.
[170] Chekhov, quoted in Andrei Kirillov, 'Teatral'naia Sistema', pp. 506–7.
[171] Byckling, *Mikhail Chekhov Zapadnom Teatre*, p. 35.

knew what all of them were feeling, wanting and expecting'.[172] The image, it seemed, had come to him from elsewhere. As Vertman puts it, according to Chekhov's summary of epigrams from Steiner and others, 'Images created by the fantasy of the artist live their own independent life.'[173] She writes that Chekhov formulated the idea of the objectivity of the creative process in the mid-twenties. Allowing the images and atmospheres to come to the actor generates true inspiration. To create from within oneself alone is mere 'materialistic brain activity'.[174] Chekhov's concept, as we have seen, however, is predicated on the existence of 'other worlds'. This is not to say that his emphasis on the imagination is invalid – it may be liberating for the actors to work from the creation of the imagination rather than have to validate their work according to Stanislavsky's nebulous Tolstoyan feeling but it could be debated as to whether the actor's imagination is fed by 'other worlds' or is, in fact is an essentially subjective capacity of the brain, with no spiritual dimension.

In assessing the differences between Stanislavskys and Chekhov's approaches, we have to consider that Chekhov's formative years were at the turn of the century, when modernism was emerging. Traditional religion, morality and law were found wanting and the idea of a second, hidden reality became prevalent. 'Divergent figures like Freud, Heidegger, Viacheslav Ivanov, Steiner, were bound by a common creative impulse – to decipher the second reality and thus improve the reality of daily life.'[175]

This was reflected in the emergence of symbolist and other plays in the theatre and the inadequacy for them of Stanislavsky's early methods. This was one of the reasons why the studios at the MAT were established, resulting in one instance in Vakhtangov's *imaginative realism*. As new views of theatre developed Chekhov firmly rejected agit-prop and also naturalistic 'simplicity as in life'.[176] Byckling sees Chekhov's response to the times encapsulated in his *Hamlet* of 1924. The actress Olga Pizhova said of Chekhov, 'Here he did not act, he performed a sacred rite.'[177] In discussing *Hamlet* Chekhov demanded 'catharsis from the actor in order

---

[172] Chekhov, *The Path of the Actor*, p. 172–3.
[173] Vertman, 'Teatral'no-pedagogicheskie Iskania Mikhaila Chekhova', p. 93.
[174] *Ibid.* p. 94.
[175] Alexander Etkind, *The Eros of the Impossible: The history of Psycho-analysis in Russia* tr. Noah Rubins and Maria Rubins (Oxford: Westview Press, 1997), p. 39.
[176] Byckling, 'Mikhail Chekhov i Antroposofia', p. 251.
[177] Byckling, *Mikhail Chekhov v Zapadnom Teatre*, p. 47.

that the public can be purified' and stated that 'inspiration is the momentary penetration of the truth'.[178]

Science versus religion

Chekhov opposed materialism with its scientific positivism, its denial of metaphysics and emphasis on scientific method, as it was anti-religious. Anthroposophy, like other occult movements, 'hoped to balance the materialism of the age by reminding man of his spiritual, intuitive side'.[179] For Chekhov, materialism also endangered art: 'The materialistic tendencies of that time began to have a noticeable influence on the artistic life of the Studio.'[180] Gorchakov states that Bolshevism and its militant materialism were alien and frightening to Chekhov. 'Danger threatened our art because of materialism. Accepted and carried out to the end, it was able to kill the living emotion of the actor, to lead him to re-evaluate the outer means of expression, and to cause him to lose the inner ones.'[181]

He maintained this viewpoint in later years:

You know, of course, that during the last third of the past century science – and later – art became very materialistic, and scientists at that time made certain statements telling us that everything was matter and materialism. Of course the beginning of the fifth century saw the rise of materialism, but the last third of the past century was the climax. The result of this is with us today. This materialistic point of view is what we are now living through . . . the whole theatre has become so materialistic for us as actors.[182]

He saw Steiner's work as scientific, as uniting mystical and scientific knowledge and, therefore, thought he had the authority to challenge scientific orthodoxy in his writings: 'Scientists . . . cannot see that it is mechanically impossible to imagine such a pump as our heart . . . The whole secret is that the blood moves and the heart follows, but our psychologists are not so well developed in science that they can accept this.'[183] What is more, scientific investigation of theatre must be done by actors and artists and not scientists and, moreover, he cites an example where a creative artistic approach is bringing great results in agriculture.[184]

[178] Byckling, 'Mikhail Chekhov i Antroposofia', p. 253.
[179] Carlson, *No Religion*, p. 34.
[180] Byckling, *Mikhail Chekhov Zapadnom Teatre*, p. 44.
[181] Gorchakov, *Theater in Soviet Russia*, p. 249.
[182] Chekhov, *Lessons for the Professional Actor*, p. 139.
[183] *Ibid.* p. 79.
[184] *Ibid.* pp. 141–2.

Chekhov's dismissal of orthodox scientific investigation, of basic anatomy and physiology, set him poles apart from Stanislavsky.

Anthroposophy and the other occult movements seemed to be the answer to personal crisis for many others as well as Chekhov: 'Theosophy appeared at a time of crisis, when it seemed to many that science and religion had become mutually exclusive.'[185] Spiritualism also claimed to be consistent with modern science and anthroposophy claimed to reconcile religion and science. It is in this context that Chekhov's rejection of contemporary science must be seen; the artist has access to higher, spiritual powers, which have a far greater authority, in his view, than that of scientific materialism.[186]

Truth as in life versus occult truth

Both Stanislavsky and Chekhov's approaches are based in empiricism in James's sense. Both offer actors a means of proceeding that, it is claimed, will enable them to have the experiences that Stanislavsky and Chekhov had themselves. From this point of view the opposition of psychological truth to occult truth is immaterial: Stanislavsky and Chekhov's followers would cite the validity of both approaches from their own personal experience. Chekhov's method can be learned without becoming an anthroposophist or subscribing to anthroposophy. His way of proceeding would enable someone else to have the experience of, for example, creating an *atmosphere*, but the interpretation of process undergone is another matter. Chekhov might have believed that atmospheres come from other worlds, but an actor could claim to create an atmosphere by going through the process Chekhov describes without subscribing to this belief; all that would need to be true was that such a thing as an atmosphere can be created.

Stanislavsky does not discuss atmosphere in the same way, but for him, mood or feeling can be generated by the actor and communicated to the

---

[185] Carlson, *No Religion*, p. 35.

[186] Chekhov's former student, the actress Mala Powers, claims that science now corroborates Chekhov's theories. 'The narrow *scientific* thinking of previous decades has gradually given way to an acceptance of certain unseen energies. Today, studies on sub-atomic particles in the field of quantum physics quote the Heisenberg Principle, which states that 'the mere act of observing something changes the nature of the thing observed'. 'The practice of visualization is now employed for improving athletic performance and for use in the field of health care.' Powers, *Michael Chekhov and the Art of Acting*, p. 6. The Heisenberg Uncertainty Principle which sets a theoretical limit to the precision with which a particle's momentum and position can be measured simultaneously does not, as far as I am aware, demonstrate the existence of 'unseen energies', or make the claim about observation that Powers asserts.

audience by going through his procedures. Again, what the actor should believe is true is that such a mood or feeling can exist and, for Stanislavsky, this would be because the actor has experienced it, or something akin to it.

Impact on Stanislavsky

In 1915, prior to Vakhtangov's complaint in 1918 that Stanislavsky sacrificed inner technique at the expense of outer technique, and Chekhov's similar complaints, Stanislavsky had concluded that when playing Salieri, his internal *experiencing* was correct, but that this was not being conveyed to the audience. He then went on to seek a way of addressing this problem. In doing so, it is possible that he did not reject Chekhov's experiments as firmly as it would seem. The higher I makes an appearance in *The System and Methods of Creative Art*, the lectures given between 1918 and 1922 at the Studio of the Bolshoi Opera Theatre. He speaks of the actor 'forgetting the personal I' in order to get the better of his own character and personality. Again, 'everything . . . an actor learns . . . is only an approach to a more flexible liberation of his creative 'I' from the clutches of his egoistic 'I' that exercises such influence over him in his private life'.[187] He recommends that in the rehearsal process you should 'see with your mind's eye whether your consciousness is as free as your body, whether all your attention has been transferred to your "Higher I".'[188] There is much discussion of the relationship between thought, word and feeling in a way that seems reminiscent of Steiner. But this mode of expression does not continue in Stanislavsky's writings.

Chekhov, like Vakhtangov, explored unresolved differences from Stanislavsky, developing his own ideas on emotion, imagination and *justification*. He experimented widely and replaced Stanislavsky's exercises on muscle relaxation with the idea of working with the 'feeling of ease'.[189] Byckling states that in his work on *Hamlet*, Chekhov anticipated Stanislavsky's *method of physical actions*: 'Chekhov's aim was for the actors to learn in practice to grasp the profound connection of movement with words on the one hand and emotions on the other.'[190] This is debatable in view of the fact that the *method* was not really a departure from Stanislavsky's earlier work. And Stanislavsky saw what was going on in the

---

[187] Stanislavsky, *On the Art of the Stage*, tr. David Magarshack (London: Faber and Faber, 1967), pp. 175–6, 110, 117.
[188] *Ibid.* p. 202.
[189] Chekhov, *On the Technique of Acting*, pp. 48–50, also Introduction by Gordon, p. xxxix.
[190] Byckling, 'Mikhail Chekhov i Antroposofia', p. 258.

studios in 1922 as the 'reverse of his teaching'. Chekhov also wanted the actor to communicate with the audience in the way Vakhtangov had suggested – acting in the way the spectators of the day demanded. 'A contact between audience and actor is established only when the actor loves the audience, *every audience* and when he offers them his stage image *as it arises today*, letting this image of the character do everything that his inspiration – in which the will of the auditorium also lives – demands of it.'[191] This would have been anathema to Stanislavsky and his Tolstoyan view.

Although Stanislavsky maintained his beliefs about *emotion*, there were a number of reasons for him to emphasise the description of action in his work after the revolution. His encounters with Vakhtangov, Chekhov and Meyerhold and their emphases in their methods may have contributed to this. He stated not long before he died, 'One must give the actors various paths. One of these is the path of action. There is also another path; you can move from feeling to action, arousing feeling first.'[192] Byckling writes that Chekhov considered Stanislavsky's *system* both more complicated than his own method and yet that it covered fewer aspects of training the actor.[193] He also stated that Stanislavsky had made his *system* his second nature and his commitment to his method provided a 'marvelous example of what it means to be trained'.[194] But Chekhov adds that Stanislavsky 'tortured' the people he worked with, in trying to get them to do what he wanted, and suggests that perhaps Stanislavsky had not found the right method of training. Clearly the major difference between Stanislavsky and Chekhov was about the use of prior personal experience to bring about authenticity of performance, which could not be resolved because of Stanislavsky's emphasis on psychology and Chekhov's spiritual beliefs. Meyerhold disagreed with Stanislavsky on the same issue, although his reasons for doing so were very different from those of Chekhov.

---

[191] Chekhov, *The Path of the Actor*, pp. 125–6.
[192] Sharon M. Carnicke, *Stanislavsky in Focus* (Amsterdam: Harwood Academic Publishers, 1998), p. 151.
[193] Liisa Byckling, 'Pages from the Past: *The Possessed*, produced by Michael Chekhov on Broadway in 1939', *Slavic and East European Performance*, 15: 2 (1995), p. 35.
[194] Chekhov, 'Chekhov on Acting', *The Drama Review*, 27:3 (1983), p. 82.

CHAPTER 5

Challenges to the system: Meyerhold

Meyerhold was an outstanding drama student at the school of the Moscow Philharmonic Society where he was taught by Nemirovich-Danchenko, graduating from there in 1898. Both he and Olga Knipper were awarded the Society's silver medal and were invited to work at the MAT from its beginnings as the Moscow Popular Art Theatre in 1898. There, he was directed by Stanislavsky, over a decade before Michael Chekhov and Vakhtangov appeared. His work on his departure from MAT involved a rejection of Stanislavsky's particular ideas of emotional truth and the subconscious, and an embrace of theatrical traditions incluuding commedia dell'arte, as sources for new theatre before the revolution. The comparison of his earlier work with Meyerhold's post-revolutionary biomechanical training system, and its purportedly scientific roots in Taylorism, reflex conditioning and William James's theory of emotion, raises interesting questions and also sheds light on the roots of the differences in perspective between Stanislavsky and Meyerhold.

Vsevolod Meyerhold (1874–1940) was born to German parents in Penza, 550 kilometres south-east of Moscow. His father ran a profitable vodka distillery and the family were patrons of theatre and music in Penza; many of his large family were musical. As a young man, Meyerhold ran an amateur group called the Penza Popular Theatre, which aimed to bring theatre to the people, an interest he pursued consistently throughout his life. In 1895 Meyerhold changed his name to Vsevolod Emilevich Meyerhold from Karl Kazimir Theodore Meiergold, took Russian citizenship and joined the orthodox faith; the year after, he married Olga Munt. He initially studied law in Moscow, like Vakhtangov, but was drawn to performance. He was taught at the Philharmonic by Fedotov (who had directed and taught Stanislavsky), as well as by Nemirovich-Danchenko.

Meyerhold's work, like Chekhov's, was suppressed in the Soviet Union from the Stalinist period onwards, although unlike Chekhov he remained in Russia, in increasingly difficult circumstances. Since the beginnings of his rehabilitation in Russia in the 1950s, and glasnost in the 1990s, more information on his work has become available, leading to a resurgence of interest in and reinterpretations of his work.

In some ways the differences between his work before and after the revolution are more clear-cut than with Stanislavsky. Meyerhold had a number of leading roles in MAT's first seasons, for example, in plays by Chekhov, Hauptmann and Alexei Tolstoy, but he left the MAT in 1902, beginning his directorial career with work in the provinces, particularly on New Drama, including symbolist plays.[1] He returned to the MAT in 1905 at Stanislavsky's invitation, to lead experimental work into new theatre forms at the First Theatre-Studio in Russia (the Studio on Povarskaia Street). Although this work was not seen as successful and Stanislavsky took a decision to close the enterprise after only a few months, 'the lessons learned at the Studio equipped Meyerhold with the experience to achieve the successes that were soon to follow in St Petersburg and which led to the establishment of a new movement in the Russian theatre'.[2] He went on to work with Vera Komissarzhevskaia, the actress famously described as 'the Russian Duse', and then for the Imperial theatres in St Petersburg. In this period he used the pseudonym of Dr Dapertutto and founded a studio on Borodinskaia Street, in 1913, which ran until 1917. He published a journal called *Love of Three Oranges*, between 1914 and 1916, which took its name from the play by Carlo Gozzi (1720–1806), who had revived commedia dell'arte in the eighteenth century.

In 1918 Meyerhold joined the Bolsheviks and was appointed as Deputy Head of Narkompros's Theatre Section. From 1918 to 1919 he taught a programme of courses in the Mastery of Stage production with Leonid S. Viven and others in Petrograd. After a period in the Crimea when he was imprisoned by the Whites in the Civil War he moved to Moscow in 1920 and ran a studio, the State Higher Directors' Workshops, which after a rapid succession of names became known as GITIS (*Gosudarstvenny Institut Teatral'nogo Iskusstva*), the State Institute of Theatrical Art in 1922. His First Theatre of the RSFSR ran briefly from 1920 to 1921, then the Theatre in the name of Meyerhold opened in 1923 and ran until 1938. In the early twenties he was lionised and his name was considered synonymous with avant-garde theatre. From 1925 the proliferation of

---

[1] See Edward Braun, *Meyerhold: A Revolution in Theatre*, 2nd edn (London: Methuen, 1998), pp. 13–14 for a discussion of the various reasons for Meyerhold's departure.
[2] *Ibid.* p. 43.

actor-training courses and studios began to die down, but Meyerhold's experiments with acting continued, in particular with *biomechanics*, as did his dialogue with Stanislavsky about acting. In 1924 Zakhava, representing MAT's Third Studio (which was in some difficulties after Vakhtangov's death), asked Stanislavsky to work with Meyerhold. Stanislavsky said that he would be interested to do so, but said 'the territory is too small'.[3] Meyerhold trained and directed a number of multi-skilled actors such as Igor Ilinsky, Erast Garin and Maria Babanova. He maintained contact with Michael Chekhov after the latter's emigration and they met in Berlin in 1930. In the thirties he met with disfavour; his training system of *biomechanics* was attacked in 1932. Stanislavsky made interventions on his behalf but he was put to death in prison in 1940 after a period of imprisonment and torture.

Meyerhold's differences with Stanislavsky: 'theatre not life'

From the beginning of his career Meyerhold had an acting style that was particular to him. Braun suggests that when Meyerhold left the MAT in 1902 it resolved the problem that 'he was finding it difficult to reconcile his angular, grotesque style of acting with the muted naturalism demanded by Stanislavsky'.[4] This situation changed, however, as Stanislavsky had struggled to develop a suitable style for symbolist drama in the early period of the MAT's development when he was also prompted by the need to find a style suitable for Chekhov's plays. Ibsen, Strindberg and Gorky all stretched the boundaries of theatrical practice and placed new demands on the actor, and such writers of symbolist plays as Hauptmann, Maeterlinck and Leonid Andreev placed an even greater demand for new forms of expression on the theatre. Briusov's article, 'Unnecessary Truth', attacked the Moscow Art Theatre in 1902, criticising the realism of the set, props and costumes and an acting style that limited the imagination of the audience. The MAT staged a trilogy of Maeterlinck plays in 1904, *The Blind, The Uninvited Guest* and *Inside*, an experiment which was deemed a failure. It was at this point that Meyerhold was asked to work in the MAT Studio to develop an appropriate style for symbolist work and although this ended abruptly, Meyerhold carried on experimenting. Meyerhold's development was prompted by both the need to find a way

[3] I. N. Vinogradskaia, *Zhizn i Tvorchestvo K. S. Stanislavskogo, Letopis* 2nd edn, vols 1–4 (Moscow: Moskovskii Khudozhestvennyi Teatr, 2003), vol. 3, p. 338.
[4] Edward Braun, (ed. and tr.), *Meyerhold on Theatre* 2nd edn (London: Methuen, 1991), p. 17.

to justify and promote his own personal means of expression, his particular style and his own unique world-view, and to uncover solutions that were not those of Stanislavsky. He took as his canon Briusov's article and its call for *conscious* conventionalisation (*soznatel'naia uslovnost'*) in production technique.[5] Meyerhold's definition of *stylisation* states that it is not the photographic reproduction of an epoch or phenomenon, but it 'is indivisibly tied up with the idea of convention (*uslovnost'*), generalisation and symbol'. All possible means of expression are to be used to reveal the hidden synthesis of the given epoch or phenomenon.[6] He argued for this as the basic principle of all art, challenging Stanislavsky's idea of theatrical truth.

The goal of Meyerhold's studio work was stylised theatricality; the rejection of what he described as Stanislavsky's naturalism and the need to find another way to achieve the theatre of mood.[7] He had a different approach to emotion than that envisaged by Stanislavsky's emphasis on the *subconscious, emotional memory* and the *feeling of truth*. He wanted the actor to be a trained and conscious artist, rather than one hypnotising and hypnotised by feeling.[8] This did not mean that he did not subscribe to a modernist view of the mystic unconscious. In many ways Meyerhold typified modernist thought in Russia. According to Leach it was a personal experience of Meyerhold's that made him mistrust 'acting by emotional saturation'.[9] In 1895, before the formation of the MAT, he had performed. A. Apukhtin's monologue *The Madman*, and found himself becoming mad. It is interesting to note that this was also Michael Chekhov's experience of working to engender emotion by drawing on personal experience, and the reason for his rejection of it. Meyerhold's note from his period of work at the Borodinskaia Studio can be taken as his central tenet. 'Why reflect it, this modern life? It must be overcome. We must improve the body of man.'[10] Later he stated that 'observations of life are necessary for us not so that we can transfer them with photographic exactitude into our work... but in order to use them as material'.[11]

[5] V. E. Meierkhol'd, 'Literaturnie predvestiia o novom teatre', in *Stat'i, Pisma, Rechi, Besedi*, 1 (Moscow: Iskusstvo, 1968), p. 123, translated in Braun, *Meyerhold on Theatre*, p. 37.
[6] *Ibid.* 'Teatr Studia', p. 105, Braun, p. 43.
[7] Meyerhold, *Stat'i*, 'Naturalisticheskii Teatr i Teatr Nastroenia', pp. 113–23, Braun pp. 23–34.
[8] Marjorie Hoover, *Meyerhold: The Art of Conscious Theatre* (Amherst: University of Massachusetts, 1974), p. 1.
[9] Robert Leach, *Vsevolod Meyerhold* (Cambridge University Press, 1989), p. 4.
[10] Konstantin Rudnitsky, *Meyerhold the Director*, tr. George Petrov (Ann Arbor: Ardis, 1981), p. 205.
[11] N. Pesochinskii 'Akter v teatre Vs. Meiekholda', in S. Bolkhontseva, *Russkoe Akterskoe Iskusstvo xx Veka* (St Petersburg:Rlll, 1992), pp. 89–90.

He was not against some form of *experiencing*, however. In 1907, Meyerhold wrote concerning the question of whether the actor should 'from the beginning reveal the inner content of the role, allow *temperament*[12] to burst out and then invest this *experiencing* in some form or other, or proceed the other way round?'[13] He argued that *temperament* should be restrained until the form is mastered. Actors of the old school recommended not speaking the role until it was mastered by heart and Meyerhold asserts that in a realistic play you should begin by reading the text to yourself and, in a non-realistic one, you should master first the rhythm of the language and the rhythm of movement. Meyerhold also appealed to traditional acting methods, as Stanislavsky did in his research.

The problems, at this stage of Meyerhold's experiments, as Briusov pointed out, were that the young actors lacked training and temperament .[14] Pesochinsky describes Meyerhold's attempts to train the actor to create the image of the character with symbolic meaning, by reducing everyday expression and movement, by getting the actor to stop and be silent and then to perform actions that conveyed the meaning, the symbolism of the image.[15] However, as Stanislavsky comments in his chapter on the Studio on Povarskaia in *MLIA*, the results of the experiments on Maeterlinck's *The Death of Tintagiles* and Hauptmann's *Schluck and Jau* convinced him that 'between the dreams of a director and their realisation there is a great distance . . . and that for the new art what is needed is new actors, with a completely new technique' (p. 362).

Meyerhold, like Stanislavsky, cited Pushkin but interpreted differently Pushkin's formula for acting. Meyerhold referred Pushkin's phrase, 'the verisimilitude of passions', which Stanislavsky interpreted as the 'truth of passions', to poetry, whereas for Meyerhold theatre has *conventionalised verisimilitude*.[16] He replaced the concept of 'the truth of passions', with 'the music of passions' in Pushkin's drama, describing the need to find all the subtleties of the melodies of the poetry, and the rhythms of the construction.[17]

[12] 'Temperament' is a term also used by Stanislavsky in this period. In a letter to the performers of Hamsun's *Drama of Life* in 1907 he writes that the play's 'main quality is temperament . . . many young artists still do not have sufficient control of unschooled temperament' (Vinogradskaia, *Letopis*, vol. 2, pp. 63–4). Apparently, both Stanislavsky and Meyerhold dropped the term as it does not appear in their later writings.

[13] Meierkhol'd, *Stat'i*, 'Pervie Popytki Sozdania Uslovnogo Teatra', vol. 1, 1891–1917 (Moscow: Iskusstvo, 1968), p. 134. See also, Braun, *Meyerhold on Theatre*, p. 55.

[14] Meierkhol'd, *Stat'i*, p. 111, See also, Braun, *Meyerhold on Theatre*, p. 45.

[15] Pesochinskii, 'Akter' in Bolkhontseva, *Russkoe Akterskoe Iskusstvo*, pp. 70–1.

[16] *Ibid.* pp. 78–9.

[17] N. Pesochinskii, '"Biomekhanika" v teorii Meierkholda', *Teatr*, 1 (1990), p. 106.

Commedia dell'arte

Because of his different emphasis, Meyerhold's search took a different direction to that of Stanislavsky. Stanislavsky sought verification from other disciplines such as psychology and yoga, but Meyerhold looked to traditions of theatre itself (at popular forms such as circus and to eastern forms such as Japanese Kabuki), the visual arts and music. Commedia dell'arte opened a number of possibilities for Meyerhold. It was a popular theatre form that provided a means of development of a theatrical, non-naturalistic style; it provided a way of exploring character that was different from that of Stanislavsky; a new way to view the relationship with the audience; and a means of training that could bring about the technical mastery lacking in Meyerhold's earlier experiments.

Meyerhold said of the 1905 Revolution that he wanted to 'burn with the spirit of the times'.[18] One way the 'spirit of the times' found its theatrical expression in the silver age of Russian theatre was in the adoption of commedia dell'arte, which became extremely popular between the revolutions of 1905 and 1917 and reached its peak between 1917 and 1921. Meyerhold, Evreinov, Tairov, Vakhtangov and even Stanislavsky (who produced Goldoni's *La Locandiera* in 1914) all directed plays with commedia elements, and many writers, such as Blok and Vladimir Mayakovsky, drew from sources in commedia. Notably, in Meyerhold's earlier period he directed *Columbine's Scarf* by Arthur Schnitzler in 1910, and *The Fairground Booth* by Blok, first in 1906 and then in 1914.

James Fisher describes the effect of the revival of interest in commedia on the development of art and literature between 1890 and 1930.

Actors and directors studied commedia as a model for improvisory and movement-oriented performance and an extraordinarily diverse group of international theatre artists sought alternatives to the pervasive realistic and naturalistic forms and techniques prevalent in the early twentieth century.[19]

Improvisatory and movement aspects were significant for Meyerhold. He called for a rebirth of the theatre of improvisation,[20] as 'improvisations of *Commedia dell'Arte* had a firm basis of faultless technique'.[21] This idea

---

[18] Leach, *Vsevolod Meyerhold*, p. 5.
[19] James Fisher, 'Commedia Iconography in the Theatrical Art of Edward Gordon Craig', in Christopher Cairns (ed.), *The Commedia dell'Arte from the Renaissance to Dario Fo* (Lewiston: Edwin Mellen Press, 1989), p. 246.
[20] Meierkhol'd, *Stat'i*, 'Balagan', p. 214; Braun, *Meyerhold on Theatre*, p. 127.
[21] Meierkhol'd, *Stat'i*, p. 217; Braun, *Meyerhold on Theatre*, p. 129.

encapsulated the essence of the actor's art for Meyerhold. Similarly to Vakhtangov, he stated, 'The actor reacts instantly by means of improvisation to all the demands of the auditorium.'[22] What he means is that the actor is able to respond consciously to the audience, other actors and the auditorium in a spontaneous way, different at each performance. This could be contrasted with Stanislavsky's idea of *public solitude*, where the actors forget that the eyes of the audience are upon them.

Through commedia Meyerhold continued to assert his political commitment to popular theatre forms. In a letter in 1911, Meyerhold claimed there was a tradition of commedia in Russia; Italian commedia dell'arte troupes had played in Russia in the eighteenth century and the tradition was firmly implanted.[23] Milling and Ley distinguish two political viewpoints that underlie the populist reclamation of theatre traditions. One adopted what was originally

a romanticised feudalism, in which festivals and publicly participatory events patronized by the elite supposedly provided an outlet for the... frustrations of the disempowered, united the people and generated a sense of national identity.

They go on to claim that Mikhail Bakhtin developed this idea, and these theories of the function of the carnivalesque and grotesque influenced Meyerhold's work.[24] 'The other political subtext to the championing of the popular culture figured it as an empowerment of the worker and with the potential for effecting social change.'[25] Arguably, Meyerhold's espousal of traditional forms was for both these reasons as well as for artistic purposes. Meyerhold's concept here is again distinct from Stanislavsky's idea of the mission of the artist being to bring the ennobling influence of art to the lower classes.

Meyerhold worked from 1911 with Vladimir Solovev a writer, researcher and teacher, and together they developed sixteen études from commedia, Elizabethan and Asian theatres, as described by Braun.[26] Commedia lent itself to the sort of pantomimic stylisation that Meyerhold wanted. He criticised Russian actors for not cultivating the language of gesture and studied the engravings of Jacques Callot (1592–1635), an etcher, engraver and painter whose representations of commedia are a major source of

---

[22] Pesochinskii, 'Akter' in Bolkhontseva, *Russkoe Akterskoe Iskusstvo*, p. 108.
[23] Leach, Vsevolod *Meyerhold*, p. 10.
[24] Meyerhold's references to the stage as a 'square' (*ploshchad'*) and his ideas of polyphony (Pesochinski'i, 'Akter', in Bolkhontseva, *Russkoe Akterskoe Iskusstvo*, p. 76) could be compared with Bakhtin.
[25] Jane Milling and Graham Ley, *Modern Theories of Performance* (London: Palgrave, 2001), p. 56.
[26] Braun, *Meyerhold: A Revolution*, p. 129.

information on the form. This was not the only occasion when Meyerhold studied art to inform theatrical representation: he studied the work of French genre painter Nicholas Lancret (1690–1743), Honoré Daumier (1808–1879) and William Hogarth (1697–1764), the English painter and printer. In this he was following a theatrical tradition where eighteenth-century performers studied and practised poses from paintings, in which Delsarte also participated in his study of Greek statues.[27] It is questionable whether Callot's images were a faithful reproduction of what commedia actors did or whether the style of the drawings was his imaginative addition. It can be conjectured that Meyerhold took the atmosphere, lively movement, poses and groupings of the painters he studied as inspiration. Moreover, Roach suggests that Hogarth painted actors in poses intended to express the passions as described by Descartes and catalogued by Charles Le Brun, whose *Méthode pour apprendre à dessiner les passions* appeared in 1702.

Meyerhold's studies of these artists, and also the work of E. T. A. Hoffman, lent themselves to his exploration of grotesque, which he, influencing Vakhtangov, saw as

the struggle between content and form. The grotesque operates not only on the high and the low, but mingles the contrasts; deliberately creating sharp contradictions . . . the grotesque deepens daily life until it ceases to represent only that which is usual. The grotesque unites the essence of opposites into a synthesis and induces the spectator to attempt to solve the enigma of the incomprehensible.[28]

Stanislavsky describes his view of grotesque, differentiating between the false grotesque and the genuine: 'Genuine grotesque is the *full, bright, accurate, typical, exhaustive, simplest external expression of a great, deep and well-experienced internal content of a role and creativity of the artist*' (*AWR*, I p. 272)

Meyerhold cites the *Bolshaia Entsiklopedia* stating that grotesque 'combines the most dissimilar elements by *ignoring their details and relying on its own originality, borrowing from every source anything which satisfies its* joie de vivre *and its capricious, mocking attitude to life*'. He adds:

This is the style which reveals the most wonderful horizons to the creative artist. 'I', my personal attitude to life, precedes all else. Everything which I take as material for my art corresponds not to the truth of reality but to the truth of *my* personal artistic whim.[29]

[27] Joseph Roach, *The Player's Passion: Studies in the Science of Acting* (Newark: University of Michigan Press, 1993), pp. 70–1.
[28] Eugenio Barba, and Nicola Savarese, *A Dictionary of Theatre Anthropology: The Secret Art of the Performer*, tr. Richard Fowler (London: Routledge, 1991), p. 156.
[29] Meierkhol'd, *Stati*, p. 225; Braun, *Meyerhold on Theatre*, p. 137.

The two statements reveal the difference in view between the two directors. Stanislavsky's truth of *experiencing* can be contrasted with Meyerhold's truth of a personal artistic vision within traditions of art, and Stanislavsky's search for the universal truth of human experience with Meyerhold's artistic experimentation, expressing a particular vision of humanity.

STYLE AND SEMIOTICS

The modernist period was a time when ideas about semiotics developed. Clayton discusses the two types of sign-systems in the Russian theatre of the time – the conflict between formalist, self-referential theatricality, and the pursuit of naturalism (such as with Stanislavsky's barking dogs). Commedia 'had a semiotic function – signifying, by the insertion of certain theatrical signs borrowed from the history of theatre, the author's or director's allegiance to the revolution in theatrical art'.[30] Meyerhold's revolution, of theatricality versus psychological verisimilitude (a theatre no longer dominated by the text), asserted conventionality (*uslovnost'*). Like Japanese theatre it relied on the audience reading and interpreting a set of signs particular to the form. As such, it posited a completely different aesthetic from that of Stanislavsky's Tolstoyan aesthetic, where the actors *infect* the audience because of their truthful *experiencing*. Before the revolution Meyerhold found in the theatricality of commedia a vehicle for his sign-system; after the revolution he attempted to develop a sign-system for post-revolutionary audiences by means of *biomechanics*.

Another reason for the use of commedia in Meyerhold's work was that writers such as Blok, and the directors mentioned, used commedia characters as symbols for humanity in contemporary society in the period before the revolution. Clayton writes about what he calls the 'master-images' of the period, which include the commedia characters – along with Russian folk tales, the Cossack Sten'ka Razin, Boris Godunov, images from the Orient, the Scythians, pre-Christian mythology, the future and Charlie Chaplin – all of which, Clayton generalises as Bakhtin's carnivalesque.

Max Nordau's *Degeneration*, published in 1895 in German, and Tolstoy's *What is Art?* published in 1898, both condemn degeneracy in art. Nordau's book, which is scientifically very well referenced, asserts that

a belief in ordered progress based on the potentialities of the natural sciences . . . is the mainstream of European middle-class thought of the late nineteenth

---

[30] J. Douglas Clayton, *Pierrot in Petrograd: The Commedia dell'Arte/Balagan in Twentieth-Century Russian Theatre and Drama* (London: McGill-Queens' University Press, 1994), p. 6.

century. The future of humanity is in its elevation not degradation. Science and progress go together and he who understands the workings of science will have an unobstructed view of the future of mankind.

Nordau explains that science operates through 'irresistible and unchangeable physical laws which apply to man as much as to nature itself.' [31] Unfortunately, according to Nordau, Tolstoy was a degenerate, as were Ibsen, Nietszche, Hauptmann and Maeterlinck. Also condemned were the 'degenerate and insane' disciples of Schopenhauer and von Hartmann, and people who dabbled in Buddhism. Tolstoy had criticised art that did not promote the spiritual aim of communion, including some of his own work in this. Tolstoy's book was also, later, taken up seriously by those guiding Soviet artistic thinking, but in early twentieth-century Russia Nordau's book had the opposite effect to that intended. Briusov popularised it, and Meyerhold and other artists revelled in the idea of 'degeneracy'. Commedia's Pierrot was seen by Briusov's contemporaries as the epitome of this degeneracy. Harlequin was often portrayed as black, embodying the modernist theme of attractiveness of the black (masked) man to the white woman:

Pierrot was the enfeebled scion of the white race, his ineffectual, homoerotic posturing contrasted with the brute animal force of the primitive races that were to sweep away Western society. The pseudo-Darwinist link between modernist art (symbolism, decadence) and the biological 'degeneracy' of European intellectuals was made explicit in Nordau's book. [32]

Pierrot can be subversive, the representation of the down-trodden classes. [33] He is the puppet of fate, death or dramatic narrative. He is the archetypal tragic hero, as found in ballet. In Meyerhold's own portrayal he represented the alienation and victimisation of the artist, a grotesque combination of comedy and tragedy, parodying and subverting bourgeois culture. The Russian Pierrot could become Petrushka the sinister clown, in whom could be seen Peter the Great or even the devil, and Meyerhold's Dr Dapertutto. [34] Clayton posits that Blok's *Fairground Booth*, with its metatheatrical devices and the images of St Petersburg, suggests God is dead and the clowns have run amok; the world is in the control of sinister forces and Dr Dapertutto himself 'had a peculiar

[31] Max Nordau, *Degeneration*, 2nd edn (New York: Howard Fertig, 1968), p. xvii.
[32] *Ibid.* p. 9.
[33] *Ibid.* p. 35.
[34] *Ibid.* p. 14.

resonance for the disorder and destruction through which Russia was passing'.[35] There was also the expression of the crisis of the individual in relation to superhuman forces. By his portrayal of Pierrot, the characterisation of a type condemned by Nordau, and hence embracing the idea of degeneracy as a positive thing, Meyerhold demonstrated a characteristic of the modernist rebellion. This was also exemplified by the Bakhtinian claiming of carnival and the grotesque as an anti-elite form of expression.

Meyerhold's rebellion could also be seen as a rebellion against Stanislavsky's bourgeois (as they were perceived), pre-modernist values of truth and beauty. Such an approach to characterisation is in sharp contrast to Stanislavsky's psychological truth. Meyerhold's characterisation of Pierrot, as the degenerate representative of the downtrodden classes, can be contrasted with Stanislavsky's Stockmann (still in repertoire in this period), the individualist defender of truth and justice. The commedia characters are types, or rather archetypes. As such, they possess a kind of sociological rather than psychological truth. Leach discusses how Meyerhold's conception of the masked characters became more sociological after the revolution.[36] Worrall relates this to formalist thinking and the rebellion against nineteenth-century concepts of fiction and character.[37] For Meyerhold, actors have an *emploi*, which in the traditional understanding means a range of characters within a certain type, which they can play but which Meyerhold used as a way to suggest characters rooted in types as a starting point for the actors' creativity.[38]

Meyerhold was fascinated, as were many of his silver age contemporaries, by the mask. He wrote in 1907, 'in the new drama, external action, the revelation of character is becoming incidental. We are striving to penetrate *behind* the mask, *beyond* the action into the character as perceived by the mind; we want to penetrate to the *inner mask*.'[39] Stanislavsky, on the other hand, writes, 'Characterisation is the mask hiding the actor-person. In this masked form he can reveal himself down to the most intimate and piquant details' (*AWHI*, p. 250). Again Stanislavsky's assertion of psychological truth, the truth of human experience and character development, is rejected by Meyerhold, who defines what lies

[35] *Ibid.* p. 14 .
[36] Leach, *Vsevolod Meyerhold*, p. 77.
[37] Nicholas Worrall, 'Meyerhold's Production of *The Magnificent Cuckold*', *The Drama Review*, 17:1 (1973), p. 19.
[38] Leach, *Vsevolod Meyerhold*, pp. 74–7.
[39] Meierkhol'd, *Stati*, p. 139; Braun, *Meyerhold on Theatre*, p. 60.

behind the mask as the character 'as perceived by the mind'; that is, he suggests, an artistic construct.

Michael Chekhov's ideas on archetype and the mask of the character no doubt emerged from the same theatrical experimentation as those of Meyerhold; like Vakhtangov and Chekhov, Meyerhold uses the term image (*obraz*) rather than character, and in Russian particularly image has wider connotations.

Another reason for Meyerhold's emphasis on commedia was located in Golub's phrase, 'the reconstruction of the spectator'.[40] Commedia exemplified the desire to cross boundaries and this extended to the actor-audience relationship.[41] A role was implied for the audience in 'co-creating' the theatrical work of art and solving the problem of the separation between the actor and the audience.[42] Leach describes how Meyerhold saw the forestage or travelling stage as the meeting point between the spectator and the commedic actor and throughout his work he experimented with non-traditional forms of staging: getting rid of the front curtain, removing footlights, exposing sources of light, using raked seating, planting actors in the audience, getting actors to use direct address to the audience.[43]

Meyerhold thought that new methods were necessary to communicate with the new audiences, who, in his view, while being impressed by the technical virtuosity of the performers, should always be conscious that they were in the theatre. Again this was a difference from what was represented in Russian theatre by the presence of the proscenium arch and Stanislavsky's idea (taken from André Antoine of the Théâtre Libre in Paris) of the 'fourth wall'. He felt that theatre should appeal, not as with Stanislavsky, to the audience's feelings, but to the spectator's imagination. His emphasis on the imagination could again be compared with Michael Chekhov and, like Chekhov, he cites Schopenhauer's statement that a work of art can influence only through the imagination and must therefore arouse it in the spectator.[44] The Russian formalists discussed the 'alienation' (*ostranenie*) of the audience and, according to Leach, Brecht coined the term *Verfremdungseffekt* (alienation effect) as a

---

[40] Spencer Golub, 'The Silver Age, 1905–1917' in Robert Leach and Victor Borovsky (eds), *A History of Russian Theatre* (Cambridge University Press, 1999), p. 287.

[41] Eisenstein discussed 'antique' and 'new' perspective or the abolition of perspective, challenging received notions of perspective in the arts and suggesting new ideas for the theatre and film and the relationship with the audience. Sergei Eisenstein, *The Film Sense*, tr. and ed. Jan Leyda (London and Boston: Faber and Faber, 1943), pp. 81–4.

[42] Clayton, *Pierrot*, p. 56.

[43] Leach, *Vsevolod Meyerhold*, p. 10, 42.

[44] Meierkhol'd, *Stati*, p. 117; Braun, *Meyerhold on Theatre*, p. 26.

result of seeing the Chinese actor Mei Lan-fang in Moscow with
Meyerhold, Eisenstein and their close associates and, he infers, as a result
of discussions with them.[45] Meyerhold cites Leonid Andreev's statement
that 'the more obvious the artifice the more powerful the impression of
life'.[46] In all of this the actor remained central. Although Stanislavsky in
his way 'authored' the text, he maintained a reverential attitude to the
idea of the text and the author, whereas Meyerhold went much further. In
his adaptations of the dramatic text from *The Fairground Booth* and
Mayakovsky's *Mystery-Bouffe*, to his *Dame aux-Camellias* in 1934, he was
the forerunner of director's theatre of the twentieth century.

TRAINING

Meyerhold undertook experiments in actor-training in 1913 in the Studio on
Borodinskaia Street, according to ideas outlined in his 1912 essay *Balagan*
(*The Fairground Booth*). Vladimir Solovev taught a course in commedia, and
Mikhail Gnesin, the composer, taught 'musical reading', which, according
to Pesochinsky, taught the basis of what was 'beyond the everyday',
encouraging the students to understand the emotional nature and structure
of theatrical action by understanding music.[47] There was also dancing,
circus acrobatics and Meyerhold's own course of movement training.

A slightly later account of the studio programme, from 1916 to 1917,
mentions, in addition to the above, athletics, fencing and recommended
sports: lawn tennis, discus throwing, sailing.[48] In 1907 Meyerhold stated
that the actor must train the body; physical sport is the basis for performance of tragedies such as *Antigone* or *Julius Caesar*.[49] The entrance
exam for the studio required a degree of musical proficiency, physical
agility, mimetic ability and clarity of diction, as well as knowledge of
theatre. Sixteen études were created from a variety of traditions including
commedia. The exercises on movement, gesture and working with objects
fed into the études, and then into pantomimes. The exercise 'Shooting
the Bow', became the étude 'The Hunt', then a pantomime in which all
involved in the Studio took part. This process was the essence of what
became *biomechanics*. Therefore, while Stanislavsky was concentrating on

[45] Leach, *Vsevolod Meyerhold*, p. 171.
[46] Meyerhold, *Stati*, p. ; Braun, *Meyerhold on Theatre*, p. 63.
[47] Pesochinskii, 'Akter' in Bolkhontseva, *Russkoe Akterskoe Iskusstvo*, p. 75.
[48] Braun, *Meyerhold on Theatre*, pp. 153–5.
[49] Pesochinskii, 'Akter', p. 130.

inner *experiencing*, Meyerhold prioritised movement forms as the way to train the actor. As Meyerhold explained in 1914:

Movement is the most powerful means of theatrical expression... Deprived of words, costumes, footlights, wings, theatre auditorium and left only with the actor and his mastery of movement, the theatre would still remain theatre. The spectator can understand the actor's thoughts and impulses of the actor from his moves, his gestures and his facial expressions.[50]

This was a radical statement for someone of his time and inspiration, no doubt, for Grotowski's poor theatre.

Braun cites the principles on which the training was based in *Love of Three Oranges*, in 1914. These included 'spontaneous control of the body in space with the whole body involved in every gesture... the ability to adapt movement to the space... and to music, imbuing each action with joy, the power of the grotesque... and self-sufficiency of form'.[51] Edward Gordon Craig, whom he respected, perhaps inspired Meyerhold here. Craig posited as an ideal the actor 'who has so trained his body from head to foot that it would answer the workings of his mind without permitting the emotions even so much as to awaken'. This is a state of 'mechanical perfection' such that 'the body is *absolutely* the slave of the mind'.[52] Craig's split way of thinking about body and mind should be noted, as should his dismissal of emotion.

Meyerhold was not as much against the 'awakening' of the emotions as Craig, but he counterpoised the actors' pleasure in their performance ('joy' as mentioned above) with the emotions of the character, which for him were far from being the cornerstone of his technique, as they were for Stanislavsky. Principles were also inherited from Delsarte and Dalcroze. Meyerhold's course, following Dalcroze, aimed to explore the rhythm and musicality of music, and 'the emergence of action not from a basic subject but from the alternation of even and odd numbers of people on the *square* and from various *jeux de théâtre*'.[53] Leach states that 'Every action and speech had to be "justified"',[54] the Delsartean principle adopted by Stanislavsky, but taken much further by Vakhtangov and Chekhov. Also, Meyerhold noted in 1915 his thoughts 'On

---

[50] V. E. Meierkhol'd, *Liubov' k trem apel'sinam*, 4–5 (1914), pp. 94–8, in Braun, *Meyerhold on Theatre*, p. 147.

[51] Braun, *A Revolution in Theatre*, p. 128.

[52] Edward Gordon Craig, *On the Art of the Theatre* (London: Heinemann, 1980), p. 67.

[53] Pesochinskii, 'Akter' in Bolkhontseva, *Russkoe Akterskoe Iskusstvo*, p. 75.

[54] Leach, *Vsevolod Meyerhold*, p. 74.

angular movements. What has come after Delsarte. The physical shortcoming of the actor. How can it be corrected? Training in *bala-gan*.'[55] The different emphases in training between Stanislavsky and Meyerhold resulted, according to Rudnitsky, in a 'painful duality' in the work of the leading theatrical innovators of the time. This was typified by the MAT's *Cricket on the Hearth*, produced in the First Studio in 1914, in which Stanislavsky's preoccupation with internal *experiencing* was in sharp contrast to Meyerhold's emphasis on external technique in his studio on Borodinskaia Street.[56] There were evidently some similar elements in Meyerhold's general training and Stanislavsky's training in *incarnation*: the use of sport, Delsarte and Dalcroze, acrobatics, dance. Meyerhold's movement training and use of études with the emphasis on technique could be compared with Stanislavsky's training in *plastique* and use of études with the emphasis on *experiencing*.

COQUELIN

In the 1880s the debate on feeling versus technical expertise started by the publication of Diderot's *Paradoxe*, in the portrayal of emotion on stage, had been joined by Henry Irving and Constant Coquelin. Coquelin was the most famous exponent of the school of *representation* and Stanislavsky frequently refers to Coquelin in his criticisms of this school. In a lecture given in 1922 Meyerhold stated in reply to an attack on his work by Ippolit Sokolov that there was no scientific basis for his work other than a book by Coquelin on the subject.[57] At other times, however, he did claim his work was corroborated by science.

Meyerhold wrote a formula, 'N = A1 + A2 (where N = the actor; A1 = the artist who conceives the idea and issues the instructions necessary for its execution; A2 = the executant who executes the conception of A1)'[58], which he derived from Coquelin. Coquelin postulated the 'dual personality of the actor' who has his first self, the actor and his second self, which is the instrument. The first self conceives the person to be created and the being that is conceived is represented by the second self.[59] Meyerhold said that the

---

[55] O. M. Feld'man (ed.), *Meierkhold i Drugie: Dokumenti i Materiali* (Moscow: OGI, 2000), p. 390.
[56] Rudnitsky, *Meyerhold the Director*, p. 204.
[57] Mel Gordon and Alma Law, *Meyerhold, Eisenstein and Biomechanics: Actor-Training in Revolutionary Russia* (North Carolina: McFarland, 1996), p. 144.
[58] Braun, *Meyerhold on Theatre*, p. 198.
[59] Constant Coquelin, *The Art of the Actor*, tr. Elsie Fogerty (London: George Allen and Unwin, 1932), p. 25.

actor must develop the ability to 'mirrorise the self',[60] by which he meant that the actors must not only act, but also simultaneously observe themselves acting. What is notable here is that both Coquelin and Meyerhold envisage the actor as having two 'selves'. This way of thinking about the human organism as split into two (A1 and A2) leads Meyerhold into difficulty, as it does Stanislavsky. Meyerhold cites Coquelin to back up his own view on emotion. In an interview in 1913 Meyerhold rejected the assertion that he belonged to the school of *representation* and denied that Coquelin did also. 'It is known that the famous Coquelin in his work on roles began with the externals but did he not experience them? The difference here is only one of method, in the manner of studying the role. But in essence the talent always experiences a role emotionally, while mediocrity only represents.'[61]

BIOMECHANICS

It is clear that Meyerhold espoused 'laws of theatricality' rather than 'laws of nature'.[62] This is not to say he did not regard his work as scientific, in the period of and after the revolution. Filippov wrote in 1924 that thanks to Delsarte, Dalcroze and Meyerhold, and other research by Russians, 'external technique is now on a firm scientific foundation'.[63] 'Scientific' before the revolution generally meant the results of experiments and observation. However, the word came to mean work supported by Pavlovian physiology, and artists had to be more careful about claiming such a foundation. In the period just after the revolution there was initially a close relationship between the arts and science. Many leading figures were both artists and scientists, such as Alexei Gastev, or Eisenstein, who trained as an engineer, or the Bolshevik Alexander Bogdanov, a scientist who wrote novels.

After the revolution Meyerhold developed from his commedia experiments the paradigmatic series of movements and études that became known as *biomechanics*, the crucial component of his actor-training method after the revolution. The term is first found in 1918,[64] and was used in an article 'On Dramaturgy and the Culture of Theatre' in 1921, which states: 'The roots of the new communist dramaturgy lie in the physical culture of the theatre which opposes to the doubtful psychological law of an out-lived

[60] Leach, *Vsevolod Meyerhold*, p. 65.
[61] V. E. Meierkhold, 'V. E. Meierkhol'd o sovremmenom teatre', *Teatr*, 1370, (1913), p. 7.
[62] Braun, *Meyerhold on Theatre*, p. 126.
[63] V. A. Filippov, *Besedy o teatre: opyt vvedenia v teatrovedenie* (Moscow: Moskovskoe Teatralnoe Izdatelstvo, 1924), pp. 95–6.
[64] Gordon and Law, *Meyerhold, Eisenstein*, p. 41.

pseudo-science exact laws of motion based on biomechanics and kinetics.'[65]
The exercises and études first developed in the studio work of Borodinskaia
Street were developed into the biomechanical exercises which Meyerhold
taught his students in the 1920s to 1930s, linking movement, emotion and
speech, synthesised with Taylorism – the American examination of the
mechanics of labouring which led to time-and-motion study.

There are a number of difficulties and paradoxes embodied in the
system of *biomechanics* and Meyerhold's attitude towards it. He made
grandiose claims about it and its place in training the revolutionary actor.
Although he became a Bolshevik, it is difficult to ascertain what
Meyerhold's political view really was. He said of himself and the futurist
Mayakovsky, 'For both of us the October Revolution was a way out of the
impasse the intelligentsia was in.'[66] Rudnitsky states that the closure of
Meyerhold's RSFSR Theatre 1 in 1921 caused Meyerhold some consternation. (Meyerhold took over the Free Theatre Company in 1920 and
renamed it RSFSR Theatre No. 1 but it was closed in the following year,
when NEP began.) His productions of Emile Verhaeren's *The Dawn* and
Mayakovsky's *Mystery-Bouffe* had been very popular with audiences but
not so popular with leaders of the revolution.[67] It was necessary to enter
the research laboratory. *Biomechanics* was a way for Meyerhold to justify
his work and argue with MAT and others.

Regarding the mechanics of *biomechanics*, the constructivist manifestos,
as described by Rudnitsky, rejected the passivity of art as a mere reflection
of reality and asserted that 'Constructivism is active; it not only reflects
reality but acts by itself.'[68] Meyerhold's production of *The Magnanimous Cuckold* in 1922 unusually included a biomechanical étude per se,
'The Leap onto the Chest' (see figure 9). The production demonstrated
the fascination of audiences and constructivist creators with machinery.
The material elements of theatre were emphasised, including the actor's
body. An article from the period states, 'Based on data from the study of
the human organism, biomechanics strives to create a man who has studied
the mechanism of his construction and is capable of mastering the ideal
and of improving it.'[69] The mechanics are where the actor begins, from
without, with motion, because in *biomechanics* the precise and fixed
external form is meant to suggest the feeling to the actor (see figure 10).

[65] Meyerhold, *Stati*, p. 25.
[66] Aleksandr Gladkov, *Meyerhold Speaks, Meyerhold Rehearses*, tr. and ed. Alma Law (Amsterdam:
Harwood Academic Publishers, 1997), p. 148.
[67] Braun, *A Revolution in Theatre*, p. 165.
[68] Rudnitsky, *Meyerhold the Director*, p. 292.
[69] *Ibid.* p. 294.

9. 'The Leap onto the Chest', biomechanical étude included in *The Magnanimous Cuckold*, 1922.

As for the 'bio' aspect of *biomechanics*, *emotion* and *spirit*, Meyerhold stated that *biomechanics* begins 'not with experience, not with seeking to plumb the meaning of the role, not with an attempt to assimilate the psychological essence of the phenomenon; in summary, it begins not "from within" but from without; it must begin with motion. This means the motion of an actor excellently trained, possessing musical rhythm and easy reflectory excitability, an actor whose natural abilities have been developed by systematic training.'[70] Biomechanical motion is of such a kind that all

[70] *Ibid.* pp. 294–5.

10. Shooting the bow. Exercises in *biomechanics*, 1927: Z. Zlolain, C. Sverdlin, I. Meierhol'd (Meyerhold's (daughter) R. Geinina (from left to right). Photograph by A. A. Temerina.

experiences (such as feelings and emotions) are an inevitable result of its process, if the actor has reflectory or *reflex excitability*, which is the 'the capacity to recreate emotional experience in movement, and in words, a task assigned from without'.[71] Its communication is the art of acting. Meyerhold stresses here that the word 'emotional' is used 'in the strictly technical sense with no loose, sentimental connotation'. Another formula of Meyerhold's states that 'the sum of A1 + A2 is the spirit of movement'.[72] For Meyerhold, therefore, emotion is motion, but motion of a particular kind, and the actor can be trained as the vehicle for this motion. For Stanislavsky, emotion is an organic, physiological reaction, brought about through an inner process; for Meyerhold the correct outer process will suffice to convey emotion or spirit as required, regardless, presumably, of the actor's inner state.

After the revolution *biomechanics* was not the only form of training used by Meyerhold. His trainees did dance, pantomime and physical culture as before. Gordon also mentions boxing.[73] He writes that Meyerhold was interested in the physical culture programme of the Red Army and from 1921 he took over a project entitled the Theatricalisation of Physical Culture, which was to set up a programme of 'work gymnastics'.[74] Biomechanical training, as taught now by Alexei Levinsky and Gennadi Bogdanov, who were both taught by Nikolai Kustov, one of Meyerhold's instructors, includes work with sticks, as in circus or music hall, as part of the training and bending, stretching and isolation exercises. The main difference in training principles after the revolution, therefore, was the development of *biomechanics* as a practical and theoretical system for acting, along with constructivism as a way of creating theatrical space.

Anatomy and physiology were taught on the courses planned from 1918.[75] Winslow Taylor, William James, Pavlov and V. M. Bekhterev were all cited in biomechanical theory. Braun states, 'however, the resemblance was superficial and was exaggerated by Meyerhold in order to show that his system was devised in response to the demands of the new mechanised age, as opposed to those of Stanislavsky and Tairov, which were unscientific and anachronistic'.[76] If the source of *biomechanics* was in commedia dell'arte, there is no scientific foundation for the training other than what was in commedia itself.

---

[71] Hoover, *The Art of Conscious Theatre*, p. 297.
[72] Pesochinskii, 'Akter' in Bolkhontseva, *Russkoe Akterskve Iskusstuo*, p. 137.
[73] Gordon and Law, *Meyerhold, Eisenstein*, p. 4.
[74] *Ibid.* pp. 30–1.
[75] *Ibid.* p. 29.
[76] Braun, *Meyerhold on Theatre*, p. 183.

Frederick Winslow Taylor 1856–1915

The founder of scientific time management, Frederick Winslow Taylor, delivered a paper outlining the rudiments of the Taylor system at the thirty-first biannual meeting of the American Society of Mechanical Engineers in 1895:

> While many of Taylor's principles meant little outside a factory, his broader outlook crossed to other fields largely intact – certainly his emphasis on efficiency and productivity. But perhaps even more, the model of applying scientific thinking to problems that on their face, were not 'scientific' at all, had never been scientific, and did not lend themselves to scientific methods. In this respect, Taylor's impact was like that of Darwin, Marx, and Freud. Each brought a deeply analytical, 'scientific' cast of mind to an unruly, seemingly intractable problem – Darwin to the chaos of life on the planet; Marx to the vagaries of social and economic systems; Freud to the swirling depths of the mind; Taylor to the physical, economic and psychological complexities of human work.[77]

Various governments and corporations took up the Taylor system, including Soviet Russia under Lenin, in order to bring about the highest productivity of labour.

Taylor studied work within a factory or workshop setting, and developed efficient systems of working. These included all aspects of work; from the management of the concern to the way each worker should carry out their particular job, using their time and capacities efficiently. 'Scientific Time Study' was the principle that for each job there is the quickest time in which a first-class worker could do it. Taylor's work was celebrated at the Paris Exhibition in 1900 and these principles spread through Europe and Russia.

Taylorism was part of a late-nineteenth-century interest in breaking down tasks or actions into their component parts. Kanigel, quoting Rabinbach, describes how European scientists with such diverse interests as Hermann von Helmholz (1821–1894 – who formulated the law of conservation of energy) and Étienne-Jules Marey (1830–1904 – who invented the chronophotograph, from which modern cinematography was developed), 'took as their starting point the decomposition of each task into a series of abstract, mathematically precise relations, calculable in terms of fatigue, time, motion, units of work and so forth ... Both rested their claims on the authority of science.'[78] Like Stanislavsky, Taylor

---

[77] Robert Kanigel, *The One Best Way: Frederick Winslow Taylor and the Enigma of Efficiency* (London: Little, Brown, 1997), p. 13.
[78] *Ibid.* p. 508.

claimed that his system had emerged from experience, not theory; 'Scientific management has been at every step an evolution not a theory', he would say. 'In all cases the practice had preceded the theory, not succeeded it.'[79]

The principles were based on Taylor's observations of workmen. Frank Gilbreth, Taylor's follower, conducted experiments with bricklaying along scientific management principles; various refinements emerged. There were recommendations, for example, of how to reduce the number of movements in a job such as bricklaying, by using both hands at the same time; that is, picking up a brick with one hand while taking mortar onto the trowel with the other. General principles emerged, such as the elimination of false, slow and useless movements so that there was no unnecessary expenditure of energy.

Gordon and Law include a list recommending movements of the hands and arms and also including the instruction that 'hand and body motions should be confined to those muscles that require the least amount of exertion (usually the hand, forearm and shoulder); movements involving a single contraction of a positive muscle group are faster, easier and more accurate than movements caused by sets of antagonistic muscle, and lastly rhythmic movements are generally the most efficient'.[80] However, these rules are based on observation and may not be true in terms of contemporary physiology and are not really like Meyerhold's rules for *biomechanics*, except in a general way.

Russian Taylorism, Alexei Gastev and Platon Kerzhentsev

Lenin studied Taylorism while living in Zurich in 1916. Russia had been laid waste by World War I and industrial production was a third of pre-war levels. He believed that Russia must be rebuilt and that capitalist science would help do this by raising productivity and improving labour discipline. In 1918 in a speech published in *Pravda*, he sought to introduce the Taylor system in Russia. Leon Trotsky supported this and by 1921 there were twenty institutions claiming to be run on principles of scientific management. There was an obvious appeal of scientific time management to those who thought they were dwelling in the age of the machine: 'In Taylor's vision, man and machine worked together like clockwork.' Aspects of Taylorism had an equally obvious appeal to the

---

[79] *Ibid.* p. 235.
[80] Gordon and Law, *Meyerhold, Eisenstein*, p. 35.

supporters of the revolution. Taylor said in 1911, 'in the past the man has been first. In the future the System must be first'.[81] Some were suspicious, as indicated by Evgeny Zamyatin's novel *We* (1920), which describes a totalitarian, dystopian future where Taylorism was synonymous with the regimentation of every aspect of life. Nevertheless, in the early twenties, the ideas of Taylorism had huge popular appeal and the revolutionary government's Five Year Plans were full of Taylorism.

Alexei K. Gastev was a Bolshevik who, when exiled in France in the war, had been a metal worker at Renault, experienced scientific management at first hand. He was the foremost Soviet Taylorist, a trade unionist and head of the Central Institute of Labour (founded in 1921). He was also a poet, and vice-president of the Council for Scientific Management. He wrote *How Should Work be Done?* which was published in 1922. It outlines sixteen rules for any sort of work; in the office, a joiner's workshop or on the land. The aim is to create 'working endurance, and make it habitual'. Again the Ja-mesian view of habit is expressed here. The rules recommend preparation, in terms of thinking through each task in advance, preparing instruments and the working area. It is recommended that you start work in a leisurely way, so that 'head and body come together', not in a rush, 'flogging the work to death', and keep working evenly, taking care when effort needs to be expended to let 'body and mind adjust'. It is important to be comfortable, to sit when possible, to take rest breaks, not to eat or smoke while working, and not to get angry if the work goes badly but to take a break and reorganise the tools. You should not go off to do another task. It is a bad habit to show off a well-completed task. At the end you should clear the workspace.[82] Again, these rules could only be compared in a very general way to the rules of *biomechanics*.

Platon Mikhailovich Kerzhentsev, a Taylorist who set up the League of Time in 1923, with Meyerhold as a board member, wanted to introduce scientific principles into all organised activity whether social or work-based. A widespread movement began, dedicated to saving time and applying principles of efficiency and there was a call, among other things, for the 'Taylorisation of the theatre'. Clearly, Meyerhold drew from Taylorism's emphasis on time. In the late 1920s Meyerhold introduced an ancient system called chronométrage, where each performance of a pro-duction was timed exactly in order to control form and tempo. Alma Law reproduces a chart showing the timings of the production of *Woe from*

[81] Kanigel, *The One Best Way*, p. 19.
[82] Alexei Gastev, *Kak Nado Rabotat?* (Moscow: Tsentral'nyi Institut Truda, 1922), pp. 5–8.

Wit in 1928.[83] Meyerhold also claimed that *biomechanics* would give the actor skills in a much shorter period that would take the ordinary actor nearly a lifetime to learn. There was a pragmatic aspect to this, in that in 1921 when Meyerhold was made director of the new State Higher Directors' Workshops, he was given a hundred young students to be trained as actors and directors.

Meyerhold's biomechanical sessions ran for an hour with a ten-minute break (as Gastev might have approved), in contrast to Stanislavsky's long training and rehearsal sessions. Therefore, Meyerhold's claim that the methods of Taylorism were applied to the work of the actor with the aim of maximum productivity could be substantiated in a general sense; the methods being that there should be rest pauses in the work process and time should be used as economically as possible (for example, the actor should not waste an hour and a half putting on make-up and costume).[84]

Biomechanical exercises

In 1922 Meyerhold organised a laboratory to explore and develop the scientific foundations for *biomechanics*. He commissioned Mikhail Korenov with defining the set of principles for *biomechanics*, of which there are forty-four. The main point of comparison with Gastev's rules is the emphasis on a calm approach. There are similarities with the pre-revolutionary principles of training in terms of economy of movement and involvement of the whole body.

The rules include the following:

All of Biomechanics is based on the premise that if the tip of the nose works, so does the entire body.
The entire body works under conditions of calm equilibrium and least tension, and a gesture is the result of the entire body.
Precision and economy of movement is achieved by conscious grasp of the instructions and attention to each element of each exercise; the performer must be aware of each change in the position of the body and its parts.
Each movement is formed of three factors: intention, equilibrium and execution. Biomechanics requires co-ordination and orientation in space and before an audience. The performer must have a reserve of *Raccourcis*.[85]

---

[83] Alma Law, 'Meyerhold's *Woe to Wit*', *The Drama Review*, 18:3 (1974), p. 92.
[84] Braun, *Meyerhold on Theatre*, p. 198.
[85] *Raccourci*, French for 'foreshortening' (a term from painting) is related, according to Gordon, to the Japanese *mie*, a moment in the general movement, a point between two movements.

Excitation arises in the work process as a result of the successful use of well-trained material.

Art is the organisation and struggle with the material.

The difficulty of acting is in the fact that the actor is at one and the same time the material and the organiser of it.

The first principle of Biomechanics; the body is a machine, the actor is the machinist.

The spectator must have a certain feeling of tension. Watching the exercise, he follows the process of the setting and turning of levers.

Giving free rein to the emotions at the beginning of the work results in spending it too soon and spoiling the entire execution.

In work, an absolute economy is essential, a total Taylorism. All the tasks must be fulfilled with a minimum number of devices, with the utmost expediency.[86]

There is a contradiction between the rule which states 'the body is a machine, the actor is the machinist', and the rule stating that the actor is 'at one and the same time the material and the organiser of it'; the first statement exemplifies a split way of thinking and the second does not. The confusion permeates biomechanical theory.

Meyerhold developed his formulae for biomechanical acting as follows:

$$N = A_1 A_2$$

$$A_1 = N \overset{o}{\diagup\!\!\bigwedge\!\!\bigwedge\!\!\diagdown}$$

$$\text{or} \qquad A_1 = N \overset{o \quad o}{\underset{n}{\diagup\!\!\overset{r \quad r}{\bigwedge\!\!\bigwedge}\!\!\diagdown}}$$

where N = *namerenie* (intention); o = *osushchestvlenie* (execution, ful-filment of the task) and r = *reaktsia* (reaction to the initial position).[87] He explains these as follows: *namerenie* is the intellectual assimilation of a task prescribed externally by the dramatist, director, or initiative of the performer. *Osushchestvlenie* is the cycle of volitional, mimetic and vocal reflexes. (Meyerhold notes that mimetic reflexes comprise all the

---

[86] Gordon and Law, *Meyerhold, Eisenstein*, pp. 135–8.
[87] *Ibid.* p. 127.

movements performed by the separate parts of the actor's body and the movements of the entire body in space.) *Reaktsia* is the attenuation of the volitional reflex as it is realised mimetically and vocally in preparation for the reception of a new intention (the transition to a new element of acting).[88] Meyerhold has clearly brought in the theory of conditioned reflexes here. Gordon and Law claim that this chain of acting elements was closely modelled on Taylor's working cycles, but what this comparison means, when for Taylor the benchmark was efficiency in the expenditure of effort rather than expressiveness of movement, is not clear.[89]

In addition, each acting element is composed of three essential moments; *otkaz, posil, tochka.* These mean literally *refusal, sending* and *full stop.* Worrall writes that *otkaz* in *biomechanics* exemplifies the Hegelian dialectic. Contradiction lies at the root of every stage action; every thesis has its antithesis.[90] Picon-Vallin reports that *otkaz* is also a musical term, meaning 'natural'.[91] Although these more complex interpretations were an important part of the theory developed around *biomechanics,* Meyerhold's intellectual justification for it, the practice, was simpler. At the root of the acting chain here is the concept, also found in Michael Chekhov's *psychological gesture,* that each movement or gesture has a clear beginning, a middle and an end.

Meyerhold was seeking to develop a conventionalised theatre language, a semiotic for an audience in revolutionary times. To develop a language of signs to which a revolutionary audience would respond, Meyerhold turned to the science of the revolution, Taylorism, and ideas of reflex action based on the work of Pavlov and V. M. Bekhterev and the James-Lange theory of emotion. Like Stanislavsky, he would have thought of the theory of conditioned reflexes as ground breaking and correct, and needed to make his theory fit with it. In the same period Kuleshov also drew from Taylor's work in the training workshop he started for film actors in 1920. He, like Meyerhold, created études with his students to practise precision and economy of movement, while also using formalist principles to create a semiotic system using the actor's body in space and time in each shot.[92] They also drew from Dalcroze's ideas on rhythm and d'Udine's synaesthesia. Eisenstein, who studied with Meyerhold, also

[88] Braun, *Meyerhold on Theatre,* p. 201.
[89] Gordon and Law, *Meyerhold, Eisenstein,* p. 40.
[90] Nicholas Worrall, *Modernism to Realism on the Soviet Stage* (Cambridge University Press, 1989), p. 179.
[91] Béatrice Picon-Vallin, *Les voies de la création théatrale, 17 Meyerhold* (Paris: Editions du Centre National de la Recherche Scientifique, 1990), p. 113.
[92] Gerry Large, 'Lev Kuleshov and the Metrical-Spatial Web: Postmodern Body Training in Space and Time', *Theatre Topics,* 10:1 (2000), pp. 65–75.

developed his theory of *Biomechanics*, and is an important source of information on the way it was conceived.

Pavlov, Bekhterev and reflexology

Leach suggests that Meyerhold's thinking is blurred.[93] The cycle of intention, realisation and reaction refers not only to the actor's technique (A2), but also to the creative process through the actor's intention (A1). Leach believes that Meyerhold brought in Pavlovian reflexes to deal with this confusion, so that the stimulus (A1) triggers a reflex action, the realisation, which in the actor with trained *reflex excitability* will be the right one. The *reaction* is a rest preparing for a new intention. Stanislavsky dealt in the same way with the problems he had in thinking about mind and body, by referring to reflexes. Meyerhold thought in much more mechanical terms, however. One of the theses of *biomechanics*, from a lecture in 1921, was that the action of the actor, according to the laws of *biomechanics* 'does not for a moment suppress in the actor the intensive flaring up of fuel in the area of sensations of A2 material, inasmuch as A1's regulator is always on guard'.[94] Gordon and Law write that Pavlov's conditioning experiments were actually employed mainly with sound stimuli; that is, with music, to perfect the actor's state of *reflex excitability*.[95]

Pavlov's assertion that 'the conditioned reflex is the basis of all man's higher nervous activity' led to the belief espoused by the Soviet government that the principles of Pavlov's theory were fundamental to the formation of motor habits, the physical qualities of strength, speed, stamina and skill, and improving the functional capacity of the organism, especially for the purposes of work. It was important, therefore, for Meyerhold to find a way to include reflex conditioning in his theory and he may, like many of his contemporaries, have believed that reflex conditioning was the key to human behaviour. Meyerhold was acquainted with the work of Bekhterev in this regard.

Vladimir Mikhailovich Bekhterev

Bekhterev (1857–1927) was the founder of psycho-reflexology, in which theories of conditioned reflexes were applied to humans, and he was

[93] Leach, *Vsevolod Meyerhold*, p. 54.
[94] Pesochinskii, 'Biomekhanika', p. 106.
[95] Gordon and Law, *Meyerhold, Eisenstein*, p. 40.

therefore the forerunner of behaviourism. Like Pavlov's, his work found favour after the revolution and he was made chair of the Department of Psychology and Reflexology at the University of Petrograd in 1918. He died in suspicious circumstances after being summoned to visit Stalin in 1927. He was convinced that complex behaviours could be explained through the objective study of reflexes.

In Bekhterev's reflexology, therefore, the external characteristics of behaviour were studied – facial expression, gesture, voice and speech – as a system of signs corresponding to both external stimuli, which could be physical, biological or social, and internal stimuli. Human beings were considered to be 'bio-social beings', whose behaviour was a response to the natural and social environment. Reflexology was the study of the collective as well as the individual.[96] The former psychology which defined mind, will, feeling, memory and attention, so necessary for Stanislavsky, was replaced by a variety of divisions of types of reflexes; higher and personal reflexes; facial expression reflexes, reflexes of concentration and so on. Some of Meyerhold's statements on reflexes may well be a result of an attempt to embrace Bekhterev's theory within his own.

William James and emotion

The popular understanding of James and Lange's theories provided further support for Meyerhold's belief that in undertaking the actions of the biomechanical acting cycle, the actor would experience automatically a range of emotions as part of a reflex reaction. As with Stanislavsky, there is no direct evidence that Meyerhold studied James, but in his notebook of 1898/99, Meyerhold wrote a list of psychology texts; Hoffding's *Notes on Psychology Based on Experience*, Chelpanov's *Brain and Thought*, Lyuss's *The Study of Psychology, its Subject, Field and Method*, James's *Textbook of Psychology* and Bain's *Psychology.*[97]

James's statement, 'I saw the bear, I ran, I became frightened', was taken as the model; Gordon and Law assert that Meyerhold expressed this as follows: 'to trigger the sensation of fear, a person would only have to run – with his eyebrows raised and pupils dilated... an automatic reflex signifying fear would be felt throughout his body'.[98] Bekhterev's influence, in terms of reflexes of facial expression, is apparent here.

---

[96] V. M. Bekhterev, *General Principles of Human Reflexology: An Introduction to the Objective Study of Personality*, tr. Emma Murphy and William Murphy (London: Jarrolds, 1933), p. 12.

[97] O. M. Feld'man (ed.), *Meierhold Nasledie*, 1 (Moscow: OGI, 1998), p. 183.

[98] Gordon and Law, *Meyerhold, Eisenstein*, pp. 36–7.

Eisenstein expanded on this, attributing to James the idea that 'a man's physical movement gives birth to excitation peculiar for the movement. Thus, laughter evokes a happy mood, tears – sadness.'[99] In a lecture on *biomechanics* in 1935, he posed the question of which comes first, the gesture or emotion? According to James, Eisenstein says, 'movement comes first, a person is sad because tears are falling, but others think the tears flow because the person is sad'. He adds that both are seemingly correct but the posing of the questions presupposes a dualistic worldview, 'ripping apart the unity of . . . the psychic and the motor as a single process'. He writes that is possible to approach the unity of motor and psychological phenomena one way or another – if you shiver as you do when you are cold, you will develop the unpleasant feeling you have when you are cold. If you place yourself in a certain emotional state you will translate it involuntarily into movement.[100] This version of James and Lange's work is an over-simplification: James said the emotion could not be divorced from the physiological state but did not claim that a physical movement would evoke an emotion.

Eisenstein goes on to state that according to James an imitative movement is made in the spectator. 'James' point of view has a correct expression in the theatre in the audience. It's not that the actor makes a correct movement and experiences a proper emotion – the audience reproduces that movement in a concentrated form and through it enters into the emotional state the actor is demonstrating. The secret of form lies here.'[101] This view of audience response was shared by Meyerhold and differed from Stanislavsky's idea of *prana* rays *infecting* the audience.[102]

The fact is that Meyerhold made statements about emotion that are often contradictory. In a talk to students in 1921 Meyerhold said:

On stage I can enter into a role so that I will suffer, cry real tears, but if at the same time my expressive means are not in correspondence with my idea, then my experiencings will achieve no result. It is possible to burst into sobs, even to faint on stage, but the public will not feel anything unless I know how to convey what I want to them.[103]

He is here describing a form of *dislocation*. Therefore, for Meyerhold, it is possible to show emotion without feeling it and the actor's own feelings

[99] *Ibid.* p. 164.
[100] *Ibid.* p. 207.
[101] *Ibid.* p. 208.
[102] I. M. Sechenov, *Reflexes of the Brain*, tr. S. Belsky (Cambridge: Massachusetts, 1965), p. 50.
[103] Pesochinskii, 'Biomekhanika, p. 104.

can be a distraction. There need be no correspondence between the personal mood of the actor and the mood of the character.

Meyerhold wrote in *Love of Three Oranges* in 1914, before the revolution, about the importance of the sphere of gesture and movement, as well as text and 'psychology': 'Look, the actor only inclines his head. "Oh, is the poor man crying?" says the spectator looking intently from the auditorium. He is sure that the actor is crying and begins to cry himself. But the actor? Perhaps he is laughing into his waistcoat, having taken a tragic pose. Here there is such power (and such deception) in the actor's pose, in the actor's gesture!'[104] Michael Chekhov is said to have possessed this particular skill of convincing an audience.

Meyerhold's fascination with theatrical illusion is apparent here, as is his ambivalent attitude towards *emotion* (i.e. he thinks it is a good thing for actors to convince the audience that they are not feeling it when they are acting it), but biomechanical theory, as described above, states that there will be a reflexive emotional response. The revolutionary science he adopted may have brought about a conflict with his own practical experience.

In a lecture in 1929 Meyerhold said:

I must portray on stage a person who is running from fright, running, frightened by the attack of a dog. So what must I do? Must I find in myself all the feelings of a person frightened by a dog's barking so then I will know how to run away from a dog well? No, I must evoke [them] in myself not before the moment when I run but when I run, the feelings of a frightened person are evoked in me.

But as Pesochinsky writes, Meyerhold did not think that the emotion of fear would appear automatically; the actor's imagination needed to be included. A person running in fright 'looks round all the time to see whether they're going to put a knife in his back. If you imagine this, there will always be the true emotion.'[105] So there is no necessary connection between action and emotion, and this very clear statement of the way an actor engenders *emotion* in practice is in essence the same as Stanislavsky's classic example of the girl looking for a brooch. The actor must use the *magic if* and *given circumstances*; that is, the actor must use the imagination to put themselves in the situation and take action accordingly.

[104] *Ibid.*, p. 106.
[105] Pesochinskii, 'Akter', in Bolkhantseva, *Russkoe Akterskoe Iskusstvo*, pp. 142–3.

The scientific basis of biomechanics

Meyerhold claimed that *biomechanics* could help the actor get rid of postural, presentation and vocal problems. If the actor could move confidently, he or she could speak the text confidently. Like Stanislavsky he used other forms of exercises in his training, such as acrobatics. Therefore, there was no more scientific basis for their inclusion as actor training than that claimed by those exercise forms. His scientific theory for *biomechanics* was more a codification of ideas, and the scientific theories he referenced are also questionable in terms of contemporary science.

In 1932, during the ideological debate on *biomechanics*, Meyerhold's theories were attacked as 'mechanistic'. He was said to be working against Soviet theatre and accused of substituting external physical action for the dialectical revelation of the social essence of the image and biologism.[106] Biologism is a deterministic social theory, which discriminates on the grounds of biological factors, like the Nazi discrimination against Jews. Meyerhold argued that he needed a laboratory to study his materials on the art of acting and claimed, 'the physiologist Ivan Pavlov is deeply interested in my scientific material'.[107]

In 1938 Stanislavsky invited Meyerhold to work as his assistant at the Opera Theatre. As Braun suggests, the reasons for the rapprochement are unclear,[108] but it may reasonably be supposed that Stanislavsky was trying to protect Meyerhold, whose theatre had now been closed. A number of commentators have drawn parallels between the *method of physical actions* and *biomechanics* (and, according to Gordon and Law, Stanislavsky even used some of the biomechanical études), but Meyerhold emphasised *biomechanics* less and less in the 1930s, perhaps because of the attacks on his work, or perhaps it was an expression of his experimentation in a particular period rather than something he saw as having lasting significance.[109]

Stanislavsky's differences with Meyerhold

Worrall states, 'just as the attack on Naturalism carried with it an attack on nineteenth-century 'individualistic' concepts of character, so bio-mechanics became orientated towards collective, integrated and non-individualistic

[106] Gordon and Law, *Meyerhold, Eisenstein*, p. 59.
[107] *Ibid.* p. 60.
[108] Braun, *Meyerhold on Theatre*, pp. 250–1.
[109] Gordon and Law, *Meyerhold, Eisenstein*, p. 81.

stage action'.[110] Meyerhold's ideas about training reflected that emphasis. Meyerhold sought to find a sign system in *biomechanics*, which was for the post-revolutionary audience what commedia had been previously. In doing so he made reference to the science of the time because the epoch espoused it; he used science for artistic purposes rather than seeking, like Stanislavsky, to find scientific corroboration for his theories.

Meyerhold did not deny psychology, or acting with emotion, but saw *experiencing* as only one of the actors means; it was 'subject to conscious organisation, technical preparation and artistic formulation, like for example, plastic decisiveness'.[111] He bypassed the problem of *experiencing*, so crucial to Stanislavsky, by saying that it was not so important, or that emotion would appear by reflex with the right action.

A further very interesting difference between Stanislavsky and Meyerhold was Meyerhold's rejection of the unconscious, the origin of emotion and *experiencing* for Stanislavsky. Meyerhold considered consciousness of stage creativity (the actor's control over his actions, physical and psychical before, during and after the action), as a necessary condition of theatre according to the laws of *biomechanics*:

The whole Biomechanical system, the whole process of our movement is dictated by a basic principle – thought, a person's brain, the thinking apparatus. This is the basic purpose of the Biomechanical system . . . we verify each movement on stage by the thought that a given scene evokes . . . Thought is the first stage of the creative process of the actor . . . the brain is the initiator of the task . . . it is what orients, what gives the series of movements, the accent, et cetera . . . Conscious control of the precision of stage action is . . . the fulcrum in acting in preparation of the role and while performing it.

The actor's biomechanical technique proposed first of all his ability:

to analyse his movements every minute – heavy thought in the laboratory or preparatory work and then on the basis of his analysis, with every minute, every rehearsal he gets lighter, his thinking apparatus becomes more mobile.[112]

In 1887 Stanislavsky, in a letter to Benois, divided traditions in theatre into those which were 'genuine and alive, coming from life itself from nature, and false, invented traditions which deform artists and turn them into mannequins'. On several later occasions, he wrote that Meyerhold

---

[110] Worrall, 'Meyerhold's Production of *The Magnificent Cuckold*', TDR, 17:1, p. 16.
[111] Pesochinskii, 'Biomekhanika', p. 106.
[112] Pesochinskii, 'Akter', in Botkhontseva, *Russkve Akteskoe Iskusstvo*, p. 140.

turned his actors into mannequins, and in 1934 he was reported to have said that Meyerhold wanted to translate feelings into an exact expression, into *representation*.[113]

Their views of the audience differed. A common goal of both Stanislavsky and Meyerhold was to free the actor from superfluous tension. Stanislavsky achieved this by the creation of the *fourth wall*, which Meyerhold dismantled. The actor was to be conscious constantly of the presence of the audience. This was also due to a change in the idea of the actor-audience relationship, from Stanislavsky's Tolstoyan ethic, that was dependent on the actor's *experiencing*, to Meyerhold's views of the alienation effect and reflex response in the audience.[114]

At least in the twenties it was possible to maintain conflicts such as those that existed between Stanislavsky and Meyerhold. In 1924, Filippov wrote as if the emphases of the two men on either internal or external technique were viable alternatives, a question of choice or style.[115] By the 1930s, however, formalism had been termed 'anti-Soviet' and its exponents were being eliminated, as Meyerhold eventually was, in order to make the way clear for socialist realism.

Although Meyerhold and others may have seen his work as bourgeois and reactionary at the beginning of the revolution, essentially Stanislavsky made the right choices politically. Kostetsky describes the Twelfth Party Congress in 1923, where Lenin's negative attitude to innovation was made clear, and it was also stated that the theatre style of the MAT could be more readily available to mass tastes, in preference to some of the experimental work going on in other theatres, if subtlety and psychological nuances (the main value of the MAT) could be avoided. This way of thinking gathered momentum. In building the road to socialist realism it was necessary to destroy the trends represented by Meyerhold, Tairov and Eisenstein.[116] Abalkin wrote that Stanislavsky's work was in accordance with socialist realism in that it placed no limit on the creativity of actors or directors; nor did it legitimate any one theatrical form.[117] Socialist realism demands of the artist a correct historical representation of reality in its revolutionary development. Kostetsky defines the common elements of socialist realism and Stanislavsky's system as nationalism, closeness to the people and the

[113] Vinogradskaia, *Letopis*, vol. 1, p. 201 (1st edn) vol. 3, p. 299 and (1st edn) vol. 4, p. 371.
[114] Gordon and Law, *Meyerhold, Eisenstein*, p. 168.
[115] Filippov, *Besedy o teatre*, pp. 102–4.
[116] I. Kostetskii, *Sovetskaia Teatral'naia Politika i Sistema Stanislavskogo* (Munich: Institut po Izucheniiu CCCP, 1956), p. 91.
[117] N. A. Abalkin, *Sistema Stanislavskogo i Sovetskii Teatr* (Moscow: Iskusstvo, 1954), p. 9.

social significance of theatre, the primacy of dramaturgy, rejection of formalism and patriotism.[118]

In summary, Stanislavsky's answer to Chekhov and Meyerhold's objections to the limitations of drawing on personal experience in acting was consistent with the beliefs about acting he had adopted early in his professional career, at the beginning of the *system*. He also refuted Chekhov and Meyerhold's claim that drawing on personal experience can lead to madness or hysteria. In a letter to Gurevich written in 1931, Stanislavsky made various definitive statements on emotion, including the statement that the artist experiences real *feeling* on stage and this is prompted by the *affective memory*. This *feeling* can be stronger than 'real living feeling' and felt more deeply, and the actor can be so immersed in it that they forget they are on stage, but this 'does not drive you mad' (*Collected Works*, vol. 9, pp. 449–53). Both Meyerhold and Chekhov stressed the importance of imagination more than Stanislavsky and attached different meanings to it.

Meyerhold and Chekhov sought solutions to the problems of acting in different spheres of knowledge than Stanislavsky. Chekhov found an answer to his spiritual quest as a performer and a human being in anthroposophy. Meyerhold looked primarily into the traditions of theatre for his answers, asking different questions to those asked by Stanislavsky, and interesting himself in questions of theatrical form rather than training. The traditions and longevity of a form such as commedia dell'arte was of interest to him in itself rather than its scientific basis. I have suggested that his interest in scientific ideas in relation to *biomechanics* arose from his desire to develop a theatrical language which would appeal to a post-revolutionary Soviet audience influenced by the Bolshevik commendation of science and work, rather than an interest in science in itself.

There are parallels between the techniques of *psychological gesture, method of physical actions* and *biomechanics*, and all emerged in a similar period, influenced by the episteme of that period. But essentially Stanislavsky looked to science, Michael Chekhov to the religion of anthroposophy and Meyerhold to traditions of theatre as corroboration for their methods.

[118] Kostetskii, *Sovietskaia Teatralnaia Politika*, p. 94.

CHAPTER 6

Theory and practice of the system

STANISLAVSKY AND SOVIET SCIENCE

The question of how Stanislavsky envisaged 'internal' and 'external' has been explored throughout this book; the problem is to be examined now in terms of what this means for the relationship between the theory and practice of the *system*. Firstly, a consideration of how a scientific basis for Stanislavsky's work that was configured in Soviet times throws further light on the trappings accumulated by the *system* and paves the way for a view of the theoretical basis for the *system* in twenty-first century terms.

Remez summarises the Soviet interpretation of the *system*. He writes that at a certain stage,

'Action' came into the arsenal of the system. It is true that at the beginning, the idea of 'internal' ('psychological') and 'external' action arose, then they became more sharply demarcated from each other, but the inculcation of the concept of 'action' into the theory and rehearsal practice of Stanislavsky itself represented an extremely spiritual stage in his research. In fact the logic of actions was to become the guiding thread to the possession of the logic of feelings.[1]

He goes on to state that in Stanislavsky's rehearsal plan for a production of *Othello*, written at the end of the 1920s, internal and external action became combined to form the concept of psychophysical action.[2] He is referring to the following statement by Stanislavsky, characteristically using a mechanical metaphor mixed with spirituality, in which the actor is an 'aeroplane with wings of belief':

Remember the way an aircraft takes off; first it travels over the ground for a long time, gaining momentum. A movement of the air is created which lifts the wings

---

[1] O. Remez, 'Istoki Teorii Stanislavskogo', in *Voprosi Teatra, Sbornik Statei i Publikatsii* (Moscow: Soiuz Teatral'nykh deiatelei, 1990), p. 94.

[2] See Jean Benedetti, *Stanislavski: His Life and Art*, 2nd edn (London: Methuen, 1999), pp. 324–30 for an account of what happened in the disastrous MAT production, where Stanislavsky's rehearsal plan was largely ignored.

and carries the machine upwards. The actor also goes along, so to speak, taking a run up by means of the physical actions and gains momentum. In this time with the help of given circumstances, and magic 'ifs', the actor unfolds his invisible wings of belief, which take him aloft into the region of the imagination, in which he has now put his trust.

But if there is no flattened ground or aerodrome, along which it can gain speed, can the aeroplane take off into the air? Of course not. Consequently our first concern is to create and flatten this aerodrome, paved precisely by physical actions, strong in their truth.[3]

Remez concludes:

Now Stanislavsky, following Pavlov, could rejoice in gaining 'general solid ground', the possibility of giving order to 'the eternal chaos of human experiences', and could fully share Pavlov's conviction that there would come about inevitably the 'natural and inevitable rapprochement and finally the merging of psychological and physiological, subjective and objective . . . and enabling this merging to happen is the great task for science of the near future.'[4]

Remez, writing in 1990, goes on to describe the *method of physical actions* as the culmination of Stanislavsky's work, saying that it came into being at the beginning of the thirties, ignoring the fact that action had always been an essential concept in the *system*. In order for Remez and others before him to make the claim that Stanislavsky's work corroborated that of Pavlov, Soviet science imposed a theory on Stanislavsky's work and obfuscated parts that did not fit with the theory. Many of those in personal contact with Stanislavsky assimilated this approach. For example, Grigory Vladimirovich Kristi was one of Stanislavsky's assistants at the Opera Studio, and worked as a director there in the forties. As one of the members of the 'Commission for the Study and Publication of the Legacy of Stanislavsky and Nemirovich-Danchenko' he was one of the editors of the first edition of Stanislavsky's *Collected Works*. His book, *The Training of the Actor of Stanislavsky's School*, published in 1968, details the training of an acting student on the MAT's four-year course. Theatre scholar Vladimir Nikolaevich Prokofiev, who was also involved with the Opera Studio and was chair of the commission, wrote in the foreword that 'Kristi's book was written taking into account the complex and lengthy evolution of Stanislavsky's views on the pedagogy and method of stage art.'[5]

---

[3] K. S. Stanislavsky, *Rezhisserskie ekzemplyary K. S. Stanislavskogo, v Shesti Tomakh, 1898–1930*, ed. by Inna Soloveva, vol. 6 *P'esa V. Shekspira 'Otello'*, vol. 6 (Moscow: Iskusstvo, 1994), p. 243.
[4] Remez, *Istoki*, p. 94.
[5] G. V. Kristi, *Vospitanie Aktera Shkoli Stanislavskogo* (Moscow: Iskusstvo, 1968), p. 12.

The members of the commission asserted Stanislavsky's supposed move from *emotional memory* to the *method of physical actions*, downplayed the discussion of *emotional memory* and referenced Pavlov. In addition, Prokofiev lists books on training actors that have appeared, including books by Maria Knebel', V. O. Toporkov, P. Ershov and others, but says that not all of these are 'incontrovertible in the scientific sense'.[6] Kristi then goes on to establish Stanislavsky's credentials as a scientist from the Soviet point of view:

His system is the work of a researcher, a scientist. In it, for the first time, the problem of conscious control of the subconscious, of the uncontrolled process of scenic creativity, has been resolved and an investigation begun of the actor's reincarnation into the character.[7]

He mentions that early on in his work Stanislavsky turned to contemporary psychology to solve the problem of achieving the creative state, and began to develop a long list of techniques on the basis of that psychology. Nevertheless, Kristi states, practice showed that it is difficult to create the proper creative state outside the process of an action, for it is little influenced or controlled by our consciousness. So in the 1930s, according to Kristi, Stanislavsky changed his approach, working not from the viewpoint of psychology, not from inner experience, but from the logic of physical actions, relying on 'the law of the organic union of the spiritual and physical in man'.[8]

Citing Sechenov, who had said that no thought occurs without being preceded by 'some external stirring of the senses; and Pavlov's theory of the second signalling system', Kristi gives to Stanislavsky the thesis that physical action is the basis for verbal action. By the first signalling system Pavlov meant external stimuli which act on our sense organs – things that we hear (except words), see, touch and so on. These stimuli are preserved in our memory as sensations and impressions of life around us. The first signalling system is common to humans and animals alike. Verbal signals are signals of signals, abstractions of reality and, therefore, speech is a second signal system, which is not shared by animals.[9]

---

[6] *Ibid.* p. 10.
[7] G. V. Kristi, 'The Training of an Actor in the Stanislavsky School of Acting', in Sonia Moore, *Stanislavski Today: Commentaries on K. S. Stanislavski* (New York: American Center for Stanislavski Theatre Art, 1973), p. 22.
[8] *Ibid.* pp. 24, 25.
[9] Hilaire Cuny, *Ivan Pavlov: The Man and his Theories*, tr. Patrick Evans (London: Souvenir Press, 1964), pp. 90–1.

In an article included in *Stanislavski Today* (*ST*), edited by Sonia Moore, Kristi writes that physical actions provide the impulses for pronouncing the words and they are intrinsic to the functioning of our first signal system. By this he means that the physical action carried out by the actor will evoke by reflex the corresponding emotional response – the words are, therefore, secondary and the appropriate way of speaking them will flow from this emotional response. He concludes that the value of what he entitles Stanislavsky's *method of physical and verbal actions* lies in the fact that it reveals to us accessible and practical ways of mastering the word on stage at the level of the first signal system. In other words, he says, Stanislavsky recommends that creativity should begin with the primary physical process of establishing a tie with the objects about us, which are the source of our sensations.[10] However, although Stanislavsky's *system* emphasises the importance of the actor giving his or her attention to stage objects or stage partners, Stanislavsky's descriptions always include the idea of the actor voluntarily focussing attention – it is not that the perception of the stage objects brings about a conditional and, therefore, precisely repeatable response in the actor (in the way he or she speaks the words, as Pavlov's dogs salivated to the sound of the ringing bell), which is what Kristi seems to be saying. In fact, Stanislavsky developed exercises for actors to focus on *objects* outside themselves and his scientific support for this was in Ribot, as discussed in Chapter 2. He read in Ribot's *Psychology of the Attention* that 'attention adapts itself to what is without, reflection to what is within'.[11] Kristi, believing in his theory of the second signalling system, emphasises that in speaking the words the whole organism must be involved: 'When a gentleman asks a lady to dance, at that moment his whole body is getting ready to dance. If when he says the words, "may I invite you to dance?" his back is bent and his legs are limp then you could doubt the sincerity of his intentions.'[12] Whether Stanislavsky thought about it quite in this way is debatable. He was influenced, after all, by Tolstoy, who distinguished between feelings, which he claimed were transmitted by art, and thought or knowledge, which is transmitted by words.[13] Stanislavsky's concept of feeling-thought-word, as discussed in Chapter 3, in no way implies that he saw words as secondary; it was rather

[10] Kristi, in Moore, *Stanislavski Today*, p. 27.
[11] Théodule Ribot, *The Psychology of Attention*, tr. from 6th edn (Chicago and London: Open Court, 1911), p. 17.
[12] Kristi, *Vospitanie Aktera*, p. 144.
[13] Leo Tolstoy, *What is Art?* tr. Richard Pevear and Larissa Volokhonsky (London: Penguin, 1995), pp. 80–1.

the opposite – words express the life of the human spirit: 'Feeling-thought-word, the spiritual image of thought, must always bear the stamp of truth.'[14]

Moreover, Kristi claims that Stanislavsky established a direct connection between the actor's *tempo-rhythm* and his creative state. He references *AWHI*, where Stanislavsky discusses the 'mechanical influence through external tempo-rhythm on our capricious, self-willed, disobedient and fearful feeling!' (p. 208), though he does not give the exact quotation, perhaps because Stanislavsky's description is worded whimsically rather than scientifically. Kristi adds that this discovery is based on the same principle of the psychophysical unity of human nature that constitutes the foundation of Stanislavsky's methods.[15] The epoch's emphasis on rhythm is questionable now, as is the idea that reflexes are central to how human mechanisms function. Also, Stanislavsky's division of *tempo-rhythm* into internal and external, as discussed previously indicates a dualistic way of thinking rather than indicating an understanding of psychophysical unity. Using the language familiar to Stalin's epoch, Kristi writes that Stanislavsky 'confessed the error' of his previous attempts to establish the creative state divorced from concrete action, and became increasingly convinced that the analysis and the synthesis, the experience and the incarnation, are a single simultaneous process and not different stages of it, as he had thought before.[16] Stanislavsky's adoption of *active analysis* is seen as an indication of this insight where the actors improvise the characters' actions, in the belief if this is done the right way, feeling will ensue, as opposed to the lengthy round-the-table analysis that characterised the early years of the MAT. However, Stanislavsky became increasingly interested in improvisory methods much earlier than this, after visiting Gorky on Capri in 1911. Gorky and he saw a show at a popular theatre which aimed to revive commedia dell'arte and Stanislavsky was very enthusiastic because the show was not scripted but improvised.[17] He encouraged the use of improvisory methods in the First Studio.

There is no reference for this 'confession' and we have noted the consistency in the discussion of action since Stanislavsky's 'artistic youth.' So far from being wedded to the idea of emotional memory at the expense of action in the early days, his experiments with *experiencing* as

---

[14] K. S. Stanislavsky *Stanislavsky on the Art of the Stage*, tr. David Magarshack, 2nd edn (London: Faber and Faber, 1967), p. 116.

[15] Kristi, in Moore, *Stanislavski Today*, pp. 30–1.

[16] *Ibid.* p. 32.

[17] I. N. Vinogradskaia, *Zhizn' i Tvorchestvo K. S. Stanislavskogo Letopis*, (Moscow: Moskovskii Khudozhestvennyi Teatr), vol. 2, pp. 274–5.

divorced from overt external expression in symbolist plays were quickly abandoned. Nevertheless, Kristi is determined to see the *method of physical actions* as an illustration of Pavlov's theories in a practical application, and the scientist P. V. Simonov goes even further.

Pavel Vasil'evich Simonov

Soviet neurophysiologist Dr P. V. Simonov, of the Soviet Academy of Science was an internationally celebrated authority on brain processes. He wrote on Pavlov and Stanislavsky in *Metod K. S. Stanislavskogo i Fiziologia Emotzsii* in 1962. Here, Simonov argues that Stanislavsky is a deterministic materialist, and argues forcefully that the *method of physical actions* is not an addendum to the *system* but permeates it from beginning to end. He states categorically that 'outside the Method there is no system' and, dismissing those who might think otherwise, writes that not to acknowledge this is tantamount to not understanding the essence of the *system*. Somewhat hyperbolically, he adds,

The Method of Physical Action is in the same relationship to Stanislavsky's system as the method of conditioned reflexes is to the theory of Ivan Petrovich Pavlov, or as natural selection is to the teaching of Charles Darwin, or the principle of accumulation of the atomic weights of the elements to the system of D. I. Mendeleev.[18]

He again argues that Stanislavsky 'discovered' psychophysical unity:

We are indebted to KSS for the materialist conception of the unbreakable bond between the psychological and the physiological, between subjective experience and its objective expression.[19]

He writes that 'with courage and logic' Stanislavsky presents the thesis that in every physical action there is something psychological, and that the most complex psychological situations are expressed through physical actions. Indeed, this is what Stanislavsky said, but Simonov then goes on to assert that, in essence, Stanislavsky's views exclude any possibility of subjective experience without physical expression. This is definitely not how Stanislavsky thought as, rightly or wrongly, throughout his life he struggled with the situation where in his perception he had a correct subjective experience but the wrong physical expression, as, for example, in the experiments with *experiencing* in the symbolist phase and the Salieri crisis.

[18] P. V. Simonov, 'From The Method of K. S. Stanislavsky and the Physiology of Emotion', in Moore, *Stanislavski Today* p. 38.
[19] *Ibid.* p. 36.

Simonov continues to claim that Stanislavsky's theory and practice of stage art was consistently materialist and that the dialectical-materialist character of his scientific research was defined by the development of Russian social thought in the second half of the nineteenth century, and by the influence of philosophical, aesthetic and natural scientific manifestations of the revolutionary democrats. He adds that Soviet socialist reality, the world outlook of the Communist Party of the Soviet Union and the classic works of Marxism-Leninism were of great significance in Stanislavsky's creativity.[20] This is far from the truth – Stanislavsky was consistent in his adherence to his idea of truth and truthful *experiencing* but there is no evidence that he read Marx or Lenin or changed his view to a materialist one.[21] Simonov writes that Stanislavsky, having developed the means for consciously generating the emotions, has gained control of how to generate the required creative state on stage. The actor communicates his experience to the spectator through the external signs of emotion, through reactions that have been provoked, and the concomitant changes in the activity of internal organs. Simonov's description here does not concur with Stanislavsky's Tolstoyan idea of the *infectiousness of feeling* which may be communicated through the external signs of emotion but also via *prana*, *raying out* and *raying in*.

These ideas, Simonov says, coincide with those of Sechenov and Pavlov on the basis of the dialectical union of the psychological and the physical, of subjective experience and objective expression and in their being conditioned by the influence of the surrounding environment. Stanislavsky recognises the importance of human behaviour and circumstances, Simonov writes, in analysing the actor's problem of reproducing an emotional experience and expressing it externally through facial expression, expression of the eyes and intonations of speech. He always starts with the cause that conditions every nuance of experience or any physical action, seeking the motivating forces of a person's psychological life not in the psychological phenomena themselves, but in the external influence of the surrounding environment, and in one's circumstances and behaviour. The determinism of the Stanislavsky *system* is a direct reflection of the theory of Sechenov and Pavlov. Our behaviour, states Simonov, is determined by physical causes. It is clear here that in order to make this claim Soviet science had to repudiate Stanislavsky's connection with the ideas of Ribot and emotional memory, and ground its

[20] P. V. Simonov, *Metod K. S. Stanislavskogo i Fiziologia Emotzii* (Moscow: AN SSSR, 1962), p. 7.
[21] *Ibid.* p. 9.

interpretation of his theory on the idea of action, and the correct action generating the correct internal emotional content.

Simonov adduces as evidence for a materialistic viewpoint that Stanislavsky stated that many of the most important facets of our complex nature are not subject to conscious control and that passions are aroused under the influence of circumstances, and cannot be commanded or forced. Simonov goes on to add that for Stanislavsky the subconscious never had any nuance of mysticism or transcendence, a statement that is just not true. Simonov adds that 'Anyone acquainted with his works can easily see that for Stanislavsky "conscious" and "subconscious" mean "controlled" and "uncontrolled".'

He further claims that for Stanislavsky the primacy of the conscious over the subconscious is characteristic. It is difficult to see how Simonov could assert this in view of Stanislavsky's many statements about the importance of the unconscious, the mysterious source of creativity. Simonov goes on to assert the superiority of Stanislavsky's view to that of idealist psychologists in the West (Sigmund Freud, for instance), for whom the subconscious is the basic motivational force in human behaviour – something elemental and incomprehensible. According to Simonov, Stanislavsky's striving to 'turn on and off' the uncontrolled subconscious physiological mechanisms, vividly demonstrates the ideological and methodological position of the author of the *system*. The Stanislavsky slogan, 'through conscious means to have control over the subconscious', contrasts in principle with the interpretation of the subconscious in the works of the psychologist idealists. Of course, Freud's understanding of the subconscious was very different to Stanislavsky's and there is much room for debate on the relative merits of Stanislavsky's concept as opposed to Freud's, but the point is that Stanislavsky's concept was rooted in nineteenth-century psychology and yoga and was one of subconscious processes as essentially mystical. Simonov goes further:

Innate and acquired paths of nerves through thousands of fibers connect physical actions with emotions and with endlessly varied nuances of human experience. Physical actions not only revive the traces of previously experienced emotions, but are themselves at the same time influenced by these revivified emotions, and so become more truthful and more expressive of the given circumstances.[22]

It seems curious to suggest the idea of nerves connecting actions with emotions as though they are in fact separate entities rather than a unified

---

[22] Simonov in Moore, *Stanislavski Today*, p. 41.

process and Stanislavsky would not have agreed that simply the repetition of a series of physical actions would necessarily make the actions more emotionally truthful – in his discussions of emotional memory he discusses the problem of the memories becoming stale and needing to be refreshed (*AWHE*, p. 291).

He wrote that

In creating a logical and consistent external line of physical actions we recognise, if we are attentive, that in parallel with that line, another one – the line of the logic and consistency of feelings – arises within us. This is understandable because they, the internal feelings, unnoticed by us, give rise to actions because they are indissolubly linked to the life of these actions (*AWHE*, p. 262).

However, he qualified this, as follows:

The secret of my method is obvious . . . the problem is not in the physical actions themselves, but in the truth and belief which these actions help us to arouse and feel within ourselves (*AWHE*, p. 262).

Stanislavsky drew his ideas of the logic and sequence of emotion from Ribot's thesis of the logic of feeling. Another problem here is that Simonov, expert though he was on the neurophysiology of emotion, appears to be taking the idea of emotions as something commonly understood, without need of definition. He writes that physical actions make accessible the emotions of the character and permit the actor to live these emotions as his own. He adds that Stanislavsky never tires of repeating that the attention must be wholly concentrated on the physical actions, on their truthfulness, logic and consecutiveness.[23] Because of this, he asserts that the 'artificial supplement' of the actor's experience is unnecessary, for the emotions will appear by themselves as soon as the physical actions have prepared the way (if the stage action is inwardly justified) and so the truth of emotions is determined by the truth of the physical actions. However, Stanislavsky continued to discuss emotional memory and the truth of physical actions is rooted in the idea of being true to life, that is, true to the actor's own personal experience.

Finally, Simonov applauds Stanislavsky's idea of the fusion of the author's intentions with the supertask of the work:

The universality of these laws is based on the fact, difficult to dispute, that the principles formulated by Stanislavsky are the reflection of the objective laws in an actor's art. It is this objectivity – i.e., independence from the will and desire of

[23] *Ibid.* p. 42.

individual – that makes these laws equally obligatory 'for all theatrical creators without exception.'[24]

However, Stanislavsky's explanations depend on the concepts of will and desire and, here again, Simonov is reading what he wants into Stanislavsky's *method of physical actions*.

He goes on to state that the *Method* has a direct relationship with a series of actual problems of human neurophysiology: the cortical regulation of the activity of the internal organs, hypnosis, the genesis of neurotic conditions, psychotherapy and the prevention of neuroses.[25] He mentions James, Cannon and Wheatley's experiments on the brain showing that a remembered emotion is a 'real' emotion.[26] Simonov's investigations are very important and Soviet work on emotion is greatly respected and needs further investigation in relation to acting. (Simonov wrote *The Emotional Brain*, published in New York in 1986.) Much of what actually happened in the 1930s in relation to Stanislavsky's work remains shrouded in mystery. But it is very important to see that Sonia Moore and some other western commentators and practitioners have taken on the Soviet interpretation, or aspects of it, without seeing the political drive behind it, or that there is no justification in Stanislavsky's writings for the assertion that the *method of physical actions* represents a rejection of his previous work. The Soviets rightly asserted psychophysical unity, following on from Sechenov's work. Indeed, twenty-first-century science has largely developed on this foundation though Sechenev and Pavlov's ideas of reflexes have been discussed, but for Stanislavsky, despite what Simonov and Kristi have to say, the mind-body problem was not fully resolved by the *method of physical actions* or, in fact, in the *system* as a whole.

Karin Jansen points out that as early as 1908 he was discussing psychophysiology and its relationship to creativity in letters to V. W. Kotliarevskaia, and also that 'physical actions as a trigger for emotions were a regular part of Stanislavsky's early rehearsal work'.[27]

I have happened to fall upon the track of new principles. These principles could transform the whole psychology of the creativity of the actor. I test this out on myself and others daily and very often get most interesting results. Most of all I

[24] *Ibid.* p. 35.
[25] P. V. Simonov, *Metod*, pp. 13–14.
[26] *Ibid.* pp. 33–5.
[27] Karin Jansen, 'Die Frühphase des Stanislawski-Systems (1906–1915) im Spiegel der Rezeption in den fünfziger Jahren', in *Konstantin Stanislawski, Neue Aspekte und Perspektiven*, ed. Günter Ahrends (Tübingen: Forum Modernes Theater, 1992), p. 29, 34.

am fascinated by the rhythm of feeling, the development of affective memory and the psychophysiology of creativity. (*Collected Works*, vol. 8, p. 83).

Significantly, Stanislavsky is discussing psychophysiology or psychophysical unity with reference to *affective memory*, in the year he discovered Ribot, much earlier than the Soviet commentators assert. The problem was that his insight was a partial one and throughout his career there are times when he discusses mind and body in distinctly dualist terms.

MIND AND BODY

Philip Zarrilli states that the language in which acting is discussed frequently implies a dichotomous way of thinking about mind and body, 'between the cognitive, conceptual, formal or rational and the bodily, perceptual, material and emotional'.[28] He suggests that many languages of acting describe the actor's body as an instrument, which they must train in order to express what is in their minds. Stanislavsky in fact used these sorts of descriptions as Meyerhold, following Coquelin, also did. For example, in *MLIA*, Stanislavsky writes that the voice and body of the actor should be obedient instruments in the sure hands of a virtuoso.[29] Zarrilli adds that the character can be seen as an object logically constructed by the mind and then put into the body. Exemplifying this split way of thinking, Leach asks the question whether the actor's brain or emotions control his voice and movement or vice versa.[30] Zarrilli writes, quoting Benedetti (and also citing Gordon, and echoing the Soviets), that 'Stanislavsky sought, through the method of physical action to overcome what divided mind from body, knowledge from feeling, analysis from action.'[31]

Roach, also following the Soviet line, says that the important division for Stanislavsky was not between mind and body but between conscious and unconscious and that the *system* cannot be understood without the science of his time.[32] Roach sees Pavlov's theory of conditioned reflexes as commensurate with Stanislavsky's view of what the actor does as a 'continuous flow of responses, where larger actions are divided into units and bits in the frame of the super-objective of the role, creating the

---

[28] Philip B. Zarrilli, (ed.) *Acting (Re)Considered*, 2nd edn (London: Routledge, 2002), p. 11.

[29] K. S. Stanislavsky, *My Life in Art*, tr. J. J. Robbins (London: Methuen, 1980), p. 70.

[30] Robert Leach, 'When He Touches Your Heart... The Revolutionary Theatre of Vsevolod Meyerhold and the Development of Michael Chekhov', *Contemporary Theatre Review*, 7:1 (1997), p. 68.

[31] Zarrilli, *Acting (Re)Considered*, p. 12.

[32] Joseph Roach, *The Player's Passion: Studies in the Science of Acting* (Newark: University of Michigan press, 1983), p. 206.

unbroken line, or score of the role'.[33] Roach echoes Kristi in saying that *affective memory* is a conditioned reflex, where 'the actor substitutes the stimuli provided by memory of certain sensations, locations or physical objects for the first reaction to actual events'.[34] Roach has Stanislavsky envisaging chains of reflexes as we adapt to circumstances and alternate between internal and external stimuli: 'To both Pavlov and Stanislavsky, behaviour consists of chains of physical adaptations, continuous transitions in the direction of the stream of consciousness caused by physical stimuli. This is the life the actor attempts to emulate by "living the role."'[35] By 'living the role' Roach means *experiencing*. He thinks that Stanislavsky experimented with various means of creating stimuli that would reliably excite the appropriate reflexive responses, whether of emotion or action. Presumably what is meant is that Stanislavsky asked what the conditions were that would enable the actor to behave in response to the stimulus of being on stage (the audience) and the stimuli of the stage situation (responding to the other actors, objects, setting, music) as if for the first time.

The problems with these readings are that there is nothing in Stanislavsky's writing that suggests he saw *affective memory* as a conditional reflex in this way, nor did his experience bear this out. If it were possible for the actor to behave as a reflex machine with emotional responses, as it were, roles such as Dr Stockmann would never go stale. The situation is more complex than that. The essential problem with conditional reflexes, as Pavlov found, is that the link created between stimulus and response is not contingent; there is the phenomenon of extinction or, as it is sometimes called, habituation, whereby for example, it is only for a certain time that the dog continues to salivate at the sound of the bell even when food is not presented. If there is no food, the connection the dog has made with the sound as a result of which it salivates, ceases to be.[36]

Pavlov bypassed the phenomenon of consciousness in his work on conditional reflexes, hoping that his findings would provide a basis for future research into the problem. He worked from the precept that mind, soul and matter are one, whatever they are, and so there could be a physiological explanation for everything. But it is possible for the conditional reflex response, such as it is in humans, to operate at an automatic level, subconsciously, so the subject reacts mechanically or habitually – the subject

---

[33] *Ibid.* p. 208.
[34] *Ibid.* p. 210.
[35] *Ibid.* pp. 206–7.
[36] Richard L. Gregory (ed.), *The Oxford Companion to the Mind* (Oxford University Press, 1987), p. 244.

may not be conscious of the reaction. Crucially for Stanislavsky, the actor should be responding on stage in a state of full attention, to be fully present, and the operation of conditional reflexes would not necessarily bring this about – the actors could go through the motions of their stage business while thinking about something else, despite the stimuli being presented.

Sechenov aimed to demonstrate that all human behaviour, including thought and emotion, could be analysed as reflex activity, wanting to resolve the mind-body problem. Even our most complicated emotional or spiritual experiences result from the associative capacities of the brain, which has learned its responses from childhood. Self-consciousness is a delusion. Following on from the work of Sechenov and Pavlov, Soviet science espoused monism. We have seen in Chapter 2 that Stanislavsky had recourse to the idea of reflexes in an attempt to overcome what was essentially, for him, a dichotomy between internal and external, mind and body, but he continued to think in a dualistic way. He was confused by the science of the day and in view of his concepts of emotion and spirit, he was not readily able to discard the notion of mind, soul or spirit as something existing beyond the body. His way of writing about mind and body is not consistent. Many of his statements indicate a concept of mind and body as separate entities, coexisting in a parallel fashion.

As an example of this, he writes that 'the true fulfilment of a physical task helps you create the right psychological state. It transforms the physical task into a psychological one' (*AWHE*, p. 218). And again, he states that

The borders of physical and spiritual bits can coincide or go apart. In the cases where a person is seized with passion as a whole, with all his being, he forgets physical tasks and they are fulfilled unconsciously, by mechanical habit. And in real life we by no means always think about how we are walking, ringing a bell, opening a door, and saying good morning. All this is done unconsciously in most cases. The body lives its own habitual life like a motor, and the soul lives its deepest psychological life. This apparent isolation, of course does not tear the link of the soul with the body. It proceeds from the fact that the centre of attention changes from the external to the internal life (*AWR*, p. 123).

In referring to *through action* Stanislavsky wrote, 'the physiological habit of the role arouses its psychology in the soul of the artist and the psychological *experiencing* of the feelings of the role engenders the physiological state of the body of the artist which is habitual for the role'.[37] In the same way as he uses the term 'reflex', Stanislavsky is here using the term 'habit' to explain the relationship between what he calls 'psychology' and 'physiology'.

[37] Vinogradskaia, *Letopis*, vol. 2, p. 149.

These descriptions are very different from Stanislavsky's occasional clear statements about psychophysical unity – the problem for him being that there can be theory on the one hand but the subjective experience or the interpretation of the subjective experience may be different. In Stanislavsky's writing, the external or physical action can bring about the correct internal or psychological task, but equally, the right thought can bring about the right action: 'From thoughts are born feeling and experiencing and from them also internal calls to action' (*AWHE*, p. 129). Importantly, without thought, acting becomes mechanical: 'If you said a word or did something mechanically on stage, not knowing who you were, where you have come from, why, what you need, where you are going to and what you will do there, you are acting without imagination ... without truth ... like a wound-up machine or automaton' (*AWHE*, p. 142). Again, in *AWHI*, he writes that physical movements are more palpable (p. 180) and that physical actions are easier to grasp than psychological ones (p. 445). These descriptions are dualist and not materialist.

Unlike some of his contemporaries, Stanislavsky did not adopt the crude interpretation of the James-Lange theory, which suggested that if you adopt a certain pose you will experience the corresponding emotion:

Of course it would be naïve to think that the bodily sensation can directly evoke the process itself of spiritual experiencing since physical sensation is only a consequence of experiencing and the experiencing itself is the cause. (K. S. Stanislavsky, MAT Archive, 676).

But this description implies that here, unlike James, he envisaged emotion as the cause of the physical expression – that he would think, for example, that we are afraid because we see the bear and therefore we run. Moreover, what is internal is often discussed as if there were separate aspects (for example thought, *experiencing* or emotion): 'The continuous chain of visual images ... creates in us a corresponding mood. It has an influence on your soul and evokes corresponding experiencing' (*AWHE*, p. 130). Stanislavsky saw the *motivators of psychic life* as a hierarchy, prioritising feeling over mind and will in the way that in the nineteenth century these were separate brain functions; the brain itself was not conceived of as one thing.

Finally, the *method of physical actions* perpetuates Stanislavsky's dichotomous way of thinking, rather than, as Zarrilli and others suggest, being a way to overcome it. For example (see Appendix), Stanislavsky writes on characterisation as follows:

All that has been done so far has achieved inner characterisation. Meantime the external characterization should have appeared of its own accord. But what is to be done if this does not occur? You should go over what has already been established but add a lame leg, terse or drawling speech, certain attitudes of arms or legs, or body, in keeping with certain externally acquired mannerisms or habits. If the external characterisation does not appear spontaneously, it must be grafted from the outside. It must take, like a lemon branch onto a grapefruit.

This rather odd simile indicates Stanislavsky's split way of thinking, as it suggests two different things being put together in a way that may not work. Further, the description of the *method of physical actions*, although the word emotion is avoided, includes concepts that had their origins in some of Stanislavsky's more esoteric ways of thinking, such as *Ia esm'* and the subconscious. There is an emphasis on avoiding speaking the text so it does not become mechanical and on *justification* and *here, today, now*. The actor is continually being urged to avoid the pitfall of mechanical acting but there are no guarantees. The 'sitting on hands' technique mentioned earlier, where the actors are asked to sit on their hands during a reading so that they do not gesture habitually, further indicates a disjunction – it appears that for Stanislavsky the actor's body is possibly out of control and the actors cannot be still simply because this is what they wish.

The way Stanislavsky separated topics in his writing again indicates the lack of consistency in the way he thought about mind and body. He writes that the inclusion of relaxing the muscles in *AWHE* is problematic: it properly belongs in a discussion of external technique, that is, with the work on the body (p. 185). This indicates that somehow he thought of body as separate from mental processes. Furthermore, splitting the actor's training into two, into inner and outer work, caused a great deal of confusion in America, as is evident from Edwards's discussion in *The Stanislavsky Heritage*. The fact that *An Actor Prepares*, the translation of *AWHI*, was published there in 1936 and *Building a Character*, the translation of *AWHE*, was not published until 1949, added to existing confusions about the *system*. In the chapter 'The Impact of Stanislavsky on the Contemporary American Theatre', she discusses 'critics who had charged that the Stanislavsky System was subjective and failed to take note of the primary task of an actor, to communicate with the audience'.[38] Stanislavsky conceives of *experiencing* and *incarnation* as separate and tries to find ways of linking them together, whereas the problem is in his dual concept in the first place.

[38] Christine Edwards, *The Stanislavsky Heritage* (New York University Press, 1965), p. 255.

Carnicke writes that Stanislavsky did not use the science of the day – his creativity was his most important resource – and adds that it was through his explorations of yoga that Stanislavsky began to perceive the indivisibility of mental and physical.[39] Stanislavsky writes on occasion that no action (including, he says, actions such as speech and thought) is purely physical or purely psychological. But he also continued to write until the end of his life (the description of the *method of physical actions* was written in 1937) in ways that drove a division between internal and external. The idea of physical action in itself is a contradiction in terms.

He was not the only practitioner to be confused. It is worth bearing in mind that Meyerhold's *biomechanics* and Chekhov's methods have both been described as 'psychophysical' and that Stanislavsky objected to the work of both men. Byckling states that in his work on *Hamlet*, Chekhov anticipated Stanislavsky's *method of physical actions*; 'Chekhov's aim was for the actors to learn in practice to grasp the profound connection of movement with words on the one hand and emotions on the other.'[40] Stanislavsky apparently did not see this connection and Vakhtangov and Chekhov's methods embodied for him the 'reverse of his teaching', as he said in 1922, and so did Meyerhold's *biomechanics*. Their emphases were in general too 'external' and theatrical for Stanislavsky and, therefore, not sufficiently expressive of inner content. But nor did Stanislavsky solve the problem of how to describe the actors's experience in consistently psychophysical terms. His purported studies of philosophy from 1929 to 1932, of which Soviet propaganda made much, did not help him to resolve his conceptual problem of mind and body.[41]

In his notes on Gogol's *Government Inspector* in *AWR*, Stanislavsky described the approach that became known as the *method of physical actions* as a 'new method, an external way of accessing the internal' (*AWR*, pp. 363–4). He did not necessarily think it was the definitive method, although it was seized upon as such in Soviet artistic theory. The *method of physical actions* prioritises external action, seeing that as key, albeit within the *given circumstances* and with 'truth' and 'belief', and as such it could be compared with Delsartean posture and gesture and Meyerhold's bio-mechanical exercises. The proponents of these techniques asserted that if these were correctly performed, the requisite emotion would be engendered.

[39] Sharon M. Carnicke, *Stanislavsky in Focus* (Amsterdam: Harwood Acadamic Publishers, 1998), p. 139.
[40] Liisa Byckling, 'Mikhail Chekhov i Antroposofia iz Istorii MKHAT Vtorogo', *Studia Russica Helsingiensia et Tartuensia*, 4 (1995) p. 258.
[41] See MAT KS Archive 544. The results of the study are just a few notes.

I am (Ia esm') and dislocation (vyvikh)

What Stanislavsky wants, whether it is by employing the *method of physical actions* or *emotional memory* is for the actor to *experience*, to be in the state of *I am (Ia esm')*.

The secret is that the logic and consistency of physical actions and feelings has led you to the truth, the truth has evoked belief and altogether this has created 'I am'. And what is 'I am?' It means: I exist, I live, I think and feel identically with the role (*AWHE*, p. 266).

Stanislavsky's use of church Slavonic *Ia esm'* indicates the highest apogee of the actor's art – a spiritual state. Carnicke asserts that *experiencing* and *infecting* the audience with the actor's emotion are synonymous with *I am*. *Experiencing* is the 'sense of self on stage as in life' and Stanislavsky wants to indicate the actor's immediacy and presence on stage, and the fact that the actor must create the role afresh each time (*AWHE*, pp. 231–2).

I am in our language refers to the fact that I have placed myself in the centre of imaginary conditions, that I feel myself situated among them, that I exist in the very depth of imaginary life, in the world of imaginary things, and that I begin to act from myself, with my fear and conscience (*AWHE*, p. 124).

Stanislavsky also uses the term *I am* as synonymous with 'inspiration' (*AWHI*, p. 440).

I am, the actor's ideal state, is opposed to *dislocation*. There are at least two kinds of *dislocation*. There is the problem where the external image of a character can be achieved mechanically: 'If you do not find a form of characterisation corresponding to the image you won't convey the life of the human spirit to the spectator' (*AWHI*, p. 225). This was what happened early in Stanislavsky's career when the external image of the character was a result of copying roles created by popular actors, and also with the role of Stockmann. The *dislocation* in the role of Salieri, as in *The Drama of Life*, was that he thought that what was going on internally was right, but it was not being conveyed externally.

Others contemporary to Stanislavsky also identified this problem. Bezpiatov wrote, 'What we call false in acting depends entirely on the lack of correspondence between the psychological content of the image (the role) and its external expression in the actor's playing.'[42]

---

[42] Evgenii Bezpiatov, *Elementi Nauchnoi Psikhologii v Teatral'nom Iskusstve* (St Petersburg: I. V. Leont'ev, 1912), p. 8.

Others interpreted a lack of correspondence – the possibility of the actor's external expression remaining accurate to the character, while the actor thinks of something different, thinks as the actor rather than the character, as a strength. But Stanislavsky's ideal was to achieve a state where there is no conflict or *dislocation*, no strain for the actor in the process of *incarnating* the role, but the actor/character are one. In this he departs from Diderot, whose view of the dual consciousness or dual personality of the actor means, for example, that Arnauld as Télaire in *Castor and Pollux* can embrace her fellow actor Pillot tenderly as the character Pollux, while whispering to him, 'Ah, Pillot, que tu pues!' ('Pillot, you stink').[43] For Stanislavsky, the situation in acting where 'the soul lives with its petty cares...and the body has to express the superconscious spiritual life' (*MLIA*, p. 374), where the actors are thinking about their own private, 'philistine' affairs (in Stanislavsky's view) while acting is dislocation. Another example of this is where the actor mechanically performs stage tricks, playing for laughs (*AWHI*, pp. 469–70).

However, there is rightly no contradiction here with the fact that the actor has two perspectives: being on stage and within the role. Tortsov cites Salvini, saying, 'I live a double life on stage, I laugh and cry and at the same time analyse my tears and laughter, so that they can more powerfully influence the hearts of those I wish to touch' (*AWHI*, p. 150). In the ideal situation actors can be aware of what they are doing and that capacity to observe oneself in activity is a different thing from the *craft* or *representational* actor who is 'concerned about the public and the audience and wants to convince them, not the actor who stands speaking with him on stage'.[44] There is no contradiction because of the capacity we have for multi-layered attention, which Stanislavsky clearly describes (*AWHE*, p. 175).

The problem, as Tortsov describes it, is 'the habit of lying, physically...which produces a dislocation of attention in young apparatus which has not yet gained strength'. The example he gives is of actors pretending to look at a point on an imaginary wall, which separates them from the audience, or at a ship on the distant horizon, when in fact they are looking at someone in the audience, and the gaze of their eyes is not where it should be (*AWHE*, pp. 175–6). Also, there is the situation where the actor is looking at an object but not really seeing it (*AWHE*, p. 400). Again, the actor is thinking about something other than what the character would think, as in the Stockmann crisis. For Stanislavsky there is no

---

[43] Joseph Roach, *The Player's Passion*, p. 135.
[44] Carnicke, *Stanislavsky in Focus*, p. 113.

I am, no *fusion*, if the actor is thinking about the audience. *Dislocation* is therefore categorised with 'coarse external technique, imitation, carica- ture, and actorly affectation' (*AWR*, p. 142). This was the source of one of his problems with Vakhtangov, Chekhov and Meyerhold, all of whom encouraged the actor to be conscious of the fact that he is performing and relate to the audience on that basis. For Stanislavsky this disrupts the purity of the actor's emotional *experiencing*. However, he does not know how to resolve the problem of *dislocation* himself. The problem is not just Stanislavsky's; this split way of thinking is endemic, as is exemplified by the voice manuals cited in Chapter 3. Stanislavsky attempted to overcome *dislocation* by his consistent emphasis on the importance of inner *experiencing*, based on 'real' emotional experience, which in his view means that the actor when performing cannot be 'going through the motions'. Only this *experiencing*, in Tolstoyan terms, can be a means of true communication with an audience.

THEORY AND PRACTICE

A practitioner's perspective

It may be that some of the problems can be resolved in the practice of the *system* and that Stanislavsky's problem is primarily one of how to write a theory of his experience as an actor and director. In this respect it is interesting to consider Zakhava's description of action and emotion in relation to Stanislavsky. Boris Evgenievich Zakhava (1896–1976) was one of the founder members of Vakhtangov's Mansurov Studio and made his first directorial attempts in the Third Studio (run by Vakhtangov), in 1921. He took over its leadership after Vakhtangov's death.

Zakhava seems to have found ways to be true to Ribot, Stanislavsky and Vakhtangov without contradicting Soviet science. He writes, 'Action is a wilful act of human behaviour directed toward a definite aim. The unity of the physical and the psychological is best seen in the action. The whole man participates in an action.'[45] He goes on to say that live, externally expressed action is the essence of the actor's art because it is through actions that the actor creates his characters. Consequently, the actor is simultaneously the creator and the instrument of his art, and the human actions which he realises serve him as the material for the creation of an action. Theatre is an art in which human life is reflected in

[45] B. E. Zakhava, 'The Mastery of the Actor and the Director', in Moore, *Stanislavski Today*, pp. 3–15.

a visual, concrete human action. The notion that the actor is the creator and at the same time the instrument of art is a helpful one, true to the principle of psychophysical unity while at the same time indicating a way of viewing the different aspects – creation and implementation. He goes on to say that the actor expresses the character with the help of his behaviour on stage. Human behaviour has two aspects: physical and psychological. These aspects cannot be torn one from another; every act of human behaviour is an indivisible psychophysical act. This is an accurate way to describe psychophysical unity. But then Zakhava goes on to articulate Stanislavsky's biggest problem. He writes that if the actor demonstrates only the external form, performance is inevitably mechanical, adding 'an actor can bang his fist on a table correctly and truthfully (according to the demands of the laws of nature) and yet with such action project the emotion of fury only if the soles of his feet are also alive'. If we take the idea of the soles of the actor's feet being alive as indicating the total engagement of the actor's psychophysical mechanism in the *task*, then what Zakhava is saying is that Stanislavsky's investigations into the laws of nature do not really resolve this – the actor can carry out the tasks required, according perhaps to the *method of physical action* but still not be fully engaged. They may be carrying out the action mechanically.

Zakhava goes on to discuss *dislocation* from the opposite end of the spectrum – where actors place too much emphasis on emotion/*experiencing* and their subjective experience is not necessarily conveyed to an audience. He writes that then the objective ties and relationships of the character towards his environment (and with this the external form of the experience) are relegated to the background. The actor should experience the thoughts and emotions of the character while also focussing his attention outwardly. Zakhava attempts to discuss emotion as 'a process and therefore [it] may have different stages of development, different levels of intensity, be of a different kind, have limitless nuances; furthermore it may be mutually involved with other processes unfolding in the man's consciousness'. Stage emotions are a poetic reflection of life's experiences. He asks what is different about stage emotion from emotion as experienced in life, and affirms that on the stage emotional memory is key. Where he differs from Stanislavsky is in his discussion of how no experience passes without leaving a trace on the nervous system. It makes the nerves that participate in a given reaction, he says, more sensitive to the particular stimulus. From a physiological point of view, emotional memory is but the revivification of the traces of what was once experienced.

He therefore asserts they are not primary according to Stanislavsky. In fact Ribot asserted that 'every recollection must be a *reversion*, by virtue of which the past once more becoming a present, we live at present in the past', and Stanislavsky expressed the same view.[46] This question seems to have been contentious: Stanislavsky wrote insistently to Gurevich in 1931, 'the actor lives on stage with such memories from the past and I will call them real' (*Collected Works*, vol. 9, p. 450). Again, in *AWHE*, he writes the actor can experience only his own emotions (p. 293–4).

Zakhava goes on to give the same example of grief that Stanislavsky gives in his chapter on *emotional memory* in *AWHE*, in discussing the fact that there is not a one-to-one correspondence between emotion experienced in life and that of the character. Grief transforms but is nonetheless authentic as time goes on; in fact it becomes purified in memory. He talks about the root of an emotion, its embryo, its physiological basis within ourselves: 'The imprints of emotions may grow and develop ... general remembrance united with a specific incident or in active work of our imagination ... connecting the hardly noticeable embryo of emotion with some imaginary circumstances.' He concludes with Stanislavsky that good emotional memory is one of the most important qualities that determine the professional competence of an actor. He follows Vakhtangov in saying that the majority of emotions are familiar to us through our own experiences in life, but these emotions were not formed in our mind in the same order, not following the same logic as required by the character.

In discussing the unity of the actor-character and the actor-creator, Zahkava writes, 'the actor on stage usually experiences two mutually active, competing, balancing and interpenetrating psychophysiological processes'. The line of the life of the character is the revivification of imprints of what was experienced many times in life, or the creation of the stage experience. The second process involves the actor's thoughts and emotions with regard to his presence on stage before thousands of spectators. The two are mutually interactive and form one complex. All the conscious efforts of the actor must have as their final goal the merging with the character. Then Zakhava asks what are the means by which the actor stirs within himself the necessary emotions on stage, and he appeals to a law – an emotion on stage cannot be stirred by addressing oneself directly to emotional memory. Instead, the emotion will come by itself during the

[46] Théodule Ribot, *The Psychology of the Emotions*, 2nd edn (London: Walter Scott, 1911), p. 171.

process of the action. Whereas our emotions arise spontaneously, our actions, on the contrary, are the result of our will:

Try to console someone honestly and you will notice in your heart a spontaneous feeling of pity. This happens as a result of the law of conditioned reflexes . . . Therefore the given action in the end becomes the stimulus which conditions the related emotion. The emotion in this case arises as the revivification of imprints of what has been experienced many times in life . . . just like experience on stage.[47]

Here, Zakhava brings in conditioned reflexes, in a way that could now be questioned. He also makes an assumption about emotion which Vakhtangov and Stanislavsky also share.

This is exemplified in Vakhtangov's statement on acting: 'Man's innate humanity comes into play the moment you give at least a bit of attention to the personal life of others.'[48] Stanislavsky was also of the view that emotion is essential to our humanity and the expression of it is part of theatre's higher purpose – a view he shared with Belinsky, who had believed that as audiences become involved with the emotional experiences of characters in a play, 'our egoism evaporates and we become better persons and better citizens'.[49] However, a wide range of different views of emotion have been propounded, a discussion of which is outside the scope of this book, but these views range from the Stoics' belief that the wise and happy life involves freedom from passions, to American philosopher John Dewey's proposition that emotions have as their antecedent some discrepancy between our expectations and the actual state of affairs in our lives.[50] It may be the case, then, that what constitutes 'innate humanity' could be disputed and it cannot be relied upon to ensure the appropriate emotional responses in acting.

Zakhava goes on to say that behind every action lies a particular purpose and you sharpen a pencil not for its own sake but to write a letter, or to draw a portrait: 'Since an action has a purpose, there must be a thought, and if there is thought there is feeling . . . an action is the union of thought, emotion and a complex of purposeful movements.' However, it may be that there is no necessary link between thought and feeling in the way suggested

---

[47] Zakhava, in Moore, *Stanislavski Today*, p. 15.
[48] Evgenii Vakhtangov, *Evgeny Vakhtangov*, (eds) L. D. Vendrovskaia and G. P. Kaptereval tr. Doris Bradbury (Moscow: Progress, 1984), p. 41.
[49] Laurence Senelick (tr. and ed.), *Russian Dramatic Theory from Pushkin to the Symbolists* (Austin: University of Texas Press, 1981), p. xxviii.
[50] Gregory, *The Oxford Companion to the Mind*, p. 220.

and again we come up against the problem that there is no definition of feeling, just the assumption that all human beings 'feel' similarly.

Practice and theory

As the *system* does not deal consistently with mind and body, it is not coherent as a body of theory, although in practical terms it continues to have much to offer the actor today. The science of the revolution may have been distracting rather than helpful to Stanislavsky, but scientific knowledge was not – and is not – necessarily important to the practical application of the *system*, as he said himself (*AWHE*, p. 41). Bentley suggested that the claims of science in acting methodology can be fallacious, but that does not necessarily invalidate acting exercises.[51] Stanislavsky used what I have referred to as 'artistic metaphors' rather than scientific terms in his descriptions of the workings of the human organism and this is not necessarily a bad thing, as long as they are recognised as such.

Longevity is an indication of practical use – the *system* or variations of it have stood the test of time and continue to be widely used in drama training. One of the reasons for this is the contribution Stanislavsky made to the development of a language of acting. As Stanislavsky said of his experience as a young actor, 'Stage directors only want the final result... They criticise, pointing out what you should not do, but say nothing about how to achieve what is wanted' (*MLIA*, p. 163). In developing a terminology Stanislavsky created possibilities for greater communication between actors and directors and found ways of explaining what he wanted from actors. The example of Maloletkova, the student who is given a task of looking for a brooch, and its demonstration of the difference between pretending or putting on a show for the audience, and acting in a convincing manner, is an excellent one, conveying the most important aspects of the *system* and how it works in practice.

Stanislavsky's *system* may work in practice and many actors would agree that it does. Unless it is the only method or system to do so it could not be claimed that it was the scientifically true one, or it would be true for all actors at all times, exclusive of all other methods. On the other hand, Meyerhold and Chekhov also have their adherents. Stanislavsky's differences with Meyerhold and Chekhov were essentially over how the actor achieves truth and the importance of this. In Stanislavsky's view of acting

---

[51] Eric Bentley, 'Who was Ribot? Or: Did Stanislavsky Know Any Psychology?' *Tulane Drama Review*, 7:2 (1962), p. 129.

it was essential that the character must be infused with the actor's *experiencing*, and this limited his outlook on acting and training to a 'naturalistic' approach. Stanislavsky's *system* is supported by certain ideas of personality and the self, whereas Meyerhold and Michael Chekhov rely on other means for authenticity, physical precision or imagination, which may limit them in other ways. If Stanislavsky's idea of the actor was as *an emotional and spiritual machine*, Meyerhold's emphasis was towards the machine, and Chekhov's on the spirit. However, the similarities in practice are on occasion surprising, such as the examples described earlier with Stanislavsky's improvisation with the brooch, and Meyerhold's idea of a person running in fright, expecting a knife in his back. Michael Chekhov and Meyerhold found different theoretical bases from Stanislavsky to corroborate their own methods. Both Stanislavsky and Meyerhold make conflicting statements about science, unlike Chekhov, who makes it clear that the science of the day has no value for him, believing as he did that anthroposophy was scientific. The problem for Stanislavsky and Meyerhold was that scientific terminology began to be more closely defined in Soviet Russia and they had to attempt to use descriptions that were acceptable within the prevailing 'episteme', and attempt to distance themselves from unacceptable science and scientists. Other psychologists such as Sukhanov and Lapshin were also an influence on the development of the *system*, but because they represent ideas that came to be disapproved of in Soviet Russia, their work was suppressed and what Stanislavsky took from them was disguised. It is important to rediscover the work of these people and other psychologists and theorists who emigrated or 'disappeared'.

Michael Chekhov stated that the *system* was over-complicated – which is indubitably the case – but there may have been practical reasons for this. Stanislavsky constantly changed his terms and descriptions as he thought of new ways to get actors to see what he wanted them to see, in order to keep the work fresh. Some of the complexity of his descriptions comes from a need to make the actor understand something in practice, not just to teach them a term. Nevertheless, it is overloaded with concepts, as demonstrated by the number of synonymous terms, such as *prana* and the *feeling of movement*, or *experiencing* and *I am*, or *subtext*. Sometimes the introduction of theoretical concepts makes more explanation necessary. *Grasp*, for example, could be described as giving full attention to something, but Stanislavsky's explanation gets rather involved.

As for theory, what is needed is an examination of the scientific basis of the *system* in its own time, and a comparison of that to scientific laws that could be verified today. Stanislavsky began referring to his *system* in 1909, planning a programme of essays under the heading '*My System*', stating that it was based on natural laws and therefore was not an invented system.[52] Although Stanislavsky set out to develop a systematic daily exercise system as training for the actor, this began to be construed as a body of theory about acting as well, and to be validated scientifically. Stanislavsky's claim that he did not invent anything is not precisely true; his acting exercises are often inventions based on a priori assumptions about the human organism and assertions about nature, which were not surprising for someone of his time. He affirmed in 1919, when still able to do so without conflict with the authorities, that the *system*'s foundation was in psychology, physiology and yoga, although it was not necessary to have that knowledge to practice it.

Creative nature has...two beginnings – body and soul...When I was im-
mersing myself in the laws of nature it was necessary for me to study physiology,
but apart from the basic elements I cannot remember anything – the same with
psychology...but perhaps this has helped me...I seized the superficial parts
which were necessary for me as an artist. It is very dangerous for an artist to be
occupied with science in the moment of creativity...(Meyerhold's triangles)...
Everything I am to say is taken and proved by both psychology and physiology
and proved and affirmed by the yogis (MAT, KS Archive 833, p. 25).

If his academic study only went so far, the breadth and scope of Stanislavsky's practical research is impressive. Sargeant writes,

Amongst the characteristics of Pavlov's research which rendered it an exemplary
model to his fellow scientists were the length of time for which his team worked
with particular subjects, the detailed and independent analysis of individual
idiosyncrasies (allowing a single aberrant instance to jettison a hitherto established theory) and insistence on the exact definition of terms.[53]

If we compare Stanislavsky's work with Pavlov's then his methodology, based on empiricism in James's sense, was a scientific one and he conducted his research over a long period of forty years. As Peter Bowler says of Darwin 'a commitment to a great idea, with a determination to test and refine it, is characteristic of great scientists but not of us ordinary busy people'.[54] Stanislavsky's commitment to an ambitious idea made him a great artist. Science is ordered by theory but what enables theory to

---

[52] Vinogradskaia, 2, p. 199.
[53] Amy Sargeant, *Vsevolod Pudovkin: Classic Films of the Soviet Avant-garde* (London: I. B. Tauris, 2000), p. 8.
[54] Peter J. Bowler, *Charles Darwin: the Man and his Influence*, (Oxford: Basil Blackwell, 1990), p. ix.

be developed is collection of data. There was insufficient information in his day on physiology and anatomy to verify his practice.

Stanislavsky's *system* is deeply rooted in associationist psychology. It has been a commonplace for writers on Stanislavsky to acknowledge the link between him and Ribot but this has not been fully analysed previously. His understanding of the relationship between attention and muscle tension, *adaptation*, the *supertask* and *communion* is owed to this link as well as *emotional memory* and mind, will, feeling to associationist and perhaps even earlier psychology. Stanislavsky was also presented with various scientific paradigms and concepts that he accepted, although they were not necessarily helpful to him and he may not have understood them. The demands of politics – the need to link Stanislavsky's work with Pavlov and Sechenov – have in fact obscured and distorted the scientific basis of the system. Reflex theory was paradigmatic and so were assumptions of the universal language of emotions and the popular understanding of the James-Lange theory. Stanislavsky brought to the development of his training methods a contradictory attitude to nature. On one hand he asserted that nature's law was unquestionable and on the other he sought ways to improve on nature. He brought a priori assumptions about the human organism, ideas about exercise and a machine model of the body (based on concepts of anatomy and physiology from his time) into his training, believing with the yogis that mastery of the body was the way to enable the development of spiritual powers. Stanislavsky also had recourse to the *unconscious*, taking his view essentially from von Hartmann. His studies of yoga and eastern philosophy corroborated his beliefs. Interestingly, this is not, as Stanislavsky may have thought, because the ideas he found in psychology are corroborated by yoga because they are correct, nor were they laws of human nature which are true for all time and all people and therefore scientific. The scientific basis of yoga needs examination – the idea of *prana* or energy flowing, although an attractive one, is not scientifically accurate. The orientalism that continues to colour western attitudes towards eastern life, which is seen as rich in spiritual values needs questioning. How does the practice of yoga contribute to an understanding of psychophysical unity?

The process Stanislavsky attempted to employ in the development of his *system* was to elaborate a theory and to test it out in practice. The validity of scientific laws, as Faddeev indicates, can be tested by seeing whether the consequences they predict actually occur. There were, therefore, parameters Stanislavsky could adopt in a scientific study of acting. As he asserted, there must be laws of nature that are the same for everyone and, therefore, necessary for everyone, whether these are physiological laws to do with voice production, for example, or inner creative processes (*MLIA*, pp. 494–5).

He adopted the introspective, empirical approach but was perhaps unaware that the results of this may be subjective. In basing his laws in nature he assumed what worked for him should be true universally, whereas in fact his view of nature was an interpretation. For example, some aspects of the *system* may have been more applicable for Stanislavsky than for people who do not experience stage fright, but his assumption was that standing on stage in front of an audience would have the same effect on everyone that it did on him, leading him to develop aspects of the *system* such as 'truth' and 'belief', *public solitude* and *the creative sense of self*. Other aspects of his thought, such as the dualistic concept of internal *experiencing* and external *incarnation*, may have been a result of his practical experience of having to correct his posture and train his voice, so that he perceived 'himself' as in conflict with 'his body'. Again, this is not necessarily a universal experience – Meyerhold and Michael Chekhov's experiences were different – and this is the problem with the introspective approach. Like the psychologist Faddeev, he observed others as well as himself, but his conflicts with Meyerhold, Vakhtangov and Chekhov indicate that he had a specific view of what good acting was, with which others did not always agree. Unlike Pavlov, Stanislavsky did not always jettison aspects of his theory if he found data that did not fit, nor did he insist on an exact definition of terms. As a result the axiomatic laws of acting that were to flow from the laws it was believed science was rapidly discovering were not fully revealed. The results of Stanislavsky's experimentation were complicated and obscured through political influence.

Stanislavsky's understanding of the mechanisms of emotion is based on Ribot's empirical psychology; it is 'physiological'. This is corroborated by other scientists of the time, Bain, Maudsley, Bezpiatov and the James-Lange theory, all showed a recognition that emotion is not separable from its expression (that is the action or reaction undertaken on receipt of an emotional stimulus). The *method of physical actions* does not contradict this. Here, there are cross-overs with the ideas of Sechenov and Pavlov.

Twenty-first-century assessments of Stanislavsky's work should address the fact that Stanislavsky's view of emotion as reflected in writing and practice reflects concepts from associationist psychology, and also the idea of the existence of universal passions as described in Darwin's *Expression of the Emotions in Man and Animals* and categorised by such psychologists as Mantegazza. There is now much more knowledge of the interpretive nature of the experience and expression of emotion.

Far more is known now about the process of learning, about habit and attention, than was available to William James. Physiology was then in its infancy. Sir Charles Sherrington, who is known as the father of physiology, published *The Integrative Action of the Nervous System* in 1906, at the beginning of his pioneering work which led to today's understanding of the nervous system, but it was not until 1931 that the invention of the electron-microscope enabled scientists to begin to be able to study the nerve synapse in detail. Although Russian science of the revolution was not simply about seeing behaviour in terms of stimulus-response, that was the central idea behind the model, which notion contemporary science has complicated. Similarly, ideas about attention, the conscious and the subconscious have developed and Stanislavsky's ideas could be corroborated or negated.

Stanislavsky was interested in processes that are still a source of fascination for physiologists now, who admit that much remains unknown, but twenty-first-century science could offer more to support the theory of the *system*. Although the mind/body debate continues today, science now is predicated on psychophysical unity, the body/brain continuum.[55] In pragmatic, empirical terms, if experiments in acting are conducted on the basis of that understanding of brain and body, and it is demonstrated that practical procedures produce expected results, those experiments would be accepted as scientific. But in his epoch, whatever his subjective experience, Stanislavsky could not have known enough to describe his work, for example, in neuronal terms.

This gives rise to the question of whether teachers of Stanislavsky-based acting, or the methods of the other Russian actor-trainers today, take into account changes in scientific knowledge, and whether a new investigation of acting could produce the same practical results as Stanislavsky, though the explanations might in future be very different. A reassessment is called for, of internal/external manifestations in acting, and of the phenomenon Stanislavsky called *dislocation*, based on current knowledge of the functioning of the human organism. The facility we have for recreating past emotional experience, identified by Ribot and so important to Stanislavsky,

---

[55] For example, Daniel C. Dennett's computational model of the mind as he describes it in *Consciousness Explained*, (London, Penguin, 1993), as opposed to Richard Swinburne's philosophy in which he attempts to reconcile theism and the existence of the soul with contemporary science, in *The Existence of God*, 2nd edn (Oxford University Press, 2004).

could be investigated in a different way now, and explanations could be found that would enable an escape from his conflict with Michael Chekhov and Meyerhold. Similarly, a re-examination of Stanislavsky's assertion, following Tolstoy, of feeling as the subject matter for art, would be interesting in view of the fact that the assumption of a universal language of emotion is not now universally held.

In Stanislavsky's period, acting and actor-training was transformed by his work and as a result of shifts across the whole episteme. Stanislavsky was instrumental in the change from viewing acting as no longer a craft but an art form, and in bringing a fresh perspective into the debate around emotion and acting. He also played a large part in the movement that took training from what had been largely the apprenticeship method in serf theatres such as Shchepkin's, or the imitation of established actors as taught in those drama schools that existed prior to Stanislavsky's time, to the development of a four-year acting course in established schools.

It is essential to look at Stanislavsky afresh, examining what has been taken for granted in the West and in eastern Europe, shifting the perception of the relationship between truth and emotion. We must also challenge current assumptions in the West and in Russia which present Stanislavsky as an icon, mythologise him, and fail to recognise how ideas from the scientific field, politics, social ideology and cultural practice, impacted on him or were appropriated by him. It is important to identify the sources of Stanislavsky's ideas; the fact that this has not always happened has contributed to misunderstandings of his pioneering work. As Kuhn and Foucault say, knowledge does not progress by accretion and it is also important to recognise the paradigms at work in Stanislavsky's time and to see how far 'an idea can spread from its original discipline into the broader currents of intellectual history and popular comprehension'.[56] On that basis there could be a new investigation, from a current perspective, into the science of acting and the contributions made to its development by Stanislavsky, Vakhtangov, Chekhov and Meyerhold.

---

[56] Roach, *The Player's Passion*, back cover.

Appendix: The Approach to the role

AWR, pp. 377–9 From Stanislavsky's notebooks, 1936–7.

1. *Story* (general, not too detailed) of the plot of the play.
2. *Act the external plot* according to physical actions. Go into the room. Do not go in unless you know: from where, to where, why. Therefore the student is justifying (his actions), the external, coarse facts of the plot. Justification of the coarse physical actions with the *given circumstances* (the most external, coarse). Actions are chosen from the play, the missing ones are invented in the spirit of the play; what would I have done, 'if' *now, today, here* . . . (I found myself in circumstances analogous with the play.)
3. *Études on the past, future* (present – on the stage itself); where I have come from, where I am going, what happened in the periods in between the exits.
4. Story (more detailed) of physical actions and the plot of the play. More subtle, detailed and deepened given circumstances and 'ifs'.
5. Provisional definition of the approximate, rough, draft supertask. (Not Leningrad but Tver or even a railway halt on the way).
6. On the basis of the material which has been developed – *carrying out* approximate, rough, draft *through action*. The constant interrogation: what would I do 'if'?
7. For this – *division into the biggest physical bits*. (Without this there is no play, without any big physical actions.)
8. *To fulfil (act out)* these coarse physical actions on the basis of the question: what would I do 'if'.
9. If a big bit cannot be taken on – temporarily *divide it into middle-sized, or if necessary, into small and very small bits. Study the nature of the physical actions*. Observe the *logic and consistency* of the big bits strictly and their component parts, unite them into whole, big, actions without objects.

10. The creation of a *logical and consistent line of organic, physical actions*. Write down this line and fix it in practice (go over this line many times; act it, fix it firmly; free it from anything superfluous – 95% away! Take it to truth and faith. The logic and consistency of physical actions will lead to *truth and belief*. Confirm it through logic and consistency and not through truth for the sake of truth.

11. Logic, consistency, truth and faith surrounded by the state '*here, today, now*' are even more firmly based and fixed.

12. All together this creates the state of '*Ia esm*", 'I am'

13. Where '*Ia esm*" is – there is *organic nature* and its subconscious.

14. Up to now you have been using your own words. Now you have *the first reading of the text*. Students or artists seize on the separate words and phrases from the author's text that they feel the need of, those that have struck them. They should write them down and include them in the text of the role among their own accidental, involuntary words. After some time, when you come to the second, third and later readings, take down more notes, more words to be included in your own accidental, involuntary text of the role. Thus gradually with separate phrases at the beginning and then whole long periods the role becomes filled with the words of the author. There remain blanks but they are soon filled with the text of the play, with the feeling of its style, language, and phrases.

15. *The text should be studied*, fixed in the mind, but avoid saying it aloud so as not to jabber mechanically or build up a series of word acrobatics. The mise-en-scene is also not fixed yet so as not to allow the line [learned] mise-en-scene to be united with the line of mechanical jabbering of words. They should act many times and fix firmly the line of logical, consecutive physical actions, truth, belief, '*I am*,' organic nature, and the subconscious. By the justification of all these actions there will be born fresh, new, subtler given circumstances coming into the mind and a more profound, wide embracing sense of through action. As this work is done, go over and over in constantly increasing detail the contents of the play. Imperceptibly you will acquire a basis for your physical actions that is psychologically subtler because of your proposed circumstances, the through action, and the supertask.

16. Continue to act the play along the lines now set. Think about the words, but when you act, replace them with *tatirovanie*.[1]

[1] See Chapter 3, p. 152.

17. The true inner line of the play has now been laid down by process of justifying your physical and other lines. Fix it even more firmly, so the spoken text will remain subordinate to it and not be jabbered mechanically and independently from it. Continue to act the play with tatirovanie and at the same time continue the work of confirming the internal line of the subtext. *Go over in your own words* (1) *the line of thought*; (2) *the line of visualization*; (3) explain them both to partners in the play in order to establish communication with them and the *line of inner action*. These basic lines form the subtext of your role. *Ground them as firmly as possible and maintain them constantly.*

18. After this pattern has been fixed, while you are still sitting around the table, *read the play in the author's own words, and sitting on your hands, convey as accurately as you can to your partners all the lines you have worked out, the actions, all the details and the score of the play.*

19. Do the same thing, *still sitting around the table but with your hands and bodies free, using some crossings and accidental mise-en-scene.*

20. Repeat the same *on the stage with the mise-en-scene blocked out provisionally.*

21. *Work out and fix the plan of the stage sets (inside four walls).* Each person should be asked: Where would he choose (in what setting) to be and act? Let each person suggest their own plan. The plan for the set will be taken from the consensus of the plans proposed by the actors.

22. *Work out and record the mise-en-scene.* [Set the stage according to an agreed plan and introduce the actors into it. Ask the actors where they would choose to make a declaration of love; where they would choose to convince the person playing opposite to engage in a heart-to-heart talk, and so forth; where it would be more convenient to cross over in order to hide embarrassment. Let the actors cross and carry out their physical actions as required by the play – hunt for books in the library, opening windows, light a fire, and so forth.

23. Test the line of the plans and mise-en-scene by opening arbitrarily any one of the walls.

24. Sit down at a table and carry on a series of conversations concerning literary, political, artistic, and other aspects of the play.

25. Characterisation. All that has been done so far has achieved inner characterisation. Meantime the external characterisation should have appeared of its own accord. But what is to be done if this does not occur? You should go over what has already been established but add

a lame leg, terse or drawling speech, certain attitudes of arms or legs or body, in keeping with certain externally acquired mannerisms or habits. If the external characterisation does not appear spontaneously (it must be grafted from the outside). (It must take, like a lemon branch onto a grapefruit.)[2]

---

[2] The last line was not included in the second edition of *AWR*.

Bibliography

Abalkin, N. A. *Sistema Stanislavskogo i Sovietskii Teatr*, Moscow: Iskusstvo, 1954.

Alexander, Albert. *Karl Marx: the Father of Modern Socialism*, London: Franklin Watts, 1969.

Andrew, Joe. *Writers and Society During the Rise of Russian Realism*, London: Macmillan, 1980.

Archer, William. *Masks or Faces*. In: *The Paradox of Acting and Masks or Faces*, New York: Hill & Wang, 1957.

Audi, Robert, ed. *Cambridge Dictionary of Philosophy*, 2nd edn. Cambridge University Press, 1999.

Auslander, Philip. *From Acting to Performance, Essays in Modernism and Post-modernism*. London: Routledge, 1997.

Babkin, Boris P. *Pavlov: A Biography*, London: Victor Gollancz, 1951.

Baer, Nancy Van Norman. *Theatre in Revolution: Russian avant-garde stage design, 1913–1935*, London: Thames and Hudson, 1991.

Bailes, K. 'Alexei Gastev and the Soviet Controversy over Taylorism, 1918–24', *Soviet Studies*, 29:3 (1977), pp. 373–94.

Barba, Eugenio. 'An Amulet Made of Memory: The Significance of Exercises in the Actor's Dramaturgy', *The Drama Review*, 41:4 (1997), pp. 127–32.

Barba, Eugenio and Nicola Savarese. *A Dictionary of Theatre Anthropology: The Secret Art of the Performer*, tr. Richard Fowler, London: Routledge, 1991.

Beacham, Richard C. 'Appia, Jaques-Dalcroze, and Hellerau', Part One: 'Music Made Visible', *New Theatre Quarterly*, 1:2 (1985).

'Appia, Jaques-Dalcroze, and Hellerau', Part Two: 'Poetry in Motion', *New Theatre Quarterly*, 1:3 (1985).

Beevor, Antony. *The Mystery of Olga Chekhova*, London: Penguin, 2005.

Bekhterev, V. M. *General Principles of Human Reflexology: An Introduction to the Objective Study of Personality*, tr. Emma Murphy and William Murphy, London: Jarrolds, 1933.

Benedetti, Jean. *Stanislavski: An Introduction*, rev. edn. London: Methuen, 1989.

'A History of Stanislavski: in Translation', *New Theatre Quarterly*, 6:23 (August 1990), pp. 266–78.

Stanislavski and the Actor, London: Methuen, 1998.

Stanislavski: His Life and Art, 2nd edn, London: Methuen, 1999.

The Art of the Actor, London: Methuen, 2005.

(ed. and tr.), *The Moscow Art Theatre Letters*, London: Methuen, 1991.

Bentley, Eric. 'Who was Ribot? Or: Did Stanislavsky Know Any Psychology?' *Tulane Drama Review*, 7:2 (1962), pp. 127–9.

'Are Stanislavski and Brecht Commensurable?', *The Tulane Drama Review*, 9 (1964–5), pp. 69–76.

Bezpiatov, Evgenii. *Elementi Nauchnoi Psikhologii v Teatral'nom Iskusstve*, St Petersburg: I. V. Leont'ev, 1912.

Binet, Alfred. 'Réflexions sur le Paradoxe de Diderot', *Année Psychologique*, 3 (1897), pp. 279–95.

Birman, Serafima. 'Life's Gift and Encounters', *Soviet Literature*, 3 (1975), pp. 74–119.

Black, Lendley C. *Mikhail Chekhov as Actor, Director and Teacher*, Michigan: Ann Arbor, 1994.

Blok, Vl. *Sistema Stanislavskogo i Problemi Dramaturgii*, Moscow: Vserossiskoe Teatral'noe Obshchestvo, 1963.

Bolkhontseva, S. ed., *Russkoe Akterskoe Iskusstvo XX Veka* (St Petersburg: Rossiiskii Institut Istorii Iskusstv, 1992).

Bowler, Peter J. *Charles Darwin: The Man and his Influence*, Oxford: Basil Blackwell, 1990.

Bowman, Herbert E. *Vissarion Belinsky, 1811–1848: A Study in the Origins of Social Criticism in Russia*, Cambridge, MA.: Harvard University Press, 1954.

Brandt, George W. *Modern Theories of Drama*, Oxford University Press, 1998.

Braun, Edward. *The Director and the Stage: from Naturalism to Grotowski*, London: Methuen, 1982.

Meyerhold: A Revolution in Theatre, 2nd edn, London: Methuen, 1998.

(ed. and tr.), *Meyerhold on Theatre*, 2nd edn, London: Methuen, 1991.

Briusov, V. 'Nienuzhnaia Pravda', *Mir Iskusstva*, 4 (Petersburg, 1902).

Brunetière, Ferdinand. *The Law of the Drama*, tr. Philip Hayden, New York: Dramatic Museum of Columbia University, 1914.

Bulgakov, Mikhail. *Black Snow: A Theatrical Novel*, tr. M. Glenny, London: Hodder and Stoughton, 1967.

'Zapiski Pokoinika' in *Teatral'nyi Roman*, Moscow: AST, 2000.

Burlakova, Tamara T. 'Leopold Sulerzhitsky and the Voyage of the Doukhobors to Canada', *Centennial Papers in Honour of Canada's Doukhobor Heritage, Ottowa Canada Museum of Civilisation*, (1995), pp. 101–7.

Byckling, Liisa. 'Mikhail Chekhov i Antroposophia iz Istorii MKHAT Vtorogo', *Studia Russica Helsingiensia et Tartuensia*, 4 (1995).

'Pages from the Past: *The Possessed*, produced by Michael Chekhov on Broadway in 1939', *Slavic and East European Performance*, 15:2 (1995), pp. 32–45.

Mikhail Chekhov v Zapadnom Teatre i Kino, St Petersburg: Kikimora Publications, 2000.

'Michael Chekhov and the Anthroposophy: From the History of the Second Moscow Art Theatre', *Nordic Theatre Research* (2006), pp. 59–71.

Cairns, Christopher (ed.), *The Commedia dell'arte from the Renaissance to Dario Fo*, Lewiston: Edwin Mellen Press, 1989.

Carlson, Maria. *No Religion Higher than Truth*, Princeton University Press, 1993.

Carnicke, Sharon M. 'An Actor Prepares/Rabota aktera nad soboi: A Comparison of the English with the Russian Stanislavsky', *Theatre Journal*, 31:4 (1984), pp. 481–94.

Carnicke, Sharon Marie. 'Stalinslavsky: Stanislavsky's Final Years', *Theatre Three*, 10/11 (1991), pp. 152–65.

'Stanislavsky: Uncensored and Unabridged', *The Drama Review*, 37:1 (1993), pp. 22–36.

Stanislavsky in Focus, Amsterdam: Harwood Academic Publishers, 1998.

Carter, Huntly. *The New Spirit in the Russian Theatre, 1917–28*, New York: Brentano, 1929.

The New Spirit in the Cinema, New York: Arno Press and the New York Times, 1970.

Chamberlain, Lesley. *Motherland: a Philosophical History of Russia*, London, Atlantic Books, 2004.

Chekhov, Michael. *Michael Chekhov's To the Director and Playwright*, ed. Charles Leonard, London: Greenwood Press, 1977.

Lessons for the Professional Actor, ed. Deirdre Hurst du Prey, New York: Performing Arts Publications, 1985.

On the Technique of Acting, ed. Mel Gordon, New York: HarperCollins 1991.

On Theatre and the Art of Acting. Four-part Tape Series edited with a Guide to Discovery with Exercises by Mala Powers, New York: Applause Theatre Books, 1992.

Chekhov, Mechael *To the Actor on the Technique of Acting*, London: Routledge, 2002.

The Path of the Actor, eds. Andrei Kirillov and Bella Merlin, London: Routledge, 2005.

'Chekhov's Academy of Arts Questionnaire' (1923), *The Drama Review*. vol 27, 3 (1983) pp. 22–33.

'Chekhov on Acting: A Collection of Unpublished Materials' (1919–1942), *The Drama Review*, vol 27, 3 (1983) pp. 46–83.

Chekhov, Mikhail. *Literaturnoe nasledie v dvukh tomakh; tom 1, Vospominania Pis'ma, tom 2, Ob Iskusstve aktera*, Moscow: Iskusstvo, 1986.

Vospominania, Pis'ma (Moscow: Lokid-Press, 2001).

Mikhail Chekhov Dom Aktiera Spetsvypusk, ed. By Gennadi Demin, Tatiana Nikolskaia. Elena Sasim, Moscow: Dom Aktiera, 1994.

Chepalov, Aleksandr. *Sud'ba Peresmeshnika ili Novie Stranstvia Frakasa*, Kharkov: AVEK, 2001.

Christian, R. F. *Tolstoy: A Critical Introduction*, Cambridge University Press, 1969.

Christie, Ian and Richard Taylor. *Eisenstein Rediscovered*, London: Routledge, 1993.

Citron, Atay. 'The Chekhov Technique Today', *The Drama Review*, 27:3 (1983), pp. 91–96.

Clayton, J. Douglas. *Pierrot in Petrograd: The Commedia dell'Arte/Balagan in Twentieth-Century Russian Theatre and Drama*, London: McGill-Queens' University Press, 1994.

Clurman, Harold. *The Fervent Years*, 2nd edn, New York: Da Capo, 1983.

Cole, Toby and Helen Krich Chinoy. *Actors on Acting*, rev. edn, New York: Crown, 1970.

Coquelin, Constant. *The Art of the Actor*, tr. Elsie Fogerty, London: George Allen and Unwin, 1932.

Craig, Edward Gordon. *On the Art of the Theatre*, London: Heinemann, 1980.

Crohn Schmitt, Natalie. 'Stanislavski, Creativity and the Unconscious', *New Theatre Quarterly*, 2:8 (1986), pp. 345–51.

   Actors and Onlookers, Illinois: Northwestern University Press, 1990.

Cuny, Hilaire. *Ivan Pavlov: The Man and his Theories*, tr. Patrick Evans, London: Souvenir Press, 1964.

Darwin, Charles. *The Expression of the Emotions in Man and Animals*, ed. Paul Ekman, 3rd edn, London: Harper Collins, 1998.

Desmond, Adrian. *Huxley: The Devil's Disciple*, London: Michael Joseph, 1994.

Diderot, Denis. *Paradoks ob Aktere*, tr. into Russian by Nikolai Efros, Yaroslavl, 1923.

Dukore, Bernard F. *Dramatic Theory and Criticism: Greeks to Grotowski*, New York: Holt, Rinehart and Winston, 1974.

Dybovskii, Vladimir. 'V Plenu predlagaemykh obstoiatel'stv', *Minuvshee*, 10 (1990), pp. 243–329.

Dzubinskaya, O. 'Dlia sebya i dlia nas', *Teatr*, 1 (1988), pp. 93–4.

Eagleton, Terry. *Marx*, London: Phoenix, 1997.

Edwards, Christine. *The Stanislavsky Heritage*, New York University Press, 1965.

Efros, N. 'The Moscow Artistic Theatre', *Russian Review* (July 1912), pp. 141–52.

   K. S. Stanislavskii, opit kharacteristiki, Petersburg: Solntze Rossii, 1918.

   M. S. Shchepkin, Moscow: Vuzovaia Kniga, 2001.

Eistenstein, Sergei. *The Film Sense*, tr. and ed. Jan Leyda, London and Boston: Faber and Faber, 1943.

Ellenberger, Henri F. *The Discovery of the Unconscious: The History and Evolution of Dynamic Psychiatry*, New York: Basic Books, 1970.

Enders, Jody. 'Emotional Memory and the Medieval Performance of Violence', *Theatre Survey*, 38:1 (1997), pp. 139–60.

Etkind, Alexander. *The Eros of the Impossible: The History of Psycho-analysis in Russia*, tr. Noah Rubins and Maria Rubins, Oxford: Westview Press, 1997.

Faddeev, Tikhon. *Shkholnaia Pedagokika; Kniga 1, Psikhologia*, Moscow: Tipografia Shtaba Moskovskogo voennogo okruga, 1913.

Fenichel, Otto. 'On Acting', *The Drama Review*, 4 (1960), pp. 148–59.

Filippov, V. A. *Besedy o teatre: opyt vvedenia v teatrovedenie*, Moscow: Moskovskoe Teatral'noe Izdatelstvo, 1924.

Fishman, Pearl. 'Vakhtangov's *The Dybbuk*', *The Drama Review*, 3 (1980), pp. 43–58.

Foucault, Michel. *The Archaelogy of Knowledge*, London: Routledge, 1972.

Frolov, Y. P. *Pavlov and his School: The Theory of Conditioned Reflexes*, tr. C. P. Dutt, London: Kegan Paul, Trench, Trubner, 1937.

Gastev, Alexei. *Kak Nado Rabotat?*, Moscow: Tsentral'nyi Institut Truda, 1922.

Gelernter, David. *The Muse in the Machine*, London: Fourth Estate, 1994.

Gladkov Aleksandr. *Meyerhold Speaks, Meyerhold Rehearses*, tr. and ed. Alma Law, Amsterdam: Harwood Academic Publishers, 1997.

Gleason, Abbott, Peter Kenez and Richard Stites eds, *Bolshevik Culture*, Bloomington: Indiana University Press, 1985.

Goethe, Johann Wolfgang von. *Rules for Actors*, tr. into Russian, *Maska*, 3 (1912), pp. 507–23.

Gogol, Nikolai. *Polnoe Sobranie Sochinenii*, Leningrad: AN SSR, 1951.

Golub, Spencer. *The Recurrence of Fate: Theatre and Memory in Twentieth-century Russia*, University of Iowa Press, 1994.

Gorchakov, Nikolai. *The Theatre in Soviet Russia*, tr. Edgar Lehrman, New York: Colombia University Press, 1957.

    The Vakhtangov School of Stage Art, tr. G. Ivanov-Mumjiev, Moscow: Foreign Languages Publishing House, 1960.

Gorchakov, N. M. *Stanislavsky Directs*, tr. Miriam Goldina, Connecticut: Greenwood Press, 1968.

Gordon Mel. 'Meyerhold's Biomechanics', *The Drama Review*, 18:3 (1974), pp. 73–88

    'Michael Chekhov's Life and Work: A Descriptive Chronology', *The Drama Review*, vol 27, 3 (1983) pp. 3–21.

    The Stanislavsky Technique: Russia, New York: Applause Theatre Books, 1987.

    'Nine Common Misconceptions about Stanislavsky and his System', *Soviet and East European Performance*, 9:2/3 (1989), pp. 45–6.

Gordon, Mel and Alma Law. *Meyerhold, Eisenstein and Biomechanics: Actor-Training in Revolutionary Russia*, North Carolina: McFarland, 1996.

Gottlieb, Vera. 'Vakhtangov's Musicality: Reassessing Yevgeny Vakhtangov (1883–1922)', *Contemporary Theatre Review*, 15:2 (2005), pp. 259–68.

Graham, Loren. *Science in Russia and the Soviet Union*, Cambridge University Press, 1993.

Gray, Camilla. *The Russian Experiment in Art: 1863–1922*, 2nd edn, London: Thames and Hudson, 1986.

Gregory, Richard L. (ed.), *The Oxford Companion to the Mind*, Oxford University Press, 1987.

Gromov, V. *Mikhail Chekhov*, Moscow: Iskusstvo, 1970.

Grotowski, Jerzy. *Towards a Poor Theatre*, New York: Simon and Schuster, 1968.

Gurevich, Liubov'. 'Khudozhestvennie Zaveti Tolstovo', *Russkagi Mysl'*, 3 (1911), pp. 117–33 and 4 (1911), pp. 127–62.

    (ed.), *O Stanislavskom, Sbornik Vospominanii*, Moscow: Vserossiskoe Teatral'noe Obshchestvo, 1948.

Hartmann, Edouard von. *Philosophy of the Unconscious*, tr. William Chatterton Coupland, London: Kegan Paul, Trench, 1893.

Hobgood, Burnet M. 'Central Conceptions in Stanislavsky's System', *Educational Theatre Journal*, 25:2 (1973), pp. 147–59.

'Stanislavski's Preface to *An Actor Prepares* and the Persona of Tortsov', *Theatre Journal*, 43:21 (1991), pp. 219–32.

'Stanislavski's Books: An Untold Story', *Theatre Survey*, 27:1/2 (1986), pp. 155–65.

Hodge, Alison (ed.), *Twentieth Century Actor-training*, London: Routledge, 2000.

Hoover, Marjorie. *Meyerhold: The Art of Conscious Theatre*, Amherst: University of Massachusetts, 1974.

'The Meyerhold Centennial', *The Drama Review*, 18:3 (1974), pp. 70–2.

Hosking, Geoffrey. *A History of the Soviet Union, 1917–1991*, London: Fontana, 1985.

Hristic, Jovan. 'Thinking with Chekhov: The Evidence of Stanislavsky's Notebooks', *New Theatre Quarterly*, 11 (1995), pp. 175–83.

Hughes, R. I. G. 'Tolstoy, Stanislavski, and the Art of Acting', *The Journal of Aesthetics and Art Criticism*, 51:1 (Winter, 1993), pp. 40–8.

Hurst du Prey, Deirdre. 'Working with Chekhov', *The Drama Review*, 27:3 (1983), pp. 84–90.

Ignatieva, Maria. 'Between Love and Theatre: Young Stanislavski', *Theatre History Studies*, 25 (June 2005), pp. 173–90.

Innes, Christopher (ed.), *A Sourcebook on Naturalist Theatre*, London: Routledge, 2000.

Ivanov, Vladislav. *Russkie Sezoni Teatra 'Gabima'*, Moscow: Artist Rezhisser. Teatr., 1999.

James, William. 'What is an emotion?' *Mind*, 10 (1884), pp. 188–205.

Principles of Psychology, London: Macmillan, 1890, reprint 1950.

Textbook of Psychology, London: Macmillan, 1892.

Talks to Teachers on Psychology: And to Students on Some of Life's Ideals, London: Longmans, Green, 1927.

James, William and Carl Lange. *The Emotions*, New York: Hafner Publishing, 1967.

Jansen, Karin. 'Die Frühphase des Stanislawski-Systems (1906–1915) im Spiegel der Rezeption in den fünfziger Jahren', in Günter Ahrends (ed.), *Konstantin Stanislawski, Neue Aspekte und Perspektiven*, Tübingen: Forum Modernes Theater, 1992, pp. 27–38.

Jaques-Dalcroze, Emile. *The Eurhythmics of Jaques-Dalcroze*, tr. Michael Sadler, 3rd edn, London: Constable, 1920.

Rhythm, Music and Education, tr. Harold F. Rubenstein, 2nd edn, London and Whitstable: The Dalcroze Society, 1967.

Kalashnikov, Yu. S. *Eticheskie Osnovi Sistemi K. S. Stanislavskogo*, Moscow: Vserossiskoe Teatral'noe Obshchestvo, 1956.

Teatral'naia Etika Stanislavskogo, Moscow: VTO, 1960.

Kanigel, Robert. *The One Best Way: Frederick Winslow Tayor and the Enigma of Efficiency*, London: Little, Brown, 1997.

Kekcheev, K. Kh. *I. M. Sechenov*, Moscow: Zhurnalno-gazetnoe Ob'edinenie, 1933.

Khersonskii, Kh. *Vakhtangov*, Moscow: Molodaia Gvardia, 1940.

Kirby, E. T. 'The Delsarte Method: Three frontiers of Actor Training', *The Drama Review*, 16:1 (1972), pp. 55–69.

Kirillov, Andrei. 'Michael Chekhov – Problems of Study', *Eye of the World*, 1 (St Petersburg, 1994).

'Teatral'naia Sistema Mikhaila Chekhova', *Mnemozina*, 3 (Moscow, Editorial URSS 2004).

Knebel', M. O. *Vsya Zhizn'*, Moscow: Vserossiskoe Teatral'noe Obshchestvo, 1967.

'Vysokaia prostota', *Teatr*, 9 (1968), pp. 46–9.

Kofler, Leo. *Art of Breathing as the Basis of Tone-Production*, Montana: Kessinger, 1887.

Konijn, Elly A. *Acting Emotions*, tr. Barbara Leach with David Chambers, Amsterdam: Amsterdam University Press, 2000.

Kostetskii, I. V. *Sovetskaia Teatral'naia Politika i Sistema Stanislavskogo*, Munich: Institut po Izucheniyu SSSR, 1956.

Kramer, Richard E. 'The Natyasastra and Stanislavsky: Points of Contact', *Theatre Studies*, 36 (1991), pp. 46–62.

Krasner, David (ed.), *Method Acting Reconsidered: Theory, Practice, Future*, Hampshire and London: Macmillan, 2000.

Kristi, G. V. *Vospitanie Aktera Shkoli Stanislavskogo*, Moscow: Iskusstvo, 1968.

Kuhn, Thomas S. *The Structure of Scientific Revolutions*, 2nd edn, University of Chicago Press, 1970.

The Essential Tension: Selected Studies in Scientific Tradition and Change, University of Chicago Press, 1977.

Kumiega, Jennifer. *The Theatre of Grotowski*, London: Methuen, 1987.

Kurtén, Martin. 'Emotion and Action'. Paper delivered at the international symposium, *Le Siècle Stanislavski*, Centre Georges Pompidou, Paris, 5 November 1989.

Lapshin, I. *Khudozhestvennye Tvorchestvo*, Petrograd: Mysl', 1923.

Large, Gerry. 'Lev Kuleshov and the Metrical-Spatial Web: Postmodern Body Training in Space and Time', *Theatre Topics*, 10:1 (March 2000), pp. 65–75.

Lauterbach, Eva (ed.), *Eurythmy – Essays and Anecdotes*, Illinois: Schaumberg Publications, 1980.

Law, Alma, 'Meyerhold's *Woe to Wit*', *The Drama Review*, 18:3 (1974).

'Chekhov's Russian *Hamlet* (1924)', *The Drama Review*, 27:3 (1983), pp. 34–5.

Law Whyte, Lancelot. *The Unconscious Before Freud*, New York: Basic Books, 1960.

Lazarowicz, Klaus. Spontaneität oder "Training und Drill" in Günter Ahrends (ed.), *Konstantin Stanislawski, Neue Aspekte und Perspektiven*, Tübingen: Forum Modernes Theater, 1992, pp. 39–50.

Leach, Robert. *Vsevolod Meyerhold*, Cambridge University Press, 1989.

Revolutionary Theatre, Cambridge University Press, 1994.

'When He Touches Your Heart...The Revolutionary Theatre of Vsevolod Meyerhold and the Development of Michael Chekhov', *Contemporary Theatre Review*, 7:1 (1997), pp. 67–83.

Leach, Robert and Victor Borovsky (eds). *A History of Russian Theatre*, Cambridge University Press, 1999.

Leontievskii, N. 'Mysli o Teatre', *Teatr*, 1 (1983), pp. 74–91.

Levin, Irina and Igor Levin. *The Stanislavski Secret*, Colorado: Meriwether Publishing, 2002.

Lewis, Robert. *Method or Madness?*, London: Heinemann, 1960.

'Emotional Memory', *The Drama Review*, 6:4 (1962), pp. 54–60.

Ley, Graham. 'The Significance of Diderot', *New Theatre Quarterly* 11:44 (1995), pp. 342–354.

Lobanova, Olga. *Dyshite Pravil'no*, Petrograd: Novy Chelovek, 1915.

MacConaill, M. A. and J. V. Basmajian. *Muscles and Movements*, New York: Robert E. Krieger, 1977.

MacIntosh, P. C. *et al. Landmarks in the History of Physical Education*, London: Routledge and Kegan Paul, 1957.

Magarshack, David. Introduction to *Stanislavsky on the Art of the Stage*, 2nd edn, London: Faber and Faber, 1950, pp. 11–87.

Stanislavsky: A Life, 2nd edn, Westport, Connecticut: Greenwood Press, 1975.

Makereva, L. F. *Masterstvo Aktera*, Moscow: Sovetskaia Rossia, 1961.

Manderino, Ned. *The Transpersonal Actor: Reinterpreting Stanislavski*, USA: Manderino Books, 1976.

Mantegazza, Paolo. *Physiognomy and Expression*, London: Walter Scott, 1885.

Markov, P. A. *The Soviet Theatre*, London: Gollancz, 1934.

Markov, Vladimir. *Russian Futurism: A history*, London: Macgibbon and Kee, 1969.

Marowitz, Charles. *The Other Chekhov*, New York: Applause Books, 2004.

Marshall Herbert. *Pictorial History of the Russian Theatre*, New York: Crown Publishers, 1977.

McAuley, Mary. *Politics and the Soviet Union*, Middlesex: Penguin, 1977.

Meierkhol'd, V. E. *Stat'i, Pis'ma, Rechi, Besedi, tomy* 1, i 2, Moscow: Iskusstvo, 1968.

Meierkhol'd Nasledie, tom 1 ed. O. M. Feld'man, Moscow: OGI, 1998.

Tom 2 ed. O. M. Feld'man, Moscow: Novoe Izdatel'stvo, 2006.

Meierkhol'd i Drugie: dokumenty i materialy. ed. Oleg Feld'man, Moscow: OGI, 2000.

Lektsii 1918–1919, Moscow: OGI, 2001.

Merlin, Bella. 'Albert Filizov and the Method of Physical Actions', *New Theatre Quarterly*, 15:3 (1999), pp. 228–35.

'Which Came First: The System or "The Seagull"?', *New Theatre Quarterly*, 59 (August 1999), pp. 218–27.

Beyond Stanislavsky: The Psycho-Physical Approach to Actor Training, London: Nick Hern Books, 2001.

Miles, Eustace. 'Physical Culture'. In: *Cassell's Physical Educator*, London: Cassell, 1904.

Miller, George A. *Psychology: The Science of Mental Life*, London: Pelican, 1962.

Milling, Jane and Graham Ley. *Modern Theories of Performance*, London: Palgrave, 2001.

Milne, Lesley (ed.), *Bulgakov the Novelist-Playwright*, Luxembourg: Harwood Academic Publishers, 1995.

Mitter, Shomit. *Systems of Rehearsal, Stanislavsky, Brecht, Grotowski and Brook*, London: Routledge, 1992.

Mokul'skii, S. 'Primer sotsialisticheskogo teatra', *Teatr* 10 (1957), pp. 135–9.

Moore, Sonia. *Stanislavski Today: Commentaries on K. S. Stanislavski*, New York: American Center for Stanislavski Theatre Art, 1973.

The Stanislavski System, rev. edn, London: Penguin, 1984.

Stanislavski Revealed: The Actor's Guide to Spontaneity on Stage, New York: Applause Theatre Books, 1991.

Muller, J. P. *My System: 15 Minutes Work a Day for Health's Sake*, tr. G. M. Fox-Davies and H. R. Murray, rev. edn, London: Ewart, Seymour, 1912.

Mumford, Meg. 'Brecht Studies Stanislavski: Just a Tactical Move?', *New Theatre Quarterly*, 11:43 (1995), pp. 241–258.

Munk, Erika (ed.), *Stanislavski and America*, New York: Hill and Wang, 1966.

Nemirovitch-Dantchenko, Vladimir. *My Life in the Russian Theatre*, tr. John Cournos, London: Geoffrey Bles, 1937.

Nietzsche, Friedrich. *The Birth of Tragedy*, tr. Shaun Whiteside, London: Penguin, 1993.

Nordau, Max. *Degeneration*, 2nd edn, New York: Howard Fertig, 1968.

Norvelle, Lee. 'Stanislavski Revisited', *Educational Theatre Journal*, 14:1 (1962), pp. 29–37.

Novitskaia, L. P. *Uroki Vdokhnoveniia: sistema K. S. Stanislavskogo v deistvii*, Moscow: Vserossiskaia Teatral'naia Organizatsia, 1984.

Odom, Selma Landen. 'Delsartean Traces in Dalcroze Eurhythmics', *Mime Journal* (2004/5), pp. 137–52.

Orani, Aviv. 'Realism in Vakhtangov's Theatre of Fantasy', *Theatre Journal*, 36 (1984), pp. 460–80.

Ostrovskii, A. N. *Polnoe Sobranie Sochinenii*, Moscow: Iskusstvo, 1973–80.

Paavolainen, Pentii and Ala-Korpela Anu (eds), *Knowledge is a Matter of Doing*. Proceedings of the symposium Theatre and Dance Artist doing Research in Practice, Helsinki, The Theatre Academy, 13–15 October, 1994.

Patterson, Michael. *The Revolution in German Theatre, 1900–1933*, London: Routledge, 1981.

Pavlov, I. P. *Selected Works*, ed. Kh. S. Khostoyants, tr. S. Belsky, Moscow: Foreign Languages Publishing House, 1955.

Experimental Psychology and other Essays, tr. Kh. S. Koshtoiants, New York: Peter Owen, 1957.

Lectures on Conditioned Reflexes, tr. W. Horsley Gantt 1, London: Lawrence and Wishart, 1963.

Pesochinskii, N. '"Biomekhanika" v teorii Meierkhol'da', *Teatr*, 1 (1990), pp. 103–12.

Picon-Vallin, Béatrice. *Les voies de la création théâtrale, 17 Meyerhold*, Paris: Éditions du Centre Nationale de la Recherche Scientifique, 1990.

Pitches, Jonathan. *Vsevolod Meyerhold*, London: Routledge, 2003
Science and the Stanislavsky Tradition of Acting. London: Routledge, 2005.

Poliakova, E. (ed.), *Sulerzhitsky*, Moscow: Iskusstvo, 1970.

Poliakova E. *Stanislavski*, tr. Liz Tudge, Moscow: Progress, 1977.
Teatr Sulerzhitskogo: Etika. Estetiko. Rezhissura. Moscow: Agraf, 2006.

Poggi, Jack. 'The Stanislavski System in Russia', *The Theatre Review*, 17:1 (1973), pp. 124–33.

Prokofiev, V. L. 'Na poslednykh repetitsiiakh K. S. Stanislavskogo', *Teatr*, 1 (1948), pp. 49–56.

Prokofiev, V. N. *V sporakh o Stanislavskom*, Moscow: Iskusstvo, 1976.

Prokofiev, V. I. 'Zapisnie Knizhki K. S. Stanislavskogo', *Teatr*, 1 (1984) pp. 92–4.

Pudovkin, V. '*Stanislavski's System in the Cinema*', tr. T. Shebunina, *Sight and Sound*, London, 22:3 (1953), pp. 115–18, 147–8.

Radishcheva, O. *Istoriia Teatral'nykh Otnoshenii*, 1897–1908, Moscow: Artist Rezhisser Teatr, 1997.
Istoriia Teatral'nykh Otnoshenii, 1909–1917, Moscow: Artist Rezhisser Teatr, 1999.
Istoriia Teatral'nykh Otnoshenii, 1917–1938, Moscow: Artist Rezhisser Teatr, 1999.

Raffé, Marjorie, Cecil Harwood and Marguerite Lundgon, *Eurythmy and the Impulse of Dance*, London: Rudolph Steiner Press, 1974.

Ramacharaka, Iog', Zhnani-ioga, St Petersburg, 1914.

Ramacharaka, Yogi. *Series of Lessons in Raja Yoga*, Illinois: Yogi Publication Society, 1906.
Hatha Yoga, or the Yogi Philosophy of Physical Well-being, London: L. N. Fowler, 1917.

Rappaport, Helen. 'Stalin and the Photographer', *History Today* (June 2001), pp. 12–19.

Rayner, Alice. 'Soul in the System: On Meaning and Mystique in Stanislavski and A. C. Bradley', *New Theatre Quarterly*, 1:4 (1985), pp. 338–45.

Remez, O. 'Istoki Teorii Stanislavskogo', in *Voprosi Teatra, Sbornik Statei i Publikatsii*, Moscow: 'Vsesoiuzny nauchno-issledovatel'skii institytis kusstvoznania i Soiuz Teatral'nykh Deiatelei RSFSR, 1990.

Ribot, Théodule. *Diseases of the Memory*, London: Kegan Paul, Trench, 1882.
The Diseases of the Will, tr. Merwin-Marie Snell, 8th edn, Chicago and London: Open Court, 1896.
La Logique des Sentiments, Paris: Felix Alcan, 1905.
The Psychology of the Emotions, 2nd edn, London: Walter Scott, 1911.
The Psychology of Attention, tr. from 6th edn, Chicago and London: Open Court, 1911.

Roach, Joseph. *The Player's Passion: Studies in the Science of Acting*, Newark: University of Michigan Press, 1993.

Rokem, Freddie. 'Acting and Psychoanalysis: Street Scenes, Private Scenes, and Transference', *Theatre Journal*, 39:2 (1987), pp. 175–84.

Roose-Evans, James. *Experimental Theatre from Stanislavsky to Peter Brook*, 4th edn, London: Routledge, 1989.

Rudnitsky, Konstantin. *Meyerhold the Director*, tr. George Petrov, Ann Arbor: Ardis, 1981.

Russian and Soviet Theatre, 1905–1932: Tradition and the Avant-garde, tr. Roxanne Permar, New York: Harry N. Abrams, 1988.

Rush, James M. D. *The Philosophy of the Human Voice*, 7th edn, USA: The Library Company of Philadelphia, 1893.

Russell R. and A. Barratt. *Russian Theatre in the Age of Modernism*, Basingstoke: Macmillan, 1990.

Ruyter, Nancy C. 'American Delsartism', *Educational Theatre Journal*, 25:4 (1973), pp. 421–35.

Sabaneev, Leonid. *Muzika Rechi*, Moscow: Rabotnik Prosveshchenie, 1923.

Sakhnovskii, V. G. Vechnye zakony tvorchestva, *Teatr*, 1 (1988), pp. 77–92.

Sargeant, Amy. *Vsevolod Pudovkin: Classic Films of the Soviet Avant-garde*, London: I. B. Tauris, 2000.

Sayler, Oliver. *The Russian Theatre Under the Revolution*, New York: Little, Brown, 1920.

Schmidt, Paul (ed. and tr.), *Meyerhold at Work*, 2nd edn, New York, London: Applause, 1980.

Schnitzler, Henry. 'Truth and Consequences of Stanislavsky Misinterpreted', *Quarterly Journal of Speech*, 40:2 (1954), pp. 3–15.

Schopenhauer, Arthur. *Essays and Aphorisms*, London: Penguin, 1970.

Schuler, Catherine A. *Women in Russian Theatre: The Actress in the Silver Age*, London: Routledge, 1996.

Schulman, Michael. 'Backstage Behaviorism', *Psychology Today* (June 1973), pp. 51–4, 88.

Sechenov, I. M. *Reflexes of the Brain*, tr. S. Belsky, Cambridge: Massachusetts, 1965.

Segel, Harold B. *Twentieth Century Russian Drama: from Gorky to the Present*, New York: Columbia University Press, 1979.

Body Ascendant: Modernism and the Physical Imperative, Baltimore: Johns Hopkins University Press, 1998.

Senelick, Laurence (tr. and ed.), *Russian Dramatic Theory from Pushkin to the Symbolists: An Anthology*, Austin: University of Texas Press, 1981.

'Stanislavsky's Double Life in Art', *Theatre Survey*, 26:2 (1981), pp. 201–11.

Gordon Craig's Moscow Hamlet, Westport, Connecticut: Greenwood Press, 1982.

'New Information on *My Life in Art*', *Theatre Survey*, 24:1–2 (1983), pp. 127–30.

(ed.) *Wandering Stars: Russian Emigré Theatre, 1905–1940*, University of Iowa Press, 1992.

Serebriakov, P. *Uchenie o Dushevnikh Dvizheniakh v Primenenii Tsenicheskomy Iskusstvu*, Moscow: Kusherev, 1891.

Serezhnikov, Vasilii. *Iskusstvo Khudozhestvennogo Chtenia: tom 1, Muzika Slova*, Moscow-Petrograd: Gosudarstvennoe Izdatelstvo, 1923.

Iskusstvo Khudozhestvennoe Chtenia: tom 2 Tekhnika Rechi, 2nd edn, Moscow-Petrograd: Makiz, 1924.

Siegloch, Magdalene. *How the New Art of Eurhythmy Began*, London: Temple Lodge Publishing, 1997.

Simonov, P. V. *Metod K. S. Stanislavskogo i Fiziologia Emotzii*, Moscow: Akademia Nauk Soiuza Sovetskikh Sotsialisticheskikh Respublik, 1962.

Simonov, Ruben. *Stanislavsky's Protégé: Eugene Vakhtangov*, tr. Miriam Goldina, New York: DBS Publications, 1969.

Singer, Peter. *Marx*, Oxford University Press, 1980.

Sladkopevtsev, V. V. *Iskusstvo Declamatsii*, St Petersburg: Teatr i Iskusstvo, 1910.

Smeliansky, Anatoly. 'The Last Decade: Stanislavsky and Stalinism', *Theater*, 12:2 (1991), pp. 7–13.

Smelianskii, A. M. (ed.), *Moskovskii Khudozhestvennyi Teatr: Sto Let*, Moscow: Moskovskii Khudozhestvennyi Teatr, 1998.

Smith, Roger. *Inhibition: History and Meaning in the Sciences of Mind and Brain*, London: Free Association Books, 1992.

Smolenskii, I. L. *Posobie iz izuchenii deklamatsii*, Odessa: B. P. Raspolov, 1907.

Socher, Zenovia. 'Soviet Taylorism Revisited', *Soviet Studies*, 33:2 (1981), pp. 446–64.

Stanislavski, Constantin. *An Actor Prepares*, tr. Elizabeth Reynolds Hapgood, New York: Theatre Arts Books, 1936.

Building a Character, tr. Elizabeth Reynolds Hapgood, New York: Theatre Arts Books, 1949.

Creating a Role, tr. Elizabeth Reynolds Hapgood, New York: Theatre Arts Books, 1961.

Stanislavskii, K. S. *My Life in Art*, tr. G. Ivanov-Mumjiev, Moscow: 1955.

Stanislavski, K. S. *Stanislavski's Legacy*, ed. and tr. Elizabeth Reynolds Hapgood, 2nd edn, London: Methuen 1981.

Theatre. Entry in *Encyclopaedia Britannica*, 14th edn, 1929.

Stanislavski produces Othello, tr. Helen Nowak, London: Geoffrey Bles, 1948.

Stanislavskii, K. S. *Moia zhizn' v iskusstve*, Moscow: Iskusstvo, 1983.

O Stanislavskom: Sbornik vospominanii, Moscow: Vserossiiskoe Teatral'noe Obshchestvo, 1948.

Besedi K. S. Stanislavskogo v Studii Bol'shogo Teatra v 1918–22 gg, noted by K. E. Antarova (Moscow: VTO, 1952) tr. David Magarshack as *Stanislavsky on the Art of the Stage*, 2nd edn, London: Faber and Faber, 1967.

lz Zapisnykh Knizhek, 1 and 2, Moscow: Vserassiskoe Teatral'noe Obshchestvo, 1986.

Masterstvo Aktera v terminakh i opredeleniakh, K. S. Stanislavskogo, ed. M. A. Venetsianova, Moscow: Sovetskaia Rossia, 1961.

Rezhisserskie ekzempliary K. S. Stanislavskogo, 1–6, ed. Inna Soloveva, Moscow: Iskusstvo, 1981–1994.

Sobranie Sochinenii, 1–8, Moscow: Iskusstvo, 1954–1961.

Sobranie Sochinenii, 1–9, Moscow: Iskusstvo, 1988–1999.

Stanislavskii repetiruet: Zapisi i stenogrammy repetitsii, ed. I. Vinogradskaia, 2nd edn, Moscow: Soiuz teatral'nykh deiatelei, 2000.

Teatral'noe Nasledstvo I: Materiali, Pis'ma, Issledovania, eds. I. E. Grabar, S. N. Durylin, P. A. Markov, Moscow: Izdatel'stvo Akademii Nauk SSSR, 1955.

Stanislavsky, K. S. *My Life in Art*, tr. J. J. Robbins, London: Methuen, 1980.

Rezisserskie ekzemplyary K. S. Stanislavskovo, tom 6, Piesa V. Shekspira 'Otello', Moscow: Iskusstvo, 1994.

Stanislavsky, Konstantin. *Konstantin Stanislavski, 1863–1963: Man and Actor, Stanislavski and the World Theatre, Stanislavski's Letters*, tr. Victor Schneierson, Moscow: Progress, 1963.

Stebbins, G. *Dynamic Breathing and Harmonic Gymnastics*, 2nd edn, New York: Edgar S. Werner, 1893.

Delsarte System of Expression, 6th edn, New York: Edgar and Werner, 1977.

Steiner, Rudolf. *Speech and Drama*, tr. Mary Adams, New York: Anthroposophic Press, 1960.

An Introduction to Eurhythmy, New York: Anthroposophic Press, 1984.

Stites, Richard. *Revolutionary Dreams: Utopian Dreams and Experimental Life in the Russian Revolution*, Oxford University Press, 1989.

Russian Popular Culture, Cambridge University Press, 1992.

Stroieva, M. N. *Rezhiserskie iskania Stanislavskogo*, 1–2, Moscow: Nauka, 1973 and 1977.

Sudakov, B. I. 'The Actor's Creative Work', *N.Y. Theatre Workshop*, 1:2 (1937), pp. 1–42.

Sukhanov, S. 'The Subconscious and its Pathology', *Voprosi filosofii i psikhologii*, 26:128 (1915), pp. 360–77.

Symons, J. M. *Meyerhold's Theatre of the Grotesque*, Cambridge: Rivers Press, 1971.

Tanner, Michael. *Nietzsche: A Very Short Introduction*, Oxford University Press, 2000.

Taylor, George. *Players and Performances in the Victorian Theatre*, Manchester University Press, 1989.

'Francois Delsarte: A codification of nineteenth-century acting', *Theatre Research International*, 24:1 (1999), pp. 71–81.

Taylor, Richard (ed.), *The Eisenstein Reader*, London: BFI, 1998.

Taylor, Richard and Ian Christie (eds), *Inside the Film Factory: New Approaches to Russian and Soviet Cinema*, London: Routledge, 1991.

Todes, Daniel. 'Biological Psychology and the Tsarist Censor: The Dilemma of Scientific Development', *Bulletin of the History of Medicine*, 58 (1984), pp. 529–44.

Tolstoy, Leo. *Ispoved'*, Poland: Bradda Books, 1960.

What is Art? tr. Richard Pevear and Larissa Volokhonsky, London: Penguin, 1995.

Toporkov, V. O. *O Tekhnike Aktera*, Moscow: Iskusstvo, 1954.

Stanislavski in Rehearsal: The Final Years, tr. Christine Edwards, New York: Theatre Arts Books, 1979.

K. S. Stanislavskii na repetitsii, rev. edn, Moscow: AST, 2002.

Trabski, A. Ya. *Sovetski Teatr, Dokumenti i Materiali*, Leningrad: Iskusstvo, 1995.

Turner, W. L. 'Vakhtangov: The Director as Teacher', *Educational Theatre Journal*, 15 (1963), pp. 318–26.

Ushakov, D. N. *Krakoe Vvedenie v Nauku o iazyke*, Moscow, Petrograd: Gosudarstvennoe Izdatatelstvo, 1913.

Vakhtangov, Evgenii. *Zapiski, Pis'ma, Stat'i*, eds, N. M. Vakhtangova, L. D. Vendrovskaia, B. E. Zakhava, Moscow: Progress Iskusstvo, 1939.

   Evgeny Vakhtangov, (eds) L. D. Vendrovskaia and G. P. Kaptereva, tr. Doris Bradbury, Moscow: 1982.

   Sbornik, (eds) L. D. Vendrovskaia and G. P. Kaptereval, Moscow: Vserossiskoe Teatral'noe Obshchestvo, 1984.

Varneke, Boris V. *History of the Russian Theatre*, tr. Boris Brasol, New York: 1951.

Vertman, Yu. 'Teatral'no-pedagogicheskie Iskania Mikhaila Chekhova', *Teatr*, 11 (1969), pp. 92–100.

Vice, Sue. *Introducing Bakhtin*, Manchester: MUP, 1997.

Vinogradskaia, I. N. 'Stanislavski Repetiruiet "Moliere"', *Teatr*, 10 (1983), pp. 75–100.

   Stanislavski repetiruet, Moscow: Moskovskii Khudozhestvenyi Teatr, 2000.

   Zhizn i Tvorchestvo K. S. Stanislavskogo, Letopis, 1st edn, vols 1–4, Moscow: Vserossiskoe Teatral'noe Obshchestvo, 1974.

   Zhizn i Tvorchestvo K. S. Stanislavskogo, Letopis, 2nd edn, vols 1–4, Moscow: Moskovskii Khudozhestvennyi Teatr, 2003.

Volkenstein, Vladimir. *Stanislavskii*, Moscow: Shipovnik, 1922.

   'Drama, kak izobrazhenie refleksa tseli', *Vestnik Kommunisticheskoi 'Akademii'*, 14 (1926).

   Dramaturgiya, Moscow, 1969.

Volkonskii, Prince Sergei. *Chelovek" na Stsene*, St Petersburg: Apollon, 1912.

   Vyrazitel'nyi Chelovek", St Petersburg: Apollon, 1913.

   Vyrazitel'noe Slovo, St Petersburg: Apollon, 1913.

Volkonsky, Prince Sergei. *My Reminiscences*, tr. A. E. Chamot, London: Hutchinson, 1924.

Volkhontsev, S. (ed.), *Russkoe Akterskoe Iskusstvo 20-ovo Veka*, St Petersburg, 1992.

Wegner, William H. 'The Creative Circle: Stanislavski and Yoga', *Educational Theatre Journal*, 28:1 (1976), pp. 85–9.

White, R. Andrew. 'Stanislavski and Ramacharaka: The Influence of Yoga and Turn-of-the-century Occultism on the *System*', *Theatre Survey*, 47:1 (2006), pp. 73–92.

Whyte, L. L. *The Unconscious Before Freud*, London: Tavistock Publications, 1967.

Wiles, Timothy. *The Theater Event*, University of Chicago Press, 1980.

Wolff, Tatiana. (tr. and ed.), *Pushkin on Literature*, London: Methuen, 1971.

Wood, Ernest. *Concentration*, 2nd edn, India: The Theosophical Publishing House, 1979, 1st edn, 1913.

Worrall, Nicholas. 'Stanislavski's Production Score for Chekhov's *The Cherry Orchard* (1904): A Synoptic Overview', *Modern Drama*, 42 (1999), pp. 519–40.

'Meyerhold's Production of *The Magnificent Cuckold*', *The Drama Review*, 17:1 (1973), pp. 14–34.

Modernism to Realism on the Soviet Stage, Cambridge University Press, 1989.

The Moscow Art Theatre, London: Routledge, 1996.

Worthen, William W. 'Stanislavsky and the Ethos of Acting', *Theatre Journal*, 35:1 (March 1983), pp. 32–40.

Zakhava, Boris. *Vospominania. Spektakli i Roli. Stat'i.*, Moscow: Vserossiiskoe Teatral'noe Obshchestvo, 1982.

Zarrilli, Philip B. (ed.), *Acting (Re)Considered*, 2nd edn, London: Routledge, 2002.

Zavadovskii, B. M. 'Darvinizm i Marksizm', *Vestnik Kommunisticheskoi 'Akademii'*, 14 (1926), pp. 226–74.

Index

Note: The transliteration system is followed except where a simplified spelling for some names is in general use in English.